QUESTIONS OF ACCOUNTABILITY

This book explores accountability from a range of perspectives, crossing traditional disciplinary, thematic and professional boundaries. It asks fresh questions about accountability and its place and importance in democratic societies.

Accountability matters. It matters because it connects the governors with the governed, and for this reason it is a hallmark of democratic governance. And yet, amidst a backdrop of concerns about democratic back-sliding, the rise of populism, the role of algorithmic governance, moral barbarism and post-truth politics – to mention just a few issues – a number of potentially far-reaching questions of accountability have been asked. It is for exactly this reason that this book explores the concept of accountability from a range of perspectives, crossing traditional disciplinary, thematic and professional boundaries. It asks fresh questions about accountability and its place and importance in democratic societies.

The book considers the questions raised by the shifting architecture of accountability. Whilst some scholars suggest that accountability processes have never been so effective – trumpeting the rise of monitory democracy with its dense array of watchdogs, sleaze-busters, auditors, legislative committees, statutory supports and investigative mechanisms – others express concern about the risk of 'overloads', 'gaps' and 'traps'. This has led to a focus on fuzzy accountability and diagonal accountability, pointing to increasing conceptual confusion.

Bringing together world-leading scholars and former politicians and public servants, the book cuts through this confusion and provides the reader with the answers to the most debated issues, including rarely discussed 'pathologies of accountability', posthuman governance and a novel focus on balance and proportionality.

Questions of Accountability

Prerogatives, Power and Politics

Edited by
Matthew Flinders
and
Chris Monaghan

• HART •
OXFORD • LONDON • NEW YORK • NEW DELHI • SYDNEY

HART PUBLISHING

Bloomsbury Publishing Plc

Kemp House, Chawley Park, Cumnor Hill, Oxford, OX2 9PH, UK

1385 Broadway, New York, NY 10018, USA

29 Earlsfort Terrace, Dublin 2, Ireland

HART PUBLISHING, the Hart/Stag logo, BLOOMSBURY and the Diana logo are trademarks of Bloomsbury Publishing Plc

First published in Great Britain 2023

A catalogue record for this book is available from the British Library.

A catalogue record for this book is available from the Library of Congress.

Library of Congress Control Number: 2023938201

ISBN: HB: 978-1-50996-422-2
ePDF: 978-1-50996-424-6
ePub: 978-1-50996-423-9

Typeset by Compuscript Ltd, Shannon

FOREWORD

As a reader of this significant book will quickly appreciate, accountability is a topic which is not only important, but it is also much more multifaceted than it appears at first sight, and some of those facets are potentially controversial in their implications. However, the various chapters in this book do not call into question, indeed they support, the basic simple and important point that accountability is a vital controlling feature of any modern civilised government.

Indeed, it appears to me that accountability is a fundamental aspect of each of the two principal pillars of our system of government – a democratic legislature and the rule of law.

So far as a democratic legislature is concerned, the UK Constitution not merely involves a democratically elected legislature in the form of the House of Commons, but also accords ultimate supremacy to that legislature within the constitutional configuration. It is therefore particularly important that MPs have to account for themselves to the electorate at least every five years. It would at least arguably be both impractical and unsettling if significantly greater or more frequent electoral accountability was required at the overall or national level. However, in an informal and rather confused way, other events and processes can, in practice, be seen as part of the web of accountability within which MPs operate. From by-elections to local elections through to opinion polls, social media and the high volume of online and offline correspondence that MPs now receive, accountability is almost chameleon-like in terms of its forms. Lord Blunkett powerfully and passionately demonstrates how it feels, both as a politician and as a human being, to be under so many accountability pressures. Such pressures are rarely acknowledged or discussed in the existing research base, and this strikes me as a major gap that needs to be filled.

Lord Blunkett is a working peer in the House of Lords. Working peers sit in the legislature on the basis of an appointment rather than on an electoral mandate which, in itself, creates a number of questions of accountability. These questions could (and have) formed the focus of many books and I cannot tackle them in this short Foreword, but it is worth noting that the House of Lords exists within a complex web of accountabilities. The Lords plays a key but often overlooked role in holding the House of Commons to account, especially in relation to legislative detail and refinement, but also occasionally in relation to constitutional, and other fundamental, principles. The creation of independent commissioners for standards in both Houses is also a significant shift in the architecture of accountability that merits more attention.

A related but possibly bigger 'question of accountability' relates to holding the executive (ie, the government of the day) to account.

At the highest level, accountability of the executive involves ministers, civil servants and other public servants accounting for their actions to Parliament, often through the parliamentary committee system. Because a large number of members of Parliament are ministers (or hope to become ministers), the executive has a worrying ability to derail or undermine any attempt by Parliament to exercise its power to require the executive to account for its actions. And far too often, when a parliamentary committee criticises a government nothing of substance really happens, save for an anodyne statement from the government department involved. Select committee reports make recommendations that, no matter how grave the findings, are too easily side-stepped by a government that knows it can rely on its legislative majority in all but the most exceptional circumstances. This is not to suggest that select committees, in both the House of Lords and House of Commons, do not matter. They matter a huge amount and exert both direct and indirect pressures over the government, but this does not detract from the fact that the balance of power is generally weighted heavily on the side of the executive. Thinking creatively and asking questions of both ministers and officials (and of the relationship between them) is therefore always a valuable exercise. Jonathan Slater's focus in this book, for example, on the accountability of senior civil servants for the policy advice they provide to ministers strikes me as an excellent example of challenging convention in ways that could have potentially transformative effects.

A focus on institutions, structures and processes raises another question of accountability that concerns the evolving political culture. This is a complex issue but the core point I would seek to make is that politicians should not only be held to account but they should also possess a cultural desire to be held to account. They should see being accountable as a core element of open and inclusive public service. As such, accountability includes not merely being held to account, but also accepting the legitimacy and importance, as well as the reasonable consequences, of the accountability processes. Recent events, in the UK and abroad, have led me to wonder if the political culture amongst many elements of the political class has mutated in such a way that they feel willing and able to simply reject 'the rules of the game'. Chris Monaghan and Josie Welsh's chapter in this collection on 'questions of control' gets to the heart of many of these concerns and serves to focus attention on the potential weakness of a system that essentially relies on the self-restraint of the government of the day not to abuse their position. The 'good chaps theory' as Professor Peter Hennessy, who communicates his deep understanding of our Constitution with elegance and humour, instructs us that our rather loose system of government only really works when those in power agree to abide by the rules (ie, when they are 'good chaps'). Constant examples of exceptions to established and conventional safeguards lead to 'eroding the rules' and fraying the fabric of effective representative democracy.

Many select committee recommendations, despite being based on a very large amount of detailed and evidence-based research and reflection, are frequently simply ignored by ministers with apparent impunity, so that, at least as it appears to me, the previously existing culture or ethos of good government has been seriously undermined. The same can be said about the way in which ministers will often respond to criticism with the declaration that they take 'full responsibility' for an error or failing but then move on as if nothing has happened. Accountability is not a charade or parlour game. Saying that one is taking full responsibility is patently not the same as actually taking full responsibility. The former without the latter simply creates a rhetoric-reality gap that risks reducing public confidence in politicians, political institutions and political processes.

Turning to the rule of law and judicial accountability it is essential that the executive is required to account for any of its decisions and actions to the courts when citizens reasonably believe that they have been unlawfully or unfairly treated. Once again, this is where accountability acts as a bulwark of open, effective and lawful government. The role of the courts is a key element of the wider accountability ecosystem. That is why any attempt by ministers, or indeed by Parliament at the behest of ministers, to curb the right to judicial review or the right to enjoy or enforce human rights, has to be examined with great care and not a little suspicion. This is not to suggest that there should never be changes in the law, the scope of jurisdictional ranges or the balance of relationships – it is simply that any such changes demand very careful thought and open discussion.

The position of the judiciary within the Constitution and its relationship with the executive have, of course, always raised many questions of accountability. Many of these are raised and explored in Se-Shauna Wheatle's chapter on a collaborative approach to constitutional accountability and in Alison Young's fascinating chapter on the 'fundamental questions' raised by the relationship between accountability and human rights. In that connection, it is worth noting that it is wrong to label politicians as accountable while judges are somehow unaccountable. Quite apart from established judicial disciplinary procedures (which in England and Wales are ultimately decided by the Lord Chancellor and Lord Chief Justice), the decisions of all judges, save those of the Supreme Court, can in some real sense said to be accountable in the sense that they can be appealed and therefore reviewed by judges in superior courts. As for the Supreme Court, it is in a rather privileged position. Its decisions cannot be appealed and the doctrine of separation of powers, at least as it applies in the UK, means that Parliament (though sovereign) cannot review court decisions. The flip-side being that the courts have to keep out of ruling on what goes on in Parliament. Nevertheless, parliamentary sovereignty means – and separation of powers does not prevent – that Parliament can enact legislation which reverses or overrides the effect of any court decision. This has happened on occasion, and it is perfectly proper.

To think of accountability in terms of government and Parliaments risks adopting a rather standard national level approach, and it should be remembered that accountability in the context of the rule of law also exists at the international level. It is therefore good to see the contribution of Kate Macdonald and Terry Macdonald on 'accountability beyond the nation state'. The questions and issues they raise pose major challenges (and possibly opportunities) for anyone thinking about accountability as it relates to both theory and practice. With this in mind I would add my concern to that of many others at the recent behaviour of ministers in the UK who seem committed to breaking international treaty obligations. One of the points made by ministers is that it is inappropriate for the UK Government's actions to be assessed, let alone criticised, by a 'foreign' court. However, just as any government has to be accountable in its domestic courts when it has breached its law duties arising under domestic statutes or common law, so it is as entirely appropriate for a government to be accountable in 'foreign' courts when it has breached its duties arising under treaties or other international law principles.

This is a book that surveys far and wide about the tricky topic of accountability. Many questions of accountability are raised and although very few are definitively answered, they are thoughtfully and informatively addressed in ways that promote new insights and provoke fresh questions. So what is the 'question of accountability' that I might bring to the table? As may be apparent from the above brief discussion, I have two main suggestions.

The first revolves around shifting the balance of power between the executive and legislature and has the aim of establishing a more constructive and transparent relationship. A wholly independent Ministerial Commissioner might, for example, complement the existing parliamentary commissioners and represent a natural evolution. Although such a 'Ministerial' Commissioner may report initially to the Prime Minister they must ultimately be responsible to Parliament. This should help to prevent inappropriate executive interference and obfuscation while at the same time underlining the reality of parliamentary supremacy and democratic accountability. I would also, as my second recommendation, seek to explore the question whether there might be some way of supervising the relationship between government departments and the select committees in the House of Commons that scrutinise them, and also supervising any proposals that emanate from the government and which seek to interfere with judicial independence or to breach international law.

These are tricky topics, which go to the heart of Whitehall and Westminster politics.

But they are also arguably more evolutionary than revolutionary. In recent years, a number of constitutional watchdogs have been established (such as the Electoral Commission and Independent Parliamentary Standards Authority) which suggests that regulating politically salient relationships is actually more common than is commonly recognised. But, quite apart from this, it seems to me that some sort of independent body which reports to Parliament on these matters is at least worth considering. In the end, we should be striving towards an improvement in the culture both in Parliament and in Whitehall: without such developments, we may be at risk of losing our bearings.

Let me conclude by offering my wholehearted support for the central thesis of this book – that accountability really matters. In this short Foreword, I have hardly scratched the surface of the important topic, which has not, in my view, been accorded the importance that it deserves. That is especially true in the present day, in light of the increasing complexity of government and the many challenges of modern life generally. In this valuable book, the topic is examined from a number of angles in depth by people who are experts in the area. It is an excellent and thought-provoking book for anyone who wants to understand the full implications of Accountability. I hope its message is recognised across and beyond academe and that it fulfils its potential in terms identifying new and critical questions, and indeed by identifying just one or two possible and actionable answers to those questions.

Lord Neuberger of Abbotsbury
President of the Supreme Court of the United Kingdom, 2012–17

ACKNOWLEDGEMENTS

Like many academic projects, this collection has its roots in a major academic conference – 'Questions of Accountability' – that took place online and was co-ordinated by the University of Worcester and the University of Sheffield. The focus of the conference was designed to resonate with a broader sense of socio-political concern, found within the UK and far beyond, that the existing scrutiny structures were struggling to contain and control a variety of pressures (populist, generational, technical, financial, etc) and seemed almost at risk of collapsing under the pressure. The global Covid-19 pandemic had added a new layer to pre-existing concerns through both the utilisation of emergency powers in many countries, and the emergence of a more existential debate about the relative merits of authoritarian regimes over democratic politics. Covid also raised basic 'questions of accountability' about how individual actors and organisations, not to mention networks and systems, had responded to the crisis.

What we hoped would be an interesting and popular conference suddenly evolved into a far larger and more diverse arena for debate and discussion than we could ever have hoped for. From our initial plans for a one-day event the conference expanded to a full week of events, panels, talks and keynote lectures. Moreover, the event expanded beyond academe and increasingly attracted contributions from politicians and policy-makers who had actually grappled with a range of 'questions of accountability' and therefore contributed valuable experiential or 'real world' perspectives that added tone and texture to the academic analyses. We would like to thank all those who helped us during the conference, and especially Janey Robins, Professor David Green, Bill Davies, and Professor Sarah Greer.

What this book brings together is a selection of those perspectives. The aim being to promote, prod and push the debate regarding why accountability matters and to maintain the momentum of the intellectual discussion that was initiated at the November 2021 'Questions of Accountability' conference. What is also noteworthy is that this is not an uncritical discussion. What accountability is in terms of '*who?*', '*what?*', '*why?*', '*when?*' and '*how?*' are all dynamic questions that demand constant reappraisal. At a more basic level the common assumption that 'accountability is a good thing' or a 'golden concept' also demands if not challenging then, at the very least, some appreciation of the need for balance and proportionality. Too much accountability can be as problematic as too little.

The commitment and energy of everyone who made the initial conference a success – speakers, participants, technological support, administrative staff, etc – needs to be acknowledged. Thanks to everyone at Hart Publishing, and particularly to our commissioning editor Kate Whetter, and Verity Stuart, the assistant editor, for supporting this collection with a rich blend of positivity, professionalism and proficiency. Special thanks also to the contributors who have made this edited collection happen by delivering their chapters. As the academic environment becomes ever more intense and challenging the significance and role of edited collections within the wider research ecosystem is easily over-looked. And yet edited collections facilitate a breadth of thinking around a core topic of focal point. In this sense they act as a crucible of ideas, perspectives and challenges which may, without a unifying method, otherwise exist in splendid isolation from each other. The bridge building role of edited collections fulfils an incredibly connective and catalysing function – laying the foundations for further collaborative analyses and inter-disciplinary investigations. Authors also generally enjoy a little more freedom to think and speculate and to fly some intellectual kites in ways that more formalised publications like research monographs and journal articles very rarely, if ever, allow for.

As we conclude these acknowledgments it is important to underline that this collection marks the beginning and not the end of this rich and fresh seam of scholarship. We intend 'Questions of Accountability' to become a living and ongoing organisation as a community of academics, practitioners and public members who share a common commitment to democratic change and renewal. Further events, conferences, publications and engagement opportunities will be developed under the '#QofA' banner.

Matthew Flinders and Chris Monaghan
June 2023
#QofA

CONTENTS

LIST OF CONTRIBUTORS

Robert Blackburn is Professor of Constitutional Law at King's College London.

David Blunkett was a British government minister from 1997–2006 and is now Professor of Politics in Practice at the University of Sheffield and a working peer in the House of Lords.

Madalina Busuioc is Professor of Governance at the Vrije University Amsterdam.

Margit Cohn is the Henry J. and Fannie Harkavy Chair in Comparative Law at the Hebrew University of Jerusalem.

Matthew Flinders is Professor of Politics at the University of Sheffield, and Vice President of the Political Studies Association of the United Kingdom.

David Neuberger served as President of the Supreme Court of the United Kingdom from 2012–17. In addition to being a working cross bench peer in the House of Lords he now serves as a non-permanent judge of the Hong Kong Court of Final Appeal and the Chair of the High-Level Panel of Legal Experts on Media Freedom.

Kate Macdonald is Senior Lecturer in Politics at the University of Melbourne.

Terry Macdonald is Senior Lecturer in International Relations at the University of Melbourne.

Chris Monaghan is Principal Lecturer in Law at the University of Worcester.

Ellen Rock is Senior Lecturer in Law at the University of Technology Sydney.

Thomas Schillemans is Professor in Accountability, Behaviour and Governance in the School of Governance at Utrecht University.

Sharon Shoesmith is a researcher and writer, and formally a Director of Education and Children's Social Care and one of Her Majesty's Inspectors (HMI) of Schools.

Jonathan Slater was Permanent Secretary in the Department for Education from 2016–20 and sits on the board of the Institute for Government and is a Visiting Professor at King's College London.

Josie Welsh is Senior Lecturer in Law at the University of Worcester.

Se-shauna Wheatle is Associate Professor of Law at the University of Durham.

Alison Young is Sir David Williams Professor of Public Law at the University of Cambridge.

LIST OF BOXES, DIAGRAMS, FIGURES AND TABLES

LIST OF CASES

1

Accountability Matters

MATTHEW FLINDERS AND CHRIS MONAGHAN

Accountability matters. It matters because it defines and mediates the relationship between the governors and the governed. Concerns regarding credibility and complexity, transparency and trust, democracy and delegation, expertise, and efficiency, right through to debates concerning symbolism, scapegoating and sacrificial lambs all share a root focus on accountability. It is therefore almost impossible to separate contemporary concerns regarding the 'health', 'crisis' or 'death' of democracy from deeper questions of accountability.

The challenge, however, in terms of engaging with these questions is that accountability is a complex concept. Sinclair's (1995) description of accountability as a 'chameleon-like concept' captures this sense of both complexity and change. There are, however, three dimensions of the conceptual debate that are worth identifying from the outset and which might be discussed under the headings of *breadth*, *beliefs*, and *blame*. The breadth dimension simply points to the manner in which, as Mulgan (2000) has noted, accountability appears to be an 'ever-expanding concept' that has come to 'stand as a general term for any mechanism that makes powerful institutions responsive to their particular publics'. 'Ever-expanding' also in the sense that concerns about distrust, maladministration and 'fugitive power' have led to the creation of ever-more sophisticated and focused tools, forms or mechanisms of accountability. This is reflected in John Keane's work on what he calls 'monitory democracy' with its complex tapestry of '[P]ower-monitoring and power-controlling devices [that] have begun to extend sideways and downwards through the whole political order.' This, in turn, explains a growing emphasis on forms of vertical, horizontal and even – as Luhrmann, Marquardt and Mechkova's work (2020) has explored – diagonal accountability. And also upon the symbolic role of accountability as an ideograph or 'rhetorical touchstone' (Romzek 2015, 27). 'The concept of accountability, in short, has become both the medium and the message of modern governance' Ciaran O'Kelly and Mel Dubnick (2014, 1) suggest 'Today, the study of governance is effectively the study of accountability.'

The 'ever-expanding' nature of accountability therefore exists across at least three dimensions. The first is structural in nature and highlights the increasingly dense institutional landscape of scrutiny processes, ombudsmen, committees of inquiry, audit mechanisms, reviews, etc. The second dimension is more normative in nature and emphasises the range of what might be termed 'accountability expectations' (ie increasing governmental efficiency, promoting greater administrative responsiveness, controlling corruption, sustaining public confidence, regulating risk, enforcing personal and organisational responsibility, allocating blame, learning lessons, facilitating societal catharsis or healing, etc). The third dimension is more theoretical and views accountability as a 'conceptual keyword' which 'are a bit like icebergs' as Jonathan Fox (2022, 7) writes – 'they turn out to be the more visible chunks of much larger bodies of ideas'. Given this expansion in relation to *institutional form*, *expected roles* and theoretical breadth it is not surprising that Dimova (2019) has written about an 'accountability explosion' – a phenomenon charted at length in Jonathan Fox's *Accountability Keywords* report of 2022. This explosion or expansion is itself explained by our second dimension and a focus on *belief*. The basic point here is that accountability is generally seen as a 'good thing'. This is based on the 'self-evident truth' that the more accountable that elected politicians and their officials are to the public, the higher the quality of democracy will be. 'There exists an almost unquestioned assumption' Mel Dubnick (2002) suggests 'that the creation or enhancement of accountability mechanisms of any sort will result in greater democracy', which explains why Bovens (2007, 448) similarly suggested that that accountability 'is one of those golden concepts that no one can be against'. The 'danger of self-evident truths' like this – as Elinor Ostrom (2000) underlined – is that they are not always true. Too much accountability, it might be argued, can be as problematic as too little which is a suggestion that allows us to touch upon our third dimension and the issue of *blame*.

The simple argument here is that it is possible to conceptualise two very different models of forms of accountability. 'Mode I' is primarily focused not on lesson-learning but on blame-attribution. It is, to return to Romzek (2015) based on 'hot rhetoric'. It is highly partisan, often aggressive in style and driven by notions of sacrificial responsibility. Mode I is therefore synonymous with what Barbara Romzek and Patricia Ingraham described as a 'Gotcha!' (2000, 249) approach to scrutiny that is likely to encourage a highly defensive response from those who are called to give an account. 'Mode II', by contrast, is imbued with an emphasis on evidence, context, rational discussion, and lesson-learning. It is a 'cool theory' (2015, 27) to paraphrase Barbara Romzek. It is therefore largely non-partisan, rather technocratic in approach and forged upon a 'good faith' model of politics whereby ministers and their officials are assumed to have acted in the public interest unless proven otherwise. This model of accountability is distinctive because in theory it could attribute both credit *and* blame. At a very broad level, the presentation of this simple Mode I/Mode II distinction is valuable for the simple reason that it underlines the way public and political accountability is generally of a 'Mode I' type, and examples of Mode II tend to be relatively rare. This explains the existence of a large and sophisticated literature on blame-avoidance behaviours, which in itself highlights the manner in which individuals and organisations generally operate within an accountability environment that is defined by the existence of multiple and cross-cutting accountability pressures rather than any single actor or process (see, for example, Aleksovska and Schillemans 2021; Eriksen 2021a).

This initial focus on *breadth*, *beliefs* and *blame* serves to underline both the complexity of accountability and why it matters in terms of democratic governance and public confidence in politicians, political institutions, and political processes. It also serves to explain why one part of the 'accountability explosion' that has occurred in recent years has actually taken place *within* academe and is reflected in a burgeoning and inter-disciplinary literature on accountability and cognate concepts (ie, responsibility, scrutiny, blame, liability, culpability, answerability, etc). Systematic reviews of accountability-focused studies in specific sub-fields (see, for example, Wieringa 2020; Grossi, Kallio, Sargiacomo and Skoog 2020) have attempted to navigate through a complex tangle of themes, debates, and concerns. The fact that some of these 'accountability accounts' focus on highly specialised topics (see, for example, the 2017 work of Hall, Frink and Buckley on 'felt accountability') underlines the existence of a vast landscape of literature.

Box 1.1 Accounting for Accountability Studies: Key Reference Points

Mulgan *Holding Power to Account* (2003) – Strom, Muller and Bergman *Delegation and Accountability in Parliamentary Democracies* (2003) – Bostrom and Garsten *Organizing Transnational Accountability* (2008) – McIntyre-Mills *Systemic Governance and Accountability* (2010) – Fox and Brown *The Struggle for Accountability* (1998) – Bovens *The Quest for Responsibility* (1998) – Przeworski, Stokes, and Manin *Democracy, Accountability and Representation* (1999), Flinders *The Politics of Accountability* (2001) – Strom, Müller and Bergman *Delegation and Accountability in Parliamentary Democracies* (2003) – Mookherjee *The Crisis in Government Accountability* (2004) – Held and Archibugi *Global Governance and Public Accountability* (2005) – Goetz and Jenkins *Reinventing Accountability* (2005) – Dowdle's *Public Accountability* (2006) – Ebrahim and Weisband *Global Accountabilities* (2007) – Gustavsson, Karlsson and Person *The Illusion of Accountability in the European Union* (2009) – Valerie Sperling *Altered States: The Globalization of Accountability* (2009)–(2010) – Bellamy and Palumbo *Political Accountability* (2010) – Bovens, Curtin and 't Hart *The Real World of EU Accountability* (2010) – Bamforth and Leyland *Accountability in the Contemporary Constitution* (2014) – Bovens (*et al.*) *Oxford Handbook of Public Accountability* (2014) – Hoque *Making Governments Accountable* (2015) – Kirton and Larionova (eds.) *Accountability for Effectiveness in Global Governance* (2018) – Rock *Measuring Accountability in Public Governance Regimes* (2020) – Mikuli and Kuca *Accountability and the Law* (2021) – Arcuri and Coman-Kund *Technocracy and the Law: Accountability, Governance and Expertise* (2021) – Eriksen *The Accountability of Expertise* (2021) – White *Held in Contempt: What's Wrong with the House of Commons?* (2022) – Blick and Hennessy *The Bonfires of the Decencies: Repairing and Restoring the British Constitution* (2022) – Pasquino and Pelizzo *The Culture of Accountability: A Democratic Virtue* (2023).

This raises two inter-related 'questions of accountability' for those intrepid intellectual explorers who wish to study this terrain. The first question concerns somehow acknowledging, drawing-upon but ultimately cutting a way through this vast body of scholarship. (Box 1.1 provides an overview of some of the key reference points.) This might be seen as *the navigational challenge*. The second question concerns novelty, originality, and innovation. This might be seen as *the distinctiveness challenge* which requires any accountability explorer to somehow either forge new routes through the existing material, identify completely new questions, develop new ways of asking old questions, or possibly of bringing new actors into the conversation as a way of, if not answering questions, then at the very least of accommodating new insights, perspectives, and dilemmas. Bovens (2010, 946–947) suggests that the navigational and distinctiveness challenges have scuppered a number of previous cartological expeditions:

> Much of the academic literature on accountability is rather disconnected, as many authors set out to produce their own specific definition of accountability. Every newly edited volume on accountability – and, even worse, each of the individual chapters within these edited volumes – uses its own concepts, conceptualisations and frames for studying accountability. Some use the concept very loosely, other produce a more narrow definition, but few of these definitions are fully compatible, which makes it very hard to produce cumulative or commensurable research … there are many scholars who talk about accountability, but few who study it rigorously.

How does this collection seek to avoid Boven's critique concerning the existence of an ill-defined and disconnected scholarly sub-field? What is the 'consistent conceptual framework' which acts as the intellectual glue that binds each contribution into a broader and more integrated analysis? How does this collection interpret and expand the notion of 'useful knowledge' in order to open-up new perspectives? The next section engages with these questions through a focus on a definition, a puzzle and an issue.

I. A Definition, Puzzle and Issue

One definition, one puzzle and *one issue*: these provide both the foundational pillars and connective strands for this collection.

A. A Definition

The definition provides our opening attempt to pin down the chameleon and to provide a starting point that contributors may well want to contextualise, develop, and refine. Having reviewed a number of descriptive debates (see, for example, Schedler 1999; Lindberg 2013; Mechkova, Bernhard and Luhrmann 2019), we accept Boven's (2007) definition of accountability:

> A relationship qualifies as a case of accountability when: there is a relationship between and actor and a forum in which the actor is obliged to explain and justify [their] conduct; the forum can pose questions, pass judgement and the actor may face consequences.

This definition has been selected for its simple logic and due to the way in which is captures both *answerability* (ie requirement to give an account) and *responsibility* (ie consequences may follow). This definition is also preferred because, unlike many others, it is neutral in tone and does not include an emphasis on failure or blame. The complexity of the concept means that accountability is to some extent destined to disappoint when it comes to definitional clarity. It is an 'essentially contested concept' (see Sartori 1964) and with this in mind it is useful to highlight three ways of immediately stretching this definitional starting point. The first relates to scale and complexity. The definition approaches accountability as a single linear principal-agent relationship when the realities of modern governance generally consists of multiple principals and multiple agents. The second way of using this definition as the starting point for a deeper discussion is to recognise that it implicitly adopts an ex post approach where accountability is a tool used to explore events or decisions after they have happened. An ex ante accountability approach might seek to reduce risks by requiring ministers or officials to explain and justify their planned course of action ahead of its implementation (see Pollman, Potters and Trautmann 2014).

The idea being that preventative measures can be taken 'before the horse has bolted' in ways that are no longer possible with an ex post accountability emphasis; but the trade-off being that the organisational agility and nimbleness of the agent is to some extent restricted by their need to secure the approval of external supervisory bodies. This flows into a third and final issue with our selected definition: the balance between *process* and *output* dynamics. As the focus on ex ante processes highlighted, accountability processes generally involve the imposition of costs. These might relate to (inter alia) organisational efficiency, the focus of senior managers, organisational anxieties about blame, distraction from core tasks, etc. This underlines the simple fact that accountability structures define relationships: low-levels of inter-organisational trust are likely to be reflected in the existence of tighter accountability webs, and vice versa (discussed below). Democratic governance, however, is generally linked to *process-based* forms of accountability where politicians, officials and public servants are expected to account for their decisions and behaviour at fairly regularised moments in the policy-process. An alternative accountability approach, however, is an *outcome-based* approach in which procedural scrutiny is removed or severely curtailed in order to allow an organisation to focus without distraction on the successful delivery of its policy or service. Put simply, an outcome-based approach believes that 'what matters is what works' and that process is secondary to performance (for a discussion see Högberg and Lindgren 2021). The benefit (theoretically at least) of an emphasis on outcomes (ie results) over process (ie how decisions were taken or by whom) is that the transaction costs of 'thick' forms of accountability are minimised through the application of 'thinner' accountability requirements which, in turn, allow delivery organisations to focus on their primary tasks without distraction.

There is, of course, a very clear 'politics of accountability' surrounding *process*-based and *outcome*-based approaches with advocates of 'new public management' promoting the latter, and critics of those reforms highlighting the risks of diminishing democratic accountability. But at the very least this brief discussion about ex ante and ex post, *process-based* and *outcome-based*, and 'thick' and 'thin' accountability underlines the value of our definitional starting point. It also allows us to move on to a discussion of the second element of this section and to a focus on what we term the accountability puzzle.

B. A Puzzle

The accountability puzzle can be set out as follows:

> If the last two decades have been associated with an 'accountability explosion' which was designed to rejuvenate public trust and confidence in politics, politicians and political processes then why has the same period been inextricably linked to growing concerns about the democratic decline, disaffection and distrust?

This 'overload but under-performance' puzzle provides a distinctive and original route into revealing, teasing-apart and dissecting a number of 'questions of accountability'. These questions serve to connect the often highly specialised and fragmented scholarship on accountability (discussed above) to far broader contemporary debates concerning (inter alia) the changing nature of democracy, the rise of anti-political sentiment and the emergence of populist pressures. Key contributions within this wider sphere of socio-political analysis include Anne Applebaum's *Twilight of Democracy* (2020), John Keane's *The New Despotism* (2020), Marcial Bragadini Boo's *The Rules of Democracy* (2022) and Mark Evans and Gerry Stoker's *Saving Democracy* (2022) and it is accurate to suggest that 'questions of accountability' (albeit with different focal points, varying perspectives and written for different audiences) provide core themes within and across these books. And yet there is an obvious naivete to the 'overload but under-performance' puzzle born from the implicit instrumental assumption that a *positive* link exists between accountability and public trust or confidence. Dubnick's 2002 emphasis on 'seeking salvation for accountability' seeks to challenge the simplistic assumption that *more* accountability will inevitably produce *better* government, *higher* levels of public trust, *improved* levels of responsiveness, etc.

Following on from Dubnick's critique and weaving it through Keane's emphasis on 'monitory democracy', during the last 50 years it is possible to identify the emergence of a constant pattern of critique and growth: *critique* in relation to the operation and performance of democracy; *growth* in the creation of new accountability processes, scrutiny systems, strengthened oversight bodies, ombudsmen, appeal processes and statutory rights to information, etc in an attempt to correct perceived inefficiencies in the management of the state and the behaviour of politicians. This is the 'accountability explosion' with its 'online and offline' dimensions, 'hard and soft' structures, 'upwards and downwards' directionality, 'ex ante and ex post' characteristics, and even 'diagonal or fuzzy' dynamics. What has arguably occurred in recent years, however, is not the systemic overview and replacement of 'old and outdated' tools of accountability with 'new and future-focused' mechanisms but a more complex process of accountability accretion and scrutiny sedimentation. The architecture of accountability has therefore become increasingly dense as new structures have been grafted onto the traditional frameworks of representative democracy.

The 'overload but under-performance' puzzle is therefore linked to the emergence of a slightly more cautious and sceptical seam of scholarship that highlights the potential pathologies of accountability. This body of work would include Robert Behn's *Rethinking Democratic Accountability* (2001), Jonathan Koppell's analysis of 'multiple accountabilities disorder' (2005), Dino Falaschetti's *Democratic Governance and Economic Performance* (2009) and Matthew Flinders work on 'politicized accountability' (2011) and Arie Halachmi's discussion of 'accountability overloads' (2014). A slightly broader and closely related body of work has explored how public sector organisations and officials cope with the 'cross-pressures' of multiple and often contradictory accountability demands. Studies on this topic would include Barbara Romzek's classic work on the Challenger Tragedy (1987, with Mel Dubnick) and the Ron Brown Plane Crash (2000, with Patricia Wallace Ingraham) through to more modern analyses such as that conducted by Marija Aleksovka and Thomas Schillemans (2021) on 'dissecting multiple accountabilities'. Taken together, what these studies serve to highlight is that too much accountability can be as problematic as too little. The relationship between democracy and accountability is therefore – as Phillipe Schmitter (2004) has emphasised – far more ambiguous than is commonly recognised. This brings us to a focus on one simple issue – *balance*.

C. A Matter of Balance

What the 'overload but under-performance' puzzle really serves to focus attention on is the challenge of achieving a proportionate 'accountability balance' between democratic scrutiny, on the one hand, and governing capacity, on the other. This is a theme that will be well-known to many scholars of constitutional change and democratic design. Sir John Laws' *The Constitutional Balance* (2021), for example, provides a set of astute observations as it explores the need to place democratic controls and safeguards on the executive while at the same time somehow ensuring that a democratically elected government enjoys the governing capacity to get things done. Simon Jenkins' *Accountable to None* (1996) was published a quarter of a century earlier but focuses on the same theme and a concern about a loss of balance. Contemporary concerns about the 'crisis', 'death' and 'twilight' of democracy all in their own ways revolve around a sense of *im*balance within a constitutional configuration.

This focus on balance or proportionality opens-up further questions of accountability that need to be if not answered, then at the very least engaged with. It is also possible to link this focus back into the previous sub-section's focus on accountability 'deficits' and 'overloads' in ways that reveal the concept's inherent ambiguities. Take, for example, Frank Anechiarico and James Jacobs' *The Pursuit of Absolute Integrity* (1996) in which they argued that the accountability explosion (discussed above) which was designed to control corruption and increase efficiency had actually seriously undermined the capacity of politicians to govern. 'Some politicians, anxious to appear morally pure, support dubious and cumbersome "reforms", regardless of the possible effect of those reforms on public administration' Anechiarico and Jacobs write (1996, 50) 'moral entrepreneurs are likely to be so consumed with stopping corruption that they rarely even consider the integrity/efficiency trade-off'. The 'integrity/efficiency trade-off' – or what other scholars prefer to term the 'accountability dilemma' (see Christensen and Laegried 2015) – simply recognises that the requirements of accountability (ie regular reporting, the use of audit mechanisms, threat of sanctions, short-term time horizons, etc) may grate against the imperatives of effective service delivery (freedom to manage, innovation, flexibility, risk taking, long-term planning, etc).

This potential trade-off is not new. It was recognised by Walter Bagehot in Britain and James Madison in the US. In 1972 Peter Self labelled it 'the classic dilemma of public administration' (277) but even this interpretation raises critical questions of accountability about form and complementarity. The 'integrity-efficiency trade-off' brings with is a set of zero-sum assumptions which themselves deserve to be questioned. The simple logic set out in Figure 1.1 is at least open to considering when and how a more positive-sum relationship between efficiency and accountability might be forged.

Figure 1.1 Trade-Off Assumptions in Accountability/Efficiency Relationships

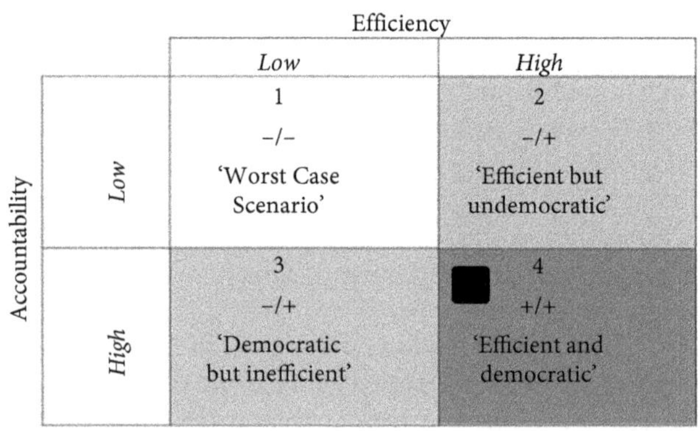

The benefit of Figure 1.1 is that it captures a great deal of the existing debate concerning accountability. Countries, sectors, institutions, or individuals placed within Cell 1 would represent the 'worst of all worlds' with serious concerns about both a lack of accountability and efficiency. The neo-liberal critiques of the post-war state that emerged in the 1970s and into the 1980s that did so much to promote an emphasis on new public management were forged on the perception that 'low-low' represented the general situation. The 'efficiency/integrity trade-off' that Anechiarico and Jacobs focus on basically represents an equilibrium point across cells 2 and 3 on the basis that any increase in democratic control must by definition come at a cost of some degree of administrative efficiency. The questions of accountability that have dominated debates about the institutions of European governance – replete as they are with concerns about technocratic dominance and democratic deficits – would chime with this perceived trade-off (see, for example, Moravcsik 2000; Sebastiao 2021). And yet the key question that Figure 1.1 is designed to focus attention on relates not to 'more' or 'less' of one component or another but on accountability can be secured *without* necessarily impinging on efficiency and effectiveness.

This is a critical point. The vast majority of existing analyses assume that a trade-off is inevitable. And yet, at least in theory, it is possible to imagine a model of democratic design that either delivered high levels of accountability and efficiency (ie +/+), or more realistically focused on achieving a clear and proportionate balance between these competing ambitions. Such an approach would, for example, chime with Francis Fukuyama's (2013) commentary on 'what is governance?'. This is because Fukuyama focuses not just on the relationship between bureaucratic autonomy, on the one hand, and quality of government, on the other, but (more specifically) on the existence of a 'sweet spot' (362) where both elements exist at optimal levels. The 'sweet spot' in Figure 1.1 is represented by the black square but even this suggestion within a simple matrix serves to underline the complexities faced by anyone engaging with questions of accountability. The reason being that identifying any optimal balance between competing pressures demands at least some consideration and agreement as to how 'benchmark' accountability which would allow participants in the debate to articulate what 'enough' (and therefore 'not enough' and 'too much') accountability looks like (see, for example, Grossi and Thomason 2015). This is where Ellen Rock's (2020) *Measuring Accountability in Public Governance Regimes* raises a distinctive set of questions concerning not just how to gauge the impact and value of different accountability processes (political, legal, professional, public, etc) but how to comprehend the cumulative influence of multiple-accountabilities (ie cross-pressures). This, in turn, takes us back to the epistemological and methodological roots of Boven's (2010) criticism of much of the existing accountability literature (discussed above). The link is provided in Rock's (2020, 1) observation that,

> Notwithstanding our apparent willingness to jump on the accountability bandwagon, the precise metes and bounds of the concept remain contested. The literature abounds

> with definitions of accountability and descriptions of the essential features of accountability mechanisms. Far from assisting in clarification, the never-ending efforts at defining accountability leave us *with many more questions than answers*. Is accountability a normative concept, or should it be defined mechanically? [emphasis added]

Three balance-related themes or issues emerge out of Rock's observation. The first theme emerges out of her concluding question and has, to some extent, been answered through Boven's (2010) identification of 'two concepts of accountability' – accountability as *a virtue* and as *a mechanism*. The former focuses primarily on the behaviour of individuals vis-à-vis democratic safeguards and holds accountability as generally 'a good thing'; the latter being predominantly concerned with institutional design. From this perspective the work of Peter Hennessy and Andrew Blick (2019) on the rejection of constitutional conventions by populist politicians – 'Good Chaps No More' – is clearly focused on accountability as a virtue; whereas Fukuyama's approach is mechanistically informed (for a discussion see Flinders, 2013). The implication being that any assessment of 'enough', 'not enough', 'too much' – not to mention 'overloads', 'deficits' and 'sweet spots' – is immediately complicated by the ways in which accountability is interpreted differently by different actors, and its constituent elements given differing degrees of emphasis. As Taylor and Buranelli's (2007) work – curiously entitled 'Ending up in Pizza' – underlines, accountability institutions, expectations and processes need to be aligned in order to avoid duplication and generally 'gumming up the works'. In reality, there are not two concepts of accountability but multiple and constantly mutating conceptualisations of account-based relationships. It is – to paraphrase David Collier and Steven Levitsky's (1997) work on a different but related topic – a concept 'with adjectives'.

To put the same point slightly differently, to cope with the innate ambiguity of accountability scholars have increasingly engaged in conceptual innovation and this has led to an almost dizzying array of adjectival sub-types. These conceptual containers are used as a way of focusing down on very specific dimensions within the far broader and complex accountability landscape. The risk with 'focusing down', however, is that moves towards analytical granularity reduces *systemic* understandings of the interplay between different accountability processes. 'We as scholars finds ourselves in a situation similar to that of the parable of the blind men and the elephant' Romzek (2015, 31) suggests 'We can feel certain parts of the animal that we touch but our limited vision leas us to capture only part of the essence of accountability.' A second insight from Rock's work – and one that takes us back to the dilemma of zero-sum assumptions (discussed above) – is that understanding accountability is unlikely to be achieved through a focus on 'more' or 'less' because the dichotomy is too crude to capture the potential complementarities or tensions *between* different forms of accountability or processes. This takes the discussion back to Mel Dubnick's (2002; see also O'Kelly and Dubnick 2014) attempt to 'seek salvation' for accountability by questioning whether every dilemma in contemporary democratic governance could really be solved by new and increasingly elaborate scrutiny structures (ie 'the promise of performance'). But what Rock (2020, 9) tries to insert into the debate is 'the argument that accountability systems encompass *a range of accountability dynamics* that must be understood in order to assess the potential presence of accountability deficits and overloads'.

A focus on balance of proportionality, therefore, cannot be achieved – this argument would suggest – through a focus on any one mechanism, relationship or process but only through an attempt to step back from the fray in order to assess how that exists and operates within the broader architecture of accountability (ie supporting, grating, reinforcing, undermining, etc). And yet even this focus *systemic* questions of accountability risks implicitly aligning and reinforcing a dominant 'reformist narrative' that unquestionably promotes 'the promise' of accountability in every setting. But it is also brings us to a third and final issue that Rock's work highlights: questions of method, range and approach.

How should accountability be studied? The most simple questions are very often the most complex and challenging to answer but the *how* question as it relates to studying and understanding accountability is not one that can be easily avoided. Our answer is one that needs to be situated within a brief (and inevitably partial) chronological account of the existing scholarship. For much of the twentieth century accountability was highlighted and discussed as an important topic in a range of disciplines. But it was generally interpreted as a secondary or consequential topic of analysis. This changed in the late 1980s and 1990s when scholars in the field of public administration began to make accountability their analytical focus, while also demonstrating its real-world effects (see, for example, Romzek and Dubnick 1991; 1993; 1987). This evolved into an increasing awareness of the existence of multiple and potentially incompatible 'accountability expectations' – as explored in, for example, Patricia Day and Rudolph Klein's *Accountabilities: Five Public Services* (1987).

While questions of accountability were undoubtedly receiving more attention and being answered in a more analytical manner the dominant case study approach – as reflected in, for example, Johnston and Romzek (1999, 2000); Romzek and Ingraham (2000); Kim (2005); Kim and Lee (2010) – meant that broader systemic insights born of common analytical approaches were rare. And yet the root issue was not so much methodological but conceptual: accountability was a term that lacked a common, stable, or meaningful foundation which made achieving analytic credibility very difficult without focusing down on a specific event, issue or episode. This explains the ubiquity within the research base of Sinclair's (1995) argument about the 'chameleon-like' nature of accountability, and Mulgan's (2000) concern about an 'ever-expanding concept'. It is also the point at which a schism emerges within the research base between those scholars who seemed content to accept and explore the innate complexity of accountability, on the one hand, and those who craved a more foundationalist and 'scientific' approach, on the other.

The work of Marc Bovens was particularly influential in terms of understanding this debate. His book *The Quest for Responsibility* (1998) harvested the insights of several disciplines to reveal how the shift to forms of networked and collaborative governance had posed new questions of accountability. His subsequent work (2007; see also 2010) was ground breaking due to its promotion of a new conceptual framework for analysing and assessing accountability. This was a framework, moreover, that could theoretically be used in any setting to answer basic questions of accountability such as – 'does public accountability work?' (Bovens, Schillemans, and 't Hart 2008). This brings us back to Boven's (2010, 946–947) critique of the academic literature on accountability (discussed above) and especially to his apparent frustration with the number of 'concepts, conceptualisations and frames for studying accountability' that had been used. Not only was the literature 'rather disconnected' but his deeper point was that 'few of these [conceptual] definitions are fully compatible, which makes it very hard to produce cumulative or commensurable research …. there are many scholars who talk about accountability, but few who *study it rigorously* [emphasis added]'. It is this notion of 'rigor' and the appropriate methods and tools with which to engage with questions of accountability that we seek to tease-apart for the simple reason that it too concerns the issue of *balance*.

'In lieu of some consensus about what accountability means, those seeking to actually "study" accountable behavior had to adapt' Dubnick notes (2011, 707) 'The only resolution was to engage in some form of methodological reductionism by narrowing the focus to the level of individual behaviour.' From this perspective the great value of Boven's contribution was that it drew upon the insights and approaches of other disciplines (notably psychology) in order to generate more experimental, behavioural and in this sense 'rigorous' and 'scientific' approaches (for a review see Aleksovska and Schillemans 2019). This has undoubtedly opened-up new avenues of insight and scholarship on, for example, 'calibrating public accountability' (Schillemans, 2016), the 'accountability cube' (Brandsma and Schillemans 2013), and the notion of 'felt' accountability (Overman, Schillemans and Grimmelikhuijsen 2021). Lindberg (2013, 203) labels this the 'Utrecht School' of accountability studies. And yet the question that Dubnick's emphasis on 'methodological reductionism' seeks to engage with is whether such a positivist epistemological position is too procrustean to capture the full 'tone and texture' – to paraphrase Isaiah Berlin – of real-world lived accountabil*ities*. It is in exactly this vein that Phillipe Schmitter (2004, 49) writes of 'measuring that which eludes measurement'.

This line of questioning could flow into a far broader and well-furrowed debate concerning the contrast between political/administrative *studies* as opposed to political/administrative *science* which, although interesting, would be of little value to this book's core focus on questions of accountability. Where this debate does help us, however, is not only in relation to the existence of questions (and concerns) as to the practical measurement and understanding of accountability but also in relation to the value of methodological pluralism. That is, the harvesting and synthesis of multiple insights through a variety of methods and approaches. In many ways the significance, originality and rigor of this book is reflected through a commitment to open-up new perspectives and to bring new voices into the debate concerning why accountability matters. The next section outlines the structure of this book and its approach in more detail.

II. Accounting for Structure

In 1978 the American Congress overwhelmingly approved the creation of a set of Offices of Inspectors-General in many federal departments in an attempt to increase accountability and root-out waste. Nearly a decade later Margaret Gates and Mark Moore would publish *Inspectors-General: Junkyard Dogs or Man's Best Friend?* (1986) as the first detailed analysis of whether these new institutions had been effective. The book sought to answer a simple question: had the creation of Offices of Inspectors-General increased the accountability of the government and improved its performance or not? Their answer was ambiguous: while the creation of the new Inspectors General had undoubtedly created new chains of accountability whether this had actually improved the performance of the federal bureaucracy was far from certain. From this perspective the work of Gates and Moore might be seen as an early example of what would become Dubnick's (2005) concern with regard to 'accountability and the paradox of performance'. Or, more specifically, of Janet Kelly's (2007, 46) 'accountability trap' where the 'pursuit of the appearance of accountability [will] sacrifice genuine accountability to citizens'; which, top follow-on, has clear links with Rock's (2020) attempt to define a 'benchmark' of accountability with which to assess claims of 'deficits' or 'overloads'. But where Moore and Gates undoubtedly make a case with contemporary resonance is when they highlight the existence of an apparently 'unquenchable thirst for accountability' (1986, 2).

The aim of this book is not to quench this thirst but to explore *why* accountability matters and *how* the socio-political relationships and structures this concept seeks to embrace have and continue to change. As the previous section explained, it seeks to cast a net across this potentially fragmented intellectual terrain through the provision of a clear definitional statement as a starting point; and a flexible but unifying framing that focuses attention on the 'overload but under-performance' puzzle and the issue of balance of proportionality. It is this three-part framing from *definition* to *puzzle* to *balance* that forms the connective tissue between each of the contributions in this collection. The aim is to provide a flexible intellectual spine rather than a tight scholarly straight-jacket, and one of the achievements of this collection is how different contributors – both academic and practitioner – are able to utilise this framing in order to engage with a number of questions of accountability.

And can there ever have been a time when questions of accountability were more pressing?

The Brexit process has, for example, raised fundamental questions about the UK's constitutional configuration and regulatory frameworks (see Lee 2017; Mikuli and Kuca 2021); while the election of Donald Trump stimulated critical concerns in relation to 'moral barbarism', 'fake news', authenticity and outright denial (see, for example, Higgins 2018; Neundorf and Pardos-Prado 2021). More broadly, the emergence of 'a populist signal' – as Anna Grzymala-Busse (2019) has written – poses distinctive questions of accountability. The Covid-19 pandemic stimulated – as Dave Cowan and Ann Mumford (2021) have illustrated – new questions of accountability regarding human rights, executive powers, and about accountability within and beyond the nation state (see, for example, Jarman, Greer and McKee 2020). These are all reflected in increasing concerns, as Stephen Haggard and Robert Kaufman (2021) have discussed, regarding evidence of global democratic backsliding in the twenty-first century (particularly but not exclusively in the wake of Covid-19). This is a theme that forms the focus of IDEA's *The Global State of Democracy 2021* report, and which poses significant questions about the ability of existing institutions and processes to respond to public concerns regarding accountability, transparency, and control. The politics of the Coronavirus has therefore raised distinctive questions about how accountability processes relate to or underpin broader socio-political forms of trust, blame and understanding (see Flinders 2021).

New questions of accountability have also emerged around perennial themes – such as the accountability of the Monarch as head of state (Kumarasingham 2020), the codification of the prerogative power to create colonial laws after instances of the questionable and largely unaccountable use of the prerogative in regards to the British Indian Ocean Territory (otherwise known as the Chagos Islands (Monaghan 2018), the use of Prime Ministerial discretion (Cladi 2022), the capacity of legislatures to scrutinise the executive (see Christiansen and Fromage 2019; Cygan, Lynch and Whitaker 2020), the need to restore public confidence in the House of Commons (White 2022), and to repair (via the way of reform) the damage done to the constitution by the Johnson administration (Blick and Hennessy 2022), and the proposed modernisation of impeachment to tackle perceived deficiencies regarding the accountability of the executive within the UK's Westminster system (Monaghan 2022) – and around completely new topics which themselves appear to challenge fundamental tenets of traditional accountability assumptions. It is in exactly this vein that Daria Gritsenko and Matthew Wood (2022) have illustrated how the use of increasingly complex computer-based models to allocate public resources (housing, healthcare, good and services) through forms of algorithmic governance pose new questions of digital transparency and political responsibility. To put the same point slightly differently, the 'quest for responsibility' – to paraphrase the title of Boven's influential 1998 (mentioned above) – is likely to grow even more complicated in the context of 'post-human governance' (see Hughes 2017).

It is this complexity that all of the chapters in this book seek to understand and unravel through a shared awareness of the 'overload but under-performance' puzzle (and other forms of trade-off) and a focus on the notion of balance or proportionality as it relates to accountable governance. More specifically, each chapter focuses on three distinct questions of accountability within its specific sphere of inquiry and investigation, and the collection is itself divided into three main parts, each containing four or five chapters.

Part I focuses on 'Framing' and its aim is to stretch the intellectual space surrounding questions of accountability by exploring the topic from several very different angles which all in their owns ways extend and expand several of the conceptual, methodological and practical debates already mentioned in this introductory chapter. Thomas Schillemans opens this section by exploring a number of 'questions of perspective' in chapter two which integrate insights from political science, public administration and psychology in order to engage with three specific questions: when do politicians and officials tend to comply with accountability expectations? In what situations might they seek to defend themselves in terms of blame-avoidance behaviour? How might politicians and officials adopt a more reflective 'accountability approach' strategy? Philip Tetlock's (2002) metaphor of the 'intuitive politician' is used to tease-apart each of these questions, specifically in relation to how politicians and officials seek to balance competing accountability demands. Real-world case studies are used to connect these questions with the book's broader thesis about 'over-supply and under-performance'. These themes are continued in chapter three as Ellen Rock focuses on the thorny issue of measurement, and the specific challenge of 'striking an appropriate accountability balance'. Three inter-related questions frame this chapter: what does it mean to quantify accountability? How could an 'ideal amount' or accountability 'sweet spot' ever be agreed upon? What basic questions would need to be resolved to maintain any sense of equilibrium? Ultimately Rock argues that if we hope to correct problems arising perceived 'deficits' or 'overloads' we must become much more explicit about the end goal we are aiming for.

In chapter four Matthew Flinders continues the discussion around balance and proportionality by reviewing and developing the debate about the 'dark side' of accountability. 'Can accountability be bad for democracy?' provides the focus of this chapter and the question that opens-up a major debate about causes and effects, and incentives and sanctions which both inform and are developed in later chapters. By focusing on *the pathology of politicised accountability* chapter four tracks the evolution of a wide-ranging debate concerning the media, psychology, populism and the need for a radical reframing of accountability. One of the most important contributions of this chapter is an advanced understanding of why – in Philip Tetlock's words – 'it is easy to look down on those who those who look soft on accountability'. This leads, in Diagram 4.1, to a psychologically informed hypo-hyper accountability continuum that helps explain the dominance of Mode I accountability approaches. Many of the questions concerning constraint and conflict are developed further in chapter five as Margit Cohn focuses on executive powers and fuzzy law from a socio-legal perspective. What Cohn identifies is not only the existence of mirror-image dynamics that relate to concerns regarding 'fuzzy accountability' but also a very specific paradox. That is, the way in which the laws and practices that instil governing capacity in the executive are very often the very same features that frustrate scrutiny and create questions of accountability. The concept of fuzzy law therefore poses questions of strategically manufactured ambiguity that urgently need to be asked, not least as they lead back to concerns regarding balance, over-load and under-supply.

These are questions that Se-shauna Wheatle continues to engage with in chapter six through an innovative approach that seeks to move beyond perennial questions about the relationship between political and legal constitutionalism. Instead of seeing political and judicial structures necessarily co-existing in a form of constant conflict Wheatle focuses on the notion of collaborative constitutionalism and explains its relevance to current questions of accountability. This chapter outlines the core features of collaborative constitutionalism, including a rejection of polarisation and a focus on the reality of inter-institutional interactions. It then makes the case for a collaborative view of the constitution by reference to constitutional pluralism and horizontal legal relationships which serves to re-orientate existing questions of accountability. This chapter challenges the view that recent examples of assertive judicial review in the UK represent excessive judicialisation and legalisation. Instead, it argues that such cases represent a turn towards collaborative constitutionalism – multiple, interdependent accountability mechanisms offer useful 'backstops' in the face of executive attempts to erode constitutional values. The chapter concludes by placing this argument back within broader debates concerning trade-offs and balance.

In Part II the focus shifts towards a more thematic approach in order to drill-down into many of the themes and issues that were raised (and questioned) in Part I. This begins – in chapter seven – with Chris Monaghan and Josie Welsh exploring 'questions of control' through a focus on the intention of the May government to trigger Article 50 of the Treaty on European Union using the arguably undemocratic prerogative powers, the prorogation controversy, long-standing concerns over judicial power, and the modernised use of impeachment. The former element highlights the potential weakness of constitutional configurations that ultimately rely on executive self-restraint, which as is argued by Monaghan and Welsh has proved to be in short supply (especially under the Johnson government), the latter element focuses attention on strengthening the processes through which a politician or public official can be held to account and potentially removed from office for misconduct. Monaghan and Welsh offer critics of judicial power a challenge – if you support accountable and responsible government, then what are you willing to do to reform the existing political system which arguably (although there are exceptions) often offers limited scope for effective parliamentary accountability of the executive.

Chapter eight shifts the focus from questions of accountability concerning impeachment to a set concerning official counsel and policy advice. This raises an area of huge significance that has to a greater or lesser extent been almost completely absent within the broader debate concerning public accountability. What Jonathan

Slater brings to the discussion – through a practitioner perspective which adds a highly distinctive lens – is a focus on three questions: how do senior civil servants come to understand and acknowledge the accountability expectations placed upon them? How do they navigate the challenges of advising ministers in a high-blame low trust-environment? Could the efficiency of government be improved if officials were made publicly accountable for the policy advice they provide to ministers? These questions open-up the accountability space in ways that produce radical and rarely voiced reform options, while also demanding fresh thinking when it comes to concerns regarding candour, trade-offs, and balance. Similarly fresh thinking emerges in chapter nine as Robert Blackburn shifts the focus from the realm of officialdom and policy advice to questions about 'accountability at the apex' and in relation to the monarchy. The absence of a written constitution in the UK has left the ancient Crown powers of state uncodified and extra-parliamentary, with much debate and considerable confusion surrounding those prerogatives still exercised or authorised directly (personally) by the Monarch. The most important of these are the appointment and removal of prime ministers, royal assent to legislation, and dissolution of Parliament. It is against this backdrop that this chapter asks: how did these precedents come into existence? To what extent are these precedents universally accepted and what factors or actors might be fuelling ambiguity? And looking to the future, could a programme of formal codification of the principles of royal accountability provide a solution to long-running questions of accountability?

Enduring debates concerning balance, ambiguity and the merits of codification also feature in Alison Young's analysis of fundamental questions concerning accountability and human rights in chapter ten. The Human Rights Act 1998 was designed to provide legal and political means of accountability over human rights decisions but to what extent has the legislation achieved its goals? This chapter tackles this question by exploring recent decisions concerning welfare benefits and discrimination. These cases concern Treaty rights (ie United Nations Convention on the Rights of the Child) that have not been incorporated into the UK as a whole, while also relating to the European Convention on Human Rights which was incorporated into UK law through the 1998 legislation. The chapter engages with three specific questions: how does the existence of multiple and interlocking chains of accountability effect procedures and decision-making? What factors ensure the effectiveness of legal accountability, especially in relation to protecting individuals from discriminatory executive or legislative decisions? Why do political mechanisms of accountability often fail to provide an effective means of scrutiny, especially when they are generally granted a wider margin of appreciation? Not only does chapter ten complement discussions that have already been opened-up in earlier chapters, but it also adds a new dimension, through a focus on accountability 'ceilings' and 'floors', to existing debates about trade-offs, balance and proportionality.

This brings the collection to Part III and to a focus that shifts from approaches and themes to a discussion of future-focused 'questions of accountability'. It is exactly this vein that Kate Macdonald and Terry Macdonald explore 'accountability beyond the nation state' in chapter eleven. In recent decades, they suggest, the ascendance of accountability discourses and practices within national governance settings throughout the Anglosphere has extended to multiple domains of global governance, promising to contain concentrations of power and provide voice and influence to stakeholders affected by global governing authority. And yet despite an ongoing proliferation of multi-layered accountability mechanisms, global accountability agendas have struggled to confront the fundamental challenge of how power is to be controlled and stakeholders empowered within a pluralist global political order that lacks a constitutionalised institutional structure for global governance. This is presented as the core question of accountability for scholars, practitioners and the publics of global governance which has yet defied clear answers. In order to tackle this question this chapter shines a spotlight on key dilemmas that arise within the interactive governance processes that characterise a pluralist global political order, focusing on challenges of dynamic stakeholder identification and the regulation of decentered power. It then argues that rebalancing relations of power and accountability within a pluralist political order demands a more explicit focus on three specific sub-questions: how can shifting configurations of stakeholders be identified? How can horizontal and networked relationships be orchestrated? How might concentrations of political power be countered through decentered strategies of social empowerment? These three questions are explored with reference to the global governance of business, development, and the environment – three governance domains in which accountability discourses and practices have played a central role in shaping ongoing struggles over power and legitimacy in global governance.

If chapter eleven focuses on macro-level questions of global governance, then chapter twelve moves to a far tighter and more personal viewpoint by looking at 'accountability from the inside-out'. 'Inside-out' in this case providing a very rare glimpse into the world of coping with multiple accountability pressures from a professional perspective, but also with coping with those pressure as an individual from a human-centred perspective: simply, *living accountability*. What David Blunkett provides is a highly challenging critique of most of the existing academic analysis. The main argument of this chapter is that too many of the 'academic' stories written about the topic of accountability – laden as they are with rich and relevant analyses of 'webs', 'overloads', 'shields' and 'deficits' – are just that: academic analyses written at a distance from the day-to-day messiness and experience of accountability processes. They are what might be termed 'outside-in' analyses where in this chapter the author utilises auto-ethnographical insights in order to provide an 'inside-out' account in order to explore three specific questions: have we gone MAD in the sense of succumbing to multiple-accountabilities disorder? How can accountability mechanisms improve their empathetic or emotional intelligence in order to overcome the challenge of 'hindsight bias'? And finally, what questions of accountability need to be asked about the mental health and wellbeing of politicians? The overall insight that chapter twelve attempts to provide is that the 'accountability problem' should not be viewed as a socio-political challenge to be 'solved' in any simple sense but one demanding greater institutional co-ordination and public understanding.

This focus on institutional co-ordination, public understanding and approaches to accountability is developed in further in chapter thirteen as Sharon Shoesmith looks at the relationship between naming, shaming and blaming in the context of tragedy and public sector failings. This is a powerful and highly personalised account not just of *how it feels* to be at the centre of a political and media feeding frenzy but also of the manner in which 'Mode I' (returning to the distinction made above) scrutiny structures generally crowd out the space for those 'Mode II' approaches that are actually more important in a crisis context. What the case study of the familial homicide of 'Baby P' reveals are exactly those negative and unintended consequences that the dominance of aggressive and blame-focused 'Mode I' systems can exert. At a more basic level, the chapter reveals the strategic game-playing by various actors in a way that resonates with Flinders' earlier emphasis on the pathology of politicised accountability. Chapter thirteen is a quite shocking study in the day-to-day realities of operating under a constant 'shadow of blame' which is either unable or unwilling to acknowledge the inevitably complex and arguably invidious nature of many of the decisions that public sector workers are required to take in the normal course of their work.

If the focus of chapter thirteen is very much on the role of street level bureaucrats, in this case through a focus on social workers, and creating an operating environment that is 'cooler' and less 'heated', then chapter fourteen shifts the analytical lens from *street-level bureaucrats* to *system-level bureaucracies* through a focus on artificial intelligence and artificial public administration. What this reveals is a sphere of technologically-orientated research and debate that is infused with 'questions of accountability' that augment and intensify traditional concerns. 'As bureaucratic discretion is removed and replaced by sophisticated algorithmic systems where does this leave us when it comes to public accountability?' Madalina Busuioc asks, 'Is public accountability on the way to becoming an outdated, archaic value in the age of the artificial administration?' The notion of 'post-human accountability' might sound far-fetched but it does go some way to identify changing decision-making processes that serve distance and delegate responsibility away from politicians and policymakers. It is for this reason that Busuioc goes to great lengths to demonstrate that what might be seen from one perspective as 'post-human' due to the existence of seemingly rational, technocratic, highly sophisticated computer-based systems are in fact imbued with the highly normative and often discriminatory values of their commissioners, designers and programmers. In this sense Busuioc attempts to (*re*)politicise an increasingly important dimension of modern public governance, while also forging links to themes and issues that have been raised in earlier chapters.

With this focus on linking and integration in mind chapter fifteen looks back across the collection of chapters in an attempt to engage with the question of 'where next?' for the analysis of accountability. This collection is founded on the principle that *accountability matters*. It matters because there is increasing evidence that a worrying gap is emerging between the governors and the governed. In this context asking 'questions of accountability' provides a way of not only understanding the existence of inevitable tensions and trade-offs but also potentially identifying measures that can promote public understanding and rebuild public confidence in political institutions, political processes and politicians. But – as this opening chapter has underlined – accountability is a broad, fluid, and multi-dimensional concept; it poses far too many questions for any single collection to try and tackle, let alone answer. Whether answers even exist is a question that needs to be asked because, as Romzek (2015, 29) has argued, '[A]ccountability is not a puzzle or a formula to be solved. In both the political and governance arenas accountability is a complex dynamic to be *managed at best* [italics in original].' This is why chapter fifteen focuses on 'questions still to be answered'. It does this by returning to this book's core focus on *a puzzle* (whether it is possible to move beyond assumptions concerning the inevitability of an accountability-efficiency trade-off) and *an issue* (the notion of balance or equilibrium). To what extent have the contributions in this collection shed new light on the overload but under-supply dilemma? In what ways might debates concerning constitutional balance vis-à-vis accountability be reconceptualised or even addressed with reference to the contributions in this collection? And finally, what are the main emergent questions concerning accountability that are likely to define the legal sphere and the social and political sciences in the future?

PART I

Framing

2

Questions of Perspective – Accountability as a Behavioural Proposition

THOMAS SCHILLEMANS

This is a book about accountability and why it matters. The previous chapter provided a broad account of some of the main criticism and concerns, dilemmas and debates within the existing knowledge base. The aim of this chapter is to explore some 'questions of perspective' vis-à-vis accountability, with a specific focus on *how* accountability is studied. It takes the discussion back to some of the topics that were raised in the opening chapter about granularity and scale, about mechanisms and virtues, and about how the existence of an accountability 'sweet spot' (see Figure 1.1, above) might ever be identified at an individual, group or societal level. These are 'big' questions but in order to be able to engage with them in a more refined or focused manner the central argument of this chapter is that accountability can be conceived of as a behavioural proposition. The implicit or explicit assumption being that the presence of accountability – either in the form of foundational values, specified norms or toothy institutions and mechanisms – will lead to the desirable behaviours and decrease undesirable behaviours in politics, public administration and democratic governance more broadly.

As such, this chapter explores a number of questions concerning the behaviour of political and administrative actors, and it does so by integrating insights in the effects of accountability from political science and public administration with those from the behavioural sciences. The purpose is to make sense of how decision-makers in the fuzzy realities of politics and public administration will behave under conditions of accountability; a question that has been answered in the abstract in crisp and clear laboratory settings. This chapter connects the insights from rather different fields of research and ultimately engages with three specific questions:

1. When do politicians and officials tend to comply with accountability expectations?

2. In what situations might they seek to defend themselves in terms of blame-avoidance behaviour?
3. How might politicians and officials adopt a more reflective, learning strategy?

Philip Tetlock's (2002) metaphor of the 'intuitive politician' is used as a basis to answer this question, to which then the 'institutional', 'professional' and 'real' politician are added, as they operate in politics and public administration. As such, in many ways – just as accountability should be discussed in terms of balance of blend – one of the key objectives of this chapter is to explore and explain how the insights of different disciplines can be balanced and blended together in order to advance our understanding of accountability-induced behaviours in both theoretical and practical terms. With this approach, this chapter seeks to underline that it is possible to combine the abstract insights of behavioural sciences with the contextual sensitivity of traditional public administration or political studies approaches, aiming also to avoid the risks of 'methodological reductionism' (see Dubnick 2011, 707).

This ambition takes the discussion back to the navigational and distinctiveness challenges that were identified in the opening chapter. The navigational challenge emerges from the existence of a large and fragmented body of scholarship that is often defined by islands of theorising and research that have for too long been almost completely disconnected. The navigational opportunity that this chapter identifies and seeks to advance revolves around building bridges between behavioural sciences, on the one hand, and public administration, on the other. The distinctiveness challenge (and opportunity) is that by attempting to blend insights, new questions, perspectives and ways of thinking about accountability (as both a mechanism and a virtue) are revealed.

In order to make this case and explore these questions this chapter is divided into three main sections. The first main section focuses on the challenges of blending and balancing different academic perspectives. What it reveals is that *the* core challenge for what might be termed the 'behavioural public administration approach' to accountability is how to combine the rigor of experimental methods with the relevance of contextual settings. The second section then explores how the approach *does* attempt to achieve this delicate balance. This involves a discussion of the 'intuitive politician' model and how methods have attempted to combine the 'cool theory' of psychological lab-based methods with the 'hot rhetoric' – paraphrasing Romzek (2015) – of day-to-day aggressive and blame-based everyday accountability lived experience. The third and final section then focuses on the three questions outlined above and seeks to theoretically understand and outlines three future-focused 'questions of accountability' that remain to be answered.

I. Two Accountability Approaches

The main aim of this section is to unite the fields of behavioural sciences and public administration in order to engage with the three 'questions of accountability' that were outlined in the opening section. This might at first glance appear like a highly technical and 'academic' endeavour, but it is also one that offers great promise in terms of understanding the relationship between breadth, beliefs and blame that was highlighted in the opening chapter. In terms of navigating between and uniting these two bodies of literature it is true that in recent years several scholars in public administration have started to bridge the previous divide by drawing upon behavioural approaches and insights from the world of psychology. This has proved a productive expedition and there is now a very large base of behavioural research on accountability offering many avenues for advancement for public administration research (for reviews see Lerner and Tetlock 1999; Hall et al 2017; Harari and Rudolph 2017; Aleksovska et al 2019). The slight paradox is that while studies that operate at the intersection or nexus between behavioural sciences and public administration exist in a relatively clear intellectual space, those on accountability wholly within public administration tend to exist in a far larger and fragmented space (hence the criticisms outlined in chapter one, above). That is not to suggest that overviews of the field do not exist (see, for example, Dubnick and Frederickson 2011; Schillemans 2013; Bovens et al 2014; Bellamy and Palumbo 2017; Schillemans et al 2021b), but it is to suggest that it is a vast and complex terrain.

The first 'question of accountability' is really 'where to begin?' In this regard possibly the most basic and important foundational insight is the manner in which public administration settings tend to differ – ontologically, epistemologically and methodologically – from those studied and enacted in behavioural accountability studies.

Almost all scholarship on accountability in behavioural sciences uses experimental methods to understand how accountability affects decisions or behaviours (or other psychologically relevant outcomes) of individuals. Psychology naturally takes a micro-level focus and studies how individuals respond to accountability. Most of these studies are conducted in the US with samples of students in laboratory settings and experimental tasks that, although relevant to real world settings, may also be quite abstract or unrealistic. To some extent this abstracted quality is not a problem and may well be seen as a strength of the approach as the aim of such studies is to uncover fundamental human traits and responses to the absence or presence of accountability expectations. Such scientific precision arguably requires the presence of tightly controlled experimental settings with a minimum of 'noise' (ie distracting contextual conditions). Using such methods, experimental scholars have – as Lerner and Tetlock (1999, 270) surmise – shown how accountability can produce 'an array of effects … only some of which are beneficial'. The obvious follow-up question posed by such analyses, however, is to what extent those findings are transferable or relevant to those likely to be observed in far more complex, intense and 'noisier', real world settings.

The starting point for public administration scholars is very much the 'noisy' end of the spectrum. The discipline emerged out of the practice of public service and seeks to support and improve public services and the business of government in terms of efficiency, co-ordination, collaboration and transparency.

Public administration is – as Walker et al (2019) have emphasised – 'an interdisciplinary social science field that emphasizes applied ("theory to practice") applications'. Unlike psychology which is less concerned with real world settings (see Brewer 2000) the root question for public administration *is* whether or not, and to what extent and when, a phenomenon occurs in specific contexts. Contextual specificity and effect is arguably the key scientific question. As such, public administration research naturally adds specific contextual, institutional, normative, organisational and professional elements to studies of accountability. This makes such studies richer or methodologically 'thicker', but also at the same time arguably more 'fuzzy', 'vague' or even 'fluid', than classic (sharper, tighter, focused) laboratory methods. It also means that behaviourally *informed* studies of public sector accountability can attempt to harness 'the best of both worlds' in methodological terms by combining the precision of behavioural sciences with the contextual sensitivity of public administration.

Having outlined the core qualities and relationship between these two perspectives it is possible to move on to a focus on the specific elements of accountability as a broad and relational concept that could be relevant to study. Or, to put the same point slightly differently, the basic definition outlined in chapter one was compromised of several elements (ie a relationship exists, an obligation to account is in place, a process of providing an account, the potential for punishment or praise) but which of these elements might be relevant or particularly attuned to what this chapter is labelling a 'behavioural public administration accountability study'? Building on Bouwman and Grimmelikhuijsen (2018), it is possible to focus on at least three elements: (i) the role of the individual; (ii) the task performed; and (iii) the accountability setting in terms of specific account-arena and applicable institutional rules. The following sub-sections take these three topics in turn.

A. Roles and Tasks

In experimental studies of accountability in behavioural science, the individual who is subjected to an accountability manipulation needs some degree of discretion or agency – some responsibility for an action or a decision – to make it a relevant scenario. These roles are not always specified, and individuals are often cast in roles they do not necessarily occupy in their professional lives. They are cast as decision-makers with clear agency for the task or decision at hand. This perspective does not always hold for individuals in public administration who are *embedded* and may enjoy different levels of formal and informal discretion and exist within a web of often contradictory expectations and relationships. As a result, from a public administration perspective it makes sense to focus individual level accountability studies on only those individuals who *do* have some formal or de facto individual responsibility for decisions. Overman and Schillemans (2022) identify four typical cases of such public decision-makers with a clear individual agency: (i) the street-level bureaucrat (see also Thomann, Hupe and Sager, 2018); (ii) the mandarin, (iii) the executive, and (iv) the professional. These are all individuals who take the types of decisions implied in behavioural accountability research. Additionally, regulators and inspectors are typically individuals in public administration with a certain individual responsibility for decisions (Dudley and Xie 2020). And, of course, politicians are individuals who take decisions in public administration (*cf* Woon 2012), although the study of their behaviour in relation to accountability is more natural in political science.

It is also important to acknowledge the existence of a two-way contradiction that spans this field of research. First and foremost, it is clear that street-level bureaucrats, mandarins or inspectors do not always have the level or type of discretion that is often assumed in laboratory studies, and yet at the same time it is important to recognise that those individuals who serve in the public sector are also likely to have professional qualities and personality profiles that make them, to some extent, unrepresentative of the population at large. This two-way contradiction – to which a range of additional complexities could undoubtedly be grafted – simply underlines why so many 'questions of accountability' seem to exist without obvious answers. The next sub-section focuses not on roles or tasks but account-arenas.

B. The Account Arenas

Chapter one drew-upon Bovens' (2017) definition of accountability which included a relational approach forged upon a four-part framework or chain. There had to be a clear relationship between an actor and a forum (Part #1), whereby an actor was obliged to render an account of their behaviour or activities (Part #2), and where an accountability forum can pose questions about and/or investigate the veracity of that account in some arena (Part #3), which leads to the final phase of passing judgement as to the standard of the accountees' behaviour or performance (Part #4). The fourth and final stage may involve the allocation of blame or the distribution of credit or praise, or even some mixture of the two. The classic experimental accountability study in behavioural science does generally neither specify the account arena or to whom accountability is rendered. Participants may also be placed in accountability settings that may not be descriptive of their professional experiences. Mostly implicitly it is assumed that the decision-maker is confronted by an account holder who has the right to demand accountability and, thus, that accountability is salient and meaningful.

In public administration settings, this condition of salient accountability is simultaneously dramatised *and* nuanced. Dramatised in the sense that organisations and individuals operate in the limelight of societal, media and political attention in which even the smallest issue, failing or problem risks becoming amplified into a major scandal, fiasco and crisis. At the same time the existence of a high-blame, low-trust context is likely to encourage a focus on blame-attribution which is reflected in a huge literature on blame-avoidance, sacrificial lambs and scapegoating (see Flinders et al 2023). At a more basic level the ethos and principles of public service place great weight on transparency and inclusive processes which means the day-to-day business of government, which is often inevitably compromise-based and messy, is far more visible than is the case with private sector governance. As Brummel (2022) has shown, the presence of at times politicised, mediatised, accountability has a strong impact in public administration. The behaviour of politicians and senior officials tends to be far more defensive, risk-averse and sometimes irrational exactly because of the socio-political context and pressures of working within the public sector (on this see Schillemans et al 2021b; Olsen 2015).

Beyond the political high stakes, public sector accountability is further marked by the presence of multiple account holders operating on the basis of multiple, at times conflictual, values or norms. These are the 'cross-pressures' of accountability that can be so distracting and pathological for some organisations. Literally all recent empirical studies on accountability in public administration at least mention, and oftentimes engage more fully, with the issue of the multiplicity of account holders, norms or processes (for an overview see Schillemans et al 2021b). What is interesting about these studies is how they tend to focus almost exclusively not on one single linear relationship to *an* accountability arena but instead focus more broadly on *extra*-organisational forms of accountability in fragmented arenas. That is, not on accountability to any one primary immediate superior but on the existence of a web or network of multi-directional accountability relationships (to Parliament, regulators, citizens, coordinating government departments, publics, audit bodies, professional associations, or others). This adds important complicating factors to the felt accountability relationship(s) in at least two ways: first, from the perspective of behavioural sciences it underlines the limits of decontextualised, lab-based experiments that secure data from non-embedded participants. Second, it also raises questions about the credibility, legitimacy and layering of these multiple arenas. Put slightly differently, when accountability is demanded from *outside* the primary relationship (for example, beyond the relationship between an arm's-length body to its parent department) the question arises whether this is at all legitimate ('What right do *they* have to question us?') and whether outsiders have the substantive expertise to interrogate account givers ('Do they actually know *what* they are on about?') (*cf* Overman et al 2020).

While the accountability context in public administration may seem more dramatic at first sight, there are also some factors that actually *nuance* the impact of accountability. Not all account-arenas in public administration are actually politically salient. The study by Schillemans and Kremer (2020) for instance has even found examples of organisations embedded in multiple accountability relationships where none of them were perceived to be particularly influential or onerous. So while there may be many account-arenas surrounding decision-makers, their impact and the level of threat they pose can be very low, or at least much lower than is normally assumed in laboratory experiments. So there may be cases with a lot of accountability yet without any salient – that is expected, effective, legitimate and authoritative (*cf* Overman et al 2020) – accountability. Also, some account holders adopt consensual styles of account holding, in which they operate more as advisors, stewards or constructive friends than as 'intuitive prosecutors' (Tetlock 2002) or critical (un)friends (Brummel 2020). In addition to that, seasoned civil servants learn to live in high-accountability contexts and may get accustomed to its presence (see Aleksovska 2021). Some particularly proactive and entrepreneurial officials or politicians may also be able to utilise dense accountability networks to their own advantage – becoming 'accountability entrepreneurs' who through shaping and framing their own position are able to engage in a sophisticated form of 'principal(s) capture'.

Taking this back into the laboratory setting of a fixed experiment utilising fictional scenarios or decision-making processes it is possible that the participant, especially if they are aware of the realities of public sector governance, may well be more intimidated and concerned by the existence of a linear one-off accountability puzzle as by definition it removes the opportunity for strategic game-playing and the engineering of different trade-offs. In public administration settings, civil servants learn in repeated games how the prevalent accountability environment operates, and they will learn how to live and cope with that. In fact, one of the key forms of tacit knowledge decision-makers in public administration learn from accountability – as Schillemans and Smulders (2016) have shown – is actually how to handle, manage and possibly pacify account-demanding processes and arenas. Therefore, when compared to the clear, sharp and precise approach of accountability analyses in the behavioural sciences, the approach of public administration is to factor in the external, dynamic, multi-dimensional and often pervasive influence of accountability (plus the way in which the political salience and risk of accountability can vary considerably at different points in the electoral cycle or in the wake of specific events).

The main focus of this section has been on outlining the core characteristics and qualities of two approaches to (or perspectives on) accountability – one derived from behavioural sciences, the second from public administration – that approach the issue of accountability from very different perspectives. In this sense the 'questions of accountability' posed revolve around not only the relative advantages and disadvantages of each approach but also the degree to which these very different ontological and epistemological positions can be reconciled to forge some form of hybrid approach. Stripped-back to its core dimension, the difference of position can be characterised as concerning 'heat' or 'noise'. Institutional rules, constitutional configurations and bureaucratic and political cultures vary from country to country and even from organisation to organisation; whereas the dilemmas of democratic competition impart specific dysfunctionalities in terms of short-term, partisan game-playing which are often played-out through accountability processes. To some extent, behavioural sciences silence the background knowledge and focus purely on individual behaviour in accountability contexts, thereby facilitating robust, rigorous and replicable studies. And yet by 'taking out the heat' and/or 'turning down the noise' – whichever metaphor is preferred – the concern amongst more qualitative-inclined scholars is that *the* defining feature of public accountability (ie, it does not take place in a hermetically sealed laboratory vacuum) is lost.

The main attraction of the behavioural approach is that it theoretically serves to develop and test causal propositions related to accountability. *The* challenge for a behavioural public administration approach to accountability then is how to combine the rigor of these methods with the relevance of contextual settings. This forms the focus of the next section.

II. Blending and Binding: The 'Cool' End of Accountability Behaviours

The theorising of accountability-behaviours in public administration has a clear baseline position and a myriad of alternatives. The baseline position is defined by principal-agent theory (*cf* Strøm 2000; Gailmard 2014). Principal-agent theory assumes the existence of rational and self-interested behaviour that, in turn, leads to a variety of theorised dilemmas within delegation-based relationships ('principal capture', 'agency shadowing', 'remaining an intelligent customer', 'shirking', etc). As such, the baseline accountability-game in a principal-agent scenario is one of a clash of interests, where the agent chooses between persistence (to their own goals or interests) or compliance (with the expected behaviour and enforced demands of the principal). This basic relationship and theorisation is itself complicated by the fact that the rationale for moving to a principal-agent relationship, especially within public sector governance, is that it provides the agent with high levels of discretion to operate. The theory of delegation in this context is that discretion facilitates responsiveness, agility, specialisation, responsiveness and, through this, higher levels of overall organisational and systemic efficiency.

In contrast to this relatively simple baseline model, scholars have proposed many alternative theoretical perspectives for accountability in public administration. These include stewardship theory (Van Slyke 2007), institutional theory (Olsen 2015), reputation theory (Busuioc and Lodge 2017) and several others; and although it is neither necessary nor possible to discuss all of these theories in detail in this section it is important to note that they all seek to posit non-rational or post-rational dimensions of human behaviour in ways that look beyond simplified assumptions about self-interest. Put slightly differently, they all suggest that behaviours can not only be understood as expressions of goal-rationality (as in principal agent theory), but also from a genuine desire to contribute to some supra-individual cause (stewardship theory) or that they are the product of institutional norms and practices (institutional theory) or can be understood through a reputational lens (reputation theory). In contrast, the behavioural science literature on accountability is considerably more empirical than theoretical. The baseline assumption here *is* very much the boundedly rational nature of human behaviours. People are capable of fully rational action, yet they are quite limited in terms of their mental ability and energies to do so. In Kahnemans' (2010) phrasing, the mind is a *lazy* machine, *jumping* to conclusions.

The notion of the lazy machine is congruent with Tetlock's (1992; 2002) 'social contingency model', which comes closest to a psychological theory of accountability. The first premise of this model is that decision-makers are generally *cognitive misers*. They will put a minimum of cognitive effort into a decision-making situation. As a result of this, they may be likely to err, fall for biases, or they may respond in particular ways to accountability. The second premise of this theory is that decision-makers are mindful of their social positions. Everything else being equal, they will be motivated to protect their social image, their self-image but also aim to acquire valuable 'goods' (such as a reputation) in accountability exchanges (Tetlock 1992). These foundational drives will guide human behaviours when confronted with accountability. Depending on some further conditions, three types of accountability behaviours (heuristics) are likely to be observed. These can be set out as follows:

1. The *Acceptability Heuristic* – adopt what is perceived to be the socially expected course of action – the behavioural process leading to compliance.
2. The *Rationalization Heuristic* – adopt a defensive position where behaviours have departed from expected norms – the behavioural process leading to blame-avoidance.
3. The *Pre-emptive Self-Criticism Heuristic* – anticipate and attempt to manage accountability pressures in advance of formal proceedings – the behavioural process leading to learning.

Decision-makers will intuitively opt for one of these heuristics, depending on the specific accountability settings in which they believe they operate. When there are clear social (accountability) norms *and* the decision-maker has not committed to a course of action yet, they are likely to adopt the *acceptability heuristic* and commit to what is perceived to be the socially easiest defendable position. The decision-maker will act as an *intuitive politician* (Tetlock 2002) who instinctively relates to its audience and tries to say whatever it is its account holders want to hear. Tetlock (1992, 340–41; see also Bouwman et al 2018) writes:

> Laboratory and field studies suggest that people frequently do exactly that: they choose the most clearly defensible action open to them. For instance, several experiments on negotiation behaviour have found that negotiators who expect to justify bargaining outcomes to the groups they represent have much more difficulty arriving at mutually beneficial compromise agreements than do negotiators who are not under such pressure.

The acceptability heuristic thus leads to compliance, even at the expense of decision-outcomes. However, when social (accountability) norms are clear but the decision-maker *has* already committed to a course of action, they are likely to become defensive and endorse the adopted behaviours or position, even while at odds with relevant social and legal norms. This is called the *rationalisation heuristic* in which the decision-maker goes on the defensive, defending their past behaviours and decisions, even in the face of the evidence of problems.

The rationalization heuristic will then easily lead to blame-avoiding and blame-shifting rhetorical strategies.

Finally, there can also be cases of salient accountability where the expectation of evaluation by a salient account-holding body hangs in the air but no formal processes have been initiated. The nature of the issue may also mean that the process and benchmarks (see chapter three) through which accountability will be enforced remain somewhat vague and opaque. In this situation the accountee is likely to resort to *pre-emptive self-criticism*. Expecting to be held accountable by a reputable other whose criteria of evaluation are not fully clear can produce powerful and useful forms of self-reflection. As such, ambiguous (salient) accountability can be seen as a 'nudge' that makes people think and *may* lead to better, or at least more properly considered, decisions. The expectation of accountability may then induce potentially valuable learning processes. Again in Tetlock's (1992, 343) words:

> Numerous studies have shown that under these conditions accountability can induce people to abandon their cognitive-miserly ways. Pre-decisional accountability to unknown audiences frequently motivates vigilant, complex, and self-critical thinking.

The three heuristics above are the main elements of Tetlock's social contingency model. Although they relate to behavioural effects of accountability which are crucial in public administration settings – ie compliance, blame-shifting and learning – very few public administration studies have explicitly utilised or sought to develop this model (but see Aleksovska, 2021; Ossege, 2012). An exception is Schillemans' (2016) CPA-model ('calibrating public accountability'), built around the preconditions for acceptability and pre-emptive self-criticism. The model explores how such strategies can be expected to be functional from a good governance perspective. It is claimed that there may be two ideal-typical types of decisions in public administration: (i) *accurate decisions* and (ii) *well-considered decisions*. Accurate decisions for instance involve deciding whether a person is eligible for some benefit or generally decisions about norm-compliance. The evaluative standard here is specific and precise and the decisions and behaviours of the agent can be evaluated from the perspective of compliance. Well-considered decisions on the other hand refer to complex and ambiguous situations, where absolute norms are absent, knowledge is (far from) finite and the presence of (multiple) open values creates evaluative ambiguity. This might refer to whether or not to enforce a lockdown in the context of a global viral pandemic or whether to fund specific 'mega-projects' (new spaceships, military technology, etc). There are no definitively 'wrong' or 'right' answers in this latter category of decisions but a host of different and competing values surrounded by imperfect information and a range of 'unknowns'. In such cases, the best we can hope for from our decision-makers is an open-minded, inclusive and thorough decision-process in which they try to learn-on-the-go.

Following up on the social contingency model, accountability for accurate decisions should be organised around clear, known norms and should focus on decision-outcomes. In a sense, the account holder or arena would want to trigger the accountees' *acceptability heuristic*. The fairly clear, standardised and mechanical nature of the decision-making function should, in theory, make such an approach optimal in function and economic terms. Accountability for 'well-considered' decisions, on the other hand, where higher levels of uncertainty and potential cost or risk exist, arguably requires a very different approach. The potential salience of the decision rationalises a sharper focus on decision-making processes in order to ensure that any final decision really has been 'well considered'. Moreover, faced with a situation of high salience and high uncertainty the decision-maker may well want to trigger some pre-emptive self-criticism as a way of highlighting the situation, collection of more data and potentially even creating a platform of engaged stakeholders who may to some extent share any subsequent blame or criticism emerging from the decision. Both routes presuppose *pre*-decisional accountability, in order to avoid the rationalisation heuristic with which individuals protect their (social) self and aim to avoid blame.

The central argument of this section has been that the generic social contingency model provides a basis for binding and blending the insights of behavioural sciences with those more contextually-oriented findings of public administration. The most developed iteration of this approach within public administration is to be found in the CPA-model which focuses on the type of decision being made and the accountability context within which the decision has to be made. The models help to understand compliant blame-shifting and learning behaviours induced by accountability settings. However, this application is still very 'cool' and 'abstract', devoid of the 'heat' and 'noise' of more realistic public administration settings. In the next section more noise will be added, by adding the 'real', the 'institutional' and the 'professional' politician to Tetlock's 'intuitive' politician.

III. Blending and Binding: The 'Noisy' End of Accountability Behaviours

To recap, so far this chapter has focused on an understanding of accountability behaviours in public administration, by blending and binding insights from abstract and cool behavioural studies of accountability with contextualised and noisy studies in public administration. This approach allows us to formulate generic understandings of how decision-makers operating within public administration are likely to behave in varying contexts. It would suggest that politicians and officials are more likely to *comply* with accountability expectations by adopting an acceptability heuristic when they face ex ante accountability to a salient account holder protecting known and precise norms. However, when they are confronted with ex post accountability they are more likely to adopt a rationalisation heuristic, leading to blame-avoidance and blame-shifting to others. And when decision-makers face ex ante accountability to a salient account-holding entity with unknown views; a pre-emptive self-criticism heuristic is more likely, leading to learning processes and well-considered decisions (which are not automatically better decisions). These insights make sense in relation to the many questions of accountability, yet they are still decontextualised from the contingencies of public administration settings.

The theoretical model of the intuitive politician does not fully capture decisional realities in public administration. This is also not surprising, the psychological model offers a baseline theory, stripped from specifics of the decision-context, the decision-maker and the decisional task. Obviously, once field-specific contents are added, outcomes might be different. To flesh out the model in a public administration context, it is necessary to add field-specific conditions. For now, we propose to supplement the intuitive politician with additional political personas. What more are public administration decision-makers than intuitive politicians? Following the broader, contextualised accountability literature, at least three additional types of decision-makers can be discerned.

1. *The Institutional Politician* – many individual behaviours in public administration are best understood as institutionalised behaviours, reproduced and modified by stable super-individual institutional structures and conditions.
2. *The Professional Politician* – many decision-makers in public administration are, in a sociological sense, professionals whose behaviours are ultimately in line with professional self-understandings, training and the primacy of professional peer-accountability.
3. *The Real Politician* – in public administration settings people are not only intuitive politicians; many of them are also politicians in reality, which has ramifications for their behaviours in a context of accountability.

Let us begin with the institutional politician (*cf* Olsen 2005; Romzek and Dubnick 1987). Public sector decision-makers have preferences which are ingrained in their roles. This is also what Overman and Schillemans (2022) were referring to by exploring the behavioural consequences of accountability for different ideal typical types of public sector decision-makers: the proverbial mandarins, executives, professionals, and street-level bureaucrats. Each of these ideal-types incorporate institutional facts and variables that may explain their behaviours when confronted with accountability. The institutional politician will have developed routinised responses to both problems of action and situations of accountability. The institutional politician is a repeat player and is accustomed to working under the spell of accountability; a condition absent from the many one-off experiments which are conducted in behavioural sciences.

This will likely mean that the impact of accountability on the repeat-playing institutional politician is relatively lower than it is on the one-off intuitive politician. The institutionalised patterns of behaviour in public administration thus lowers the effects of accountability. Evidence to this effect is that sizes of experiments with practitioners are significantly lower than for studies using students as participants (*cf* Aleksovska et al 2019). Additionally, the institutional politician is also the 'guardian of normalcy'. The institutional politician generally operates according to the logic of appropriateness (Olsen 2015). As such, decision-making even in the face of accountability, may tend to be status-quo protecting or enhancing.

As such, the institutional politician can be expected to protect the status quo when confronted with accountability or exploit it as an external push with which foundational values can be protected. Finally, the institutional politician operates in a complex politico-administrative field. If you work for a government department or large governmental agency, you are used to working under conditions of permanent and mulitiplicitous critical scrutiny. Accountability is omnipresent but not always omni-salient. After some time, participants learn to shrug off some external criticisms, unless they are likely to have a major impact. Institutional politicians will thus pay selective attention to accountability. In many cases, where accountability is not highly politically salient, institutional politicians are likely to pay very little attention to it. But when accountability is highly (politically) salient, the institutional politician will pay very close attention. Thus, the varying degrees of salience of the accountability settings will moderate the effects of accountability in a hyperbolic way: magnifying some and nullifying most demands for accountability.

All in all, compared to the proverbial intuitive politician, the institutional politician is likely to be more selective in responding to accountability and they can draw on routinised and standardised behaviours. Institutional politicians are also the ones most likely to be compliant with external accountability demands, as long as they are not in conflict with institutional norms. Second, quite some important decision-makers in public administration are in a sociological sense professionals (*cf* Freidson 2003). The chief scientists modelling the likely progression of Covid-19 or the effectiveness of vaccines are first and foremost (research) professionals. In the same vein, the lawyers in the office of prosecution, psychologists doing assessments of staff, the engineers developing infrastructures, data-specialists designing digital systems, professors at public universities, and many others in public administration; these are all professionals. Additionally, seasoned decision-makers in public administration will be comparable to some extent to professionals in the sense that they form a relatively closed group fostering joint norms of appropriateness.

Two elements of the theory of professions are relevant in relation to accountability-induced behaviours First of all, a profession is self-regulating. The (theoretically) main form of accountability for professionals is peer accountability: accountability to one's peers on the basis of professional standards. From a classic professional perspective, only other professionals will be legitimised and have the required expertise to evaluate one's behaviours. As such, legitimacy and expertise will be crucial conditions for the effective accountability of professionals. Additionally, a key concern for professionals is jurisdiction (Freidson 2003). In political terms, the chief issue for a profession is to acquire and defend a unique decisional jurisdiction. The research professionals decide what is relevant to investigate and when a hypothesis is corroborated; the legal professionals decide how to interpret the law, the engineering professionals decide when a bridge is sufficiently safe and virologists decide if and when the prevalence of a virus merits the qualifications of a 'pandemic'. External accountability claims by citizens or politicians that the bridge is (not) safe, the virus is (not) a pandemic or a hypothesis has (not) been proven, are not taken seriously. From a professionals' position, even when working in public administration, only fellow professionals have the expertise and legitimacy to pass such judgements.

Translated to public sector accountability, these two elements would imply that the more a decision-maker is and understands themselves to be a professional, they can be expected to first of all respond sharply and protectively to accountability demands that challenge jurisdictional uniqueness. Accountability exchanges are also contests about dominance and power to set norms and standards (Greiling 2010). Professional decision-makers are likely to be most protective of their specific professional turf and to be the hardest nuts to crack for external account holders. Second, as professions yield autonomy to individual professionals, when facing accountability they will set relatively higher demands on the legitimacy of the account holder and its ability to demonstrate sufficient professional knowledge and expertise. Only under this condition, a cooperative response can be expected from a professional politician.

Compared to intuitive politicians, professional politicians are thus in principle much less likely to be compliant and certainly not when accountability norms are at odds with professional norms, understandings and routines. However, if the account holder manages to establish their authority, more self-reflective and learning heuristics are the likely result.

Finally, public administration is not first of all the realm of the intuitive politician – a metaphor aiming to describe how people in general respond to accountability – but it is of course the realm of real politicians. The executive is spearheaded by politically appointed ministers – who may, depending on the national system, appoint a few or a very large number of appointees in influential positions. The principal accountability-relations in public administration are between the people and its representatives and between the legislative and the executive. Also, for public administration employees to climb the rungs of hierarchy, considerable political skill is required, even though bureaucrats are not officially politicians. As such, the institutional context of public administration is marred by real politicians taking crucial decisions under varying conditions of accountability.

Compared to the cognitively minimising intuitive politician, the real politician will have goals and values in mind that they will vigorously pursue and defend against the demands from account holders. While the intuitive politician is a bit of a push-over – they will 'switch preferences' and align with the account holder – the real politician is a more stubborn customer. The real politician will be more inclined to resist accountability demands than intuitive politicians when they are at odds with their political preferences and positions. In addition, the real politician will have much more political skill than the average person, their ability to appease the account holder will thus be much higher and their ability to get away with what is essentially a rationalisation heuristic will also be much bigger. The real Machiavellian politician will furthermore also be able to *use* external demands for accountability to boost the course of action already envisioned. While the account holder believes their behaviour to be compliant the real politician may in reality increase the pace of whatever they were working on. Simultaneously, as accountability is a permanent game on many levels in politics, real politicians will have to be selective in terms of picking their battles. They are likely to invest a disproportionate amount of attention in a few high salient accountability exchanges while they are, conversely, much more flexible, pragmatic and talented to 'give in' on many other minor accountability episodes. Their ability also to pass the buck, shift blame to others or frame acceptable excuses will also be above average.

Figure 2.1 The Behaviours of Intuitive, Institutional, Professional and Real Politicians under Conditions of Accountability

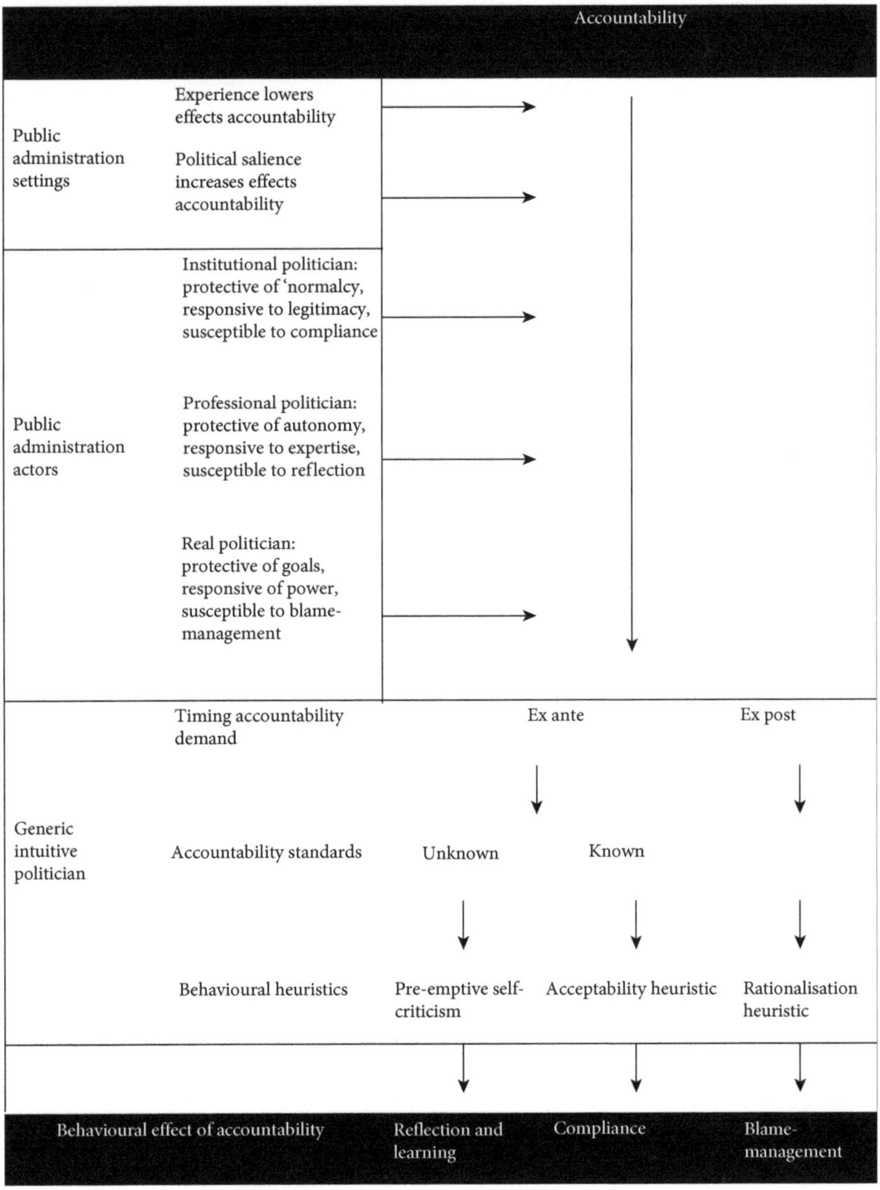

This chapter has theorised the behaviours of political and administrative actors when confronted with accountability. It has done so by blending insights from behavioural sciences and public administration and ultimately binding these together in an expanded model of political behaviours in response to accountability. Figure 2.1 (above) summarises the arguments advanced in this chapter. It reads as a collection of behavioural propositions related to accountability, highlighting when accountability is more likely to produce compliant behaviours, when blame-management and -shifting strategies are more probable and under what conditions it may make decision-makers reflect and induce learning processes.

3

Questions of Measurement: Striking an Accountability Balance

ELLEN ROCK

The previous chapter looked at a number of 'questions of accountability' by comparing and contrasting two very different perspectives. One drew upon the insights of behavioural psychology, focusing on individual behaviour and rationality; the second explored the field of public administration and the complexities of contextual factors. In many ways Thomas Schillemans' chapter sought to strike an epistemological and methodological balance that blended and bound the advantages of both perspectives together, while still recognising the existence of inevitable limitations. This chapter continues this focus on balance and blend but from a very different analytical direction. Instead of focusing on disciplinary perspectives, this chapter focuses on the very different – and yet at the same time closely connected – issue of measurement. The basic rationale for this approach is that 'questions of accountability' are very often framed (as chapter one illustrated) as relating to issues of 'too much' or 'too little'. Too little accountability (an *accountability deficit*) is a perception that existing accountability mechanisms are insufficient to deliver on expected accountability outcomes; too much accountability (an *accountability overload*) arises where the number or operation of accountability mechanisms produces unintended negative consequences.

The existence of these two poles is itself, however, founded on the highly questionable assumption that it is possible to measure accountability with a view to defining an ideal amount between these two extremes, which could presumably stand as a reference point to recalibrate or re-engineer the system towards some form of optimal 'sweet spot' (Figure 1.1 in chapter one). This chapter draws out this implicit assumption, highlighting the inherent difficulty of striking a proportionate balance that avoids the problems of imposing the 'wrong' amount of accountability. More specifically, this chapter focuses on three questions that are each in their own way relevant to a focus on measurement:

1. What does it mean to quantify accountability?
2. Can we ever successfully define an 'ideal amount' of accountability?
3. What difficulties must we resolve in striking a balance between accountability extremes that addresses deficits without producing overloads?

The central argument of this chapter is that if the practice of politics and public administration is ever to get beyond fairly broad and crude interpretations of deficits and overloads then there is a need to be far clearer about the end goals and ultimate role of accountable governance. This sets the debate far beyond 'hot rhetoric' and 'cool theory', or 'mechanisms and virtues', and opens fresh intellectual and empirical terrain in relation to fundamental objectives and institutional trajectories. In order to develop this argument this chapter is split into three main sections. The first section explores the existing debate on deficits and overloads in more detail, identifying the need to have some form of gauge, measuring tool or 'normative yardstick' if progress beyond 'hot rhetoric' and towards 'cool measurement' is ever to occur. The second section then explores how such a 'yardstick' might be crafted. More specifically, it seeks to illustrate how such a yardstick could (in theory) be developed around each of the main goals of accountability (ie, transparency, control, restoration, punishment and reform). The reason for setting out these goals is less about producing some formula for an optimal accountability equilibrium but, if anything, to underline the complexity of the challenge given the existence of numerous and often contradictory goals. Having explored the inner dimensions of the measurement challenge, the third and final section returns to the twin themes of tensions and balance.

I. Quantifying Accountability

Accountability has been aptly described as a chameleon concept (Sinclair 1995, 219). Its content shifts depending on the use to which it is put, which is one of the reasons why theorists have had some difficulty agreeing on a functional definition (Rock 2020, 13–20). What is generally agreed, almost irrespective of context, is that accountability is a 'good thing'; it is a 'golden concept that no one can be against' (Bovens 2007, 448), a 'hurrah-word' (Sinclair 1995, 219) with which '[n]obody argues' (Mulgan 2000, 555). In democratic societies, accountability represents an ideal of government under law and according to the mandate of its people. As this volume highlights, the supposed intrinsic value of accountability has encouraged the call for ever-increasing levels and types of accountability, but not always with expected outcomes. In more recent times academic attention has evolved away from the assumption that there can never be too much of a good thing. While a shortfall in accountability is undoubtedly a matter of concern, the inverse problem of excessive accountability can produce problems of its own (Halachmi 2014). Research in legal and political theory has tended, then, to cluster at these two extremes; identifying and solving accountability deficits at one pole and responding to accountability overloads at the other. With so much attention being paid to the identification and resolution of accountability deficits and overloads, it is perhaps surprising that so little work has been done to unpack the assumption on which these accountability claims rest – namely, that accountability is a measurable commodity. It is this question of accountability measurement that is tackled in this chapter.

Discussions of accountability (and particularly government accountability, with which this chapter is concerned) have frequently been framed by reference to the concept of accountability deficits. If accountability is a democratic ideal, the perception of a lack of or shortfall in accountability is a threat to that ideal. Concerns over accountability deficits often target perceived shifts in the status quo. In many cases these may be structural shifts, where an alteration to the existing structure or makeup of government impacts the reach of existing accountability mechanisms. For example, the ever-expanding size of the executive branch has given rise to accountability concerns due to the inability of ministers to practically oversee those operations, rendering traditional ministerial responsibility principles an inefficient and ineffective form of control (Ng 2020, 465–67). Similarly, the move towards greater outsourcing of public functions to private contractors has raised the spectre of accountability concerns where traditional judicial review mechanisms are unable to supervise the exercise of public power by private bodies in the same way as public actors, or in some cases, at all (Daintith and Ng 2020, 307–09). In more recent times, the incorporation of artificial intelligence technology into the fabric of government administration has – as the focus of chapter fourteen on accountability in the age of artificial intelligence illustrates – again raised the spectre of accountability deficits, with traditional administrative law controls struggling to accommodate shifting understandings or modes of 'decision-making' processes (see Boughey and Miller 2021).

Alongside structural changes, concerns about accountability deficits may also arise in response to shifts in practices or standards, exposing new fault-lines in the existing structure. This may be the case where a long-standing (but questionable) practice is used to political advantage. The Australian Auditor General's 2020 report into 'pork barrel politics' and the selective distribution of funding grants to support partisan rather than public interests provides an apt example. Accountability concerns may also be raised where loopholes in existing systems are perceived to have been exploited, such as where creative legal or accounting practices are used to circumvent the accountability protections that may ordinarily have been engaged. Again, from the Australian context, a possible example would be former Attorney-General Christian Porter's failure in 2021 to disclose the identities of donors who funded his personal defamation case against the national broadcaster in respect of its reporting on an historical sexual assault allegation. Mr Porter's use of a blind trust mechanism to facilitate anonymous litigation funding was found not to be in strict violation of parliamentary disclosure obligations, but the responsible parliamentary committee resolved to amend the rules going forward as this was not thought to be consistent with the spirit of those obligations.

From a functional perspective, the identification of accountability deficits offers a foundation to critique existing accountability arrangements. For those who are normatively inclined, that foundation paves the way for an argument to either extend the reach of existing mechanisms to reinstate the status quo, or to introduce new forms of accountability to ensure that perceived gaps are closed. The proliferation of accountability mechanisms that have been layered into the structure of government over time – ministerial responsibility mechanisms, parliamentary processes, general elections, Auditors-General, integrity commissions, Ombudsmen, review tribunals, legal challenges to government action via judicial review, tort, criminal law and so on – are testament to this effort.

While sharing the accountability task amongst numerous bodies and via numerous processes offers important failsafe benefits in line with Scott's (2000) 'redundancy' model of accountability, there comes a point of diminishing returns and eventual regression. This is because the flipside to ever-expanding and new forms of accountability processes is the production of the opposite type of accountability problem – an accountability overload. Researchers have identified numerous different manifestations of accountability overload, being a phenomenon in which the over-reach and excessive application of accountability mechanisms produces unanticipated results. Actors who are subject to accountability overload may be torn between the conflicting expectations of different accountability mechanisms (Halachmi 2014, 561). For example, where one mechanism emphasises accuracy and another efficiency, an actor may struggle to work out which goal to pursue with the result of failing to meet either standard. Excessive accountability processes may also tend to generate obfuscation problems, where – as Mulgan (2003) has discussed – actors engage in forum-shopping to bring themselves under the auspice of the least demanding of the applicable processes. An over-emphasis on accountability may also lead to 'blame games' as actors attempt to avoid subjection to the processes of accountability (for a wide review see Flinders et al 2023), or may seek to 'game the system' with a view to fulfilling accountability expectations in a superficial sense rather than focussing on performing the task on which the actor is being measured (see Halachmi 2014). More generally, it is clear that subjecting actors to an excessive range of accountability processes will impact the time available to perform the core functions of government; actors may 'spend half their time explaining to all sorts of accountability forums what they intend to be doing' as Bovens, Schillemans and 't Hart have argued (2008, 227–28) 'and the other explaining to them why they did not get around to doing all these things'.

Beyond risks to the practical effectiveness of accountability mechanisms and pragmatic impacts on government time and resources, this collection highlights a far more insidious danger arising from accountability overloads. If the underlying purpose of accountability is to support the legitimacy of government then there would seem to be a real risk that diminishing returns in the effectiveness of accountability mechanisms may also manifest as diminishing returns in public trust. As discussed in further detail in section III (below), if the accountability processes designed to secure government accountability fail in this task, the public may not only lose faith in those mechanisms but also in the government itself. This problem may only be compounded if there is a perception that these mechanisms are failing *by design*, such as where a mechanism is deprived of the powers or resources required to perform its functions effectively, or where accountability processes take the form of apparently empty, box-ticking exercises.

Taking the above observations together, the problems of accountability deficits and accountability overloads can all be reframed as concerns about *quantifying* accountability. Too little accountability (where officials are insufficiently hemmed about by accountability in their exercise of public power) is an *accountability deficit*, and too much accountability (where officials are subjected to a degree or forms of accountability that negatively affects the performance of their core roles) is an *accountability overload*. This chapter is concerned with the implicit assumption that underlies both concepts of deficit and overload – namely, that accountability is a measurable phenomenon. This implicit assumption seems to hold that it is possible to analyse a given situation, power, official or institution and determine whether it is subjected to too little, or too much, accountability. With few exceptions (see Bovens, Curtin and 't Hart 2010; Brandsma and Schillemans 2013; Rock 2020), the difficulty is that many of those who make claims of accountability deficit and overload tend to gloss over the detail of how accountability has been quantified. As Bovens, Curtin and 't Hart (2010, 230) have noted 'few if any of the parties to the debate specify which standards they employ. The literature is remarkably light on assessment tools and methods'. Without such precision it is more than feasible that different analysts, academics or practitioners may come to very different conclusions as to whether an *appropriate* balance exists when asked to assess the same situation. Defining a tool could bring consistency and rigour to that assessment process. That said, there is a need to manage the expectations associated with this chapter, which does not provide a neat solution to the puzzle of accountability measurement. Rather, its purpose is to prompt deeper consideration of whether, and (if so) how, we might move towards a shared understanding of the nature of the measurement task.

With this in mind the issue becomes one of 'units of measurement' within any single accountability space. Capacity, length and mass can all be discussed with a shared vocabulary of litres, meters and grams which facilitates shared meaning and therefore the generation of cumulative knowledge. But when it comes to accountability the situation is far more complex. Uncertainty surrounds what an ideal *unit of accountability* looks (or feels) like. The complicating factor being that accountability is – as Bovens clarified – more than a mechanism. The 'unit' in this case is as *relational* as it is institutional, structural or any other manifested type. The existing research base therefore lacks what Bovens, Curtin and 't Hart (2010, 49) once labelled a 'normative yardstick' that might somehow inject agreed precision into the arguments of 'too little' or 'too much', just as a tailor rolls-out yards of cloth. Even if it were possible to give some agreed shape to those units, however, that is not the end of the measurement problem but the beginning of another. This is because identifying the quantity of units *present* in a given context is only meaningful when we compare it against the quantity of units *needed* in that context. After all, we can only say that two eggs is sufficient to bake a cake if we have already (i) read the recipe, and (ii) considered the number of guests we plan to feed. In the accountability context, meaningful use of the accountability value descriptors of deficit and overload depends on a clear understanding of what accountability is intended to achieve. This forms the focus of the next section.

II. An Accountability Ideal

The identification of accountability deficits and overloads rests on the implicit assumption that there is some midway 'sweet spot' of accountability for which we are aiming – the presence of 'too much' accountability in some cases and 'not enough' in others presupposes that we have in mind an ideal of 'enough' accountability in between those poles. However, as the previous section suggested, many claims of accountability deficit and overload are conclusory in character in the sense that they posit a situational interpretation without explicitly identifying exactly what they believe is missing, absent or under-developed within the situation. 'Accountability angst' (on this specific socio-political malady see Dimova et al 2023) is therefore very often rudderless in the sense that concerns are rarely tied down or anchored to a specific diagnosis of the problem or the outcome being sought. Moreover, value-laden normative assumptions will to some extent inevitably confuse and complicate ideals around the simplistic *quantification* of accountability. To suggest, for example, that a minister or official has been sufficiently or *in*sufficiently held accountable we are implicitly measuring that outcome against a normative benchmark.

To take an example, some might argue that the unavailability of damages in judicial review proceedings represents an accountability gap because an applicant whose licence is illegally cancelled is left with a loss that cannot be remedied (see Panetta 1999). Perhaps implicit in this argument is the assumption that accountability demands the restoration of harm and that wrongs be made right. Rather than leaving this assumption implicit, we have much to gain from bringing it to the forefront. To begin with, this would provide the rudder that is otherwise missing from our accountability assessment. If we argue that accountability demands the restoration of harm, then there may indeed be a potential accountability gap if an applicant who successfully challenges an invalid government decision is left unrestored. Rather than simply a conclusory assessment or statement of rhetorical appeal, this argument might then be said to have a firm foundation. However, by making the assumptions behind this measurement assessment explicit we also enable ourselves to critically debate the merits of the assumption – does accountability indeed demand restoration of harm? For what kinds of losses, and in response to what kinds of wrongs? It is only once we fully flesh out and test this assumption that we can legitimately use it as a benchmark to identify accountability deficits and overloads. Perhaps more importantly, however, if we make our accountability demands explicit, then we also have a firm foundation to advocate for effective change. If accountability demands restoration of certain types of harm caused by certain types of wrongs, this allows us to define a targeted response to correct any *under*- or *over*-performance with respect to that goal. To put the same point slightly differently, we are in a far better position to prescribe an appropriate cure if we: (i) understand what 'full health' looks like; and (ii) have effectively diagnosed the condition we are treating.

How, then, might we go about defining the accountability 'ideal' that can serve as a benchmark for our assessment? To begin with, we must be able to state what accountability demands. What is the overarching objective or purpose of accountability? When we say that someone should be held accountable, or has not been held accountable, what is it that we are saying should be, or has not been, done? A review of academic work in this area reveals a number of possible accountability objectives that could inform our benchmark. Perhaps the strongest argument is that the purpose of accountability is to secure the legitimacy of government and support public trust in its operations: accountability is, as Barnard (2001, xi) rather powerfully suggests, a 'gravitational centre in the legitimation of democratic governance'. The effectiveness of accountability mechanisms is key to securing this legitimacy objective. On this view, when accountability mechanisms operate as designed, they would be capable of fostering public faith in the system of government (the accountability ideal). Conversely, when accountability problems arise this presents a very real threat to the ongoing legitimacy of government.

Traditionally, ineffective accountability as a threat to legitimacy has most often been raised in the context of accountability deficits. Accordingly, public perception of the accountability of government is threatened when existing mechanisms are unable to attach to new or shifting governance models (eg moves towards outsourcing of government functions or reliance on artificial intelligence technologies). The 'Robo-debt' scandal in Australia is a strong example of this issue, with the federal government coming under heavy scrutiny for its use of automated technology to issue debt notices to social security recipients who were determined to have under-reported their earnings following a data-matching process undertaken across government databases. As it transpired, many such assessments were erroneous and the debts ought not have been levied. Traditionally, errors in administrative decision-making of this type would be regarded as the core territory of judicial and merits review mechanisms, allowing tribunals and courts to overturn decisions made in excess of power. However, the application of these traditional accountability mechanisms to this new breed of government decision-making is by no means straightforward (Boughey and Miller 2021). Part of the public furore over Robo-debt has arisen from the apparent accountability fault-lines that allowed the unlawful practice to carry so far as it did, notwithstanding that it was subject at various points to numerous forms of merits review challenges, legal challenges, Ombudsmen investigations, parliamentary committee inquiries, and, most recently, a Royal Commission inquiry. Public and academic concern around the risks posed by technology-enhanced government decision-making remains high (see, for example, Braithwaite 2020; Whiteford 2021; Akter, et al 2021).

While accountability deficits pose definite threats to the legitimacy of government, legitimacy may also be threatened when the proliferation of mechanisms produces an overload in accountability. When we overload our accountability system to the point that it is bloated and sluggish in its operation, it is inevitable that public perception of that system will be negatively impacted. The same issue arises where accountability mechanisms take on the character of empty processes or box-ticking exercises – mechanisms of this character risk eroding public trust in not only in the mechanism itself but also in the government it purports to hold accountable. Citizens are unlikely to build trust where there is a perception that accountability mechanisms are applied in a lip service fashion, or where hollow mechanisms are being used as a form of shield to avoid subjection to more genuine accountability processes. Even more problematically, sub-par accountability arrangements may lead to a regression in legitimacy; public trust may well erode over time where a government is routinely seen to be escaping effective accountability. For all of these reasons, we must treat concerns about accountability overloads no less seriously than concerns about accountability deficits – both forms of accountability problem are capable of undermining public trust in our system of government.

Supporting legitimacy is a potentially compelling explanation for the objective or purpose of government accountability. However, this does not tell us very much about the appropriate means to reach this end. In many ways the 'legitimacy of government' provides a grand narrative which demands granularity if it is to be in some sense measured. This creates a need to drill-down into the goals, ambitions or purposes of accountability in a practical sense. After all, when people complain that a government official has escaped accountability, or that the government needs to be held accountable for a policy debacle, this does not really tell us *what* those complainants are seeking. What goals or anticipated outcomes are hidden within these calls for accountability? What is the missing accountability ingredient in cases where we say that there is an accountability gap? The value of asking these 'questions of accountability' in the context of a broader focus on measurement is that it facilitates a process of dissection. While 'accountability' in toto does not lend itself to measurement, its more specific functions or goals may. A review of the literature reveals a number of common threads which could be framed as goals or rationales of accountability. These may be summarised as *transparency, control, restoration, punishment* and *reform*.

A. Transparency

There are many who view transparency as a core purpose of accountability. Koppell (2005, 96) has gone so far as to indicate that transparency is 'the literal value of accountability'. On this view, the function of accountability would be to facilitate access to information and explanation from the government and its officials. In turn, accountability deficits might arise where the government denies access to information, immunises certain categories of information from review and public knowledge, refuses to provide reasons for its decisions and, more generally, governs behind closed doors. There are a number of examples of transparency-oriented disclosure regimes that are linked with the facilitation of government accountability. For instance, members of Parliament in Australia are required to disclose their pecuniary interests and receipt of benefits or gifts via a publicly available register, allowing public awareness and scrutiny of conflicts of interest and potential sources of influence over parliamentary decisions.

Perhaps the most well-known transparency mechanisms are freedom of information regimes, which provide individuals with a legally enforceable right to request access to government documents. The Australian Commonwealth regime establishes a relatively user-friendly process, under the Freedom of Information Act 1982, that allows individuals to freely request access to broadly defined 'documents' held by government agencies. These must be produced unless they fall within an exemption category, such as where the release of documents might impact national security or destroy legal professional privilege. Alongside creating rights of request, the Australian Commonwealth regime also imposes an obligation to proactively release certain categories of information, such as details of agency structure, decision-making powers, and adopted policies, procedures and guidelines. Freedom of information regimes such as this one are frequently linked with the objective of securing government accountability, with one member of the Australian High Court describing their purpose as being:

> to reinforce 'the three basic principles of democratic government, namely, openness, accountability and responsibility'. The central objective is to strengthen constitutional principles of governance not always translated into reality because of a lack of material information available to electors. Fundamentally, the idea behind such legislation is to flesh out the constitutional provisions establishing the system of representative government; to increase citizen participation in government beyond a fleeting involvement on election days; and to reduce the degree of apathy and cynicism sometimes arising from a lack of real elector knowledge about, or influence upon, what is going on in government (*Osland v Secretary, Department of Justice* (2008), [62] (Kirby J)).

Other mechanisms that facilitate transparency in government operations take on a stronger investigatory role. For example, anti-corruption commissions, Royal Commissions and ombudsmen are empowered to investigate instances of government wrongdoing, including through the exercise of compulsory powers to enter premises, gather documents and interview witnesses. In addition to uncovering relevant information, such agencies may facilitate public awareness of issues through the publication of reports on their findings.

Accepting that transparency is one of the objectives of accountability, it is unsurprising that concerns of accountability deficit are raised in circumstances where transparency is under threat due to the exploitation of loopholes in existing transparency regimes or the failure of existing regimes to keep pace with new developments. So, for example, accountability concerns were recently raised in Australia when a resigning minister passed significant documents on to the National Archives rather than to the incoming minister, thus excluding them from the coverage of the applicable freedom of information regime. Similarly, accountability concerns were raised when it became unclear whether freedom of information would extend to documents held by the so-called 'National Cabinet', a government agency comprising heads of the Commonwealth and State governments formed to manage the Australian pandemic response.

But excessive transparency may also be linked with the potentially negative outcomes of accountability overload. Two examples suffice to make this point. The first is a practical one; the size and responsibilities of modern government produces a proliferation of documents and data, far beyond the capacity of individuals to grasp. If government were to be an entirely open book in its operations it is possible that transparency could be undermined by the sheer volume of data; it might become impractical for individuals to locate and collate relevant information from within that broader set. The second example of a potential transparency overload problem is linked with public perception. If we were to publicise not only every *significant* error and misjudgement in government operations but also every *insignificant* and innocuous error, there is a possibility that rather than increasing trust in government we might see the inverse outcome. Instead of fostering public belief that government mistakes will be revealed and put right, we risk eroding public belief that the government is capable of performing its functions with any degree of competence. The practice of politics – as David Blunkett underlines in chapter twelve in this volume – is messy. It grates and grinds. It is built on favours and compromises and sub-optimal deal-making that can be hard for the public to understand from the outside. Some issues have specific security dimensions, others are just 'super-wicked' policy challenges that bring with them a multitude of complexities. As highlighted at Section III below, accountability may sometimes be in tension with alternative (but no less legitimate) goals, and being completely 'open' or 'transparent' when it comes to practical everyday politics might from this perspective be viewed as a slightly naïve or idealistic ambition. In short, some questions of accountability bring their own issues of balance and proportionality that are rarely discussed openly. The same might also be said for the ambition of control.

B. Control

A second objective that is sometimes linked with accountability is that of control. On this view, the underlying purpose of accountability is to ensure that the government acts within the constraints of the law. We might also consider this to be a 'rule of law' perspective of accountability (see Tamanha 2009), ensuring that the government and its officials are subject to the ordinary laws of the land. There have been a number of theorists – Strom's (2003) work on delegation and Lupia's (2003) equally influential work on the 'perils' of autonomy, to mention just a couple of key reference points – who link accountability with conceptions of control. Mulgan and Uhr (2001) go so far as to describe control as accountability's 'core purpose'. Many who subscribe to this view adopt a principal-agent perspective in which the political sphere is interpreted and modelled on a 'chain of delegation' whereby different powers, responsibilities and mandates are devolved within an arm's-length relationship. From the public to politicians via elections, from politicians to their officials through ministerial instructions and framework documents, from officials to private and third sector organisations through contracts, etc, the key role of accountability from this perspective is to control those to whom public power has been divested and to prevent the occurrence of 'fugitive power' operating beyond the control of democratic structures.

There are a number of different accountability mechanisms that operate in support of this control objective. One of the most well-known is judicial review. The underlying purpose of judicial review is to ascertain and police the legal limits that apply to the exercise of government power. The Australian adherence to a procedural conception of judicial review is particularly well-aligned with the control objective, being concerned with enforcing the boundaries that apply to the exercise of power rather than the interests of the individual:

> The duty and jurisdiction of the court to review administrative action do not go beyond the declaration and enforcing of the law which determines the limits and governs the exercise of the repository's power. If, in so doing, the court avoids administrative injustice or error, so be it; but the court has no jurisdiction simply to cure administrative injustice or error (*Attorney-General (NSW) v Quin*, 35–36).

Another key accountability mechanism that we might link with the control objective would be the principle of responsible government, pursuant to which Parliament can exercise control over the executive branch of government through mechanisms such as Question Time (written and oral), the power to call for 'papers, persons and records' and even in extreme circumstances to hold members in contempt.

Many of the complaints about accountability deficits appear to be concerned with changes that impact the capacity of existing accountability mechanisms to control the exercise of new and emerging forms of government power. Thus, for example, the evolution, expansion and fragmentation of the executive branch of government may be claimed to produce an accountability deficit because the traditional mechanisms of responsible government are not capable of adapting to the demands of a large and complex state. In this situation, ministers are free to claim that although they have a constitutional duty to account to the House this does not mean that they are in any way responsible for the content of that account. In essence, ministers claim that what occurs way down the 'chain of delegation' is not something of which the minister can realistically be expected to have had personal oversight. At the same time, however, those officials to whom responsibility is to some extent assigned are themselves not constitutionally or directly accountable to Parliament. Increased moves to address complex social issues that reach across the purview of any one government department (ie, the 'joined-up government' agenda) also creates challenges in terms of teasing-out *who* was in control of *what* and *when* within a complex network of multi-level collaborative governance (see Bache et al 2015). Increased reliance on private contractors to perform outsourced public functions – as Eckersley and Ferry (2020) have demonstrated – is another focus of accountability deficit complaint, as the traditional mechanisms of control such as judicial review are inapplicable. The increased use of algorithmic governance in public decision-making processes adds, as has already been indicated, yet another set of 'questions of control' that sit within a broader concern about the changing nature of accountable governance.

The flipside of the control dilemma, however, is that too much control, oversight and interference can prevent politicians and decision-makers from getting on with the job of governing. This is a particular concern in highly adversarial and aggressive majoritarian polities where the capacity of opposition parties to frustrate the government of the day for partisan reasons needs to be balanced against the need for an effective and efficient administration. The convention of individual ministerial responsibility – as Flinders (2000) has illustrated – was therefore designed as both an *accountability sword* (ie, to allow parliament to scrutinise and control the executive) but also as an *accountability shield* (ie, to allow the executive to be able to govern while addressing a proportionate degree of scrutiny). This is an important but generally overlooked point. Accountability mechanisms can be designed to act almost like valves – moderating and controlling the degree of scrutiny and not simply facilitating a one-way flow. This focus on design principles (valves and flow) reintroduces the topic of multiple-accountabilities disorder and the pressures of accountability 'cross-pressures' that were discussed in chapter one. Trying to march to too many drummers – as Langford (1984) argued nearly four decades ago – all playing different songs to different beats, is only ever going to end in chaos. This brings the discussion to a crucial pivot point and a shift in focus from control to restoration.

C. Restoration

The third objective that seems to rest at the heart of calls for accountability is a demand of restoration or redress. Put simply, for some, accountability demands that wrongs be made right. Thus, Oliver (1991, 22) views accountability as an 'amendatory' process pursuant to which an actor should be liable to 'undertake to put matters right if it should appear that errors have been made'. Similarly, Mulgan and Uhr (2001, 153) state that 'effective' accountability 'requires the possibility of remedies and sanctions so that … damage can be repaired'. Without redress, Mulgan (2003, 10) suggests, 'accountability seems frustrated'. While this broad idea of 'restoration' underlies many calls for accountability, it is not always clear what practical form that is expected to take. An obvious example of redress is the provision of a remedy that either reinstates what has been lost (eg, returning property that was improperly taken), or offers an equivalent of its value (eg, compensatory damages). A number of mechanisms are able to offer those types of specific redress. Within the legal sphere this function is served by causes of action that provide a remedy in damages for harm occasioned by government wrongdoing. So, for example, the torts of misfeasance in public office, false imprisonment and negligence can offer a remedy for certain failings in government operations (see Rock and Weeks 2018). The government can further be liable for damages in contract and equity.

Outside the legal frame, ombudsmen and ex gratia compensation regimes can offer further access to monetary redress for harm caused by maladministration. Merits review proceedings may also offer redress in the form of a 'different outcome' where a person's grievance relates to an unfavourable government decision. However, the concept of restoration is broader than this legalistic understanding of remedies. A wider view of restoration would include less tangible forms of redress, such as the provision of apologies (Allan 2008) and even the cathartic experience of participating in the accountability process itself – an 'airing of grievances'. While most accountability mechanisms can offer some form of that experience, public inquiries are particularly well-adapted for that role. Truth and Reconciliation Commissions are a prime example of this broader focus on transitional justice. It is at this point that accountability mechanisms can be recast as therapeutic tools for social catharsis and forms of inter-community, inter-ethnic or inter-generational healing. At those outer edges, the backwards-looking focus of restoration merges with the forward-looking objective of reform (see section E).

Returning to the task of measurement, the failure to offer a means of restoration to those harmed by government wrongdoing may give rise to concerns of accountability gaps or deficits. Some perceived 'restoration' deficits may target structural concerns about a mechanism's inability to deliver redress in appropriate cases. This may be due to limits on its powers (eg, a judicial review court which has no power to award damages), or the reach of its jurisdiction (eg, excluding errors by private contractors from the coverage of Australia's dedicated 'maladministration' ex gratia compensation scheme). Other deficit concerns may reflect the 'quality' of redress that can be obtained. In some contexts, the notion of redress is able to draw on a rich body of principle that defines the type and extent of remedy that can be expected. The award of damages and other restorative remedies by the courts is a good example. However, for less tangible forms of restoration – such as apologies, catharsis and healing – calculating deficits is a much woollier task because the character of these goals is so subjective. It may be simple, for example, to identify whether an apology has or has not been made. It is much harder, however, to assess whether that apology is sufficiently meaningful to support a goal of restoration (Allan 2008, 370).

What is interesting is that an excessive focus on restoration may produce negative consequences which could be viewed as a manifestation of an accountability overload. Many of the concerns about 'opening the floodgates' in the legal arena are underpinned by the reality that government pay outs in court cases are sourced from public funds, and increasing demands on those resources to assist individuals comes at the expense of the ability to direct funds to other public services: 'the more extensive governmental damages liability becomes, the more significant its implications for public spending' (Cane 1999, 491). In a similar vein, it might be thought that the threat of legal liability might produce an 'overkill' or a 'chilling effect', whereby public officials might exercise their functions in an overly defensive manner. These types of concerns may also travel into the looser restorative goals of personal or social catharsis. As Minow (2007) has shown, the space between vengeance and forgiveness can be very narrow and highly contested, and pushing the pursuit of restoration too far can potentially bleed into other (perhaps unanticipated or unwanted) outcomes. Concerns about restoration can therefore be linked to wider concerns about accountability deficits and overloads. This brings the discussion to a focus on a fourth goal of punishment and blame.

D. Punishment

A further objective that appears to underlie some demands for accountability is the expectation that wrongdoers will be punished. Without that possibility, there is concern that accountability falls short of ideal – it is 'weak, toothless, "diminished"' as Schedler (1999, 15–16) has noted. Mulgan (2003, 10) puts this point plainly:

> In many cases, particularly when mistakes have been made and things have gone wrong, we want to see something more than just transparency and communication, important though these functions are … Particularly when an institution has caused a major disaster and loss of life, heads should roll. If heads stay stubbornly in place, as often happens, we think that accountability has been denied. In other words, accountability implies an element of retributive justice.

Retributivist theories of justice, as Zaibert (2006, 7) has explained, are premised on the notion of desert: we impose punishment on the basis that the wrongdoer *deserves* hard treatment. In this context, punishment is imposed to 'underlie the importance of the norms that were contravened' (Bovens 1998, 39) and 'as an expression of community outrage' (Rock 2020, 112). Possible means of achieving this goal include traditional punitive remedies such as termination of employment, fines, civil penalties and jail terms, and lesser sanctions such as embarrassment, humiliation and withholding of political support. These consequences may be delivered through official legal channels such as criminal and civil penalty proceedings, anti-corruption commission investigations and more broadly through public and social media. Some would further view the process of subjection to certain accountability mechanisms (ie, being required to provide an account) as punitive, irrespective of their outcomes. This explains the link between 'naming and shaming' and accountability but possibly the biggest insight to be made is simply this: accountability is generally associated with the allocation of blame. This is particularly true in relation to politics and public governance where a well-documented negativity bias tends to ensure that accountability is about attributing fault rather than distributing credit or praise.

If punishment is an underlying objective of accountability, concerns of accountability deficit may arise where there is a disconnect between community expectations that an incident of wrongdoing warrants punishment and that consequence not being delivered. This may be the case where the nature of an official's conduct does not fit currently defined descriptions of wrongdoing (such as 'grey area' corruption), or where an official is protected or shielded from punitive consequences (such as where a leader protects senior officials by refusing to ask for or accept their resignation). Concerns of deficit may also arise where punishment is not thought to 'fit the crime', which may be the case where community perception of the degree of wrongdoing does not match the severity of the punishment meted out. For example, there might be claims of accountability deficit where an official is temporarily suspended from their position over a serious allegation of corruption rather than being terminated or prosecuted for a criminal offence.

On the other hand, over-zealous punishment may also produce concerns of accountability overloads, especially where concerns also suspect that an individual is taking more blame than they should (ie, being scapegoated or sacrificed to sate the public hunger for sacrificial responsibility). Accountability's negativity bias can foster a low-trust, high-blame environment in which actors might rationally adopt a defensive and highly risk-averse mindset. This is an argument that weaves through, for example, Weaver's (1986) classic article on 'the politics of blame avoidance', Pierson's (1996) work on the 'new politics' of welfare state retrenchment, Christopher Hood's (2002) work on 'the risk game and the blame game', Boin, 't Hart and McConnell's (2009) work on blame and crisis exploitation, and Markus Hinterleitner's (2020) more recent scholarship on 'policy controversies and political blame games'. The common strand connecting these works is that accountability is linked to blame and punishment and, as such, is to be avoided. It is therefore possibly not surprising that threats of being 'hung out to dry' by their political masters might encourage officials to adopt defensive practices in performing their roles, notably shying away from making 'tough decisions' in favour of self-protection. This leads to a fifth and final focus on reform.

E. Reform

The final objective highlighted in this chapter is that of reform, which encompasses the forward-looking goals of accountability. Bovens (2007, 466) is a strong advocate of this purpose of accountability, describing it in the language of 'learning'. On this view, one of the concrete objectives of accountability is to 'enhance … the learning capacity and effectiveness' of government officials and agencies. One aspect of this reform-oriented goal is the deterrence of undesired behaviour, sanctioning wrongdoers both to discourage them from committing future infringements (specific deterrence) and also to disincentivise others from following suit (general deterrence). In Behn's (2001, 14) words, holding a specific wrongdoer accountable 'seeks to influence the behaviour of all future public officials'. As for punishment, the tools associated with deterrent objectives include criminal and employment-oriented punitive sanctions (eg, firings, fines and more general public admonition). While deterrence is often offered as a justification for the imposition of such sanctions, there are many who doubt whether they are an efficient means to achieve this objective, particularly in the public sphere. Braithwaite (1997) is one such scholar, arguing that 'big sticks often rebound' when deployed as a tool of deterrence, sometimes encouraging a defiant reaction instead of the desired adjustment to behaviour. In the language deployed in this chapter, the phenomenon of *reactance* (see Brehm 1966) might be thought of as a manifestation of accountability overload. Instead, Braithwaite (1997, 319) encourages consideration of non-punitive means to deter abuse of power, such as offering incentives, reintegrative shaming strategies and fostering dialogue.

In addition to the immediate goals of deterrence, the forward-looking objectives of accountability might also be thought to include the broader pursuit of systemic reform with a view to improving the underlying systems and processes that provided the occasion for wrongdoing to occur. So, for example, we might look to accountability mechanisms to make recommendations for reform of existing systems, the establishment of new processes and standards of conduct to improve governance going forward. There is a range of accountability mechanisms charged with these types of roles. Key examples include Royal Commissions, ombudsmen, anti-corruption commissions and auditors-general. It is within the remit of such agencies to investigate instances of maladministration, corruption and wrongdoing and to make recommendations for future reform. The challenge, however, as Resodihardjo (2020) illustrated at length in *Crises, Inquiries and the Politics of Blame*, is that an emphasis on blame-attribution very often emerges to crowd-out more positive and future-focused lesson-learning. But what this point underlines is really the argument of this section and chapter: measuring accountability and developing useful yardsticks is complicated by the existence of highly normative, often partisan and frequently incompatible intentions.

Assessing claims regarding *deficits* and *overloads* therefore requires an incredibly sophisticated analytical antennae. With no broad acceptance of what constitutes an accountability ideal – or what a 'sweet spot' might look like – academic claims for more 'rigor' or 'systemic foundations' that can facilitate cumulative learning across sectors, countries and time spans starts to look, if not highly problematic, then at the very least challenging. Indeed, such an argument brings the dialectical inter-relationships between individual behaviour and contextual dynamics which featured in chapter two back into sharp relief. Nevertheless, the state of both academic and political debates concerning 'questions of accountability' would undoubtedly be improved and clarified if proponents on all sides were more explicit in relation to their primary accountability objectives. This leads the discussion to a final focus back on the themes of proportionality, tensions and balance.

III. Proportionality, Tensions and Balance

The main argument of this chapter is that 'questions of accountability' often arise not so much due to the existence of 'gaps' or 'traps' – or 'deficits' and 'overloads' – but due to the absence of agreed measurement criteria that might allow some shared, balanced and precise discussion of when and why accountability expectations have become problematic. Part of this lack of specificity is, as the previous section illustrated, a reflection of the range of accountability objectives that people may have in mind, and which may also pull in very different directions. It is possible that an accountability 'overload' might exist in relation to one dimension (ie, punishment and blame) and, to some extent, veil the existence of an accountability deficit in relation to another dimension (ie, reform and lesson-learning). Making this point helps underline the measurement challenge, while also complementing the previous chapter's focus on different perspectives and false promises. The core insight, however, is that accountability is what might be called a 'compromise concept'. Trade-offs, delicate balances and a sensitivity to context serve to inject exactly the dynamic and fluid quality that was discussed in chapter one. As such, the aim of this concluding section is to reflect upon the inevitable tension points that are likely to inform a focus on balance and proportionality.

The first and most clear problem or tension point with achieving an accountability balance is the inherent difficulty of identifying when 'enough' accountability tips to a point of 'too much'. For each of the potential accountability objectives explored above (*transparency, control, restoration, punishment, reform*) it was noted that the failure to deliver on *that* specific objective might constitute an accountability deficit. If there is no means to access information held by a certain government agency, for example, or about a certain area of government operation, concerns about a lack of transparency may well emerge. However, the intensity of transparency obligations may reach a point of diminishing returns if shining a bright spotlight on errors big and small causes the public to view the government as incompetent – that would be an accountability problem in its own right. If we fail to recognise that accountability problem as an issue of *imbalance*, we risk compounding it, because the usual public response to concerns about accountability is to demand the imposition of even more or even tighter accountability controls.

Striking the right balance between accountability extremes is an inherently difficult task in respect of which very few scholars or practitioners are able to offer ready answers or reform proposals. Simply recommending *more* accountability is plainly not the answer. What is clear, however, is that debates and discussions that may flow through into design proposals would be improved if we are explicit about the underlying accountability objective(s) we have in mind. To reiterate, effective prescription is dependent on proper diagnosis.

A second tension exists for the simple reason that accountability objectives, as this chapter has attempted to stress, do not always align. For example, dialling up transparency may in turn dial down the effectiveness of reform-oriented objectives such as innovation – when we place an official under a public microscope, it would be unsurprising if they were to adopt a defensive and risk-averse approach to their role. In O'Neill's (2002, 19) words, 'plants don't tend to flourish when we pull them up too often to check how their roots are growing'. The discussion of proportionality and balance might therefore be framed as a two-level game: level 1 relates to the amount of accountability – secured through a range or mixture of tools, methods and processes – in relation to a *specific* goal or objective; but level 2 relates to the blend or balance *between* different objectives. Dissecting 'questions of accountability' in this manner is rarely undertaken and yet it offers significant analytical and practical purchase. Seen from this perspective, Figure 1.1's (chapter one) identification of a 'sweet spot' is working on a simple two-dimensional framing that cannot really capture the range of cross cutting pressures that are in play. In this regard, an adapted version of Brandsma and Schillemans's (2013) 'accountability cube' might offer a more sophisticated framing of sweet-spot dynamics. Thinking of accountability in terms of a two-level game with first order questions focusing on the tactics and tools selected to achieve a *specific* accountability objective, and second order questions focusing on the potential (in) compatibility between *broad* objectives, may well offer a new perspective.

A third tension point resonates with many of the insights and arguments of chapters two and three in the sense that there needs to be some way of acknowledging and assessing the external circumstances or context within which accountability processes exist. In times of crisis, for example, the (level 2) broad objectives of accountability might shift to a focus on performance, efficiency and outcome-based measures. At the same time, specific (level 1) tools and procedures might also be paused or lessened in order to facilitate government action. A changing context may well affect the appropriate mix or blend; the 'accountability space' may become permanently or temporarily reconstituted. Established modes of measuring or evaluating accountability may be left obsolete by the pace and nature of new demands. This brings the discussion to a final focus on institutional design.

Accepting that the pursuit of an 'ideal' amount of accountability – not too much, not too little – might pull us in different directions, we might gain some assistance by splitting up our accountability tasks. If it is not possible to charge a single mechanism with a broad suite of conflicting accountability goals, it might instead be possible to hive off different mechanisms to prioritise different objectives: 'accountability can, and should, take several forms' as Elliott (2013, 258) argues '… [which] demands that accountability be supplied by a range of functionally-complementary institutions applying a diversity of criteria and approaches'. The courts, for example might focus on the control objective via judicial review proceedings, freedom of information regimes with transparency, criminal law with punishment of abuse of power, etc. These mechanisms might support other objectives in a secondary or complementary way, but points of internal tension are reduced through prioritising a core focus. On this basis, for example, we might not be concerned that judicial review fails to address restoration of harm caused by maladministration, because this mechanism is primarily concerned with controlling and policing limits on government power. Similarly, we might not be concerned that the government shields a wrongdoing employee from punishment by footing the bill in vicarious liability tort cases – the primary focus of tort law may be restoration rather than punishment of abuse of power. To put this point more simply, accountability might simply be a situation of 'horses for courses'.

Adopting this type of approach to accountability certainly produces some benefits; a 'belt and braces' (Scott 2000, 53) model of accountability. However, such an approach may also lead to unwanted accountability problems. First, from the perspective of the general public, the proliferation of accountability mechanisms will not necessarily equate to a strong perception of government accountability. The public may not necessarily appreciate the difference in task or focus of the various mechanisms, leading, for example, to criticism of the ombudsman as a 'toothless tiger' or of anti-corruption commissions as 'kangaroo courts'. The belt and braces model may also be problematic from the perspective of the government officials being held to account. This may be the case where accountability reaches a point of critical mass where multiple mechanisms overlap with one another and over-deliver on certain outcomes, reaching a point of 'overkill' (on this see Barendrecht 2011).

Further, hiving-off accountability functions to different mechanisms does not address the tension between objectives for the individual who is subject to them – tension is still present if transparency is demanded through one mechanism while improved performance is demanded by another. As Koppell (2005, 95) puts it, the official may be left to 'oscillate … between behaviours that are consistent with conflicting notions of accountability'. Finally, from the perspective of accountability mechanisms themselves the fragmentation of accountability functions does not necessarily resolve those tensions. Mechanisms that operate independently from one another in pursuit of their own accountability objective may not necessarily be aware of, or responsive to, the risks of tension or overlap that arise with other mechanisms. What all of this tells us is that striking an accountability balance *at the systemic level* must be an exercise in careful institutional design.

Assuming that we can reach consensus on what accountability outcome(s) we are aiming for in the context of public governance, we should then consider how best to achieve those objectives through the appropriate distribution of functions across a system of accountability mechanisms. In so doing, we again need to be aware of the need to strike a balance between these mechanisms not only in terms of the accountability objectives they might serve, but also in their operation as a system. As explored at length elsewhere (Rock 2020), the institutional design of accountability systems requires us to be aware of two different considerations.

The first is the *characteristics* of mechanisms within our accountability systems. Mechanisms may differ as between their functions and features across a range of criteria, such as their degree of autonomy, cost, accessibility, flexibility, coerciveness, independence, permanence, etc. In the context of discussions about accountability deficits, these types of characteristics are often thought about in terms of strengths and weaknesses. For example, the free ability to complain to an ombudsman might be thought consistent with supporting accountability, whereas the high costs and accessibility hurdles in legal challenges might be treated as a potential accountability 'deficit', 'gap' or 'hurdle'. Similarly, the highly coercive and enforceable remedies available through the courts might be thought desirable in the delivery of accountability, whereas the 'weaker' non-coercive powers of the ombudsman might be framed as a threat to accountability. However, when adopting a systemic approach to accountability it should be clear that the appropriate response to 'accountability angst' is not to simply maximise the range, number and power of accountability processes and actors. On a systemic and more sophisticated view, the ombudsman's lack of coercive powers may be framed as a positive strength within the overall blend or mix because officials are more likely to comply with requests and recommendations. To achieve our accountability objectives, we must consider the range of possible variables in features or characteristics and ensure that these appear in appropriate balance across the system.

The second point of institutional design which might inform efforts to achieve balance across and within accountability systems is to appreciate the nuances of the *relationships* between accountability mechanisms. As noted above, there is a very real risk of accountability overload if numerous mechanisms operate independently in their pursuit of overlapping accountability objectives. To limit this possibility, it is necessary to understand that mechanisms may operate and relate to one another in a range of different ways. Supreme audit institutions will often undertake fairly technical and regularised 'accounts' in ways that act as a 'fire alarm' for parliamentary scrutiny committees who lack the time and resources to undertake 'police-patrol' approaches to accountability (see McCubbins and Schwartz 1984). It is therefore also possible that mechanisms may operate in a staged manner (with one acting as a precondition to another), or a co-operative style (sharing information or resources), or mutually exclusively (where the operation of one cancels out the operation of another). Other possibilities include interdependent relationships (where mechanisms interplay or build on one another) and reciprocal relationships (where mechanisms hold one another accountable). Appreciating the nature of the relationships *between* mechanisms is important, as it should inform any assessment of the presence of accountability gaps and overlaps.

The failure of one mechanism may not in itself produce an accountability deficit if there are other complementary structures in place. There is no deficit, for example, in the inapplicability of judicial review to private contractors if effective control can be achieved through the law of contract; and there is no deficit in the unavailability of damages in judicial review proceedings if the applicant has access to a statutory compensation scheme. To a similar end, the presence of two accountability mechanisms does not represent an accountability overload if they do not in fact overlap but simply complement each other. There is no excess in accountability, for example, if tort proceedings against a government official are permanently stayed following the commencement of a criminal trial, and there is no overlap between the provision of damages in tort law and ex gratia compensation payments if the latter are available only in a 'gap filling' capacity. Again, our efforts in institutional design and our analysis of accountability systems must take into account the nuances of the relationships between mechanisms in order to identify potential accountability deficits and overloads.

If the overarching goal of accountability is to support the legitimacy of government and public trust in those systems, then there is clearly merit in seeking to 'measure' accountability with a view to identifying areas of accountability deficit and overload. This represents the central argument of this chapter. But measuring accountability and coming to any clear sense of agreement on systemic design is complicated by an array of dynamic factors. At the same time, *the politics of accountability* (ie, the manner in which the blame-based emphasis of accountability tends to fuel defensive behaviours) creates very few incentives for actors in positions of power to pro-actively seek more integrated systemic structures. Analysts of accountability should not be naïve to the fact that the existence of 'deficits' or 'gaps' may not be completely accidental. Strategic ambiguity can be a strategic asset for those seeking to evade or manage the accountability demands placed upon them. With this in mind, 'questions of accountability' relating to perspective and measurement are likely to continue for some time.

4

Loss of Balance? Exploring the 'Dark Side' of Accountability

MATTHEW FLINDERS

In the previous chapter Ellen Rock explored 'questions of measurement' and, more specifically, how questions of 'too much, or too little' could be settled. Her conclusion focused attention on the underlying rationale for accountability in any given context, and the primary goals being sought through the application of accountability processes. This chapter continues this focus on proportionality and balance – themes that define this whole collection – while expanding and complementing Rock's approach. It achieves this through a novel emphasis on excess and asks: *can accountability be bad for democracy?* Although Bovens, Schillemans, and 't Hart (2008) suggest that accountability 'is one of those golden concepts that no one can be against' this chapter seeks to explore *how*, *why* and *when* accountability might be detrimental to the broader health of democracy. More specifically, it seeks to construct and interrogate an argument regarding whether a link exists between *increasing* levels of public accountability and *falling* levels of public confidence in politics in advanced liberal democracies. This is clearly a wide-ranging argument. It embraces a range of debates and discussions which although difficult to settle in a definitive sense do at least deepen our understanding of the interplay between individuals, institutions and society vis-à-vis accountable governance. In doing so this chapter helps provide the foundations for later chapters that drill-down into more specific concerns and controversies. It is also a chapter that innovates in the sense of embracing, presenting and developing its core six-word 'question of accountability' (ie, *can accountability be bad for democracy?*) by returning to an influential text and then exploring how the debate it set in train has evolved over time.

In 2011 Matthew Flinders wrote an article entitled 'Daring to be a Daniel' which crafted a controversial argument concerning the pathologies of too much accountability. It was defined to stimulate a debate and a series of response pieces subsequently critiqued, revised and refined Flinders' core thesis. Moreover, over the subsequent decade, a large number of research projects and academic publications have attempted to test – or, at the very least, explore – Flinders' core thesis through applied empirical analysis in a range of settings. These three stages of debate and discussion (initial intervention, immediate response, incremental analyses) provide a framework through which to range from micro-political questions of institutional inertia or reform, through to far larger macro-political questions concerning the changing socio-political context, the role of academics in society and the ontology of 'accountability spaces'. In order to capture and present this breadth this chapter is divided into three question-focused sections:

1. *Initial Intervention* – Why might accountability be 'bad' for democracy?
2. *Immediate Response* – How was this 'dark side' of accountability thesis initially received?
3. *Incremental Analyses* – What do we know about the pathologies of accountability ten years on?

In seeking to explore questions of excess, salvation and sorrow this chapter is not, of course, arguing in any way against the concept of accountability per se. Accountability, and the relationships through which this concept is enacted and made real, provide the core essence of legitimate democratic governance. The 'be bad' dimension of this chapter's primary question is therefore partial in the sense that it accepts and recognises the core centrality of accountability processes but simply seeks to provoke a debate about *dis*proportionality, excess, overloads and imbalance. In order to start this debate, the next section provides a precis of Flinders' original 2011 article.

I. Why might Accountability be 'Bad' for Democracy?

'Accountability' Flinders suggests (2011, 595) 'is not always a good thing'. In this regard he draws inspiration from two key sources: the first being Elinor Ostrom's (2000) warning about 'the danger of self-evident truths', and the second being Melvyn Dubnick's 'seeking salvation' argument concerning the limits of accountability. 'The fact that something is so widely believed' Ostrom (2000, 33) suggested 'does not make it correct.' Furthermore, reforms 'based on overly simplified views of the world have led to counter-intuitive and counter-intentional results'. For Ostrom there was an urgent need for social and political scientists to question dominant self-evident truths, accepted foundational assumptions and simple 'common-sense' understandings. The link across to Dubnick's work was that he sought to expose the danger of a core and dominant accountability assumption within advanced liberal societies. 'There exists an almost unquestioned assumption' Dubnick (2002) suggested 'that the *creation or enhancement of accountability mechanisms* of any sort will *result in greater democracy* [emphasis added].'

This implied logic of 'more accountability equals greater/better democracy' was the 'self-evident truth' (*qua*. Ostrom, 2000) that Dubnick sought to question, and that Flinders sought to explore in his 2011 article. As such, Flinders surveyed a vast seam of scholarship and identified a common four-step logic-process (see Box 4.1, below) that tended to dominate debates, almost without question:

Box 4.1 The 'Self-Evident Truth' of Accountability

Step 1
The transition from *government* to *governance* has undermined traditional mechanisms of democratic accountability;

⇓

Step 2
As a result, politicians have become more untrustworthy and bureaucracies less responsive;

⇓

Step 3
New modes and mechanisms of accountability therefore need to be implemented; and

⇓

Step 4
Any individual or organisation that argues against greater accountability must have something to hide.

Steps 1 to 4 were from this perspective imbued, as Dubnick (2002) had argued, with the 'unquestioned assumption' that more accountability would result in greater/better democracy. Flinders sought to question this assumption through a focus on caution and proportionality. Caution in the sense that accountability processes can mutate into self-fulfilling prophecies. If rational-choice theoretic assumptions are accepted about the behaviour of politicians and bureaucrats (ie, Machiavellian rationality that they are intrinsically self-interested and not to be trusted) then there is a risk that healthy *dis*trust may mutate into corrosive cynicism (discussed below) in ways that squeeze-out any possibility of recognising or acknowledging of virtuous or selfless behaviour (see Hay, 2004). If normative caution about *always* prescribing self-interested motivations for public service provides the first of Flinders points, then the second focuses on proportionality and the capacity to govern. Put simply, politicians and the officials who work within the public sector must be able to make decisions. Overly demanding or complex accountability requirements born out of excessive *dis*trust can suffocate the capacity and morale of any organisation. Governing capacity is therefore a requirement of any political system. 'My point is that we cannot bind the hands of politicians by placing more and more limits on their governing capacity, or by subjecting their every decision to forensic analysis' Flinders (2011, 599) suggested 'and then attack them for failing to govern with conviction or take decisive action.'

In highlighting the themes of caution and proportionality Flinders was able to draw upon British constitutional history. In *The British Constitution*, for example, Walter Bagehot (1867 [2001]) went to great lengths to explain that the convention of ministerial responsibility was intended not simply as a sword of accountability but also as a shield *from* accountability. The convention's role was to deliver an acceptable degree of accountability while at the same time protecting ministers from 'the busy-bodies and the crotchet-makers of the House' thereby preventing 'the incessant tyranny of parliament over public offices'. Constitutional texts from the nineteenth century that considered the birth and risks of representative democracy were almost defined by a focus on how to deliver an acceptable balance between *representative government* (emphasising accountability, transparency, and public participation) and *responsible government* (emphasising stability, executive capacity, and control). AH Birch's *Representative and Responsible Government* (1964) and David Judge's *The Parliamentary State* (1993) provide astute analyses of how this balance has gradually evolved to the benefit of the executive over the legislature (for a review see Flinders and Judge, 2017).

Flinders was able to draw-upon a thin stream of more recent analyses when seeking to emphasise the themes of caution and proportionality, and in this regard the focus on Anechiarico and Jacobs' (1996) discussion of the 'integrity/efficiency trade-off' provided a particularly important reference point (discussed in chapter one, developed in Figure 1.1). 'Some politicians' Anechiarico and Jacobs (1996, 59) suggested

> [were] anxious to appear morally pure, support dubious and cumbersome 'reforms', regardless of the possible effect of those reforms on public administration … moral entrepreneurs are likely to be so consumed with stopping corruption that they rarely even consider the integrity/efficiency trade-off.

What might from this perspective be termed *the accountability dilemma* at the heart of the 'integrity/efficiency trade-off' revolves around the simple recognition that the requirements of accountability (ie, regular reporting, audit mechanisms, threat of sanctions, short-term time horizons, etc) may grate against the imperatives of effective service delivery (freedom to manage, innovation, flexibility, risk taking, long-term planning, etc). The simple point that Flinders was attempting to highlight was that this dilemma or trade-off too often appeared to have been overlooked against a backdrop that Moore and Gates (1986, 2) had correctly described in terms of an 'unquenchable thirst for accountability'.

Unquenchable thirsts are rarely a sign of good health and Flinders supported this concern with reference (inter alia) to a range of studies and perspectives that had each in their own ways questioned simplistic 'accountability-is-good' assumptions. This began with Romzek and Ingraham's (2000) exploration of the 'cross-pressures' of accountability and ended with Falaschetti's (2009) analysis of the economic costs of accountability – with works including Behn's (2001) *Rethinking Democratic Accountability* with its emphasis on dysfunctional incentive frameworks, O'Neill's (2002) philosophical 'question of trust', Koppell's thesis about 'multiple-accountabilities disorder, Hood and Heald's (2006) questioning of the link between transparency and better governance, and Philp's (2009, 43) warnings about 'delimiting democratic accountability' providing important intervening reference points.

All of these studies, Flinders suggested, presented reasons for why accountability *might* be bad for democracy in certain forms, contexts or quantities. Or, to put the same point differently, these studies posed critical questions about the need for design-based thinking and discussions when considering the introduction of new or enhanced scrutiny systems. But in addition to these predominantly economic or administrative analyses, Flinders attempted to make a distinctive *democratic* contribution by highlighting the implications of a changing socio-political context or, more specifically, *the pathology of politicised accountability.*

For Flinders the *pathology of politicised accountability* consisted of three interwoven dimensions that, when taken together, risked creating a negative spiral of cynicism – possibly even the hollowing-out of democratic governance. The first element was the emergence of an increasingly dominant form of aggressive 'Gotcha!' accountability. The ultimate ambition of this mode of scrutiny was *not* to find out *what happened, why and what might be learnt to prevent similar problems in the future* but to enforce sacrificial accountability (ie, to claim a political scalp). In theory accountability revolves around the balanced review of information and the subsequent allocation of credit or sanctions for performance; in reality, Flinders argued, it had become synonymous with naming, shaming and ultimately blaming. 'Accountability means punishment' as Behn (2001, 3) had argued, and Flinders (2011) sought to explain how the dominance of such a one-dimensional blame-focused accountability emphasis could be 'bad' for democracy. 'Bad' in the sense of failing to identify 'lesson-learning opportunities' or 'what works', 'bad' in the sense of encouraging defensive behaviours on the part of politicians and public servants, 'bad' in the sense of not facilitating balanced or evidence-based discussions, 'bad' in the sense of generating risk-averse cultures and blocking innovation and 'bad' in the sense of encouraging an emphasis on scapegoating individuals when often it was structures and systems that were often at fault.

Accountability is an inevitably political process. It revolves around the control of political power and public resources. But the point Flinders was making emphasised the emergence and dominance of a particularly pathological and highly partisan form of 'attack politics' in which the tools and processes of public accountability were increasingly used as little more than weapons of party-political point scoring (see Buell and Sigelman 2009). This flows into a second shift that Flinders initial analysis sought to emphasise: the changing role of the media.

The emergence of 24/7 rolling media with a vast number of online and offline channels all competing for a slice of a finite and increasingly fluid viewing public had, Flinders suggested, created an additional layer to the *pathology of politicised accountability* discussed above. The 'if it bleeds, it leads' approach of key outlets reflected a media sphere that had become increasingly imbued with a culture of negativity that ignored success or balanced reporting in favour of crisis amplification and personalised attacks. Thomas Patterson's (2003) award-winning work, for example, linking increasing news media negativity bias with the phenomenon of 'vanishing voters' and in many ways what Flinders sought to hypothesise was the relationship between an ever-expanding (but largely negatively inflected) accountability universe and concern about the 'death', 'end' or 'suicide' of democracy. In this hypothesis what might be termed 'the dark side' of accountability mattered because: (i) it provided the public with a heavily distorted view about the performance of political institutions, political processes and politicians; which (ii) could have major implications in terms of fostering 'disaffected democrats' and nurturing anti-political sentiment; (iii) while at the same time also rationalising a reform agenda based on the movement of powers, responsibilities and decision-making capacity *away* from elected politicians (on the basis of their untrustworthiness, inefficiency, etc) towards 'depoliticised' arm's-length agencies or actors in an attempt to solve a perceived 'credibility crisis' (see Fawcett et al 2017).

Too much accountability, particularly of the wrong kind of accountability, can be as bad for democracy as too little. This was the simple argument Flinders attempted to craft in his 2011 'Daring to be a Daniel' article. To make such an argument was not to deny the concept's 'golden' qualities but it is to highlight the existence of a 'dark side' which can become highly problematic if allowed to evolve without requisite *caution* and *proportionality* (discussed above). Accountability might be 'bad' for democracy – to return to the core focus of this section – if it over-exaggerates or over-inflames the societal 'negativity bias' in ways that are in fact misleading, inaccurate or simply a gross misrepresentation of the realities of democratic governance. Accountability is also likely to be 'bad' if it cannot distribute credit, praise or reward; and if it fosters defensive and risk-aversive cultures within the public sector. This in itself underlines the basic chameleon-like quality of accountability structures with different systems having different aims, ambitions and unintended consequences. As such, and returning, to Dubnick's (2002) 'seeking salvation for accountability' argument – the answer to every governing dilemma is therefore unlikely to be found in the imposition of ever-greater and more strident scrutiny structures.

'This is clearly a wide-ranging article and, like painting on a large canvas, this has required the use of a fairly broad brush, in analytical and empirical terms' Flinders (2011, 597) noted

> However, it is hoped that by daring to challenge the normative assumptions that underpin the development of increasingly dense accountability webs and locating this perspective within a number of broader debates concerning public attitudes and the evolution of democracy, this article will stimulate more scholarly interest in this topic.

The next section explores the initial response to Flinders' focus on the 'dark side' of accountability and how these criticisms and refinements relate to issues and themes that have surfaced in earlier chapters in this collection.

II. How was the 'Dark Side' Thesis Initially Received?

Too much accountability can be as problematic for democracy as too little. This was the basic argument that Flinders had presented. This was not a new argument.

Although phrased in different ways at different times, the 'integrity/efficiency' trade-off (discussed above) had been a feature of scholarship for at least a century and basically highlighted that 'the pursuit of *absolute* integrity' [emphasis added] – the title of an Anechiarico and Jacobs 1996 book on the topic – was likely to impose major financial and administrative costs. The issue here not being about accountability per se or the demand for high-standards in public life but how to achieve some sort of balance between effective scrutiny, on the one hand, and governing capacity, on the other. The search for *absolute* integrity – the very highest levels of propriety and public service – may serve as an honourable ideal but may in practice create little more than a low-cost, high blame operating environment. What Flinders added to this thesis was an emphasis on the changing socio-political context at the end of the first decade of the twenty-first century. More specifically, his concern about the *pathology of politicised accountability* sought to underline how scrutiny structures appeared to have become more aggressive, personalised and partisan in nature. This, in turn, was linked not only to a changing political climate but also to shifts in the political economy of the media which risked providing the public with a misleading sense of political life and public service that may, over time, lead to democratic *de*consolidation (ie, the evisceration of public commitment to the core values and principles of democracy).

How then was this thesis received, and what did the tone and content of those responses indicate about other 'questions of accountability' that may deserve consideration?

Table 4.1 Main Immediate Responses to the 'Dark Side of Accountability' Thesis

Respondent	Discipline	Argument
Yannis Papadopoulos	Political Science	Flinders' etiology (ie, causal interpretation) suggests but does not demonstrate the negative influence of the media, and it over-inflates the penetrative capacity of monitory democracy.
Philip E. Tetlock	Political Psychology	The micro-mechanisms underlying the accountability excesses that Flinders identifies will not be curbed by well-intentioned pleas for proportionality.
Melvin J. Dubnick	Public Administration	Flinders adopts an institutionalist approach that fails to grasp the role of socially mediated relationships. Understanding the 'accountability space' requires a radical reframing.

The immediate and direct replies came in the form of response pieces that were all written by leading and internationally renowned scholars specialising in accountability-related issues. The main thrust of their arguments is set out Table 4.1 (above) and the remainder of this section provides a very brief precis of each author's thoughts, criticisms and counter-claims. The reason for this review is to expand the debate and questions concerning the 'dark side' of accountability, before looking at how these issues and themes have developed and evolved over the last decade in the next and concluding section of this chapter.

A. Papadopoulos: A Salutary Note of Caution about Media Influence and Monitory Penetration

'Notwithstanding [the] undeniable merits of Professor Flinders' critical piece on the pathologies of accountability' Papadopoulos (2012, 240) notes

> I am afraid there are some weaknesses in his line of thinking … They are concentrated, in my view, in two partly inaccurate descriptions: one on the role of the media and one on the impact of 'monitoring' in contemporary governance.

In relation to the media Papadopoulos suggested that Flinders exaggerated the negative impact of the media, or at the very least failed to acknowledge the heterogeneity of media regimes and practices in different parts of the world and due to this presented an overly 'Americanised' (ie, market-driven, sensationalist, conflict-focused, a culture of negativity, etc). Papadopoulos also suggested that when it comes to media accountability and its effects on public trust and confidence in democratic politics, what Flinders was really offering is 'insightful inductive hypothesis' that demands substantial empirical testing. The reason for this being that in advanced liberal democracies, Papadopoulos suggested, the public are increasingly well-educated, interested in politics and highly distrustful of the media to the extent that cognitive mobilisation may not inevitably lead to cynicism and disaffection in the way Flinders assumed.

A second area where Papadopoulos suggests the 'dark side' of accountability might be over-stated related to Flinders concerns about the emergence of 'monitory democracy' in which a vast range of watchdogs, integrity commissions, sleazebusters, flash mobs, civic associations, public assemblies, ethical guardians, ombudsmen, etc, utilise transparency regimes, freedom of information legislation, social media and communicative technology to enforce post-electoral and frequently direct forms of public accountability. These are the specialised accountability institutions – 'power-monitoring and power-controlling devices' – that John Keane (2009) argues are focused on 'checking-on, goading, and humbling' those elected to power. The impact of these organisations is, however, over-stated according to Papadopoulos. The heavily mediatised and therefore 'frontstage' visibility of such monitory organisations has limited reach, he suggested, into the deeper structural 'backstage' dynamics of political life. The internationalisation of rule-making also complicates, Papadopoulos suggested, the capacity of monitory bodies to penetrate policy-making structures, and extreme information asymmetries still define the relationship between the governors and the governed. Moreover, private international regulatory regimes proliferate in many sectors and 'probably even less than in other forms of governance beyond the nation state' Papadopoulos (2012, 246) suggests 'private governance activities are not much the focus of monitory democracy.'

What is interesting, however, is that where Flinders is critical of 'monitory democracy' for potentially creating an *excess of accountability*, Papadopoulos drew upon his previous work (2010) to suggest that in some contexts *more accountability, might lead to less democracy*. 'In a democracy, the monitoring agents are the citizens who compose the demos. But in "monitory" democracy' Papadopoulos notes (2012, 246) 'this is not true any longer.' For Papadopoulos the perceived pluralism that Keane promotes is, in fact, a form of 'advocacy democracy' in which monitoring agents or institutions claim to represent the people or to act in their interests. But the link between monitory bodies that claim to work for the public interest or for specific communities is often tenuous at best, and spurious at worst. The 'dark side' of accountability in this interpretation relates to the unequal distribution of resources and the mirroring of embedded structural inequalities within monitory structures.

> In my view, the major current pathology of accountability is not that there is too much monitoring in policy-making but that there is an increasing number of governance areas in which there is either too little monitoring or monitoring that lacks democratic credentials (2012, 247).

B. Tetlock: It's Too Easy to Look Down on Those Who Look Soft On (Accountability)

By focusing on the influence of the media and the legitimacy of monitory bodies Papadopoulos focuses on large macro-political or structural issues. Tetlock, by contrast, focuses on micro-political matters. 'As a research psychologist' he notes (2011, 694)

> I approach the proliferation of accountability mechanisms from a micro-vantage point. My focus is on the cognitive and emotional processes that drive smart social-system designers to keep upping the accountability ante and demanding increasingly intrusive and expensive monitoring of the performance of various classes of political and economic actors.

The critical element of Tetlock's response, however, did not lie in its critique of Flinders' thesis but in its explanation of the 'micro-mechanisms underlying accountability excesses' and why it will be 'impossible to curb these excesses via Flinders well-intentioned but inadequate pleas for proportionality (694)'. What Tetlock highlights is the existence of a vast seam of psychological scholarship on motivated reasoning and cognitive dissonance that demonstrates why advocates of heavy-handed forms of accountability will feel no dissonance in simultaneously agreeing with the need for proportionality and balance *in theory*, while at the same time challenging the moral character and ideological agenda of those who seek to apply the proportionality principle *in practice* (see Tetlock et al 2007). 'The core problem' Tetlock suggests (694) 'is that the line between "healthy skepticism" and "corrosive cynicism" is much blurrier in the policy trenches than it is in political theory.' More specifically, there are few incentives on the part of the potential architect of more stringent accountability measures to exercise caution. Imparted inefficiencies and transaction costs are likely to fall most heavily upon those from whom an account is demanded; while pushing back and resisting the imposition of additional accountabilities is likely to be interpreted as evidence that the accountee has something to hide (see Box 4.1, above).

Tetlock uses subjective expected utility theory and signal-detection theory to help identify the causal drivers for accountability punitiveness. The former focuses attention on your base-rate belief about the trustworthiness of an individual or organisation; in short, the more suspicious you are, the tighter accountability net or web you would want to put around them (limited discretion, high penalties, etc). Signal detection theory, by contrast, focuses on political values that are enacted within an accountability framework. Signal sensitivity means that system-designers need to be aware of the risk of *false-positive attribution errors* (in which they hold role incumbents responsible for outcomes beyond their control) and *false-negative attribution errors* (in which they fail to hold role incumbents responsible for outcomes that they could have controlled). 'All else equal' Tetlock notes 'the less you care about avoiding false positive attribution errors and the more you care about false-negative errors, the greater the likelihood of your endorsing a system that transfers risk to, and places onerous demands on, role incumbents.' This two-dimensional approach facilitates the creation of a grid-based *hypo-* to *hyper*-accountability continuum.

Diagram 4.1 Hypo- and Hyper-Accountability Continuum

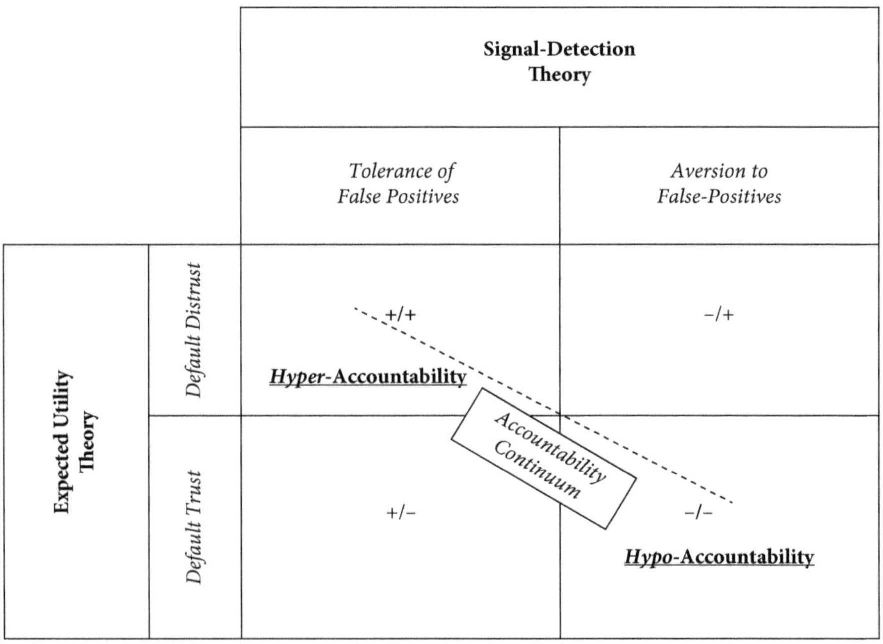

At least four issues emerge out of Diagram 4.1. First, in a political context defined by aggressive competition (ie, for votes, for party funding, for viewing audiences, control of the agenda, etc) a systemic incentive-system emerges – or form of bounded rationality – around *hyper*-accountability. This is because (second) levels of default societal distrust has increased in many countries over the last decade (discussed below) while the costs of 'false negatives' is not necessarily 'negative' in the sense that account-demanders will very often receive credit for keeping potential miscreants 'on their toes', and the announcement of an investigation, inquiry or court case provides valuable agenda-setting and policy-framing influence. (In a low-trust, high-blame environment 'false negatives' are also likely to be interpreted or perceived as 'unproven positives' through recourse to the (in)famous adage that 'there is no smoke without fire'.) A fourth and related issue relates to the 'social psychological problem of competitive self-righteousness' (Tetlock 2011, 700) whereby those who argue for tighter accountability and new scrutiny safeguards adopt the moral high ground ('better safe than sorry'). While those arguing in favour of proportionality and balance are vulnerable to accusations of political weakness, regulatory capture, undue influence or being hopelessly naïve: promoting 'obfuscationalist rhetoric that gives far too much wiggle room to untrustworthy actors' (Tetlock 2011, 702).

The need to acknowledge the existence of a theoretical inflection point where the costs of over-correcting for accountability outweigh the likely benefits, let alone arguments about the 'dark side' of accountability, are simply too 'academic' to cut through and influence contemporary politics and policy. 'Cut through' not because politicians and policymakers do not understand the basic accountability argument (ie, 'too much can be as bad as too little'); quite the opposite, they deploy a form of motivated reasoning involving cognitive dissonance on the basis of their ideological disposition towards distrust. And yet arguably, the key issue that Diagram 4.1 attempts to illustrate is that there are very few incentives for accountability agencies of any kind to moderate their scrutiny. The existence of perverse incentives to be hyper-vigilant increase as actors or organisations become enmeshed within or in some way responsible for complex networks that are rife with co-dependencies (the system goes 'MAD' to reintroduce Koppell's work on multiple-accountabilities disorder). This is exactly why Tetlock argues that irrespective of the theoretical or practical value of Flinders' arguments, 'pleas for proportionality and invocations of integrity/efficiency trade-offs will often fall on deaf ears' for the simple reason that 'accountability zealots do not see themselves as zealots. They see themselves as thoughtful rational actors responding to a social problem that others have – for far too long- pretended does not exist (Tetlock 2011, 702)'.

C. Dubnick: We Need Some 'Accountability Space'

'It is not accountability that is undermining our aspirations for an effective democracy' Dubnick (2011, 705) argues 'but the reformist aspiration for an effective democracy that is undermining accountability.' What Dubnick proceeds to offer is a more cautious approach to accountability-based reforms based on the existence of what he labels the 'reformist-paradox'. 'This paradox holds that any effort to improve accountability through reforms generates consequences that in fact alters and often undermines existing forms of accountability already in place' (706). The rationale for presenting this paradox is to be found in Dubnick's (2005) rhetoric-focused study of 'accountability and the promise of performance' which uncovered a set of common but theoretically vacuous and untested assumptions or 'promises' about what the imposition of higher levels of accountability could and would achieve.

> This brings me to my current view of the accountability problem and the conclusion that what we are dealing with is an ontological issue from which all other problems – analytic, conceptual, and theoretical – flow. Perhaps the problem is the way we view accountability and the role it plays in our governance universe (707).

The mistake Dubnick suggested Flinders had made in his argument about the *pathology of politicised accountability* was to adopt an overly narrow and conventional view of accountability as consisting of three basic and nested attributes: macro-level structures (eg, constitutional frameworks including checks and balances); meso or mid-range processes (eg, investigations, review, etc) and micro-level tools or mechanisms (eg, reports, sanction, etc). Seen through this lens – in this 'ontological world' as Dubnick (2011, 708) claims – accountability is defined as an instrument of governance, management and reform which Dubnick claims 'blinds us to an even more significant place for accountability in our lives'.

> The 'alternative reality', I would argue for, is not one in which accountability relationships (as institutions, mechanisms, and processes) play a secondary or corrective role in governance, but rather where they (i.e. account-demanding and account-giving relationships) constitute the very essence of social arrangements that comprise governance.

What Flinders had implicitly adopted and presented was, according to Dubnick, an argument born of a substantialist or foundational view of governance whereby observable empirical objects and structures formed the primary interest. What Dubnick sought to promote was a relational view with accountability acting almost as the glue which builds and binds the social order within which the structures, processes and tools operate. Instead of viewing the architecture of accountability in mechanical or machine-like terms, accountability becomes the oil or lubricant that facilitates the human interactions on which governance arrangements depend.

> Conceptually, from a relationalist perspective, accountability constitutes what sociologists and social geographers would call a 'social space' – a milieu of account-giving and account-demanding human relationships that constitute what, for our purposes, would be more appropriately 'accountability space' (2011, 709).

This shift in ontological approach mattered according to Dubnick because the 'promise' of accountability was forged on a substantialist narrative which links *pre factum/ex ante* accountability as the key to 'good governance' which was increasingly operationalised through performance management and measurement regimes. In a phrase that resonate with Tetlock's focus on 'accountability zealots', Dubnick suggested that the ever-expanding reach of reformers who believe in and promote such narratives 'borders on a fundamentalist faith that is intolerant of sceptics (2011, 710)'. From Dubnick's perspective, Flinders emphasis on 'too much' accountability does not go far enough because although it questions the excessive demands of reformers it fails to expose and question the very notions that underpin such 'promises' (ie, underlying substantialist narratives). Flinders was, in essence, buying into the reformist mind-set.

In emphasising the relational dimensions of accountability, Dubnick focused on morality, sentiment, social capital and trust over structures, processes and tools. In doing so he drew on Sinclair's (1995) emphasis on the social construction of accountability, Hall's et al (2007) focus on the accountability 'lens' in society, and how contributions by Fairclough (2011), Hochwarter et al (2005) and others focused on the role that 'affective' or 'felt' accountability played in shaping everyday social interactions. The 'reformist narrative' that all problems relating to public governance can be solved through the application of new, more and tighter accountability *structures* needed, from this perspective, to appreciate the inevitable unintended consequences this reform agenda was likely to have on the more informal and less visible bonds of trust-based social and professional accountability that may already exist.

III. What Do We Know about the Pathologies of Accountability Ten Years On?

The first part of this chapter set out Flinders' simple suggestion that 'too much accountability can be as bad as too little'. This is an argument that had been made before but to which Flinders sought to draw greater attention due to concerns about *the pathologies of politicised accountability* in the twenty-first century. His core concern was that an excess of aggressive, sensationalist and very often partisan blame-driven accountability risked undermining public trust in democracy. The second section reviewed how this strong statement of concern was originally received: Papadopoulos suggested Flinders had overstated the influence of the media and the penetration of monitory democracy, Tetlock explained why Flinders' 'plea for proportionality and balance' was essentially doomed, and Dubnick emphasised a relationalist perspective in order to reveal the full 'accountability space'. This section: (i) explores whether if Flinders' warnings about 'the dark side of accountability' became more-or-less relevant during the last decade; (ii) what subsequent research has revealed about some of those issue raised in the initial responses; and (iii) how this debate resonates with the broader 'questions of accountability' raised in this collection.

The main argument of this section is that developments in the second decade of the twenty-first century have resonated with Flinders' basic argument about *the pathology of politicised accountability*. The well-documented emergence of populism in many parts of the world has generally been fuelled by an explicit, carefully crafted and three-dimensional set of accountability arguments. At the first level are a set of generic accusations about the existence of an unaccountable and morally suspect 'elite', which is attached to an antagonistic logic concerning 'them-and-us' (see, for example, Mudde 2010; Moffitt 2016); at the second level are a set of more focused accusations concerning the failure and corruption of exactly those horizontal accountability actors (watchdogs, court systems, central banks, audit institutions, independent commissions, etc) that are supposed to protect 'us' from 'them' (see, for example, Ruth 2018; Guasti 2020); and the third element is a relational dimension bound to faith in a 'strong leader model' that generally emphasises direct, vertical or plebiscitary accountability (see Körösényi 2019; Subedi and Scott 2021).

Enacting accountability under populist pressures, as Wood et al (2021) demonstrate in great detail, is based on a moral or emotionalised form of blame-attribution which is systemic in nature, arguably nihilistic in nature, highly mediatised and sensationalist, designed to fuel and funnel democratic distrust and anti-political sentiment, and linked to evidence of democratic backsliding which resonates with Flinders' original pre- 'populist signal' (Chwalisz 2015) concerns about the potential manipulation and politicisation of accountability. In the context of populist pressures, Orhan (2022) finds that the global growth in affective polarisation and electoral hostility is highly correlated with *less accountability*. Put very simply, populism represents a very extreme version of exactly the *pathologies of politicised accountability* that Flinders sought to warn against. As such the central argument of this section is that his warnings about 'the dark side of accountability' have become more relevant during the last decade.

The politics of populism also facilitates a link back to Papadopoulos' concerns that Flinders over-estimated the influence of the media, and the reach of monitory democracy. In terms of the media, while not uncontested, increasing evidence has supported the 'malaise theory' and found evidence of 'sleeper effects' (Kleinnijenhuis, van Hoof and Oegema 2006) whereby negative news *does* appear to stimulate political distrust (see, for example, Borah 2014; Klein and Robison 2020; Zoizner 2021; Jones-Jang, Kim and Kenski 2021). The effects are interwoven with relatively recent concerns regarding social media and the socio-political implications of fake news, misinformation, conspiracy theories and 'post-truth'/'alt-truth' framings. In short, and not withstanding Papadopoulos' caveat about the exceptionality of an overly 'Americanised' emphasis (see Suiter and Fletcher 2020), the current evidence base would broadly seem to support Flinders' initial concerns about negative news fuelling political distrust, with the emergence of populism adding a distinctive and generally anti-democratic dynamic.

Papadopoulos' emphasis on the failure of 'monitory democracy' to penetrate the 'off-stage' dynamics of elite politics provides another link to what might be termed *the politics of populism*. Papadopoulos suggests Flinders over-stated the influence and scrutiny capacity of horizontal accountability actors, especially at the international level and within transnational networks (the focus of chapter eleven in this volume). This is a position that would indirectly chime with populist arguments concerning the existence of unaccountable technocrats, complicit politicians and non-majoritarian institutions (on this see De Cleen et al 2020). What is interesting, however, is that as Wood et al (2022, 311; see also Rooduijn 2018) note, 'there has been limited cross-fertilization between research on populism and research on public accountability'.

Where a rich cross-fertilisation of theories and approaches has, however, taken place is at the intersection between Tetlock's work on political psychology vis-à-vis accountability and Dubnick's emphasis on relationships and the 'accountability space' (as discussed by Schillemans in chapter two in this volume). This has emerged through the emergence of a seam of scholarship on 'felt accountability' which seeks to acknowledge and understand the position of account-givers and how they feel about the legitimacy and credibility of the accountability expectations placed upon them. 'Felt accountability denotes the expectation that one's decisions and behaviours will be evaluated by an "able" accountability forum with authority' Schillemans et al (2000, 893 note 'Felt accountability has been translated to public administration research from psychology, where its effects on individual decisions and behaviours have been studied in hundreds of experimental studies. Individually felt accountability is conceived as a *response* to the accountability environment in which the individual operates.' Elsewhere Overman and Schillemans (2022) demonstrate that effective accountability mechanisms must acknowledge the beliefs of account-givers about their own professional role, about the perceived authority of the account holders, and about the contents of the accountability demand. It therefore emphasises relational dimensions of credibility, reputation and expertise and how the perceptions of future accountability that account-givers hold are the result of the internalisations of (in)formal norms. In this sense the recent emphasis on 'felt accountability' embraces elements of Dubnick's (2011, 704) call for 'a radical reframing of the accountability space'.

Moving back towards a focus on Flinders' original focus on the dangers of 'too much accountability' a number of subsequent studies have provided substantive empirical data that supports his core concern. The work of Tu and Gong (2022), for example, explores how local government officials in China cope with multiple-accountabilities disorder and conflicting expectations. They reveal that although public officials tend to put more effort into tasks that are aligned with citizens' interests, over-stringent accountability requirements that crowd-out intrinsic public service motivations and incentivise mechanical but sub-optimal behaviour. 'Intensified accountability' they (2022, 1779) conclude 'may not necessarily lead to better policy outcomes'. Wang's (2022) research also explores how intense, top-down monitoring tends to reduce the operational efficiency and performance of those subject to such procedures. Wang reveals the existence of a 'chilling effect' which disincentives the use of informal practices by local officials when completing daily tasks. In a conclusion that resonates with Ostrom's arguments about the dangers of 'self-evident truths', Wang (2022, 1807) notes, '[A]lthough scholars of state-building equate low corruption with effective bureaucracy, these findings present a paradox where intensive state-led efforts to lower corruption [via tight accountability structures] may further undermine bureaucrats' productivity.'

Aleksovska, Schillemans and Grimmelikhuijsen (2021) provide a related analysis by exploring how public servants manage multiple accountabilities. What they find is that a hierarchy of considerations exists, with the avoidance of sanctions, particularly material and reputational, taking primacy over all other considerations. However, in a finding that resonates with analyses of felt accountability they also found that account-givers tend to prioritise the demands of stakeholders that are seen as highly knowledgeable and with which there is a history of a positive working relationship. The critical finding, however, is arguably that operating in a context of 'multiple accountabilities' and 'cross-pressures' is neither exceptional for public servants nor necessarily pathological. Its deleterious impact on performance being dependent on the management of relationships which are, in turn, frequently highly dependent on contextual dimensions.

Continuing with this more positive interpretation, Li, Qin and Koppenjan (2022) explore a major experiment in direct public accountability – the ten-thousand citizen review in Nanjing, China. What this demonstrated was the challenge of grafting new bottom-up forms of public accountability onto existing top-down frameworks of political accountability (on this see chapter five's discussion of Type I and Type II, bottom-up and top-down structures). 'Our findings show that citizens' involvement initially resulted in a practice in which types of accountability were mixed and resulted in a situation of multiple accountabilities disorder.' However, what the analysis also revealed was the gradual alignment, refinement and recalibration of the overall accountability system towards an integrated balance. Szydlowski, de Boer and Tummers (2022) build upon Flinders' (2011) focus on 'bad accountability' to explore the relationship between 'bureaucrat bashing' and eliciting public compassion. In a major study that is rooted in concerns about the populist politicisation of accountability they find that increasing public understanding around the everyday challenges faced by public servants motivates the public to be more compassionate and less critical. This emphasis on how levels of public understanding can mediate accountability pressures is critical to the overall focus of this collection on balance and proportionality. It is a theme that flows through Lord Blunkett's chapter on 'Accountability from the Inside Out' and Sharon Shoesmiths's contribution on 'positive accountability' (chapters twelve and thirteen respectively) and is explored in more detail in the concluding final chapter as Matthew Flinders and Chris Monaghan explore 'Questions Still to be Answered' (chapter fifteen). But in order to continue this focus on framing 'questions of accountability' the next chapter explores the relationship between executive powers and fuzzy accountability.

5

Fuzzy Law, Executive Powers and the Problem of Accountability

MARGIT COHN

Although a title such as 'fuzzy law and fuzzy accountability' might seem a rather odd opening line for a chapter on the challenges of modern governance, the central argument of this chapter is that critical 'questions of accountability' very often have their basis in statutory or constitutional ambiguities that grant power to executive bodies of the government. The previous chapter concluded with an emphasis on 'the politics of accountability' and the way ambiguities can be exploited and even strategically created and manipulated by those obliged to render an account in order to deflect responsibility and blame. The paradox this chapter focuses on is how the laws, rules and conventions that are supposedly designed to confer clarity and control over those who wield public powers are themselves often the root source of confusion and criticism. The central 'question of accountability' tackled here can therefore be set out as follows: how are the requirements for government accountability thwarted by the laws and practices of the executive branch? This chapter expands the usual focus on the unavoidable unclarity of law and legal rules, and argues that fuzziness is presented as a feature that supports the ability of governments to act under law but without much of its constraining features. No less than 13 modes of law that are fuzzy, indeterminate or difficult to grasp are identified in order to expose the link between fuzzy law and fuzzy accountability.

To talk of accountability in terms of fuzziness is not in itself new. Wilkins (2002), for example, identified 'fuzzy accountability' as part of his analysis of Australian government and attempts to foster greater inter-organisational collaboration. Foreman (2004) explores fuzzy accountability in relation to performance management'. Pollack (2009) explored the same issue in relation to social work and care services, while Verbruggen and Havinga (2015) explored fuzzy accountability and regulatory relationships in relation to food safety controls. Bache (2015) and his colleagues emphasised the fuzzy nature of accountability in their analysis of complex and opaque governing structures vis-à-vis climate change mitigation strategies. Bostrom and Garsten (2008, 1) targeted the term itself; exploring transnational governing structures, they concluded that '[A]ccountability is a sought-after ideal, yet fuzzy concept.' What is interesting about the existing literature on 'fuzzy accountability', however, is that the specific meaning or deeper roots of the fuzziness are rarely discussed. 'Fuzzy accountability' is used almost as a short-hand descriptor for the consequences of network governance. It is also a term that is found primarily within the fields of public policy and public administration but what this chapter seeks to contribute is a mirror-image explanatory concept in the form of 'fuzzy law'. Not only does this term take the debate into the fields of public and constitutional law but it adds depth by revealing exactly how and why those legal structures that are intended to provide clarity often fail. By doing this it raises a new set of 'questions of accountability' and the three that are explicitly tackled in this chapter can be set out very simply as follows:

1. What is fuzzy law?
2. Why does it matter?
3. Can anything be done to counter fuzziness and ensure proper accountability?

This chapter is divided into five sections. The first section explores the concept of fuzzy law and locates it within the existing scholarship on fuzzy accountability in order to tease-out its relevance and significance. The next three sections develop this line of argument and theoretisation by focusing on different types of fuzzy law, generated by the constitution, legislation and executive action. These sections offer insights that show how control mechanisms often fail to deliver the expected levels or forms of accountability, and offer examples from the United Kingdom and the United States. The final section looks to the future and asks what might be done, if anything, to tighten-up legal structures in a way that brings accountability more sharply into focus.

I. Enter 'Fuzzy Law'

In many ways the focus of this chapter is on the role that rules play in structuring and delivering accountability. Often framed in terms of the 'rule of law' these rules exist to provide clarity in relation to who does *what, why, how* and the avenues for *redress*. It could, of course, be argued that the 'rule of law' was itself a fairly fuzzy concept with notoriously varied meanings of the concept ranging from a principle that focuses on minimal formal requirements to its equation of law as a morally-laden agent (hence the common distinction between 'thin' and 'thick', or 'formal' and 'substantive' versions of the term (see, eg, Dicey 10th edn 1977, 183–205, Hayek 1944, Fuller 1964, Tamanaha 2004). And yet even under the most restrictive definitions of the terms there is a consensus that the rules that govern and control those to whom public powers are delegated should be clear and accessible. In many ways this focus on the rule of law and the rights of the individual vis-à-vis the state adds an extra dimension to the definition of accountability provided in chapter one of this volume. That definition is very forum focused in the sense that power-holders are primarily expected to account to an institution or arena (a court, auditor or legislative committee) that exists, as it were, to accept and assess and account on behalf of the public.

This 'fuzzy law' perspective emphasises the arguably *unavoidable* fuzziness of law and legal rules and offers an account on how this opacity potentially allows governments to act *under law but without its constraint*. It enables us to understand how the constraining features of public law frameworks, be they hard or soft or constitutional or legislative, are generally far less restrictive and more pliable than originally intended. Thus, enter 'fuzzy law'.

In *A Theory of the Executive Branch* (2021) I suggest that governments in established liberal democracies have been given an almost impossible task due to the manner in which they are expected to 'imperially' direct the life of the nation in the face of rising public expectations and wave-after-wave of crisis (economic, technological, social, viral, etc) while at the same time being subservient to and acting in accordance with the legal restrictions and processes set down by a sovereign legislature. I therefore offer a distinctive model of executive governance based on a general argument from constitutional theory that prioritises dispersal of power under irresolvable tensions emerging from concepts of hierarchy. The key element of this approach that this chapter seeks to highlight and develop is the way in which the law can offer public bodies the option to both *act under law but without its restrictions*.

This 'within the law but without restriction' resonates with the central 'overload but under-performance' puzzle that was set out in chapter one. This focused attention on the fact that at a time when there are more accountability processes – watchdogs, auditors, sleaze-busters, constitutional watchdogs, citizen groups, active media, judicial protections, freedom of information legislation, etc – than at any other point in history, public faith and confidence in politics, politicians and political processes has never been lower. The specific insight that law can be – at one and the same time – both *empowering without effectively constraining public actions* draws on David Dyzenhaus' (2006) notion of 'grey holes'. These 'holes' exist when a façade of legality masks the absence of any substantive limitation of power. Extending Dyzenhaus' original focus beyond action in emergencies and the breaching of individual rights it is possible to make the concept travel into the area of executive action in ways that reveal while also explain the existence of 'fuzzy law'. This might range from what is often referred to as 'everyday' or 'mundane' policy right through to constitutional provisions.

A central element of this emphasis on 'fuzzy law' is the understanding that what might even be termed the notion of 'fuzzy legality' reaches well beyond the indeterminacy of text. Indeed, few rules can be applied in an automated fashion; and even the most prima facie 'simple' rules often become far more complex and contestable once their underpinning details are examined. Take, for example, the minimum age for receiving a licence to drive a car. In the UK the age is set at 17, in France 18, in Mexico it is just 15 and in the US and Canada the age varies from state to state and province to province. At one level it might appear that the legal age to drive is not an area to be characterised in terms of 'fuzzy law'. But other provisions that underpin and support this rule may well be more subjective or debatable. In all the countries mentioned, anybody wanting to drive must successfully complete a competence test in order to drive unaccompanied. Details of the nature of these tests are generally set in a highly detailed set of regulations. In the UK, for example, the regulations set out the requirements for two tests, one theory, one practical. Under the relevant section of these regulations:

> 40C. – (1) A person shall be treated as having passed the theory test … if he satisfies the person conducting the test—
>
> (a) in respect of the standard test of driving theory, of his knowledge and understanding of the specified matters; and
>
> (b) in respect of the standard test of hazard perception, that his performance in the test demonstrates an ability to perceive hazards on the road.

No numeric 'pass' grade is found in these regulations; however, under information provided on the dedicated government website, specific numeric thresholds are outlined (at least 43 points out of the 50 on the theory test, 44 out of 75 in the hazard perception test). The key issue here is that there is no clear explanatory source material for why the threshold has been set at each specific level. Moreover, passing the practical driving test is a matter where the designated examiner enjoys a very broad discretion. This indeterminacy is to some extent understandable, but the bigger point being demonstrated here is that discretion forms a core element of most grants of power in the administrative state. Over a century ago, Kocourek (1914, 225; see also Davis 1969; Galligan 1997) underlined that discretion was 'a standing and permanent characteristic of the law, and one of the great levers of legal evolution' and to some extent the growth in the size and complexity of the modern state has expanded the discretionary space. As such, the need to interpret most texts is part and parcel of the nature of law and the realities of public governance. The central argument being – and one that resonates with Rock's arguments concerning 'questions of measurement' (chapter three) – that 'fuzziness' is more than mere interpretability: it emerges in the absence of benchmarks, or in the absence of a clear formal rule. As Box 5.1 illustrates, 'fuzzy law' can emerge in a variety of forms and types.

Box 5.1 Types of Fuzzy Law

I. *Constitution-generated fuzzy legal forms*:
   a. Highly open-ended provisions in written constitutions;
   b. Conventions and other recognised sources of power under an unwritten constitution;
   c. Judicial-recognised doctrines that are constitutional by nature but do not rely on the text of a constitution.

II. *Legislature-generated fuzziness*:
   a. Highly open-ended provisions in legislation;
   b. Extensive grants of discretion;
   c. Extensive authority to delegate power;
   d. 'Patchwork legislation' – the existence of several legislative sources of power;
   e. Existence of a large, or indeterminate number of grantees of power;
   f. A 'lopsided' statute – enabling but not constraining, or otherwise covering only part of the regulated field.

III. *Executive-generated fuzziness*:
   a. Selective enforcement of a legal regime;
   b. Introduction, and reliance, on extra-legal parallel regimes;
   c. Dead-letter law and 'floating' statute, which is yet to enter into force;
   d. Secondary rules that rely on multiple, mixed sources (constitutional and statutory).

It is neither necessary nor possible to provide a detailed analysis of every one of these types within the contours of this chapter (but see Cohn 2021). Nevertheless, the main aim of the next two sections is to provide a brief account of this legal landscape, before connecting the focus back into fuzzy accountability in the fourth and final section.

II. Constitution-Generated Fuzziness

Constitutions are essentially open-ended. A base document that may be drafted in the background of disputes over key elements, it is also designed as a long-living entrenched text immune from continuous amendments. Hence, the constitutional text will necessarily be broadly-termed which, in turn, creates the space for interpretative contestation. The very few countries with (in)famously unwritten constitutions, like the UK, promote an emphasis on flexibility, agility and adaptive capacity as the rationale for not being bound by the structures of a formal constitutional document, especially when amendment processes are designed to be difficult. The critical point, however, is that even where written constitutions exist, such as in the US, it would be a mistake to think that fuzziness is somehow prevented. With this in mind it is useful to very briefly examine these cases in a little more detail.

A. The United Kingdom

Instead of being subject to a constitution, the British legal system operates under an amalgam of statutes that contain provisions of a constitutional nature. A list of such statutory benchmarks might begin with the Magna Carta of 1215 and end with the European Withdrawal Act 2018, with the Petition of Right 1628, the Bill of Rights 1689, Act of Settlement 1701, Act of Union 1707, Parliament Acts 1911–1947, the European Communities Act 1972, the Scotland Act 1998, the Human Rights Act 1998, the House of Lords Act 1999, the Constitutional Reform Act 2005, the Constitutional Reform and Governance Act 2010, the European Union (Withdrawal) Act 2018, and the European Union (Withdrawal Agreement) Act 2020, forming critical statutory stepping-stones in between. These statutes are complemented by a body of case law and a collection of unwritten understandings and rules of practice known as 'constitutional conventions' (see, eg, Loveland 2021). In the latter context, the work of Geoffrey Marshall (1984) and Brian Galligan (2015) provide important analyses. Marshall's *Constitutional Conventions: The Rules and Forms of Political Accountability* provides a historical and detailed review of the constraining power of conventions, whereas three decades later Galligan's *Constitutional Conventions in Westminster Systems: Controversies, Changes and Challenges* writes from a far more tentative position as to the binding capacity of rules which essentially rely on the self-restraint of those in power (for an overview see, eg, Loveland 2021). All of these aspects of the structural constitution enjoy a historical pedigree; even those seemingly governed by a statute of Parliament are coloured by past practice.

When a constitutional framework, or field, is unwritten, fuzziness is unavoidable: definite understandings of an unwritten arrangement, even when firmly supported by history and practice, are always susceptible to rereading and manipulation.

Focusing more specifically on the executive, the best-recognised form of unwritten source of power is the Royal prerogative, which pertains to Crown powers that were not taken away by Parliament. By their nature, prerogative powers are fuzzy. No one, at least since the early nineteenth-century (see Chitty 1820), has dared present a complete list of prerogatives, although recent government and parliamentary reports have offered versions. The House of Commons Public Administration Select Committee's March 2004 report – *Taming the Prerogative: Strengthening Ministerial Accountability to Parliament* (HC 224) – offers a detailed review and critique (see also Ministry of Justice, 2009; House of Commons Library, Briefing Paper 03861, 2017). Scholars provide lists that are carefully supplemented by a caveat such as 'it is not possible to give a comprehensive catalogue of prerogative powers', followed by a discussion of the classically acknowledged ones (see, for example, Bradley, Ewing and Knight, 18th edn, 2022, 286–98). The legitimacy of the prerogative remains a constitutional convention and an element of constitutional practice that generates extensive controversy due to the discretion held by the executive and the limited control capacity of the legislature. Fuzziness often exists in relation to whether and how an executive *may* have agreed to 'tying their own hands' by agreeing to greater legislative oversight.

Some prerogatives concern inter-branch matters, such as the power to summon Parliament and the power to grant assent to Bills passed by Parliament. More important for our discussion are prerogatives that pertain to administrative powers. Historically, all prerogative powers were directly linked with the Crown. This link has not been formally severed, but centuries of practice have established, under constitutional conventions, that all prerogatives of an administrative nature are in fact exercised by the Prime Minister and his government. Some of these, such as coinage, the setting of territorial waters, and the maintenance and management of the civil service have been legislated, the latter only in 2010. The passport regime, powers linked with foreign affairs and national security, the appointment of high-level officers, the power of mercy, and legislation in colonies and overseas territories are the best-known remaining prerogatives. In these fields, then, the government retains freedom to act, constrained mainly by the possibility of judicial review and the looming threat of future legislation, all under a recognised, albeit unwritten, element of the constitution.

The fuzziness of the prerogative has enabled governments and courts to squeeze new powers into the existing framework by being rediscovered as 'old' prerogatives. Some of this stretching is rather innocuous – for example, the inclusion of modern warfare and technology within the ancient prerogative of war would attract no criticism (compare *Re Petition of Right* with *A-G v De Keyser Royal Hotel)*. But some judicial reasoning has gone much further, to the extent of arguably reinventing the past, as in the case of the (re)discovery of the 'historical' power to keep the peace of the realm as a well-grounded prerogative, one that enabled the court to approve an extension of police powers beyond statute.[1] Other non-statutory powers currently invoked in the UK and recognised as 'prerogatives', such as ex-gratia payment schemes and government dissemination of information (adjudged in *Criminal Injuries Compensation Board ex parte Lain* and *Jenkins v AG)*, were likewise newly recognised prerogatives, but are in fact different, 'third source' powers, to be now discussed.

[1] *R v Secretary of State for the Home Department, ex parte Northumbria Police Authority*; *R v Secretary of State for the Home Department, ex parte Northumbria Police Authority* (power of central government to supply anti-riot equipment to local police stations in the argued absence of such authority in the Police Act. The Court of Appeal found sufficient basis in the statute, but addressing the question of the continued existence of a prerogative to maintain 'the peace within the realm', the court adopted the lower court's reasoning that the Act did not create a 'monopoly' that excluded central government action in this field).

Initially, the pairing of 'non-statutory' powers with 'prerogative' powers may have been intuitive, since the prerogative does not derive from statute. The prerogative, nevertheless, is really something else, as it is deeply embedded in the historical unwritten basis of the English Constitution. As noted above, some such powers have relatively recently been identified as age-old prerogatives, most notably the prerogative to maintain the peace of the realm, which supported twentieth-century judicial recognition of police powers that initially found no basis in statute.[2] Yet, as most commentators have recognised, many non-statutory powers currently invoked in the UK cannot, or should not, be linked to this historical source of power. Such identified non-prerogative powers included the creation and operation of ex-gratia payment schemes, the issue of governmental pamphlets, government policy-making by contract, and, potentially, guidance published by ministries. These powers are sometimes titled 'the third source' of power (see Harris 2007; but see Cohn 2009), in addition to other parallel titles, but their provenance is still undecided. Aiding the legitimacy of such 'third source' powers, the concept of 'personification' equates governments' power with individuals' freedom to act. In *Malone v Metropolitan Police Commissioner*, arguments that police telephone-tapping was unlawful due to the absence of statutory authorisation were curtly rejected in court by equalising the individual's freedom to act unless prohibited by law with the government's power. In the words of Sir Robert Megarry VC, responding to the contention of illegality:

> [T]he underlying assumption of this contention, of course, is that nothing is lawful that is not positively authorised by law. As I have indicated, England is not a country where everything is forbidden except what is expressly permitted. One possible illustration is smoking. I inquired what positive authority was given by the law to permit people to smoke … (366).

The fact that governments as such cannot smoke was apparently immaterial to the decision. Recognising that the practice 'cried out for legislation', the court ruled that in the absence of a recognised right to privacy at the time, telephone-tapping could be carried out without the breach of the law both by individuals and public bodies, and was thus safely within the scope of government action. Although this practice was subsequently found unlawful in the European Court of Human Rights, and was later regulated by statute, the route to recognition of such

[2] *R v Secretary of State for the Home Department ex parte Northumbria Police Authority*, most notably Nourse LJ's opinion, tracing this prerogative 'probably' to the Norman Conquest: ibid 58. For criticism see HJ Beynon, 'Prerogative to Supply Plastic Baton Rounds and CS to the Police' [1987] *Public Law* 146; AW Bradley, 'Police Powers and the Prerogative' [1988] *Public Law* 298. Likewise, and earlier, the Criminal Injuries Compensation Scheme, non-statutory for more than two decades. Challenged in 1967, was reaffirmed by the court as an exercise of the prerogative in *R v Criminal Injuries Compensation Board, ex parte Lain* [1967] 2 QB 864.

a source of power had opened, and is still available. The fuzzy and creative nature of such routes was demonstrated some years ago when the government unearthed a 1945 legal memorandum that, it is still argued, has provided a basis of power equivalent to these inhered in an individual or a body corporate (see HL 47/HC 38, 2008). The memorandum, recognised as 'the Ram doctrine', was penned by First Parliamentary Counsel Sir Granville Ram, was disclosed in a Cabinet Office report only in 2002, and was further debated in the House of Lords a year later (see Lester and Weait 2003). According to this memorandum, beyond express statute-based powers and implied powers incidental to the exercise of such statutory powers and implied powers, 'a department can do anything that a natural person can, provided it is not forbidden from doing so'. Emphasis on corporatisation of the Crown remains central in the government's reading of this memorandum (see HL Hansard, WA 25 Feb 2003, Vol 645, col 13). But are written constitutional configurations any less fuzzy?

B. The United States

Unlike articles I and III, relating to the legislature and the judiciary, which include close-list vesting clauses (clauses that precede a closed list of powers), article II of the US Constitution is an open-ended statement providing a seemingly inconclusive list of executive powers. This includes the command of the armed forces, the grant of pardons, the making of treaties under Senate advice and consent, and the ambiguous 'take care that the laws are faithfully executed' clause. All are open for interpretation, notably the 'take-care' and commander-in-chief clauses, which have offered promising bases for expansionist executives (see Barron and Lederman 2008; Goldsmith and Manning 2016; Cohn 2021). However, under the general clause '[t]he executive power shall be vested in a President of the United States of America', other powers have been recognised by proponents of executive aggrandisement.

Beyond reliance on the text of the Constitution, the President, Congress and the courts have generally recognised the exercise of presidential unilateral power under four distinct doctrines: (i) political reality; (ii) history as providing a 'gloss' on the constitution or otherwise embedding the recognition of governmental action on past use; (iii) the state's sovereignty; and (iv) conceptions of 'aggregation', under which the general tenor, and collection, of various sources suffice for the recognition of specific executive powers.

First, justifications drawing on political reality carry a long pedigree. US Presidents have justified some of their contested action, especially during emergencies, by referring to urgency and the need to answer crises. The best-known example of such practices are President Lincoln's measures taken during the Civil War, some of which were contrary to the Constitution. In his message to Congress on 4 July 1861, Lincoln justified his unilateral suspension of the habeas corpus by referring to the exigencies of the rebellion and the need to preserve the nation and the Constitution (see Basler 1953).[3]

Under the next constitutional doctrine, history, past practice and precedent have operated as generators of fuzziness and have enabled the extension of executive powers beyond textual authorisation. History has supported US presidential power, albeit in the absence of Congressional objection, and has served in not a few cases to offer not only a tool for expanded interpretation of the constitutional text, but also an alternative theory that considers inter-branch interaction over time as a generator of legitimacy. In *US v Midwest Oil* the legality of executive orders issued for the temporary withdrawal of mineral-rich public lands from private access was found to be embedded in a practice that 'dates from an early period', 'known to Congress, and as principal, and not in a single instance … disapproved' (459, 469, 475). 'Gloss' and undisturbed executive practice feature in Justices Jackson's opinion in *Youngstown Sheet & Tube v Sawyer* (579, 637) and in Justice Frankfurter's oft-cited dictum concerning the impact of 'a systematic, unbroken, executive practice, long pursued to the knowledge of the Congress and never before questioned, engaged in by Presidents who have also sworn to uphold the Constitution' as a 'gloss on "executive power" vested in the President by S.1 of Art. II' (*Youngstown* 610–11; see also *Dames and Moore v Regan*, 654, 686; Morrison and Bradley 2012).

Under the third doctrine, state sovereignty as a predecessor of the formal Constitution has served as a basis for the recognition of unilateral powers invoked in the context of foreign relations. The source and mainstay has been Justice Sutherland's opinion in *Curtiss-Wright* (1936), in which Justice Sutherland offered a three-pronged argument that supported the President's power to act unilaterally in the field of foreign affairs. Under the third count, sole presidential power derived from the nature of the US 'as a member of the family of nations', which had received sovereignty on independence; since 'the Union existed before the Constitution', and the states were not granted power in this field, these powers 'did not depend upon the affirmative grants of the Constitution' (*US v Curtiss-Wright*, 317–18, a challenge to the constitutionality of a ban on sale of arms to warring entities. See, in the same vein, *US v Belmont*; *US v Pink*, 223–24).

Finally, under the fourth doctrine, power may be recognised in the existence of 'aggregated' powers – a collection of sources which, combined, may uphold

[3] See also Lincoln's 1864 letter to Albert G Hodges, editor of the *Commonwealth*, regarding his emancipation proclamation (claiming that the president's oath 'to preserve the constitution to the best of [his] ability, imposed upon [him] the duty of preserving, by every indispensable means, that government – that nation – of which the constitution was the organic law'. Basler, Vol 7, 281–82; and President Roosevelt's 'stewardship theory' which relied on political responsibility rather than authorisation by the Constitution or Congress to support his claim that 'every executive officer, and above all every executive officer in high position, was a steward of the people, and not to content himself with the negative merit of keeping his talents undamaged in a napkin'. T Roosevelt, *An Autobiography* (Macmillan, 1916) 372.

powers that are not easily traceable to any single source of power. The main judicial endorsement of the idea is found in Chief Justice Vinson's dissenting opinion in *Youngstown*. Upholding President Truman's order to seize steel mills on strike during the Korean War, Chief Justice Vinson recognised the longstanding practice of presidential action during emergencies, discussed separately above, but he also cited a statement written by the Attorney General at that time, Robert Jackson, who was one of the Justices on the *Youngstown* bench, in which Jackson opined inter alia that '[t]he Presidential proclamation rests upon the aggregate of the Presidential powers derived from the Constitution itself and from statutes enacted by Congress' (695–96).

Although this alternative source of action has not attracted much attention since, it has been well-internalised by all presidents. One clear example is found in virtually all recitals of executive orders issued by presidents since the mid-twentieth century. Executive Order 10340, which authorised the seizure of the steel mills in *Youngstown*, contained the following recital:

> … by virtue of the authority vested in me by the Constitution and laws of the United States, and as President of the United States and Commander in Chief of the armed forces of the United States, it is hereby ordered as follows ….[4]

Similar citation sources are found in all such orders made in the past decades; in fact, the majority of orders made in the past two decades simply cite 'the constitution and laws of the United Sates' – the fuzziest formula available.

C. Analysis

The UK and US provide insights into the link between fuzzy law and fuzzy accountability that this chapter seeks to emphasise. The fuzziness of these *constitutional* sources makes it difficult to challenge their use by the executive. How can members of the public and other players in the political sphere know the extent and limits of the exercise of such powers in the absence of a clear framework? What is the *true* basis of unilateral executive action, and, what are its limits? Is personification a proper basis for the action of government in the absence of statute? How could an individual assess whether a long-standing practice that has no explicit basis in a written legal text will be recognised, before a court rules on the matter? Does such 'gloss', when recognised provide sufficient basis for individual reliance on the practice? None of these, and other questions, are easily answered: the resulting fuzziness effectively eliminates the conduct of a proper accountability process. This flows into a focus on a second type of fuzzy law and to a consideration of legislation-generated accountability ambiguity.

[4] Executive Order 10340, Directing the Secretary of Commerce to Take Possession of and Operate the Plants and Facilities of Certain Steel Companies, 8 April 1943, 17 FR 3139.

III. Legislative-Generated Fuzziness

While constitutions are generally written in fairly broad terms, statutes are designed to deliver a higher degree of clarity in relation to both those granted public powers and those subject to these powers. The degree of precision is, however, often far less clear when that legislation grates against the inevitably messy realities of political game-playing and public life. Box 5.1 (above) outlines six types of fuzziness that emerge from legislation and, as such, contains some well-known forms of fuzziness. Much has been written on statutory interpretation, delegation and discretion and the intention in this section is not to repeat that relatively well-known literature. Instead, I focus on a different, less discussed fuzziness found in legislation: 'Patchwork legislation'.

A. Patchwork Legislation

Beyond interpretation and statutory grants of discretion and delegation, an unclear legal regime can be the result of the existence of a multitude of statutes that treat a single field of governance. Patchworking emerges not due to the *absence* of statute but rather due to the *proliferation* of legislation in a specific area. (In this regard there exist clear links back to the notions of *deficits* and *overloads* discussed in the previous chapter and the Introduction.) Attention to this legislative practice has generally focused on emergency law, but it is actually far more commonplace than is generally acknowledged. There are two ways that generate this type of fuzziness: *piling-up* and *dispersion*.

(i) Piling-Up

This form of patchwork legislation exists when several arrangements, each of which could singly address the regulated field of action, lead to the existence of a collection of statutes and rules, some overlapping, some at least potentially offering alternative paths for action which may contradict each other. The main issue here is not only the inherent danger of over-expansion of power; fuzziness exists even when a new arrangement is *not* stricter than its precursors, since the executive retains the ability to choose from the existing menu of power sources, or to opt for a novel arrangement.

As an example, consider the piling-up of UK anti-terrorism laws. British legal sources relevant to national security and emergency range from international law, through constitutional law, a few international conventions incorporated into domestic law, primary legislation, and some EU law, which, post-Brexit, is either introduced directly into domestic law or is bound to expire. Setting aside any discussion of international law and international treaties due to reasons of space, in the domestic sphere the British system has amassed a particularly large number of anti-terrorism statutes. Described as a 'messy' collection of 'knee-jerk' reactions to contingencies (see Anderson, 2012, 133; see also Neal, 2012). The scale and extent of the legislative terrain reflects a gradual process of legislative accretion. The Civil Contingencies Act 2004, the Anti-Terrorism, Crime and Security Act 2001, the Terrorism Act 2006, the Counter-Terrorism Act 2008, the Terrorist Asset-Freezing Act 2010, the Terrorism Prevention and Investigation Measures Act 2011, and the Counter-Terrorism and Security Act 2015, are the main arrangements, but others exist. Some of these statutes target specific terrorism activity but, all-in-all, the pattern of piling-up of several alternative arrangements is clear.

This state of affairs is not unique to the United Kingdom. The pressure on politicians to be seen as responding to a situation very often means that each and every emergency generates some form of new legislation, during or after the actual emergency or incident. Furthermore there are very few procedures and very few political incentives to invest precious time and energy into reviewing the legislative landscape or repealing outdated measures (see, for example, Questiaux, 1982).

(ii) Dispersion

Under the second form of patchworking – so common that it is rarely considered a fuzzy legislative practice – redundancy is replaced by dispersion. Usually, scholars interested in regulation depict the legal treatment of the regulation of any single sector as organised under a single 'legislative mandate'. However, even when a commitment to such an overarching and conclusive framework is expressed, the law on the ground will be messy. The so-called central legislative mandate, when it exists, is never the sole source of executive authority. The focus here is not on secondary legislation and other executive rules made under the legislative mandate, as they draw their force from the parent statute and can be easily traced. Other legal rules that have no direct link to the so-called legislative mandate are usually in existence. Beyond statutes that pertain to the regulated field, unilateral measures, and, in a federal system, state law, often complement (and possibly, contradict) the legal measures considered as the core governing rule. Riders (ie, added legislative provisions) in the annual appropriations acts that set substantive limits on the use of appropriated funds or introduce programmes not authorised elsewhere, are possibly the least discoverable and most fuzzy form of legislation-generated fuzziness.

For example, to understand the law of air pollution in the United States, one needs to trawl through the statute book, in addition to searches of rules originating from transnational sources. Even under the US Code, which organises federal law by areas, the rules are dispersed. Some statutes are coded in Title 42 of the US Code – concerned with public health, social welfare and civil rights – or in its chapters dedicated to the environment; others, that directly or indirectly affect the field, are located in other Titles of the US Code. Some statutory provisions have escaped inclusion in the Code, as have some executive orders and other unilateral measures that impact, directly or indirectly, on the regulatory framework. The Clean Air Act is indeed the central legislative arrangement concerned with air pollution but attention only to this mammoth statute would not enable those who wish to understand the law to reach their goal.

B. Analysis

Focusing on patchwork legislation, both forms of patchworking – piling-up and dispersion – create fuzziness. When several routes of executive action are available, executives are granted a choice of sources, while other players in the public sphere may find it very difficult to plan ahead. In the absence of rules that limit patchworking, such fuzziness may grow in time. Similarly, fuzziness-by-dispersion renders any arrangement difficult to grasp and necessitates trawling through the entire legal system. This could be interpreted as the legal equivalent of creating structured ambiguity in order to evade accountability, the creation of complex delivery networks by governments in this strategy serving to distance and dilute their responsibility for performance. These common features of the legal system almost always ensure that the deciphering of a legal arrangement requires a high level of legal expertise; even when relied upon, the potential of supplementing the arrangement with additional legislation, when not twinned with a commitment to pare down existing relevant law, remains. Easy reliance on the law, which is required for planning ahead, is thus seriously impaired.

Like other types of fuzziness, both forms are arguably unavoidable. The first for convenience and political reasons, the second simply due to the complexity of realities which law attempts to organise. Both lessen the hold of substantive legality and enhance the executive's freedom to act within formal legality in the absence of easy access to the rules, thereby underpinning the core 'under law but evading constraint' argument of this chapter.

IV. Executive-Generated Fuzziness

Out of the four types of fuzziness that emerge from executive behaviour vis-à-vis rule-making and rule-application selective enforcement has received a significant amount of scholarly attention. From housing (see Fagan, Davies and Carlis 2012) to counter-terrorism measures (see Huq 2011), the asymmetrical application of public law, often by local officials or 'street-level bureaucrats' is the topic of a significant body of research and writing. A different, rarely discussed executive-generated fuzziness, included under type III. c. in Box 5.1, concerns the usage of commencement clauses. British statutes often contain commencement provisions under which the statute, or parts of it, enter into force on a future date. Sometimes the future date is set; for example, the commencement section may designate its entry into force at an exact date or on the expiration of a designated period. In other cases, commencement is effected by ministerial order (usually in the form of a statutory instrument). In these latter situations, the question of *if* and *when* to trigger specific legislative powers, and all the concomitant issues concerning power and enforcement, remain entirely at the discretion of the executive.

One may argue that postponement of entry into force for a short period, even a year or two, may be excusable, as sometimes elaborate arrangements are needed before commencement. More so when provisions are contingent on external forthcoming conditions, as in the case of the carbon emissions tax. However, some statutes or portions thereof have remained floating for much longer periods, or, considering the time lag, may be declared as provisions that have never entered into force and are unlikely to change their status. Such commencement orders may be a complex set of directions. For example, the commencement provision of the Counter-Terrorism and Border Security Act 2019, a substantial collection of amendments to no less than 25 statutes applicable to England which also introduced a new arrangement of border control, presents all possible permutations:

27 Commencement

(1) The following provisions come into force on the day on which this Act is passed—

- (a) section 21;
- (b) section 23(2) to (7);
- (c) section 26;
- (d) this section;
- (e) section 28;
- (f) paragraph 19 of Schedule 4 and section 23(1) so far as relating to that paragraph;
- (g) any other provision of this Act so far as necessary for enabling the exercise on or after the day on which this Act is passed of any power under Schedule 3 to make regulations or to issue codes of practice.

(2) The following provisions come into force on such day or days as the Secretary of State may by regulations appoint—

- (a) sections 16, 17 and 18;
- (b) section 19 and Schedule 2;
- (c) section 22 and Schedule 3 (so far as not brought into force by subsection (1)(g) of this section);
- (d) paragraphs 17 and 18, 20 to 26 and 28 to 33 of Schedule 4 and section 23(1) so far as relating to those paragraphs.

(3) The other provisions of this Act come into force at the end of the period of two months beginning with the day on which this Act is passed.

(4) The Secretary of State may by regulations make transitional or saving provision in connection with the coming into force of any provision of this Act.
(5) Regulations under this section are to be made by statutory instrument.

Here, then, a host of meticulously selected provisions enter into force only after a minister so declares in a statutory instrument. The entry into force, thus dependent on executive discretion or goodwill, may not be forthcoming – some of the examples below show a worrying pattern. In such a case, the chimera that is a statute can mislead those who rely on the law in the books: the statute merely 'floats' above the legal system, at best offering some guidance as regards the original intent of the legislature at the time of legislation.

Even when as of 30 May 2023, more than five years after its enactment in February 2019, two relatively minor provisions of the Counter-Terrorism and Border Security Act 2019 are yet to enter into force (both are amendments to orders applicable in Northern Ireland). Yet some of the provisions which did finally enter into force, have only been partially so. The commencement order of the 2019 Act, issued on 22 July 2020, more than a year since its enactment in February 2019, contains the following commencement provision:

2. Commencement

The following provisions of the Counter-Terrorism and Border Security Act 2019 come into force on the 22nd day after the day on which these Regulations are made—

(a) section 16 (evidence obtained under port and border control powers);
(b) section 17 (persons detained under port and border control powers);
(c) section 18 (detention of terrorist suspects: hospital treatment);
(d) section 19 (retention of biometric data for counter-terrorism purposes etc) so far as relating to the provisions brought into force by paragraph (e);
(e) paragraphs 1 to 4 and 6 to 17 of Schedule 2 (retention of biometric data for counterterrorism purposes etc);
(f) section 22 (port and border controls) so far as relating to the provisions brought into force by paragraph (g);
(g) Schedule 3 (port and border controls) to the extent it is not already in force, except for paragraphs 44 and 45 in relation to Northern Ireland;
(h) section 23(1) (minor and consequential amendments) so far as relating to the provisions brought into force by paragraph (i);
(i) the following paragraphs of Schedule 4 (minor and consequential amendments)—
    (i) 17 and 18;
    (ii) 20(2) to (8) and paragraph 20(1) so far as it relates to those sub-paragraphs;
    (iii) 21 to 26;
    (iv) 28 to 33.

Some of the provisions, then, have entered into force only for 'specified purposes'. In other contexts they continue to 'float' in the stratosphere that contains statutes yet to enter into force.

Both features are not unique to this Act. Twelve of the 31 Public General Acts passed in 2019 contain a commencement provision that authorises a Secretary of State to enter specified provision into force by an order. One of these four is worth mentioning further: as of June 2023, almost all the provisions in the Mental Capacity (Amendment) Act 2019, which introduces substantial changes to the regime of depriving persons of their liberty for mental health reasons, is yet to be entered into force by the Secretary of State. Without considering whether the amending provisions further protect, or further constrain, the liberty of mental health patients, knowledge of the fact that most of the act is not in force requires professional expertise.

Since so many statutes enacted in the UK enable late entry into force of their provisions, and, in some cases, only partially, databases offer updates to those considering legislation. The website managed by the National Archives, legislation.gov.uk, contains references to both patterns of fuzziness. Provisions yet to enter into force are coloured in the PDF texts of statutes, and information on the commencement of each provision is stated. If entered into force by an order, reference to the order is provided, and when a provision is only partially enabled, it is stated that the particular provision has entered into force 'for specified purposes'. Practitioners and scholars can thus trace the status of an act's provisions at any given time. This is a helpful feature; however, knowledge of these patterns, and the need to conduct a research every time a statute is considered, obviously hinders one of the main requirements of an accessible statute: its clarity.

In sum, the entry into force of previously approved legislation is heavily dependent on executive discretion and goodwill. Where legislation has been passed without coming into force it exists in a liminal space between the political and legal spheres, 'floating' in a manner that provides some sense as to the original intent of the legislature at the time of legislation but little more in terms of hard substance. As in other types of fuzziness, this type of 'fuzzy law' raises a multitude of 'questions of accountability'.

V. Accountability and Fuzziness: What Can be Done?

High levels of fuzziness are, to a large extent, unavoidable features of laws granting powers to public bodies. Beyond the needs of the administrative state, under which law should be flexible enough to answer exigencies, other factors contribute to fuzziness. The aim of this final section is to tentatively explore these factors, with a view to engaging with the question as to 'What can be done?'

Political preferences, which have little to do with a bona fide intent to ensure optimal governance, may be classified as exogenous to the lawmaking process, and include interests concerning the amassing of relative power, disagreement over the content of a rule which may lead to its ambiguity, the existence of political or transnational pressure to make a rule in the absence of a true commitment to its application, and the marginalisation of the need to set a detailed arrangement due to its relative unimportance or the relative importance of other pressing issues.

In other words, the existence of competitive electoral forces, partisan game-playing, and a contextual negativity-bias combine to ensure that for politicians and public officials, accountability is interpreted very much as generally only being of the 'Gotcha!' variety (ie, the Mode I version discussed in chapter 1; see also Kloby 2012. On the other side, forces that drive towards the dissipation of fuzziness, and its related dangers to the proper operation of the public sphere, are much less likely to succeed. The push towards greater clarity thus grinds against a counter-pressure to sustain and exploit fuzziness. This chapter's focus on fuzzy law has simply exposed and placed this clash of values and incentives squarely within the legal sphere. But if this tension exists and fuzzy laws frustrate and hinder accountable governance *what might be done?*

Rather than merely argue for recognition of the ingrained difficulties of finding a body accountable to the laws that regulates its powers, an alternative approach might consider adopting a more sophisticated design under which fuzzy accountability structures are established as a counterweight to fuzzy laws. Taking the discussion back to a focus on blending, balance and proportionality, the intention would be to adopt a multi-dimensional approach to closing down the gaps, such as those relating to commencement provisions or patchwork law should explicate more clearly the core objective of accountability and how success or failure might therefore be measured. The idea of, as it were, fighting 'fuzzy law' through the pro-active design and development of 'fuzzy accountability' is not as intellectually outrageous as it might first appear. In many ways, established and traditional accountability processes have for some decades been attempting to evolve and adapt to fit new circumstances. If there is a challenge here it is that in most political systems the implementation of more systemic and joined-up approaches to accountability would implicitly or explicitly require the support of the executive. The existence of a strong risk-aversion and defensive attitude towards accountability by that executive is unlikely to lead to the provision of such support.

Beyond this direction, further attention should be granted to the possible benefits of enhanced judicial review of fuzzy executive action. In itself, the judiciary offers an alternative and important forum for the strengthening of the clarity and accountability of executive action. Review by courts is only part of accountability, but indeed is not a minor part.

6

Collaborative Constitutional Accountability

SE-SHAUNA WHEATLE

So far the chapters in this collection have ranged far and wide in exploring a number of 'questions of accountability'. This has included discussions of disciplinary perspectives and methods (chapter two), the challenges of measuring accountability (chapter three), an analysis of the 'dark side' of accountability (chapter four), and the extent to which 'fuzzy law' facilitates 'fuzzy accountability' (chapter five). What has united each of these chapters has been, apart from an emphasis on 'cool theory' over 'hot rhetoric', an emphasis on proportionality and balance. As such, they have engaged with the navigational challenge outlined in chapter one by forging new routes through the existing scholarship in ways that pose fresh questions and, in some cases, new answers to perennial challenges. This chapter seeks to continue this process and to develop the focus on balance, blending and proportionality by exploring a novel way of looking beyond dominant existing debates. It does this through a focus on *collaborative constitutional accountability*.

Questions of accountability under the UK constitution typically involve debate over political and legal constitutionalism. The two ideas are presented as competing opposites, with political constitutionalists advocating political controls exercised by political institutions and legal constitutionalists privileging the role of law and the courts in regulating state power. While some of the core features of this debate are useful in helping us work out the landscape of the UK constitution, the course of the debate has become too polarised. This polarisation has, at times, obscured points of commonality between the two models of constitutionalism and distracted us from important questions about the actual nature of interactions between institutions, the values that the constitution does, and ought to, uphold and the real-life impact of constitutional norms and decisions on society.

Partly in answer to this polarisation, and its negative effects on constitutional discourse, some commentators now advocate a more collaborative vision of the constitution. Instead of viewing different elements of a constitutional configuration as somehow co-existing in a state of constant antagonism, this approach moves away from what tend to be highly polarised conceptualisations and instead focuses on the mutually supportive and sustaining nature of interlocking accountability institutions and relationships. In this sense, collaborative accountability is more systemic in approach and dovetails with analyses that focus on the 'accountability space' (Dubnick 2011) or more specifically the 'accountability ecosystem' (see Halloran 2016). This chapter synthesises and advances the collaborative approach and adds to the literature by providing evidence of constitutional collaboration in practice. The three main questions this chapter seeks to engage with can be set out as follows:

1. What are the contours of the conventional accountability debate in the UK?
2. What are the core constitutive features of *collaborative* constitutional accountability?
3. Where is the evidence that collaborative constitutional accountability is emerging in the practice of constitutional actors?

This chapter is divided into three main sections, each focusing on one of the questions outlined above. As such, the next section outlines conventional UK accountability discourse and explains the need for a change in approach.

I. Political *or* Legal Constitutionalism

Khaitan (2019 349) argues that 'In a liberal democratic constitution institutional accountability is the main guarantor of liberal and democratic guarantees.' That accountability is performed through a web of institutions, processes and relationships. Constitutional accountability therefore encompasses an intermixture of legal and political checks, both to ensure that state organs fulfil their constitutional responsibilities and that they act consistently with the fundamental principles of the constitution. As such, the entire web or network of institutional checks operating in modern constitutions form an integral part of liberal constitutionalism. However, accountability mechanisms for executive power are particularly essential in both enabling the fulfilment of constitutional objectives and restraining unconstitutional exercises of power. The executive has been justifiably described as 'the most dangerous branch' (Flaherty 1996) of government due to the manner in which the growth in the size and scope of the modern state has generally empowered the executive, often without counter-balancing increases in the power of other constitutional actors. This explains the arguments about 'constitutional balance' that have been made by Sir John Laws (see chapter one), and also why theories and doctrines – as well as research and writing – tend to focus on the accountability of the executive. This concern is particularly pronounced in relation to 'Westminster-style democracies'. As Gardbaum (2020, 1,438) explains:

> [I]in parliamentary systems … the absence of direct public election, and the less institutionally separated power, of the executive means that political accountability and

responsibility to the legislature play a larger role in legitimating its exercise of public power.

UK constitutional discourse on the accountability of the executive customarily involves adopting either political or legal mechanisms of accountability. Although the debate between these two accountability frameworks has been present either on the surface or as an undercurrent in UK constitutional law for decades, recently it has become more prominent. Specifically, the debate is now prevalent in conversations about the role of the courts, the foundations and principles of judicial review and the common law constitution. This, in turn, has raised critical 'questions of accountability', while also reflecting the existence of a more generalised 'accountability angst'.

Each model of constitutionalism (ie, *political* or *legal*) has both descriptive and normative dimensions. Political accountability prioritises the use of political norms such as constitutional conventions, with regulation by political actors and arenas. Notable political constitutionalists, whose worked helped shape the doctrine and guide its direction, include Griffith (1979), Bellamy (2007), Tomkins (2007), Gee and Webber (2010). Under the political constitutionalist model, democracy is the primary value and, in the UK, the principle of parliamentary sovereignty is, as Ewing (2018) notes, 'the core legal principle of the political constitution'. First, democracy supplies the normative underpinning for the political constitution; as Michael Gordon (2019, 231) explains, '[i]t is the legitimacy of majoritarian democratic politics, which provides the principled rationale for political constitutionalism.' Second, democracy provides the conditionality for the exercise of power: 'what receives democratic support, in principle, can be achieved; what does not receive democratic support, in principle, cannot be achieved' (Gordon 2019, 131). The argument for political methods of accountability is not merely based on normative preference but also, as Griffith (2001) has argued, on assessments of the relative effectiveness of political modes of accountability. Thus, political accountability is said to be more effective because it is ultimately secured by the removability of politicians (for a discussion see Goldoni and McCorkindale 2019; Griffith 2002). Legal accountability mechanisms are from this perspective viewed – as Griffiths underlined in his classic 1979 article 'The Political Constitution' – as anti-democratic and ultimately dangerous, as politically illusory and offering false comfort.

The political constitutionalist model, as observed in the UK, also requires respect for the supremacy of Parliament as the unassailable and most fundamental rule of the constitution (see Ewing 2013). Specifically, parliamentary sovereignty has been positioned as central to the accountability of the executive. As Ewing (2018) notes, 'The legal principle of the sovereignty of Parliament provides both the source of legal authority, and the source of legal restraint of the power of government in a political constitution.' Gordon (142) goes even further to note that parliamentary sovereignty does more than empower public authority; it also facilitates the accountability of public power 'by preventing the emergence of absolute legal limits, and thereby establishing room for politics'.

Legal accountability, on the other hand, urges the development and use of legal norms to regulate the executive, and in some accounts, the legislature. The focus and starting point for legal constitutionalists is the imperative of fundamental principles such as the rule of law and respect for human rights. Law becomes centralised under more ardent legal constitutional theories, with Allan (2013, 77) maintaining that 'accountability means, above all, compliance with the rule of law'. For legal constitutionalists – including Allan (2013), Craig (1998; 2000), and Laws (2014) the courts ought to play a significant role in defining the terms of the constitution and ensuring that state organs comply with constitutional principles and rules. Moreover, under the legal constitutionalist model, 'Courts go beyond merely supplementing the legislature's control over the executive.' As Young (2017, 58) notes, this model maintains that 'courts have their own, independently justified controls'. Legal constitutionalism does not deny the operation or role of politics; neither does political constitutionalism deny that there is a place for law in the constitution. Rather, the division is a question of priority.

There is an understanding in the UK that political accountability represents the dominant constitutional orthodoxy in the sense that the constitution *is* and *ought to be* predominantly political. Judicial accountability is therefore a secondary and subservient process to the primary role that forms of political accountability play. Against this background, legal accountability can be accommodated within the orthodox political framework but must be rigorously justified when used. This perspective and the accompanying desire to restrain legal constitutionalism motivated the responses of Griffith (2000) and Tomkins (2005) to waves of 'legalisation' of the UK constitution. Over the years, the debate between political and legal constitutionalists has become polarised and at times febrile. It has become a debate typified by 'hot rhetoric' rather than 'cool theory'. As Young (2017) has illustrated, the discourse is populated with battle-laden metaphors intertwined with reductionist accounts that reduce opposing viewpoints to little more than caricatures. This state of affairs has undoubtedly arisen in part as a consequence of constitutional reforms that have, as Flinders (2005; 2010) has shown, undoubtedly shifted the nature of the British constitution towards a form of 'modified majoritarianism' where the potential for judicial ventures into political or politicised areas had increased.

Yet the real issue regarding varying accountability mechanisms is one of *priority, not exclusivity.* Accordingly, binary discourse is generally unhelpful and too crude to capture the more subtle interplay of multiple and multi-layered relationships. However, as the current nature of the debate often presents political and legal actors as opponents (see, for example, Ekins 2019, Loughlin 2020, Craig 2020), it runs the risk of obscuring areas of – and the potential for – cooperative engagement and diverting attention away from the constitutional principles at stake. There is some recognition within each 'camp' that the dichotomised framing and debate may have diminishing returns. For instance, Goldoni and McCorkindale (2009, 74) identify what they see as a third wave of political constitutionalism which seeks not to defend political constitutionalism against legal constitutionalism, but to contemplate 'what it is that is political about the political constitution'. For Goldoni and McCorkindale (2009, 74–75), the implications of this wave could include 'the freeing up of a political constitutionalism fixated on the role of Parliament vis-à-vis the courts in order to examine a broader and a deeper set of constitutional questions'. In this vein, Gee and Webber (2010, 12) have cautioned that political and legal constitutionalism are not realistic objectives or observed in practice in any one jurisdiction, but that they provide 'an explanatory framework' for understanding and evaluating constitutions. Nonetheless, as Kavanagh (2019, 62) explains, this 'approach nonetheless perpetuates the problem of polarisation engendered by the very idea of two separate, one-dimensional models'. There is also lip service to the rejection of a perception of judges and political actors as rivals. It is in exactly this vein that Ekins (2019, 11) notes that 'Judges and parliamentarians are not and should not be rivals.' However, this statement was made in a report that referred to the *Miller II* prorogation judgment (discussed below) as 'an affront to the political constitution' (Ekins 2019, 13) and recommended that Parliament legislate to increase ministerial involvement in judicial appointments and rename the Supreme Court in order to address concerns about 'constitutional primacy'. Such language unhelpfully reinforces a confrontational positioning of legal and political institutions.

Moreover, despite intimations of a critique of the legal-political constitutionalism divide, there are at least two reasons that a new paradigm (ie, *collaborative constitutionalism*) is needed. First, the main contemporary political constitutionalists, a group of scholars and practitioners who tend to orientate themselves with the Judicial Power Project, continue to issue scathing and sometimes vitriolic critiques of assertive judicial review that very much echo battle metaphors and antagonism. As a result, although the existing research base does contain concern about the need to move beyond an adversarial and generally aggressive binary vision of the constitution, the 'rivalry' framing persists. To be clear, there is no expectation or desire to jettison conflict and debate; conflict is a *sine qua non* of constitutionalism and governance in a modern state. What is mooted is an approach to the inexorable conflict of modern constitutional governance that focuses on constitutional principles and objectives and the well-being of the people, rather than institutional posturing. Second, subtle acknowledgement of the flawed nature of the current debate is welcome but insufficient. There is a need for a theory – or theories – that offers a reconfiguration of our understanding of accountability in the UK constitution. Collaborative constitutionalism is one such proposal that may shift the discourse in a more fruitful and realistic direction.

The aim of this section has been to explain, compare and contrast two main forms of constitutionalism – *political constitutionalism* and *legal constitutionalism*. The key distinctions between these two visions concern power and position and the question of which constitutional actors sit at the apex of polity-elected politicians or appointed judges. The main argument of this section has been that the existence of a binary either/or debate has generally been unhelpful in terms of promoting a deeper understanding of longstanding questions of accountability that urgently need, if not answering, then at the very least *re*conceptualising to facilitate new perspectives, choices and understandings. In this context, collaborative constitutionalism provides just that fresh approach. The features and merits of the collaborative approach form the focus of the next section.

II. Collaborative Constitutionalism

This chapter advocates a move *beyond* the divide between models of political or legal accountability. It argues in favour of a reframing of language, debate and discourse around constitutional accountability. Movement in this direction has in recent years been promoted by a number of leading scholars, including Eoin Carolan (2015), Alison Young (2017) and Aileen Kavanagh (2019, 2023), and although variations in approach and emphasis exist, it is possible to identify a number of common features. First and foremost, collaborative constitutionalists reject the polarity between legal and political accountability mechanisms, arguing that the debate often over-simplifies each set of mechanisms. Instead of focusing on conceptualisations of 'dominance' and 'supremacy', collaborative constitutionalism encourages 'fruitful conflict' (Carolan 2015) and mutual constructive engagement between institutions with differing priorities and perspectives. Though conflict remains a feature of constitutionalism under this approach, there is no expectation that conflict will result in battle or lead to a final winner-takes-all result. Instead, constitutional collaboration 'discourages', as Carolan (2015, 226; see also Benhabib and Fredman 1994; Fredman 2013) notes, '… [us from reducing] constitutionalism to a conflict between the Politician and the Judge.'

Second, these authors focus on examining the *actual* day-to-day interactions between the central institutions of state as they occur in the real world. Collaborative constitutionalists depart from a fixation on models or ideal types, as models are too remote from – and indeed distract from – the actual dynamics that occur in the lived life of the constitution. While acknowledging that they are 'highly stylised' and admitting that neither can be fully realised in practice, Gee and Webber (2010, 298) defend the value of models on the basis that they can at least provide an organising perspective through which some understanding of the constitution might be secured. The risk, however, is that such perspectives become reified as theoretical anchor points that become difficult to recast or move, a dynamic which might, in turn, explain some of the more stringent critiques of recent Supreme Court decisions. Further, models do not have superior evaluative value in instructing us about the *objectives* of the constitution or effective means of pursuing and protecting constitutional values, let alone measuring or gauging success or failure (an issue that takes us back to themes raised in chapter three about measurement and chapter four about 'false promises'). The core contention of collaborative constitutionalists is that by shifting the analytical focus away from models and towards what actually happens in the sphere of public governance, we have a clearer view; we can observe the institutions of state working interdependently in furtherance of the fulfilment of fundamental public values.

This is not to suggest that institutional actors may not disagree about how to achieve or uphold specific values, or even how and whether a precise constitutional balance should be struck. But collaborative constitutionalism does start from the basic position that: 'In the working constitution, all three branches of government have to work together, collaborating at a respectful distance in the general promotion of important public values Kavanagh (2019, 66).' So, for instance, expressed in terms of adjudication, courts will recognise the importance of parliamentary will as an expression of democracy and seek to give effect to Parliament's intentions as expressed through legislation. However, alongside this effort, courts will also seek to give effect to fundamental constitutional rights and principles by conditioning their interpretation of legislation by reference to these constitutional norms.

Collaborative constitutionalism sits alongside related theories such as the new Commonwealth model of constitutionalism articulated by Gardbaum (2013), bipolar sovereignty championed by Stephen Sedley (1995) and CJS Knight (2009) and the 'mixed constitution' recently suggested by Tomkins (2013). These theories all recognise that the realities of modern constitutional practice require a complex, non-dichotomised understanding of institutional relationships. Yet, despite common themes that connect these views with collaborative constitutionalism, collaborative constitutionalist theories seek to move beyond the conceptual assumptions on which these cognate theories rest. For instance, Gardbaum's model still accepts the utility of political and legal constitutionalist models and places the new Commonwealth model along a spectrum that is partly defined by the political and legal ideal types. On the other hand, one of the appeals of collaborative constitutionalism is the opportunity to look beyond both polarised models and hierarchical constitutional orderings.

In sum, collaborative constitutionalism involves four core features:

1. Overlapping and inter-mingling legal and political norms and methods.
2. Each institution conducts its own accountability processes and according to its own normative priorities.
3. Each institution's accountability process allows space for other institutions to contribute to deliberative engagement and resolution of issues.
4. There is no requirement for one institution to be supreme or have the final word – this is in partial recognition of the ongoing nature of constitutional disputes.

There are several reasons to support this collaborative constitutionalist framing. The first is that it arguably provides a more convincing and realistic account of constitutional developments in the UK from the 1950s onwards. That period has seen the expansion of judicial review, the incorporation of European Union (EU) law through the European Communities Act 1972 (along with the adoption of EU law supremacy), and the duty of the courts to reinterpret legislation to achieve rights consistency under the Human Rights Act 1998. These changes have all seen a flow towards greater legal control within the constitution which has, to some extent, inevitably increased the visibility of the judiciary vis-à-vis the executive. And yet this process has occurred *within* the edifice of the traditional political constitution. This process has been analysed and discussed by Matthew Flinders (2008) through the concept of 'bi-constitutionality'. The impact of these changes means that an account of the constitution as strictly political does not work, but neither does an account that sees the constitution as overwhelmed by legal norms and actors. An understanding of the constitution that embraces an interdependent and mutual relationship between the branches of state – as this chapter's focus on collaborative constitutionality does – is a much less convoluted and more realistic way of explaining current rights arrangements under the Human Rights Act, common law developments, as well as the relationship and between the UK and the EU as channelled through the European Communities Act and European Union Withdrawal Act.

Second, a collaborative understanding of accountability mechanisms is also more conducive to the safeguarding features of constitutional*ism*. An understanding that there are several sites of accountability across the constitutional landscape facilitates a failsafe in case of the failure or inability of one site to supply the requisite safeguards. One of the analytical benefits of collaborative constitutionalism, as noted for instance by Carolan, is that it looks beyond a dyadic vision of the constitution as divided between Parliament and the judiciary and engages with the accountability role of the executive. Nonetheless, the theory is most convincing and most useful in its conceptualisation of the relationship between Parliament and the courts. Specifically, it is a useful frame for understanding the dual functions of the political and legal arms of the state in holding the executive to account. It could be argued that both political and legal constitutionalism already accommodate some capacity to appreciate such parallel processes. Collaborative constitutionalists, however, might reject such a suggestion on the basis that the fixation with dominance and supremacy within and between those competing visions effectively crowds-out the space for a more mature and sophisticated focus on systemic inter-dependencies and value. Building on this conceptual groundwork, the next section moves from theory to practice by exploring how collaborative constitutionalism takes practical form in relation to both political and judicial action.

III. Collaborative Constitutionalism in Practice

Chapter one of this book suggested that 'accountability angst' was rarely addressed through simplistic statements about 'more' or 'less' but was, in reality, more concerned with issues of blend, balance and proportionality. The way this chapter has cut into this discussion is by seeking to dissect or look beyond questions that explore either 'the demise of the political constitution' or the 'emergence of legal supremacy'. A focus on collaborative constitutionality, it has been argued, provides a far more accurate and constructive account of constitutional relationships. The aim of this concluding section is to demonstrate this argument through a brief focus on collaborative constitutionalism in political practice and then on a collaborative turn in the courts.

A. Collaborative Constitutionalism in Political Practice

The evolution of political accountability methods reveals the co-existence and interdependence of legal and political standards, the mutual influence of legal and political characteristics and the development and increase of political scrutiny alongside legal scrutiny. Political accountability systems have steadily been adopting – or accommodating – 'legal' solutions and influences. Processes for parliamentary accountability now recognise explicitly legal constitutional concerns through the mandate and work of the Joint Committee on Human Rights (JCHR) and the Constitution Committee in the House of Lords, both of which simultaneously conduct activities through a political process that takes account of wider constitutional concerns.

The Constitution Committee's appointment in 2001 demonstrates that a period of 'legalisation' of the constitution – through, for instance, the Human Rights Act 1998, the devolution statutes and more intrusive judicial review – was accompanied by a broader shift towards assessing and evaluating the constitutional implications of government proposals at the pre-legislative stage. The Constitution Committee's various reports have all in their own ways sought to increase ex ante accountability of the government's plans. For instance, the Committee has emphasised 'the importance of Cabinet government and the essential role that the Cabinet committee system plays as part of the system of collective ministerial responsibility' (Cabinet Office, 2010). By also pushing for a 'clear and consistent process' for introducing and enacting major constitutional reforms the Constitution Committee has sought to bolster parliamentary or 'political' accountability. And yet at the same time by seeking to ensure that legislation with potentially far-reaching constitutional implications is subject to closer inspection and review, this process also limits the need for exercise of judicial accountability as clear and constructive pre-legislative scrutiny is likely to reduce the number of subsequent judicial review challenges. In this sense 'good scrutiny makes for good governance' as Robin Cook, Leader of the House of Commons from June 2001 to March 2003, was fond of saying (see Evans 2019).

The parliamentary role in protecting constitutional standards is also highlighted by the JCHR. Its articulation of parliamentary responsibilities and activities reflect a collaborative understanding of the relationship between judges and political actors, with the ultimate objective of respecting human rights standards. The Committee has therefore avowed the basic principle that 'the will of Parliament includes an intention that legislation should not be incompatible with Convention rights', noting that the government's intention 'that new Bills brought before Parliament should not be incompatible is made clear on their face' (see HC89/HL31, 2021–22, 36–37). In relation to the legislature's interaction with the courts, the JCHR has rightly noted that Parliament's 'central role' in protecting rights continues *after* an adverse human rights judicial decision as Parliament then needs to scrutinise the government's response and determine whether a change in law is necessary. In its second report of the 2009–10 session (HL 10/HC 92, para 22) the JCHR explained that 'Parliament is central to the Human Rights Act. Ministers must report on the human rights compatibility of every Bill and it is Parliament, not the courts, which must decide how to deal with legislation which is not compatible with the Act.' The Committee's report on Enhancing Parliament's Role in relation to Human Rights judgments maintains that:

> [I]n many jurisdictions with constitutional bills of rights, courts are deemed to have a monopoly of interpretive wisdom and there is little scope for parliamentary involvement in ensuring that the executive complies with the supreme judicial will.
>
> Under the UK's institutional arrangements for protecting human rights, however, Parliament, as well as the courts, has a central role to play in deciding how best to protect the rights which all are agreed are fundamental. This means that in our system, when a UK court decides that a law, policy or practice is in breach of human rights, Parliament still has an important role to play in scrutinising the adequacy of the Government's response to the judgment including, in some cases, asking itself whether a change in the law is necessary to protect human rights and, if so, what that change in the law should be.

The JCHR 'undertake[s] the lion's share of Parliament's scrutiny of the Government's performance on human rights issues' and it has a broad remit to consider 'matters relating to human rights in the United Kingdom'. In light of the design and role of the JCHR, it is unsurprising that the Committee has been described as part of a 'quasi-judicial' approach to parliamentary scrutiny (see Klug and Wildbore 2007), while at the same time being praised by Tomkins (2013) as a fortification of the political constitution. The Committee's work interacts with the legal process at several stages in terms of both scrutinising government Bills for consistency with human rights and reviewing government responses to judicial human rights decisions. The Committee's processes are directly representative of the interweaving of legal and political mechanisms of accountability with legal standards – in the form of legislation and case law – guiding the scrutiny of Bills and the examination of governmental responses to judicial decisions. These processes see the JCHR interacting with and using judicial decisions while maintaining the character of a political accountability arena (ie, it does not consider individual cases). In short, the JCHR's role facilitates effective and sustained legislative involvement in the accountability of both Parliament as a whole and the executive, as well as in the enforcement and protection of human rights. In this sense it provides a practical example of collaborative constitutionalism in action, which brings us to a focus on the collaborative turn in the courts.

B. Collaborative Constitutionalism in Judicial Practice

Alongside parliamentary processes that facilitate mutual engagement, judicial decisions indicate a turn towards collaborative constitutionalism in the courts. The UK Supreme Court decision in *R (Unison) v The Lord Chancellor* [2017] UKSC 51 on access to justice is a useful exemplar of the courts depicting the interdependence and mutual engagement of institutions under the constitution. The *UNISON* case called on the Court to determine whether an Order made by the Lord Chancellor imposing fees for access to employment tribunals and employment appeal tribunals undermined access to justice. The Supreme Court found that the fees rendered employment claims unaffordable and thereby unlawfully prevented access to justice. The judgment in *UNISON* signalled a collaborative direction in the judicial development and exposition of common law rights. Lord Reed cast the Court's constitutional role as part of a collaborative enterprise shared with the political arm of the state:

> At the heart of the concept of the rule of law is the idea that society is governed by law. Parliament exists primarily in order to make laws for society in this country. Democratic procedures exist primarily in order to ensure that the Parliament which makes laws includes Members of Parliament who are chosen by the people of this country and are accountable to them. Courts exist in order to ensure that the laws made by Parliament, and the common law created by the courts themselves, are applied and enforced. That role includes ensuring that the executive branch of government carries out its functions in accordance with the law. In order for the courts to perform that role, people must in principle have unimpeded access to them ([68]).

The institutional narrative presented by Lord Reed is one of collaboration and mutual problem-solving, rather than institutional confrontation and antagonism. Battle-laden framings are set aside for a more sophisticated account of the interplay between different actors. Lord Reed's formulation sees rights claims as an avenue for a collaborative means of assessing the content of a right, and determining whether and in what circumstances the right can be limited in the pursuit of other public goods. This approach begins from the premise that both political and legal organs have a role to play in this endeavour. Moreover, in this framing, there is respect for multiple constitutional values – democracy, rule of law and fundamental rights – and each institution plays a role in safeguarding those values.

Despite concerns that cases such as *UNISON* demonstrate a form of judicial over-reach, the Supreme Court has generally been very careful to emphasise the confines within which common law constitutional adjudication is maintained. For example, despite reliance on *UNISON* by the applicants in *R (O) v SSHD*, in support of an argument that fees regulations made under the Immigration Act 2014 for a child or young person to be registered as a British citizen were unaffordable and accordingly ultra vires, the Supreme Court rejected the argument and applied ordinary rules of statutory interpretation. Lord Hodge explained that the calibration of the judicial role relative to Parliament and the executive was, at least partly, occasioned by the choice of interpretative approach. The applicants in *O* sought to rely on the principle of legality, according to which fundamental rights and principles can only be overridden by clear, unambiguous words. However, this principle, with its attendant flexibility for judicial construction of statutory terms, was held to be inapplicable as the case did not engage fundamental rights. Two limits or guidelines were observed. First, interpretation under the principle of legality is only reserved for fundamental or constitutional norms (where there are no relevant constitutional norms, ordinary statutory interpretation, with its more limited role for courts, remains operative). Second, the category of constitutional rights is 'kept within narrow bounds' (*R (O) v SSHD* [43]), reflecting rights which 'everyone living in a democracy under the rule of law ought to enjoy' (see *R v Lord Chancellor, ex p Lightfoot*, 609). Notably, both foundational pillars of democracy *and* the rule of law play a role in identifying which rights should be classified as fundamental or constitutional.

Box 6.1 Constitutional Moments: *Miller (No 1)* and *Miller (No 2)*

The decision in *Miller (No 1)* concerned the question of who had the power to trigger Article 50 of the Treaty on European Union which notified the President of the European Council of the UK's formal decision to leave the Union. The legal challenge had a consequence of bringing significant public attention to the question of whether the executive (using the prerogative powers) had the power to unilaterally trigger Article 50 or whether the government must first receive Parliament's authorisation through primary legislation. Both the High Court and the Supreme Court held that the government could not trigger Article 50 using its prerogative powers. The initial decision of the High Court was met with significant public and media acrimony, including the infamous 'Enemies of the People' headline in the *Daily Mail* newspaper on the 4 November 2016.

The decision in *Miller (No 2)* concerned the Prime Minister's request of August 2019 to the Monarch to prorogue Parliament. The prorogation would have the effect, so the Supreme Court held, of preventing parliamentary scrutiny and accountability. The legal challenge in 2019 was led by a coalition of parliamentarians and activists including Gina Miller. In a unanimous decision the Supreme Court enhanced the substantive effect of parliamentary sovereignty by applying it to limit the power to prorogue Parliament. Essentially the judicial system bolstered parliamentary accountability and the 'political' constitution in a manner which reinforced checks on executive power.

In addition to roles in safeguarding constitutional rights, constitutional dynamics are also revealed in judicial understandings of institutional principles at common law. The *Miller, Cherry* case (*Miller II*) provides useful evidence of judicial views on the development and protection of fundamental institutional principles. Extensive engagement with the case is also useful as the Supreme Court's judgment has been cited as proof of judicial overreach and of the legalisation of the constitution. Indeed, the decision has been identified as a motivation for the government's launch of the Independent Review of Administrative Law, which culminated in the Judicial Review and Courts Act 2022. Moreover, as one of the most significant constitutional cases and constitutional moments of recent decades an examination of *Miller II* also provides meaningful insight into constitutional collaboration in practice.

The case arose from extraordinary circumstances. In the run-up to the UK's scheduled exit from the EU, the Prime Minister advised the Queen to prorogue Parliament for five weeks. Businesswoman and activist Gina Miller and a cross party group of MPs challenged the lawfulness of the Prime Minister's advice to the Queen. The government, however, argued that the matter was not justiciable. The government maintained that the only appropriate accountability mechanisms for the Prime Minister's advice to the Queen were political and to be exercised by Parliament. In a significant contribution to discourse on constitutional accountability, the Court rejected the idea that the existence of political accountability for a particular act or decision displaced the necessity for, and lawfulness of, legal or judicial accountability. Lady Hale and Lord Reed defended the idea of concurrent legal and political accountability. The Court's two reasons for concluding that 'the Prime Minister's accountability to Parliament does not in itself justify the conclusion that the courts have no legitimate role to play' involved a *practical* argument about the realistic effects of proroguing Parliament, and second a *principled* constitutional argument resting on the role of the courts and the distinction between legal and political assessment benchmarks. In a practical sense, the Court observed that:

> The effect of prorogation is to prevent the operation of ministerial accountability to Parliament during the period when Parliament stands prorogued. Indeed, if Parliament were to be prorogued with immediate effect, there would be no possibility of the Prime Minister's being held accountable by Parliament until after a new session of Parliament had commenced, by which time the Government's purpose in having Parliament prorogued might have been accomplished (*Miller, Cherry*, [33]).

Effectively, and as Sinclair and Tomlinson (2019) have illustrated, the lengthy prorogation made it impossible for Parliament to scrutinise government decisions surrounding the withdrawal from the EU at a time of fundamental constitutional change. The Court's recognition of this fact is consistent with its increasingly realistic approach to constitutional questions. As Wheatle (2020) argues, the Supreme Court is now going beyond formalistic techniques and instead taking cognisance of the real-world practical impact of governmental decisions. Moreover, such a pragmatic approach is highly consistent with the collaborative focus on the real-world interactions of the institutions of state.

While the first argument made by the Court was that the impact of the lengthy prorogation was to render accountability by Parliament impossible, more fundamentally the Court firmly defended the co-existence of legal and political accountability by outlining the distinctions between the constitutional functions fulfilled by the courts and Parliament. So 'the courts have a duty to give effect to the law' while Parliament will judge the government according to policy imperatives. The Court also recognised the constitutional obligations of the executive to the legislature, explaining that as the person who advises the Monarch on prorogation, the Prime Minister bore 'a constitutional responsibility to have regard to all relevant interests, including the interests of Parliament' (*Miller, Cherry* [30]). This is a critical point. In framing their decision in this way the courts were not attempting to usurp the role of any other constitutional actor but, if anything, to underline the constitutional obligation of the executive not to seek to avoid parliamentary accountability. Therefore, the decision did not reflect judicial over-reach; rather, it reflected a commitment to supporting and ensuring the political facets of the constitution and parliamentary sovereignty.

The role of the courts in relation to Brexit, and the specific debate around the prorogation of Parliament in 2019, will be explored from a range of perspectives in several later chapters. As such, the remainder of this section focuses on identifying the dynamics of collaborative constitutionalism in the *Miller, Cherry* decision. It does so through a focus on three thematic couplets: measurement and benchmarks, conventions and conversion, and evolution and adaptation.

As chapter one underlined, accountability is a complex concept. This is reflected in apparently endless debate and discussion about '*Who?*' '*How?*', '*When?*', '*For what?*', which are themselves to some extent complicated by the way in which the concept contains mechanistic and normative elements. What *Miller, Cherry* brings to the discussion is a practical example of the contestation of the meaning of accountability, particularly from the perspective of different institutions of state. Accountability centres on applying normative standards to actions and decisions. But the normative standards applied and the methods by which they are applied depend on the institution in question. The accountability standards in Parliament are political standards – including policy objectives, democratic principles and budgetary constraints. For the courts to exercise accountability, there must be legal standards against which courts can assess governmental action. Accordingly, part of the challenge made by critics in contested cases is to cast doubt on the very existence of relevant legal standards that can be applied to the decisions and actions at issue. This is evident in responses to *Miller, Cherry*, where critics of the decision argue that there were no relevant legal standards for the Court to apply as the question was exclusively a political question, or that the relevant legal standards were expanded beyond their proper boundaries. In essence and returning to Ellen Rock's emphasis in chapter four on measurement and the need for 'normative yardsticks', the courts were accused of creating their own measures. Loughlin (2019), for example, distinguishes between parliamentary supremacy as a formal and functional principle and argues that it 'has always been understood to be a formal legal rule that grants supremacy to the laws enacted by the Crown in Parliament'. And yet, as argued above, the Court's judgment reads as a rejection of constitutional formalism. Further, the Court was arguably on solid constitutional ground in viewing parliamentary sovereignty as a normative or functional principle. For instance, the continuing nature of parliamentary sovereignty – whereby one Parliament is unable to bind a successor Parliament – has long been used as justification for the interpretive doctrine of implied repeal (see Thoburn [37], [42], [59], and Perreau-Saussine 2002). The effect of continuing sovereignty is the presumption that where two ordinary statutes conflict, the later in time will prevail – the will of the successor Parliament prevails over that of the previous Parliament.

A second objection to the use of normative standards applied by the Court has been that the Court converted *political conventions into legal rules*. Critics challenged the Court's finding that not only parliamentary supremacy, but also the requirement of ministerial accountability to Parliament – was a constitutional principle enforceable by judges. Ministerial accountability, both individual and collective, has been traditionally understood as a constitutional convention and, as such, *is* – or *was*, prior to the *Miller, Cherry* decision – a political norm, to be observed and enforced by political actors. Under orthodox constitutional law, as recently reaffirmed by the first *Miller* decision in 2017, 'Judges … are neither the parents nor the guardians of political conventions; they are merely observers' ([146]). The apparent conversion of the normative character of ministerial accountability has, accordingly, generated critique for converting a political convention into a legal norm. As Ekins (2019) argues:

> The principle [of political accountability] underpins a range of conventions and practices which make up our political constitution, in which the Government is formed by and accountable to the Houses of Parliament, especially the Commons. The principle is sometimes noted by courts but it is not a legal principle and cannot justify novel judicial intervention.

Similarly, Finnis (2019) criticised the Court for 'suddenly transforming the historic principle of Parliamentary accountability into a legal principle'. Paul Craig offered a thoughtful response to this critique in which he highlighted the use of parliamentary accountability and responsibility by judges to explain and justify the exercise of deference to the state in judicial review and human rights case law. This is a salient point and there are many examples of this practice. For instance, the Supreme Court's 2014 decision in *R (Nicklinson) v Ministry of Justice* not to grant a declaration of incompatibility in relation to existing law and policy on assisted dying was partly premised on existing parliamentary activity and responsibility for the issue. The response from Ekins is that there is a distinction between the use of parliamentary accountability in such cases and the use of the principle in *Miller, Cherry* in that the former case law activated the principle to limit judicial power whereas in the *Miller, Cherry* the principle was used to augment judicial review. This response is arguably unconvincing. The salient factor is that the core of both uses of parliamentary accountability was to protect parliamentary power. As such, both uses are fundamentally consistent and reflective of the interrelationship between political and legal norms.

There is, however, a more challenging counter to Craig's analogy – in deference cases, parliamentary accountability is only used indirectly to affect the law. That is, the use of parliamentary accountability in such cases is not as a legal principle in itself, but as a political norm or practice that is used to affect the level of scrutiny applied by the court. However, *Miller, Cherry* goes beyond indirect legal effect by affording direct legal effect to parliamentary accountability as a legal constitutional principle that can limit the extent of a prerogative power. This concession does not, however, mean that the entire judgment is misguided. The judgment could be read as *evolution* of the normative role of parliamentary accountability – from having indirect to direct legal effect. On this understanding, the treatment of parliamentary accountability is part of the incremental evolution of the common law constitution. Alternatively, the reasoning could suggest that parliamentary accountability has both political and legal dimensions, with the legal dimension capable of application by the judges to, as it were, bolster the political constitution.

The central argument is therefore that *Miller, Cherry* does not represent a displacement of the political constitution, as some critics have claimed. It reflects a Court that sees itself as acting alongside other institutions to protect fundamental constitutional norms. While the Court ruled the prerogative unlawful, it did so in defence of Parliament's constitutional role. The judgment also acknowledged the existence of political space and capacity that had simply not been utilised – by suggesting that prorogation *would* have been lawful if reasonable justification was presented, the Court exercised a form of deference to the government. The judges afforded space to the government to provide reasons for its interference with Parliament's constitutional duties (on this see Masterman and Wheatle 2019). When viewed in this light, the *Miller, Cherry* judgment represents a collaborative approach to constitutionalism rather than a form of judicial supremacy or over-reach.

Finally, it is also worth noting that the criticisms of those who claimed the political constitution had been displaced by *Miller, Cherry* have not been supported by subsequent post-2020 judicial decisions. If anything, the attitude of the courts to the executive has been more favourable, possibly even somewhat deferential. Decisions such as *R (Begum) v Secretary of State for the Home Department* in which the Supreme Court refused to overturn the government's decision denying Shamima Begum leave to enter the UK to challenge the deprivation of her citizenship provides a case in point. Such decisions have prompted some commentators to argue that the Court is actually currently *overly* deferential, almost as a counter-reaction against the controversy surrounding *Miller, Cherry* (see Graham 2022). Recent case law suggests that, as the Supreme Court underlined in *Miller, Cherry*, that decision and the circumstances that prompted it were highly exceptional. The decision did not signal a new age of judicial supremacy.

There is, of course, a more subtle and contextual discussion that needs to take place but which often remains lost beneath a fixation on judicial activism. An approach that might deliver answers to pressing 'questions of accountability' might focus upon *which cases in which contexts* prompt judges to restrain governmental action, or to engage in constitutional innovation. Comparing *Begum* to *Miller, Cherry*, for example, exposes deep cleavages. The former dealt with the very foundations of responsible government, *Begum* with national security and terrorism. *Begum* touched on issues of contingent and insecure citizenship for ethnic minorities and, as Prabhat (2023) has demonstrated, these are topics where British law and institutions have very often adopted a restrictive – and conservative – approach. Such contextual analysis and awareness should certainly supplement, if not define, the debate concerning judicial activism and restraint.

IV. Conclusion

So where does this leave us in terms of understanding both the theory and practice of democratic accountability? First, this chapter has argued that framing longstanding questions of accountability in simple polarised terms of 'politicians *versus* the judiciary', 'supremacy *versus* subservience', etc is generally unhelpful. It tends to produce more heat than light, or more 'hot rhetoric' than 'cool theory'. It is in this context that this chapter has explored the theory of collaborative constitutionalism. This theory encompasses an emphasis on understanding the complementary and interdependent nature of different accountability processes and arenas. It is therefore *systemic* in approach and seeks to acknowledge and understand the full accountability space rather than focusing on which institution is (or is not) 'supreme'. In this sense a collaborative emphasis does fit with the navigational challenge that was outlined in the opening chapter in the sense that it forges new routes, identifies gaps in the knowledge base and poses new questions. There are, of course, lingering questions about the practice of collaborative constitutionalism and its interaction with the wider constitution. Such questions include the definition and interaction of the shared constitutional values of the institutions of state. There are also avenues to explore the potential relevance of collaborative constitutional theory well beyond the confines of a focus on the UK and beyond law and into comparative political and socio-legal studies. It is likely, for example, that more consociational or power-sharing democracies might be more aligned with reflecting and refining a more collaborative approach. Certainly, as multiple democracies around the world grapple with the pluralistic realities of modern governance, there is a strong case for the relevance of collaborative constitutionalism and similar theories.

PART II

Themes

7

Questions of Control: Accountability in the Shadow of Prorogation

CHRIS MONAGHAN AND JOSIE WELSH

Several chapters in the framing section of this book underlined the role of accountability not in terms of blame-allocation or lesson-learning but in relation to control. Accountability as facilitating the control of those who wield power in a democracy, and possibly removing them from power, is possibly the most basic function of accountability governance. Without being able to effectively threaten the prospect of removing the empowered from power, a system that purports to demonstrate any sense of meaningful accountability, risks being but a mirage and one that discourages self-restraint by those in power. Basically, and to put it bluntly, why should the empowered (those who exercise executive power) bother to conform to the expectations of accountable government (underpinned within the British tradition by constitutional norms) when there is little detrimental incentive? This chapter focuses on one specific question as the central hook in which its contribution to this collection hangs – what does the Brexit experience tell us about the state of accountability in the UK? Underneath this core Brexit focus exist a range of related and secondary questions such as – what does Brexit suggest about the realities of political power and the nature of fuzzy or fluid accountability? Are new processes and forms of accountability needed to control fugitive power? What do we mean by fugitive power? We believe that within the context of Brexit fugitive power means the exercise of executive power (given to the government by legislation or the prerogative) that is not held to account and therefore exceeds the expectations of the accepted constitutional norms.

Furthermore, how might Brexit aid understanding in terms of the 'over-supply but under-performance' thesis that was presented in chapter one? In situations of legislative 'deadlock' how valuable is an emphasis on proportionality and balance? What relevance might Brexit have for understanding accountability in theory and practice beyond the UK, and what post-Brexit 'questions of accountability' remain to be answered? These are 'big' questions, and it is not possible to engage in great detail about each and every one of them in this chapter. As such a more modest approach has been adopted that focuses on three 'questions of control':

1. Does the British executive really enjoy 'unbridled' power in the sense suggested by extreme majoritarianism?
2. What do recent events suggest about the role of the judiciary in ensuring 'bridled' power and is the current relationship sustainable?
3. What might be done to innovate in relation to accountable governance, what are the 'barriers' and 'blockages' to reform?

These questions take the debate from a focus on Brexit to a fresh and distinctive discussion about the politics, power, and potential of impeachment. The first of the three sections that form this chapter provides an account of power and the British constitution and seeks to identify a number of core 'truths'. This approach is almost designed to be controversial; many analysts and observers will disagree with both the diagnosis, prognosis and prescription for change that is presented. The aim is not, however, to add to the 'hot rhetoric' that already pervades many 'questions of accountability' but simply to set down some clear and unavoidably normative benchmarks to provide a foundation for the second section's focus on changing patterns of judicial power.

The second question shifts the analytical focus to the courts and judiciary to assess their role and legitimacy in a traditionally 'political constitution'. This will enable a critical discussion of the Brexit litigation and the consequences of *Miller (No 1)* and *Miller (No 2)* and how this readily taps into concerns about judicial power. These concerns are long standing and were famously articulated by JAG Griffiths (1979, 2010) and have consequently received considerable attention within the academe and politics, through Policy Exchange's decision to establish the Judicial Power Project and whose reports often include forewords by senior judges, such as the Lord Chief Justice of England and Wales (Burnett 2018). The point being that the judiciary are aware of these concerns and have to some extent engaged in the debate (which is mainly limited to extra-judicial speeches and fettered by the constraints of judicial office).

The third question looks beyond binary debates concerning the judiciary and politicians and offers a more fundamental focus on control within a constitution which is (in)famous for its power-hoarding dynamics. By exploring these three questions, this chapter confronts uncomfortable truths, explores tentative reforms, and calls for a reappraisal of our existing understandings of power within the constitution. In a way that resonates with Wheatle's (chapter six) call for a more nuanced and detailed understanding of roles and relationships, the second section dissects the different rationalities that underpinned controversial Brexit-related judicial decisions. The third and final section then looks beyond existing analytical framings and asks 'questions of accountability' about impeachment processes that despite their long history in the British context are rarely raised.

I. Constitutional Flux and Constitutional Truths

This chapter is concerned with a very specific set of 'questions of accountability'. Specifically, the legal and constitutional questions of: (i) who had the power to trigger Article 50 of the Treaty on European Union which gave official notice to the European Council that the UK was leaving (ie, the *Miller (No 1)* case); and (ii) whether the executive had the prerogative power to prorogue Parliament in the final stages of the UK leaving the European Union (ie, the *Miller (No 2)* case). In both cases, and putting a very complex set of issues in simple terms, the government attempted to use its *extra*-statutory prerogative powers to achieve its ambitions. This prerogative power is the residual power of the Crown (for a definition see Dicey 1915) and in both cases it was either exercised by the government (*Miller (No 1)*), or exercised by the late Queen Elizabeth II upon the advice of her government *(Miller (No 2))*. This resulted in litigation and the ultimate decision by the Supreme Court that the executive could not behave in such an 'unbridled' manner.

Before we consider precisely what we mean by 'unbridled' manner it is important to state that both cases demonstrate first some key similarities about the exercise of power, and second some important differences. *Miller (No 1)* arguably was the most justifiable of the two in terms of the May Government's use of prerogative powers. Arguably it made sense that the prerogative could be used to bring the UK's membership of the European Union to an end, just as the prerogative had been deployed to allow the UK's membership of what is now the European Union in 1973. Yes, due to the UK's dualist legal system the legal realities of membership required the enactment of the European Communities Act 1972, yet it was not inconceivable that the prerogative could be utilised to unilaterally trigger Article 50. This is the case, even though we disagree with the legality and constitutional probity of the use of the prerogative in these circumstances (see Monaghan 2019). Whereas *Miller (No 2)* could be viewed as an outright attempt by the Johnson Government to remove parliamentary accountability and make a mockery of the foundations of responsible government and the parliamentary system.

The term '(un)bridled' is a carefully selected descriptive term, especially in the case of understanding the shifting balance of power in majoritarian power-hoarding democracies. The key reference point being Geoffrey Palmer's 1989 analysis of New Zealand's Constitution – *Unbridled Power* – with its interpretation of an executive that operated with excessive freedom and inadequate safeguards. The fact that Palmer had himself been both a professor of constitutional law and an MP, minister and even the Prime Minister of New Zealand gave the book's focus on questions of accountability and proposals for reform particularly persuasive. But what makes the New Zealand experience particularly relevant for this chapter's focus on 'questions of accountability', in general, and on the UK, in particular, is that it was broadly recognised across the party system and amongst the public that the constitutional balance of power had become as unbalanced as it was unsustainable. A change in the electoral system was agreed via a binding referendum in 1993 and the simple plurality system was subsequently replaced by a mixed-member proportional system. The constitutional equilibrium was shifted considerably as a result of this reform, and this was reflected in the title of Palmer's subsequent book – *Bridled Power* (1997). The New Zealand experience demonstrates the need for a frank discussion by those in power about the shortcomings and merits of the political system and whether the current framework is up to scratch. It is not so much as speaking truth to power, but the empowered speaking truth to themselves and actively listening. The use of the referendum which gave a voice to the electorate, albeit binding unlike the use of referendums in the UK context, offers a way to facilitate meaningful (and we daresay ambitious reform), even the use of referendums has not been to be unproblematic in the UK.

The main argument of this section is that the UK has in recent years undergone a particularly extreme period of constitutional flux, which have, at times, led to debates concerning the power of the executive and whether the balance of power needs to be shifted towards a slightly different equilibrium point. Since 2010 the UK has enjoyed somewhat of a constitutional rollercoaster ride: the indecisive 2010 general election, the coalition and the agreed package of political and constitutional reforms, the realities of the Scottish independence referendum (which is still unresolved), Brexit, and not to mention internal party and leadership dynamics within the Conservative party. Brexit, in particular, and the judicial challenges it stimulated, represented a particularly stark 'constitutional moment'. The aim of this chapter is not to review this period in descriptive detail but to attempt to look beneath and beyond the constitutional chaos in order to identify the core self-evident truths. To talk about constitutional governance and democratic politics in terms of 'truths' is clearly a controversial approach to adopt. As Elinor Ostrom (2000) argued, the social and political sciences are dominated by 'self-evident truths' and dominant assumptions but just because something is widely believed does not mean it is true or beyond challenge. But as a starting point to this chapter's focus on what might be termed 'bridling, blockages and barriers' some initial scoping of dominant or broadly accepted understandings is useful. With this in mind five inter-related 'truths' might usefully be identified.

Truth #1 – at a national level there is generally fairly weak control of the executive. This is a key element of majoritarian Westminster-style politics, and is inscribed to some extent in both the institutional framework and culture of Westminster and Whitehall. The pre-democratic legacy of the UK's institutions remains, as David Judge (2005) has argued, relatively 'thin' in democratic terms. That is not to suggest that the executive exists with complete autonomy. The parliamentary decline thesis has, for example, been re-evaluated in recent years (see Kelso and Flinders 2011; Russell and Cowley 2016); while, as chapter six has noted, a series of constitutional reforms have produced a system of what Flinders (2009) has labelled 'modified majoritarianism'. But it is to suggest that at a basic level, and especially when viewed through a comparative perspective, that the executive wields significant power within the British polity. More specifically, the executive's capacity to control its legislative majority in all but the most extreme situations creates something of a constitutional trap for 'questions of accountability' (examples of when MPs can control the legislative agenda of the House of Commons in face of executive opposition is rare, with one such example being the European Union (Withdrawal) (No.2) Act 2019 which resulted in Prime Ministerial 'threats' to disregard the law and an implicit rebuke from the Lord Chancellor).

This 'trap' reflects the manner in which reforms that are intended to enable scrutiny and shift the balance of power away from the executive must generally be supported by the executive that they seek to bind or disempower. Few executives are going to voluntarily cede power, strengthen the opposition or make the business of government harder. In terms of the prerogative what incentive is there for a government (or indeed the governing party) to voluntarily give away or introduce statutory regulation of contentious prerogative powers. Yes, there have been instances of reform such as Gordon Brown's Constitutional Reform and Governance Act 2010 and the coalition government's Fixed-term Parliaments Act 2011 (now repealed), but arguably in the case of the latter this was driven by expediency (ie, the need to reassure both parties of the intent to govern together without an early general election being called), rather than an altruistic desire to improve accountability.

In this context and with the theory of collaborative constitutionalism in mind it is possibly unsurprising if other accountability arenas attempt to seek to assert increased control. This brings the Supreme Court's decisions in *Miller (No 1)* and *Miller (No 2)* into sharp focus. The argument being that the legislature's lack of capacity to control or scrutinise the prerogative powers of the executive inevitably brought the judiciary into the debate as one of the few institutions with the capacity to demand answers to critical 'questions of accountability'.

Truth #2 is simply that although the accountability of the executive to the legislature is the primary or core scrutiny system within the traditional 'political' Constitution, this principal-agent relationship exists within a web of alternative and multi-layered relationships that all play a role in the broader accountability space. This matters because these alternative processes facilitate forms of bottom-up and diagonal accountability which, in turn, can buttress and sustain parliamentary processes. What is interesting about both *Miller* decisions is that although they involved macro-political questions, they were in fact generated through individual citizen challenge. The litigation is most associated with the businessperson Gina Miller, but it in fact represented a broad coalition from across the political spectrum. Indeed *Miller (No 2)* involved one former conservative Prime Minister (Sir John Major) being a party in a judicial review against the then current conservative Prime Minister (Boris Johnson). Again, what is interesting here is that although the reasoning in *Miller (No 1)* was not novel (see, for example, Baker 2021 who points to legal opinion – even prior to Sir Edward Coke – that envisaged legal limitations on the Crown's prerogative powers) in *Miller (No 2)* the reasoning was more unique as the courts attempted to remedy what it interpreted to be a deficiency in the political constitution. 'The Supreme Court's decision may be thought a bold one' Monaghan (2019, 7) notes 'but boldness does not negate constitutional probity … the Supreme Court … delivered a mature and contemporary decision based on its understanding and articulation of the present state of the United Kingdom's constitution.' Yes, it is conceded that not everyone will agree with the assertion of 'constitutional probity', but it is hard to support the alternative account, in which the legitimate exercise of executive power has been thwarted by the activist judges.

Our third 'truth' is therefore simply this: judicial accountability has an important and legitimate role to play *within* a political constitution. To put the same point slightly differently, the court's role can be seen as the guardians of the political Constitution.

Truths #4 and #5 can also be stated in rather parsimonious terms. Truth #4 is simply that any constitution that relies upon executive self-restraint and an implicit willingness to play by the 'rules of the game', as constituted through the history and role of constitutional conventions, is inevitably vulnerable to the whims of those politicians who refuse to recognise the existence of valid restraints. Although certain constitutional conventions may be viewed as unbreakable, such as the fact the Monarch will not use his prerogative powers to refuse Assent to a Bill presented to him by Parliament (as despite concerns that George V would refused Assent to the Irish Home Rule Bill, the last Monarch to *actually* refuse Assent was Queen Anne in 1708 and this was upon the advice of her ministers), others are clearly not, and operate at the discretion and subject to the conscience of actors within the constitution, such as the convention of individual ministerial responsibility (Lord Carrington's resignation in 1982 being an example of when the convention was followed). Such behaviour, in refusing to recognise the existence of valid restraints, have been particularly associated with, though certainly not limited to populist politicians who engage in an explicitly antagonistic performative style characterised by the 'flaunting of the low', a political style characterised by slang, swearing, being more 'colourful' in their fashion, gestures, language and bodily self-presentation as potential ways to invoke bad manners and 'with "the middle finger" defiantly raised' as Pierre Ostiguy (2017, 84) puts it 'to the well brought up, the proper, the accepted truths and ways associated with diverse world elites'. An example of a non-populist politician affected by populism is Theresa May. May's Government was the cause of the original *Miller* litigation, yet the agenda of many within her own party and their allies within the media, if not of May herself who can be perceived as a politician in the traditional mould, was arguably driven by a fatalistic populist wave – that is, to get Brexit done no matter the cost. This explains just why judicial control, which in *Miller (No 1)* fettered the executive fiat, was perceived as being anti-democratic and heavily resented.

On the other hand, in terms of a leader who plays the populist, there is Boris Johnson, who has cultivated a 'cult' of the academic outsider-insider, who was not afraid of taking on global figures whilst serving as Mayor of London (ie his response to the then US Republican presidential candidate Mitt Romney in 2012, in response to Romney's criticism of the preparation of London's planning for the 2012 London Olympics). The Johnson Government arguably played fast and loose with the Constitution and its norms, and a rhetoric was constructed both within the government, the party, and the right-wing media to essentially vilify any restraint. This vilification predated Johnson, as can be attested by the 'Enemies of the People' saga (*Daily Mail* 2016). But it was not for nothing that Johnson boasted in his farewell speech as Prime Minister to the House of Commons, that 'with iron determination we saw off Brenda Hale and we got Brexit done'. One would struggle to find an example of such an overt Prime Ministerial (or indeed monarchical) attack on such a senior judge, since at least the reign of the Stuarts in the seventeenth century.

Truth #5 brings the discussion back to poise and proportionality, balance and blend in the sense that if: (i) concerns exist regarding the over-centralisation of power in the executive; but (ii) the existence of judicial control mechanisms is for some reason interpreted as anti-democratic and illegitimate; then (iii) the natural response would appear to focus on somehow strengthening Parliament's capacity vis-à-vis the executive. The latter, however, being something which would implicitly demand the support of the government of the day (hence the notion of 'the trap'). A resetting of the balance between Parliament and the executive would arguably require a constitutional moment of such magnitude that events compelled reform, either in the face of executive opposition (we can get a sense of this in the Brexit saga of 2018–19) or at the instigation of a reform minded executive (which would need to do more than tinker with the House of Lords, the office of the Lord Chancellor, the appellate courts, or indeed the personal powers of the Monarch).

In the context of global concerns regarding 'democratic backsliding' and more specific concerns about the turbulence of British politics in recent years any attempt to identify even the most preliminary list of core features, let alone 'truths' might appear somewhat foolhardy. And yet at a broad level the main argument of this section is that these five positions do provide an accurate account of the core, if not, 'questions of accountability' then 'problems of accountability'. As such they provide to the first core question of this chapter and allow us to move on to explore the second question's focus on the role of the judiciary.

II. Judicial Power

It is worth stepping back and very briefly contextualising this chapter's focus on 'questions of control' through a focus on Bruce Ackerman's (1991) work on 'constitutional moments'. Simply stated, Ackerman seeks to solve one of the most pressing questions of accountability in legal and democratic theory – the counter-majoritarian difficulty. How can a democratic society justify empowering unelected, relatively unaccountable judges to invalidate the policy choices of more democratically selected legislators? (especially, when the judiciary can be characterised by it critics as out-of-touch and drawn from certain types of backgrounds) (for an evidenced based assessment see Darbyshire 2011). For Ackerman, the counter-majoritarian difficulty is premised on a misconception that courts invoking the Constitution to invalidate legislation are frustrating 'the People's' will. From Ackerman's position, ordinary day-to-day legislation does not represent the genuine 'voice of the people' in any genuine or real sense and is simply the result of messy machine politics generated by political agents. The 'voice of the people' is only genuinely heard, according to Ackerman, during very rare moments of 'constitutional politics'. Only by recognising the 'dualist' nature of our political regime, Ackerman argues, will we see the counter-majoritarian problem for what it is: an illusion.

The dualist democrat in Ackerman's approach therefore distinguishes between *normal* and *constitutional* politics. 'Apathy, ignorance and selfishness' (1991, 265) characterise the former, while considered popular judgments on 'the rights of citizens and the permanent interests of the community' (1991, 240) mark the latter. By forging such a distinction Ackerman poses fresh questions that rotate and pivot around the issue of accountability, but the relevance of his approach to the UK is clearly limited by the existence of very different constitutional configurations. But at a broad level Ackerman's work can be used as a touchstone through which to begin to explore debates and controversies in the UK, especially those surrounding what Colin Hay (2020) labels 'Brexistential angst and the paradoxes of populism'. The decision to hold a referendum on the UK's membership of the EU essentially created a 'dualist' polity in the sense that a form of *direct* democracy was used within the confines of an *indirect* representative polity. How the potential tensions and clashes between direct and indirect modes of public engagement would be reconciled was never considered ahead of the actual vote. The result was not therefore a deeply divided polity, especially at the territorial level, but also a more basic misalignment between the basic viewpoint of most MPs (ie, *pro*-EU membership) and the result of a referendum, which had itself been held without any of the normal constitutional safeguards relating to numeric and territorial thresholds. This may shock commentators from other jurisdictions as to how such a fundamental political change can be justified by a simple majority, even if the referendum was only advisory in nature, as the yes vote left the May Government (Cameron having resigned) with arguably very little room for manoeuvre. The Brexit referendum is hardly novel, as arguably a more 'traumatic' (for the future of the UK), or indeed significant, result could have been achieved had the Scottish electorate voted in favour of independence in 2014.

In many ways the people had spoken but what they wanted was not overwhelmingly clear. This created a constitutional moment that cannot be interpreted in terms of 'normal politics' and was explicitly concerned with the rights of citizens and the permanent interests of the community. And yet this was a moment when the courts did not 'invalidate' the policy choices of the executive but simply ensured that due process was followed and that parliamentary accountability could not be avoided. As such, the central argument of this section is that *Miller (No 1)* and *Miller (No 2)* can be interpreted, in many respects, as critical constitutional moments. Moments, that is, where the counter-majoritarian problem was at its most obvious and explicit, and therefore where a debate about the appropriate boundaries between politics and the law. In this regard Richard Ekins (2016) comments ahead of the *Miller (No 1)* decision proved prescient:

> The legal proceedings now underway are dangerous. The courts have no choice, thus far, save to allow the arguments to be made before them. But if the courts are perceived to be helping to frustrate Brexit, to be standing in the way of the Government's intention to honour the referendum result, then this will undermine public confidence. And the simple act of hearing the challenges at all risks fuelling this perception, for there is at least a risk of delay, which is partly the point of the legal action. It would be best if the challenges are rejected clearly and quickly.

The courts did not reject the cases 'clearly and quickly'. If anything, the strength, and clarity of the decisions, especially in relation to *Miller (No 2)*, seemed almost intended to prod and provoke not only the executive vis-à-vis Brexit but also a far wider public debate about questions of power, accountability and control. In terms of the public debate, this perhaps unsurprisingly led to an obsession (of sorts) with the physical manifestations of 'judicial control', as embodied by Lady Hale's spider brooch (later to be referenced in her autobiography, *Spiderwoman: A Life* (2022).

But when viewed from a position of 'cool theory' rather than the very 'hot rhetoric' that the decisions provoked, what do these cases suggest about the role of the judiciary in ensuring 'bridled' power, and whether the current relationship is sustainable?

First and foremost, scrutiny of these cases has fallen against a backdrop of a pre-existing debate about judicial power in the UK and across the common law world. Books such as Kate Malleson's *The New Judiciary: The Effects of Expansion and Activism* (1999) through to Jonathan Sumption's *Trials of the State: Law and the Decline of Politics* (2019) or Joshua Rozenberg's *Enemies of the People? How Judges Shape Society* (2020) – not to mention academic analyses like Rickard Ekins and Graham Gee's (2018) 'Putting Judicial Power in its Place' – have covered this debate in great detail. But what was arguably interesting and distinctive about the *Miller (No 2)* and *Miller (No 1)* cases is how they triggered a public reaction. This is a critical point. The role of the judiciary was not only politicised in a highly public manner due to the extreme salience of Brexit but also became enmeshed in a set of broad pre-existing narratives or 'folk theories' that framed the debate in a very specific manner. Central among them was the basic assumption that judicial power 'is on the rise' (see, for example, King 2009; Elliott 2017), and that the *Miller* cases were both somehow unconstitutional and therefore illegitimate and democratically dangerous. 'The Supreme Court's prorogation judgment proves that it is not just hard cases that make bad law' Richard Ekins and Stephen Laws (2019) wrote in *Prospect* magazine

> If the Court had faithfully upheld the law of the constitution, it would have ruled that UK courts had no jurisdiction to quash advice to prorogue parliament, let alone to declare that a prorogation carried out in parliament was null and of no effect. Unfortunately, the

> Court did *not* uphold the law of our constitution. The Supreme Court worked a radical change in our law, one that makes significant inroads into the political constitution.

But beyond the hyperbole do these cases really represent a significant, possibly even fundamental shift, in judicial power? The argument of this section is that such framings fail to capture the nuance and subtlety to judicial decision-making, while also failing to appreciate significant contextual factors.

First and foremost, both *Miller (No 1)* and *Miller (No 2)* demonstrated that the Supreme Court is able to provide a form of constitutional accountability. But on both occasions the provision of such accountability proved highly controversial. This is hardly surprising, as what government enjoys having its powers limited and controlled by the courts, even a government who might support increasing the 'power' of the judiciary through the enactment of a Human Rights Act 1998 (such as the first Blair Government did), can quickly grow tired of judicial scrutiny. Yet, that is not the point, the role of the judiciary is hardly irregular, or a cuckoo in the constitutional nest. Rather judicial scrutiny is a product of the incremental development of the Constitution (in the absence of a written document) with high-profile judicial scrutiny of the executive stretching back to the reign of James I of England. The judges have also been the recipients of increased statutory powers and the instructions to use these to achieve the aim of the legislation (such as the European Communities Act 1972 and mostly notably sections 3 and 4 of the Human Rights Act 1998).

However, despite the clear relationship between *Miller (No 1)* and *Miller (No 2)* in light of their broader constitutional genesis, these cases each tell a different tale in terms of accountability and the relationship between judicial, executive and parliamentary powers. *Miller (No 1)* was controversial when viewed from a contextual position as the salience of the Brexit debate was so intense, but at the same time the legal reasoning that led to the decision was fairly orthodox – more 'vanilla than thriller' to paraphrase Young (2017). The question raised in *Miller (No 1)* was *exceptional* if looked at in light of its circumstances: the first Member State to withdraw from the European Union and legal questions as to the correct constitutional procedure for achieving this (both within the UK's constitutional arrangements and within the European Union as to Article 50 itself and whether a Member State might be able to subsequently withdraw its letter triggering Article 50). *Miller (No 1)* was *unusual* if considered within the context of the Brexit referendum and unique in terms of the specific legal question being asked of the courts – not least given the peculiar nature of the UK Constitution and its own relationship with international law. And yet, in reality, the Supreme Court's use of judicial review procedure, of the treatment of prerogative powers and of the principle of parliamentary sovereignty would have aligned with expectations if such a scenario had been presented as a hypothetical situation. It is telling that the then Secretary of State for Exiting the European Union, David Davis, had himself privately decided at the time that Article 50 should be triggered by Parliament (through legislation) and not the prerogative. This is hardly surprising given Davis' parliamentary career and his views on civil liberties, but nonetheless demonstrates the plurality of opinion within the government.

Miller (No 2) was similarly controversial, but the controversies were very different. The Supreme Court played an arguably more novel and to some extent audacious role which placed its decision beyond more traditional constitutional jurisprudence. More overt, novel and potentially significant 'questions of accountability' were at play. In a way that dovetails with collaborative constitutional theory, the judiciary was stepping-in to fill an accountability gap that the legislature could not fill without its support. The subtly that was often overlooked in the subsequent outrage about the Court's decision was that the judiciary were not seeking to harvest additional powers or responsibilities for themselves, but simply to ensure that the principles and values of the political Constitution were not trammelled by unbridled executive power. The absence of a more formalised constitutional court in the UK also means that it falls to the (non-supreme) Supreme Court to come to decisions that inevitably draw it into political debates. Putting the same point slightly differently, if a political Constitution wants to maintain an appropriate level of democratic accountability, then it would have to either ensure that Parliament *does* have the capacity to scrutinise executive decisions, especially in relation to constitutional decision-making (and this has been frequently suggested by parliamentarians and academics), or the courts will be utilised as a constitutional safety net. This brings the chapter to a focus on its third and final question and to the topics of innovation and prorogation.

III. Doing Things Differently

The previous section suggested that the *Miller* cases of 2017 and 2019 (respectively) did illustrate the role of the courts in terms of militating against unbridled executive power. It also suggested that *Miller (No 2)* was constitutionally exceptional, but that it should not be interpreted in terms of judicial 'supremacy' or 'overreach', as the judgment was explicit about the rationale for the decision focusing on sustaining political and parliamentary accountability rather than judicial or legal accountability. The rationale given for protecting parliamentary sovereignty from executive overreach, that is, from denying Parliament the scope to exercise its legislative sovereignty during the extent of the prorogation, may appear strained as it moves beyond more traditional judicial protection of Parliament's legislative sovereignty, but can be justified on the basis of the judicial approach since the 1990s. The Constitution Unit rejected the decision as judicial overreach, as it argued in 2021, that the role of the courts was to '[protect] the public from the risk of exposure to arbitrary executive authority'. That the executive might not interpret the Court's decision in quite this way is arguably not surprising. Constitutional innovations often trigger counter-reactions as different constitutional actors seek to push back or augment their own positions. Constitutional politics is, when all is said and done, an arena concerning the raw distribution of power in a society. The government's reaction took the form of the commissioning of an Independent Review of Administrative Law (IRAL) in July 2020 to consider the scope of judicial review and the need for changes: 'to ensure the right balance is struck between citizen's rights and effective governance'. One key element for the review was whether 'certain executive decisions should be decided on by judges' or left in the hands of politicians.

For some commentators the IRAL – plus the Independent Human Rights Act Review of December 2020 – were examples of where the 'principal target is, in reality, alleged judicial over-reach in relation to review of discretionary power' (Craig 2021).

The IRAL may be one example of the management of judicial power through 'striking back' and 'clamping down' – to paraphrase Harlow and Rawlings (2016) – by the executive against the possibility of judicial over-reach. Just as the Supreme Court's decision in *Miller (No 2)* may itself be seen as an example of constitutional functionality and the judicial management of executive power. What this reveals is exactly the ebb-and flow or push-and-pull of not only the boundary between politics and law, but more broadly the healthy tensions that should exist within the wider accountability space or ecosystem. More provocatively, if the *Miller* cases highlight anything it is less about Brexit and more about the changing socio-political context and possibly even the existence of parallel processes of constitutionalism within the UK. With this in mind the manner in which Brexit has arguably exposed and maybe even deepened territorial tensions (increasingly see in debates about the dis-United Kingdom) is likely to ensure further challenges to the constitutional configuration, which may ultimately be placed at the door of the Supreme Court rather than the Houses of Parliament to resolve. The announcement by the Scottish First Minister in June 2022 of plans to hold a second referendum on Scottish independence (ie, indyref2) provided a case in point. The question of whether a referendum can take place without the UK Government's agreement was referred to the Supreme Court by the Lord Advocate, as it is unclear whether the Scottish Parliament can unilaterally legislate under the powers devolved to it by the Scotland Act 1998 for an independence referendum. The key insight not being the court's ultimate decision in *Reference by the Lord Advocate of devolution issues under paragraph 34 of Schedule 6 of the Scotland Act 1998*, that there was no such devolved power, but how it has once again been utilised to settle a politically salient matter concerning the legitimate use of power within a democracy. Tellingly, the outcome has been met with a positive reaction by the UK Government (as the judges can take responsibility and serve as a convenient scapegoat, and the judicial decision buttresses the position of the government), whereas the criticism of the decision has been from those who support Scottish independence.

This role of judges in settling such issues within a representative democracy could take the discussion *back* to the 'counter-majoritarian difficulty' discussed above; whereas mention of Scotland could itself take the discussion *forward* to a more detailed review of constitutional dynamics and bi-constitutional processes, due to the manner in which a consociational power-hoarding democracy has essentially been constructed *within* a highly majoritarian 'mainframe'. But in many ways both cases – whether seen as *forward* or *back* in any sense – focus attention on the simple theme of 'doing things differently'. Tellingly, there was no accusation by the UK executive (or sections of the media that have been largely supportive of the government and its conservative predecessors) of either judicial overreach or constitutional improper decision making by the Supreme Court in *Reference by the Lord Advocate*, which reinforces the view that what is seen as constitutionally proper and appropriate depends on whether you stand to lose or gain by the decision (ie, had the decision in 2022 been different, then it would have been more difficult to deny Scotland a second independence referendum).

If delegating questions concerning executive control to the judiciary is broadly viewed as a 'bad thing' in the UK (and this once again must be viewed through the subjective lens of gain and loss for the executive and other critics), then what might be done differently to bolster Parliament's control capacity and reduce judicial dependence? This is a question that must be answered by all those who are critical of 'judicial power' and the *Miller* decisions. If you do not think this role of quasi-constitutional guardian belongs to 'unelected' judges, then short of increasing Parliament's role in the appointment of the senior judiciary (which is not to be advised), then what can be done to buttress the current mechanisms in place to improve the level of scrutiny and accountability at Westminster. There is clear support for reform, as Blick and Hennessy observed '[there is] an apparent willingness of senior figures to depart from constitutional norms [which] has in turn revealed frailties in the protections against such conduct' and they are argue that 'Mr Johnson's legacy' could be the need for 'a serious look' at the Constitution (Blick and Hennessy 2022, 125, 145).

This 'bad thing' narrative does not, of course, reflect the central argument of this chapter. The position presented is that *Miller (No 2)* afforded legal protection to the political Constitution. But how might alternative and more politically orientated protections be put in place? There are, of course, may different possible responses to this question that range from relatively minor reforms to the select committee system to more macro-constitutional measures that might adjust the electoral system to make it less disproportional and, by doing so, prevent the creation of artificial governing majorities in the House of Commons. However, a rather modest change to the electoral system was rejected in a nationwide referendum in 2011, and it is difficult to see any government go-ahead with, when faced with the realities of maintaining a majority, the introduction of proportionate representation (even if they support it prior to taking power, such as Labour in September 2022). Therefore, what next? Do select committees and parliamentarians propose small reforms in the hope of gaining the support of the government and/or their peers, or should we look for something more radical?

But one option that is rarely discussed but which has strong historical precedents, as Monaghan (2022) has revealed, is that of impeachment where a legislative process is able to remove senior executive office holders for incompetence or the misuse of public office, thereby providing both an ex ante accountability deterrent and an ex post accountability process. Monaghan has proposed the reimagining of impeachment and one which places the House of Commons as a guardian of the Constitution (although the Supreme Court would be a co-guardian). Thus, MPs would have the tools to tackle executive abuse of power and become empowered (however, it is important to note Hannah White's (2022) analysis of the House of Commons, where White's account, if applied to impeachment raises issues about public confidence in MPs' ability to use this in a way that engenders trust). How this would work in the real world of Westminster politics remains to be seen. However, the potential for real deterrent and the prospect of impeachment being brought once a government has left office, would remove the safety net of the in-built majority in the House of Commons.

Finally, it is important to see that ultimately the question is who *should* guard the Constitution and are they *capable* of fulfilling this vital role. It is not simply a binary choice between caricatures of the political Constitution and legal Constitution, but rather acknowledging that we should be willing to look at empowering the actors or elements of the Constitution on whom we place these responsibilities.

8

Questions of Counsel: Accountability and Policy Advice

JONATHAN SLATER

This is a chapter written from the position of someone who has spent their professional life not studying politics or public administration, but as a professional practitioner of practical politics. This is a career that spanned local government and central government and which was, to some extent, almost defined by 'questions of accountability'. This practical experience may well explain why this chapter does not focus on a critical question – that of accountability for the policy advice given by officials to ministers, but also on a potential solution. Highlighting questions of accountability is a relatively easy endeavour, identifying workable solutions to those questions far more challenging and urgently required. There are, of course, no easy answers to complex questions; plus the manner in which public accountability processes are very often utilised as tools for party political game-playing helps ensure that defensive cultures and strategies become almost embedded into day-to-day political life. This explains the vast literature on 'blame-avoidance', 'blame games' and all the other tricks and tactics that are employed on an almost daily basis to ensure that ministers and their closest advisers remain unblemished by the failures and inefficiencies that remain rife in public service.

'How are permanent officials held to account for the quality or veracity of the policy advice they provide to elected ministers?' This is the core 'question of accountability' that this chapter engages with. In terms of situating this question within the existing research base there are three particularly important reference points. The first is the bibliometric meta-analysis conducted by Gergana Dimova, Mel Dubnick, Matthew Flinders and Chris Monaghan (2023) as part of their 'Accountability with Adjectives' project. This revealed not only a massive growth in the sheer quantity of accountability focused scholarship in recent decades, but also the emergence and existence of hundreds of accountability sub-types (ie, adjectivised accountability) as scholars had sought to grapple with the concept's chameleon qualities by focusing-down on one specific form, sector or arena. This leads us to Jonathan Fox's extensive 2022 study of 'accountability keywords' and, more specifically, his comment that this approach 'identifies accountability adjectives – and addresses some of the many different ways in which the idea is understood and *how adjectives can add precision* [emphasis added]'. Fox's study is highly relevant for the simple reason that it underlines the significance of cultural context, and even how the word 'accountability' is not easily translated into many dialects and languages. What is also interesting about Fox's broad review is that it does focus on *policy* accountability (ie, accountability for policy advice and decision-making) when, as the bibliometric analysis by Dimova, Flinders and Monaghan illustrates, this is not a topic that academic analyses have generally clustered around.

The rare exception, and therefore our third reference point, is Susan Rose-Ackerman's (2005) study of 'policy-making accountability and democratic consolidation' in which she argues that 'full democracy cannot be attained unless the policy-making process is accountable to citizens through transparent procedures that seek to incorporate public input'. The notion of 'weak policy-making accountability' is therefore developed in the context of new and transitional democratic regimes. The core argument of this chapter is that 'weak policy-making accountability' is also a feature of advanced liberal democracies and I seek to illustrate this point with reference to my experience at the top of the bureaucratic system in the UK.

In order to explore this focus on *policy-making* accountability as a very specific sub-form or process this chapter is divided into three main sections. The opening section provides a short biographical sketch of my career in order to underline how different the operating cultures tend to be between local and central government. There are, of course, issues of scale and size that might be used to explain and justify such differences, but these are, I suggest, secondary to cultural variables which service to create a gap between the governors and the governed at the national level. There is no innate need for a gap of this size to exist or be tolerated. If anything, this gap serves to insulate officials, whose job it is to provide the very best policy advice to their ministerial masters, from being held accountable for the quality or accuracy of that advice. This theme is developed in the second section but now from a solution-oriented perspective. If weak policy-making accountability is a core problem at the heart of British government, as it is in many countries around the world, then what might be done to close this 'gap'? Having outlined a number of potential reform options the third and final section returns to the linkage between politics, policy, and power. Is it realistic to expect senior officials to 'speak truth unto power' when it comes to policy-making? This is arguably the ultimate or most basic 'question of accountability' from which a host of other questions flow.

I. Distance, Divides and Disconnects

One of the most interesting and obvious shifts in the dynamics of policy-making in recent years has been an explicit shift to draw-upon and utilise different forms of knowledge. Peer-reviewed 'scientific' knowledge is therefore important as a source of evidence and insight, but so too is tacit knowledge, experiential knowledge and 'everyday' lived experience. Policy-makers should, this logic suggests, synthesise inputs from many disciplines and sources in order to generate a full understanding of the nature of the problem that a specific policy is attempting to tackle, and the full range of choices that exist within the potential reform repertoire. The great challenge, as Geoff Mulgan (2021) has skilfully revealed, is that the absorptive and synthesising capacity of governments is very often weak. Mulgan identifies the problem as an 'imbalance between inputs and digestion' and to some extent this focuses attention back on the synthesisers and knowledge-brokers who are employed to provide specialised policy-advice to ministers. In order to underline this point, it is useful to draw upon the tacit knowledge and my own everyday lived experience as I progressed from senior local government management to the top of the British civil service.

My last job before joining the civil service in 2001 was Director of Education at the London Borough of Islington. At the time there were not enough primary school pupils to sustain all of the local schools, so it was my job to advise the local politicians what to do. After considering all the options, my advice was to close the Angel primary school. Clearly this was going to be very disappointing for the staff, pupils and parents, and so it was only right that I should explain to them – personally and directly – the basis on which I had come to my view. I went to the school along with the elected councillor who chaired the Education Committee, as it was his responsibility to make the decision. Neither of us found the meeting remotely comfortable, and I still remember the unhappy pupils sitting at my feet as if it were yesterday. This was real accountability of a very direct and raw type, the local community was disappointed, confused and angry, but as the primary policy advisor I knew and accepted that it was my job to account to the local community and not seek to hide behind the anonymity of officialdom. And although this was possibly the most difficult and challenging public meeting that I had ever attended it was in no ways unique. Throughout a decade in local government senior management accounting for my actions, decisions and advice was a fairly regular and central part of my role.

The distance between local officials, local councillors and local communities was relatively small. It was hard for accountability gaps to emerge, just as it was relatively clear about the respective roles of officials (ie, advice and implementation) and local politicians (ie, decision-taking and strategic oversight). Engaging with the public – directly and without fear or favour – was, however, not simply part of the job. It was far more than that. It was through public accountability processes that I stayed in contact with the local communities that I was employed to serve. I gained an insight into the tone and texture of how different parts of the community viewed different issues and could therefore use that knowledge to build bridges, form connections and design policy that really was fit for the locality. I could also work with local communities in the design of that policy which, in turn, generally led to greater community 'buy in' and ultimately to greater policy effectiveness. I am not suggesting that local government, in general, or Islington, in particular, was a panacea for the challenges of local public service development.

It was not. Things went wrong, lessons were learned. Demand always out-stripped resources and difficult decisions had to be taken. But I am suggesting that a culture of community engagement existed and that senior officials were publicly accountable for the quality and accuracy of the policy advice they gave to politicians.

And then I arrived in Whitehall.

I thought the transition would be reasonably straightforward. Central government was, of course, much bigger than local government, with a spread of policy responsibilities I had not previously been involved with. And yet the basic model of permanent senior officials employed to advise elected politicians in relation to policy decisions seemed, at least at a structural or institutional level, much the same. This core and basic assumption proved to be almost completely wrong. The culture of officialdom has little interest in what the public actually thought about the range or standard of services being delivered. A gap existed that went way beyond the territorial and scalar difference between local and central government; it was culturally embedded to the extent that not only were officials generally disinterested in what the public thought they also lacked access to any form of data on, for example, what patients thought of the health service, pupils thought of schools or what the unemployed thought of job centres. In fact, when I used the word 'customers' most of my new colleagues looked puzzled, even though this was just a few years after the customer-focused reforms of John Major during his time as Prime Minister from 1990 to 1997. Looking back, my approach to public service was almost exactly the opposite of the dominant culture in Whitehall. For many senior civil servants there was an assumption that ministers were their 'customers' and therefore all lines of communication went up to the minister's office through the Permanent Secretary as the most senior official in the department. Many were therefore somewhat confused and crestfallen as I explained to them (repeatedly) that our customers were the public who received or benefitted from the policies we design, implement and oversee. Ministers were our masters and certainly not our customers. Such thinking was almost heretical for anyone schooled through the traditional civil service fast track structures; it also demonstrated the benefit of bringing people in from the outside and who possessed what I came to realise was a very non-traditional perspective.

This upward focus towards the minister and the machinations of political life dovetailed with a related and equally striking feature of the culture I suddenly encountered: a near obsession with 'policy' over everything else. This activity called 'policy' was the only topic people seemed able or interested in talking about. Statements were prepared, briefings written, meetings held, cross-departmental conference calls held but this vast body of activity seemed to almost exist above-and-separate to any practical emphasis on delivery. Operational issues were almost completely absent from the discussion, as were officials who had experience of actually running schools, health centres or social housing. Focusing on 'policy' was seen as the realm of senior, ambitious and future leaders of the civil service, whereas focusing on delivery or operational issues was viewed as almost second-class, certainly not second nature. Added to this was the fact that what a lot of people referred to as 'policy' was nothing of the sort. Helping ministers answer parliamentary questions, preparing ministerial visits or making sure that the media grid is populated with a sufficient number of 'announceables' has nothing to do with policy-making in any real or serious sense. If anything it is part of a hyperactive tendency towards being seen to be busy instead of actually focusing on the core business of government in a serious or sustained manner.

And then I discovered executive agencies.

They were quite different parts of the civil service – 'hived-in' (rather than 'hived-out') as business units but still formally part of the civil service and of their 'parent' department. They worked under the auspices of a published framework document and they certainly knew their customers. These were the engines of the civil service where over 95 per cent of staff were based and where the greater part of departmental budgets were actually spent. The agency chief executives did understand delivery and the operational dynamics of public service delivery. And they were as sceptical about 'policy' as I was becoming. It would at this point be possible to provide a brief history of how a 1988 report from the Prime Minister's Efficiency Unit entitled *Improving Management in Government – The Next Steps* (Jenkins, Caines and Jackson 1988) led to the creation of 'Next Steps' agencies and a debate about the implications of this process for the convention of ministerial responsibility, but all of this has been documented extensively elsewhere (see Flinders 2002; McLaughlin, Osborne and Ferlie 2002). It is sufficient for the purposes of this chapter to note that the creation of agencies was explicitly designed to inject a sharper delineation in Whitehall between 'policy' and 'operational' concerns. The idea being that the small core of policy-focused officials would exist at the centre of departments overseeing the strategic co-ordination of a vast network of delivery-focused agencies (this model of governing is referred to as the 'hub-and-spoke' model of public governance). The benefit in terms of improving management in government was that instead of focusing on policy and 'looking up' to ministers the agencies would develop specialist knowledge and 'look down' to focus on the needs of their customers.

I really got to see how this arm's-length governing logic operated in practice when I found myself working alongside the Prison Service Agency, first at the Home Office and then at the new Ministry of Justice. I was really impressed. Prison Service staff understood their core 'customers', despite the fact that as prisoners they might have been reluctant beneficiaries of the state's services. Agency staff knew which prisoners were at most risk of escaping, or of committing violence; they knew which were most likely to reoffend as soon as they finished their sentence, and which were most likely to be persuadable not to do so again. And yet there seemed to be a considerable amount of tension between the agency and their more policy-focused civil service colleagues, despite the fact that they were all formally in the same department. Furthermore, my outlook on policy-making meant that I felt naturally more inclined towards the more practical and delivery-focused emphasis of the agency than I did with the more generic interest of my colleagues in the core department. There was no doubt about what agency staff did, how they did it or why it mattered. Their social value was therefore clear. The operated operating prisons, kept prisoners safe, prevented escapes and offered as much as their resource-package allowed in terms of providing educational or rehabilitative opportunities. But what did the (higher paid) policy-focused officials in core departments actually do? Where was the demonstrable public value? How could you define their role, let along evaluate excellence in the performance of their duties?

During my time as a policy official with responsibility for prison-related matters, I advised no less than four different Secretaries of State on how best to reduce reoffending. But surely it was the Prison Service staff that possessed the most accurate understanding of such issues? Not least as 'policy' officials in departments were rotated at fairly regular intervals on the basis of some sense of building 'cross-departmental' knowledge and skills. In reality this meant that just as a senior civil servant had developed not only the specialist knowledge about an area of policy but also those high-trust informal relationships across the sector that often furnish information and insights they would be deployed to a new post and the cycle would start all over again. Policy officials came and went, agency staff stayed and learned. And yet the former rarely, if ever, utilised the latter. There is, of course, always a need for new talent, new ideas, strategic thinking and so on. But I was far from convinced that the department needed a completely separate and well-resourced policy division, full of people – like me – who knew *much less* about rehabilitation than Prison Service staff did and yet were seen as having the lead responsibility for advising ministers, and then telling the service what to do as a result. When I started asking questions about the model, I learned that it had been criticised in precisely these terms for many years, most famously in the Fulton report for Harold Wilson in 1968, which concluded:

> The Service is still essentially based on the philosophy of the amateur (or 'generalist' or 'all-rounder'). This is most evident in the Administrative Class which holds the dominant position in the Service. The ideal administrator is still too often seen as the gifted layman who, moving frequently from job to job within the Service, can take a practical view of any problem, irrespective of its subject matter, in the light of his knowledge and experience of the government machine (Cmnd.3638, p.11, para.15).
>
> There is not enough contact between the Service and the rest of the community. There is not enough awareness of how the world outside Whitehall works, how government policies will affect it (Cmnd.3638, p.12, para.19).

So far as I could see, the situation certainly didn't seem to have improved very much at all in the intervening 40 years, at least in this respect. In fact, while the Next Steps reforms had clearly improved the capability of the 'delivery' arms of the civil service as intended, I was beginning to wonder if they hadn't accidentally made the policy 'generalist' problem more acute. After all, if it's the job of the agencies to talk to their customers and to deliver, then why would policy people need to? I thought the answer to that question was easily answered with a question of its own: how can you possibly design an effective rehabilitation policy if you don't spend a lot of time with prisoners? To be fair, I learned subsequently that in some parts of government, good work had been done to encourage policymakers to collaborate with their delivery colleagues (discussed below), but Fulton's 'generalist' seems just as visible in Whitehall today as 50 years ago, and provides an excellent description of what it takes to get to the top.

Shortly after my time in the Ministry of Justice, Anthony King and Ivor Crewe published *The Blunders of Our Governments* (2014) in which they describe a long list of failures and fiascos that had occurred from broadly 1980 to 2010. Having done so, they turn to the question of why all these failures happened and I was fascinated to read their description of two key disconnects. The first was the '*cultural disconnect*' between ministers and their civil servants on the one hand, and the public on the other, by which King and Crewe meant that the former all too often failed to understand the way that the latter would actually behave when what might seem like a jolly good policy idea in Whitehall was actually rolled out. The second disconnect was *operational* and simply highlighted that policy was very often reviewed, evaluated and made without the slightest understanding of the delivery challenges that were being completely over-looked. This focus on a cultural and operational disconnect chimed almost perfectly with my experience and concerns on moving into central government. Cultural disconnects were inevitable if policymakers didn't spend their time with the customers. And operational disconnects were equally inevitable if they saw themselves as quite distinct from 'delivery' people and agencies.

As King and Crewe made clear, this is a problem for ministers as well as civil servants. I certainly have my own perspective on the former, and agree with those who have argued that the increasing trend over recent years for politicians to go straight from university to think tank to special adviser to MP to minister is making things worse. I also agree strongly with the case for much more ministerial training. But I reject the argument sometimes offered rather defensively on behalf of the civil service that it can't address its weaknesses unless ministers do so too. Or that these weaknesses are the fault of ministers. Clearly civil servants are more effective when their ministers are highly capable. But I have never seen any minister standing in the way of policymakers trying to improve their understanding of the reality on the ground. Quite the reverse, such expertise is typically welcomed.

In May 2016 I was appointed Permanent Secretary at the Department for Education and the experience only reinforced what I had already come to see as Whitehall's policymaking problem. The problems about various forms of 'disconnect' that Crewe and King had written about were so clear to be blatantly obvious (although I accept that my background and experience *beyond* central government may have made it easier for me to recognise these challenges). The department's handling of a new policy based around 'Individual Learner Accounts' provided all the evidence I needed. The basic policy idea was that adults without qualifications would be encouraged to gain them by being given money to spend on retraining. What actually happened was that the money was spent instead largely by two other groups of people. The first group already had lots of qualifications and simply fancied collecting some more at the state's expense; the second group were professional and experienced fraudsters who invented fake courses as a mechanism for fraudulently channelling the funding into their own private bank accounts. Anyone with experience of practical politics and the implementation of policies, particularly across vulnerable communities, would have picked-up on these foreseeable challenges from the first moment the idea for 'Individual Learner Accounts' was mooted. Policy makers in the Department for Education had not foreseen either of these problems until it was too late. The scheme had been launched in September 2000 but was closed with immediate effect in November 2001 due to concerns about effectiveness and particularly about large scale fraud. The Comptroller and Auditor General concluded that

> In some respects, this was a very good and innovative scheme: it was popular and encouraged many people to acquire or update much needed skills. But the speed with which the Department implemented the scheme resulted in corners being cut. Poor planning and risk management by the Department led to weaknesses in the system which made fraudulent activities possible. And the Department did not keep their eye on the quality of the learning and on the indications that a few unscrupulous providers were taking advantage of the inadequate security arrangements (see HC1235, 2002).

Cultural and operational disconnects really do matter. But so does basic business management and financial competence. The highly critical National Audit Office report of October 2002 found total expenditure on Independent Learner Accounts to be £273 million but that no business model for the policy had ever been drawn-up, no clear cost-benefit-analysis, security requirements had been overlooked and the relationship with the delivery partner (Capita) had been far too lax. As a snapshot of fairly common government policy-making and innovation the Independent Learner Account fiasco provides a perfect case study of the 'questions of accountability' that tend to swirl around British government. Always there, but rarely answered. The Public Accounts Committee published a highly critical report. The Permanent Secretary at the time of the policy, Sir David Normington, was embarrassed and apologetic about the whole affair: 'I say again to you, this is a very bad story, I am quite ashamed of it and I am quite ashamed of it on behalf of the Department. I am very sorry for it too, and we have to put it right' (HC 544, 2003, Q13). But no ministers or officials lost their job as a result of the fiasco. This is not to suggest that sacrificial responsibility should be sought on every occasion something goes wrong, but it is to suggest that the UK is generally an example of 'weak policy-making accountability', to return to Rose-Ackerman's phrase.

But have things been getting better since then? A second policy case study should help answer this question.

In 2017 I inherited from the Department for Trade and Industry (DTI) responsibility for the apprenticeships programme which was a priority policy for the then Prime Minister, Theresa May. Two teams transferred across – a 'policy' team from the DTI head office, and a 'delivery' team based in one of the agencies. As normal, the delivery team was headed by someone who was hugely knowledgeable about and committed to the subject, with strong connections across the sector, but without much experience of 'managing' ministers. And just as normal, the policy team was headed by someone without any background in the subject matter at all, but very good at working with ministers. As Permanent Secretary with overall responsibility for the effective and efficient management of the department, I decided that this was one team too many, and merged them. The challenge was that I then had to choose which official should lead the newly amalgamated team. I decided it would be a lot easier for the one with deep subject-matter expertise to learn how to communicate with ministers than for the ministerial-friendly one to learn deep subject-matter expertise, so I chose the former. I then invited the new head of the team to accompany the Secretary of State on an overseas trip as an opportunity to not only get to know the minister but also to learn how ministers think, behave and assess options. Although possibly something of a 'baptism of fire' this strategy worked well and under the selected official's leadership the apprenticeship team ensured that the department's work on the programme was well grounded in what was achievable in practice, as well as informed by a rich understanding of employers' and employees' training needs.

There is an important aside to this story, and one that illustrated the existence of a subtle but significant 'disconnect'. Shortly after merging the 'policy' team and the 'delivery' team into one integrated unit, I decided that it would be a good idea for me to meet the new team and underline the importance of apprenticeships not just for the department but for the government as a whole. For me with a background that straddled policy and delivery in equal measure the meeting was fascinating for the simple reason that the previously policy-focused staff were clearly dismayed and unhappy about joining a delivery-team. 'If I'd realised this is what you were going to do' one particularly disgruntled official told me '[then] I wouldn't have come because I wanted to do policy'. 'I thought you wanted to do apprenticeships' was my reply. Seeing policy as an end in itself was and to some extent remains precisely the problem.

My last major project before leaving the Department for Education in September 2020 was on the response to the first months of the Covid-19 pandemic. A public inquiry is the right way to try and get to the bottom of what was done well and what badly, by whom and why. But I have no doubt that it will find plenty of cultural and operational disconnects. It will presumably explore my own department's record on opening and closing schools, for example, and on providing support (or not) to those left at home, to say nothing of the exams fiasco (on the latter see Kippin and Cairney 2022). This chapter is not the right place for me to offer my own assessment of what happened and why but given the broader focus of this contribution I do think it is appropriate for me to acknowledge that during the initial stages of the Covid crisis there was a huge disconnect between the conversations that were happening in Whitehall and those that were happening on the ground in local communities. While ministers and their senior officials are quite within their rights to announce that, for example, pupils with special educational needs should continue going to school, or that primary schools should reopen to all pupils while the rest of the population are required to abide by social distancing, there is, in reality, a need for a more integrated and emotionally-attuned approach that is alert to the day-to-day challenges that people face in their lives.

With the benefit of hindsight, one of the most significant cultural disconnects of all looks to have been the difficulty that ministers and senior civil servants seem to have had in imagining how today's public would change the way they went about their daily lives in response to the threat of a deadly virus. That Exercise Cygnus, a three-day stimulation exercise carried out by the government in October 2016, had showed that a major pandemic would cause the country's health system to collapse, with a lack of medical ventilators highlighted as a core concern, is equally worrying from a basic preparedness perspective. There was also quite a lot of commentary at the beginning of the pandemic to the effect that the British people couldn't be expected to accept authoritarian demands from their government to stay home. But that was to miss the point – the ultimate cultural disconnect – that people would take action to save themselves from catching a potentially fatal illness by staying away from others wherever possible, whether the government told them to or not. And there was also no shortage of very serious operational disconnects, of which testing and personal protective equipment are only the most high-profile examples. Whereas, as Kate Bingham (see Smyth 2021) – the UK's Vaccines Tsar – has argued, the success of the UK's vaccination development programme seems to have been down in large part to operating *outside* Whitehall's constraints, the success of the rollout belongs to the NHS and the problem for the civil service has been groupthink.

There are, of course, encouraging examples of civil servants operating differently. It is also possible to identify specific phases when departments in Whitehall did try and shift the dominant culture towards something far more inclusive and engaging. Sure Start, for example, was a potentially transformational policy that connected local authorities, agencies and communities into a shared support structure. During the late 1990s and 2000s the Department for Education reached out to schools and colleges in a way it had never done before, not least because of the influx of new leadership from local government (such as Michael Bichard, Michael Barber and Peter Housden). And over the years I've worked for the civil service I've certainly seen example of civil servants at all grades who were clearly very connected to operational realities, and constantly thinking about what would work in practice but never a critical mass with the capacity to push beyond a certain tipping point and towards a very different way of 'doing' policy. I remember speaking to a hugely impressive policy director who seemed to be driving positive change. My initial positivity was to some extent dented when on talking to her I discovered the number of barriers and blockages that had been placed in front of her every move, and that she had needed to adopt a determined counter-cultural approach in order to achieve even the smallest change. The support of her permanent secretary had been crucial in allowing her to at least test new processes and methods, but she knew that such an approach would be impossible in a more traditional department or if her permanent secretary left the department.

That this extraordinary official had previously worked outside the civil service did not surprise me, but my concern is that anyone with passion, energy and a commitment to bring in new ways of working to the civil service will quickly become frustrated and disillusioned as the cultural and operational disconnects become more obvious. So tackling disconnectedness needs more than one-off examples, good intentions, individual enthusiasts and external recruits. Important though each of these are, they will never be enough without great, sustained leadership which promotes, encourages and incentivises different ways of working over the medium term. It is to this more solution-orientated emphasis that the chapter now turns.

II. Wiring It Up

This book is dedicated to the analysis of public accountability. What works, what doesn't work, and what might be done differently. This section focuses on this latter element and to how the issues concerning disconnects and weak policy-making accountability might actually be addressed. This is in itself a fairly unique contribution to the broader discussion about various 'questions of accountability' for the simple reason that academic analyses have generally adopted a *problem-orientated* approach to the topic. As a result, we know a huge amount about 'gaps', 'traps' and all the other generally negative and problematic features of modern governance that were highlighted in the opening chapter. What's generally all but absent from the existing academic knowledge base is a more *solution-orientated* approach that gets into the actual detail of how to, as it were, 'close those gaps' or 'avoid the traps'. This is not a peripheral or insignificant point. Academics have a key role to play in challenging dominant assumptions, exposing group think and contributing fresh perspectives to perennial challenges. In this sense the design-based and solution-orientated approach to political science and public administration that Gerry Stoker (2013) has advocated as a largely untraveled 'road to relevance' for those disciplines is almost certainly ripe with potential. In many ways this scientific theme takes us back to those questions of balance and proportionality that were raised in chapter one, but now from two very different angles. The first being the balance of analytical power and resources being dedicated by academe into working with practitioners to think through and address some of the relatively well-known 'questions of accountability'. In a way that mirrors the emphasis of the senior civil service on policy instead of implementation, a similar argument could be made that too many academics focus 'up' on questions of high 'theory' instead of focusing 'down' on more applied questions of applied service delivery and inter-institutional co-ordination. The second (and related) issue of balance and proportionality brings us back to a core focus on policy-making accountability and shifting from the current weak emphasis to something not only slightly stronger but also possibly more systematic (hence the use of 'Wiring It Up' as the title of this section).

In terms of achieving this shift there are three main elements that this section seeks to promote.

1. *Leadership* – An emphasis on determined leadership from the administrative apex;
2. *Incentives* – An emphasis on how incentives shape behaviour; and
3. *Visibility* – An emphasis on public accountability for policy.

It is, of course, only possible to briefly introduce the relevance and role of each of these three dimensions – *leadership, incentives* and *visibility* – within this section but the argument is that when taken together as part of a broader integrated approach these dimensions would serve to deliver effective policy accountability, with insights and implications that may be of interest far beyond the UK.

A. Leadership

Leadership from the top has been essential for changing the way the civil service works in the past and is needed today to challenge its established culture of remoteness. I have seen at first hand the impact that a determined and self-aware head of the civil service can have. When Sir Gus O'Donnell (now Lord) became Cabinet Secretary and Head of the Civil Service in 2005 I was based in the Delivery Unit within the No.10 Policy Unit. What really struck me was when he gave an introductory talk in which he emphasised the importance of four 'Ps' – *pace, passion, pride* and *professionalism*. I was very struck by the first two Ps in particular for the simple reason that whatever the UK civil service was famous for it certainly wasn't speed, and it prided itself on being *dis*passionate. But O'Donnell wanted something different, and it wasn't just words. I remember an email from the new Cabinet Secretary in which he asked me to write to every permanent secretary in Whitehall about new plans to undertake departmental capability reviews (for a review of this initiative see HC 123, 2009). The tone and style of the email was striking: I was to ensure the memo had gone out to all departments by the end of that week for the simple reason that pace was more important than perfection. Or, to put the same point slightly differently, if new plans, policies and initiatives were crafted to the point of some sense of perfection then in all likelihood very little, if anything, would actually be done. But *perfection before pace* had until that point almost defined civil services ways of thinking and working.

More than anything else, Gus O'Donnell tackled the absence of collaborative leadership head-on. We saw it in the way he modelled his leadership of the top team, working in partnership with senior colleagues, and with the support of expert coaching, something which might previously have been seen as a sign of weakness rather than the strength it clearly was. We also saw it in the way he worked with the next tier down – bringing the most senior 200 civil servants together regularly to lead and work together. It wasn't just internal either – a major part of the argument was that people needed to work together across silos if they were going to meet the needs of the public, whose issues typically don't fit neatly within individual departments' boundaries. So, he sent us out to the frontline too. A few of my senior colleagues were, of course, dismissive of such attempts to foster an understanding of what academics often label 'street level bureaucracy'. 'What are we doing at a job centre in Hounslow of all places?', I remember one exclaiming, thereby providing an almost perfect example of the dominant administrative culture. But whether they liked it or not, with clear and direct leadership coming from the Cabinet Secretary a shift in the expectations around culture and what mattered was clear.

It was also clear in relation to the tangible changes that Gus O'Donnell brought in relation to tackling male dominance at the top of the civil service. Slowly but surely, the proportion of female permanent secretaries rose to 50 per cent. Or to take another example, it was O'Donnell who pushed the civil service to add behavioural economics to its armoury – in essence, the importance of thinking about why people behave as they do, and what would it take for them to change these behaviours. Interestingly, O'Donnell didn't have any more operational experience than his predecessors or successors before becoming Cabinet Secretary. What he did have, however, was a huge amount of self-awareness, and the confidence to reach out for help and support when it was needed. His reform agenda for the civil service clearly needed ministerial approval and this was something he was able to not only achieve but to sustain which, in turn, shows what clear and consistent leadership can achieve itself *if* the willingness to change is there.

A similarly comprehensive and determined approach could be really effective in tackling the systemic challenge of cultural and operational disconnects. So long as it confronts the reality of why these disconnects exist head-on, rather than – as so often in the past – papers over the cracks. The unintended consequences of constant staff movement (ie, the 'churn problem' as it is generally described) needs to be addressed, but progress will only be made if leaders tackle the cause of the problem, not its symptom. There have been many attempts to tackle the 'churn' of Whitehall's policymakers: civil servants who, as Lord Fulton argued over 50 years ago, move from job to job far too quickly. And indeed, reducing churn would make an important contribution to tackling disconnects, as the longer you stay in post, the better you understand your subject matter. But excessive churn is a symptom of the service's disconnectedness from delivery and the public, not its cause. If your success as a policymaker is measured in large part by your ability to help ministers with short-term fixes, then you are going to want to have as many of these opportunities as possible, working for as many ministers as possible, and churn will be inevitable. Hence a problem described in 1968 by Fulton as follows:

> It cannot make for the efficient despatch of public business when key men rarely stay in one job longer than two or three years before being moved to some other post, often in a very different area of government activity (Cmnd 3638, 1968, para,16, 11).

This issue has actually become *more* significant since the late 1960s, as Tom Sasse and Emma Norris from the Institute for Government illustrated in 2019:

> In six departments, a new minister will find four in ten of their senior officials have been in post less than a year … Such brevity in role compares poorly with other civil services around the world and equivalent private sector organisations (12).

Critically, they point out that:

> [O]fficials think that promotion prospects are enhanced by acquiring generalist policy skills and gaining experience of working in a variety of high-profile roles on Ministerial priorities … Mid-ranking policy officials told us that they are strongly encouraged by managers to move on after 18 months in a job and get experience in a range of roles (36).

Excessive churn creates an accountability gap or trap that is very rarely acknowledged let alone addressed. The rapid turnover of staff creates and reinforces weak policy accountability as no official takes clear and personal responsibility for seeing a policy from inception through to delivery and evaluation. What might be termed the 'policy baton' is generally passed through the hands of many officials with the result that the development of a personal and professional sense of clear and visible ownership of that policy is rare. This contributes to the blurred or 'fluid' accountability that has already been discussed in several chapters. Adherents to the core foundations of the British Constitution might respond that the convention of ministerial responsibility ensures that such concerns regarding opacity and fuzziness cannot occur: the minister is always responsible. Although quaint, adherence to such constitutional fictions serves us poorly. Ministers may well be accountable for everything that happens within the auspices of their department, but they are rarely *responsible* in the sense of willing to take the blame for errors or omissions. At the same time officials can use the very same convention as what David Judge (1993) has termed 'an accountability shield' to shelter behind the protection of their minister and, in all but the most extreme circumstances, avoid having to take personal responsibility for failure. Excessive churn can be tackled successfully, officials do not have to move around at anywhere near the current frequency, and the system seems almost designed to ensure weak policy accountability. Appointing officials to posts on the basis that they will stick with the policy from design, roll-out and evaluation would address many of these 'questions' and help address the disconnect that currently exists.

It would, however, be wrong to think that the cultural disconnect and the operational disconnect can be addressed purely through stability in post. Solutions in the public sector are rarely, if ever, that simple and the root of the issue in relation to the civil service arguably goes far deeper and to a basic lack of diversity. Despite the achievements of a raft of recent initiatives and investments, the lack of diversity amongst the senior civil service remains as problematic as it is multi-dimensional. From class and ethnicity, through to sexual identity and where you grew up, the lack of diversity amongst policy makers sustains a powerful cultural disconnectedness. Put very simply, we are much less likely to understand the concerns of people very different from us, and if most of us are very similar to each other, we are much more likely to fall into the 'groupthink' trap. I have seen no shortage of plans to improve things, and indeed I worked hard on this myself at the Department for Education. I was proud of our success in promoting many more black and Asian staff into senior roles. But I remember the department's first non-white director general saying that, despite this progress, he was confident that he wouldn't have reached this level of seniority if he hadn't been to the 'right' university and spoken with the 'right' accent.

The Social Mobility Commission analysed this issue extensively in their 2021 report *Navigating the Labyrinth* and concluded that 'the proportion of senior civil servants from high socio-economic backgrounds is higher today than in 1967 (although this partially reflects the widespread expansion of professional and managerial jobs since the 1960s)'. After interviewing a large number of civil servants at different grades and with different backgrounds, they coined the phrase 'studied neutrality' to describe a 'cross-cutting and unwritten behavioural code that underpins notions of "merit" in … prestigious professions like policy, and within the Senior Civil Service'. Returning to the explicit leadership style of Gus O'Donnell as Cabinet Secretary it's interesting that 'passion' *was* one of his key watchwords, the very opposite of 'studied neutrality'. The report describes 'studied neutrality' as:

> [I]incorporat[ing] a particular received pronunciation accent and style of speech, an emotionally detached and understated self-presentation, and an intellectual orientation to culture and politics … synonymous with an advantaged background. In contrast, regional accents are cast as impinging on this embodiment of neutrality, with those from working class backgrounds frequently reporting 'feeling misread as aggressive, loud or too passionate' (60).

Transforming the diversity of the policy profession can only be done successfully if we reject the primacy of 'emotional detachment' and 'an intellectual orientation to culture and politics'. And what is emotional detachment if not a cultural disconnect? Likewise, intellectual orientation equals operational disconnect. Tackling these disconnects will improve diversity; leaving them in place will prevent things from changing, however hard we might try. At its most straightforward, people 'not like us' will be rejected. But once recruited those individuals from a wide range of backgrounds also need to find themselves in a professional environment where the incentives are aligned to deliver clear and coherent policy accountability.

B. Incentives

The previous sub-section argued that leadership matters, and the main argument of this sub-section is that incentives matter. At present there is no real or explicit incentive, let alone requirement, to have worked in an operational or delivery-focused role as you progress through the ranks of the senior civil service. But there is no reason why such a requirement could not be introduced as part of a future-focused talent management strategy. Just as academics are increasingly expected, and in some cases required, to gain experience in non-academic but research-related environments so too might civil servants. Anyone applying for promotion to the post of policy director general (the most senior policymaker in each department) would, under this proposal, must have developed a strong sense of operational realities by spending time in customer-facing delivery roles that have required them to have engaged actively and regularly with the public. Traditional skills in terms of managing ministers would also be required but the critical point is that policy skills and operational experience should not be seen as in any way incompatible. One of the benefits of the creation of 'Next Steps' agencies (discussed above) is that there are lots of opportunities for officials to gain operational experience without having to leave the civil service.

There are also examples of positive leadership within the civil service to draw upon. When Robert Devereux became permanent secretary of the Department of Work and Pensions (DWP) in 2011, he inherited a silo-based departmental model. I had taken part in the DWP's first Capability Review in 2006, and we were struck by the way in which each of its agencies – responsible for benefits, pensions, child maintenance, etc – operated very much at arm's-length. We concluded:

> Strong individual leadership does not consistently lead to strong collective role modelling – Executive Team members were described [by staff] as a group of chief executives and the team as a holding company with low visibility. Unless the centre, agencies and stakeholders work as well together as they should, quality, accuracy, customer service and value for money will suffer.

Devereux took a very deliberate decision to bring the agencies into the heart of the department and through this forged far closer links, inter-relationships and mutual understanding between policy and operational specialists. The shift in culture and agility was far-reaching. A new policy idea could be developed in the department and tested in practice within a matter of days.

Devereux also saw the opportunity to develop the careers of his senior people in ways which would enable them to grow a combination of policy and delivery skills. The career of John-Paul Marks is a good example as he is now Director General (Work and Health Services) in the DWP with responsibility for over 60,000 staff and service delivery to around 10 million people. And yet Marks had begun his career within a very traditional, policy-focused, fast-stream framework as speechwriter for the Chief Secretary to the Treasury and then Principal Private Secretary to the Secretary of State for Work and Pensions. What Devereux identified was the need for Marks to broaden his skills and experience through gaining senior operational experience, and then through leadership of large change projects. All of this has enabled Marks to understand organisational leadership and delivery from ministerial, strategic and frontline perspectives and due to this combination of skills play a leading role in shaping and delivering key policies during

Covid. (Marks was appointed Permanent Secretary to the Scottish Government in January 2022). This is precisely the sort of career development that should be pursued right across the civil service. And in both directions, of course – enabling people with strong delivery skills to improve their understanding of policy, just as much as the other way round.

It's easier to organise for those departments like the DWP which manage both policy and delivery, rather than those, like the Department of Health and Social Care, which don't deliver services themselves. Arranging three-year secondments between the civil service and the NHS or local government is more difficult than switching people between different jobs in the same department. But it can and, I suggest, must be done if the civil service is going to really tackle disconnectedness and improve policy accountability. Making this a reality also requires a more thoughtful approach to open, external recruitment than is sometimes demonstrated. Clearly there is a lot of benefit in testing the market when filling a post (and I am a beneficiary of that myself!). But there is also a lot of benefit in developing the careers of civil servants so that they become more effective. So we should avoid the 'self-evident truth' that open recruitment is *always* the right thing to do. As Elinor Ostrom (2000) argued, herself a Nobel Prize winning economist, just because something is widely believed does not make it true.

In this regard my own experience within the Department for Education was revealing. The Department for Education I joined in May 2016 was very much policy-focused in a fairly traditional manner, despite the great raft of managerialist and market-led reforms that had been implemented throughout the 1990s. This may be a slight exaggeration, but my sense was that the department had resisted embracing any clear reform agenda and 'normal service' had been resumed. Most of the more reform-minded officials who had been appointed during the last decade had, possibly due to a combination of frustration and exhaustion, certainly left the department by the time I arrived. The department's main arm's-length agency was the Education Funding Agency which managed a budget of over £54 billion a year to support all state-provided education for children aged 3–16. The 'arm' in the arm's-length relationship was very long: its chief executive didn't even report to the permanent secretary. And while there was a 'school immersion' programme to help policy officials understand the day-to-day realities of running a school, liaising with parents, caring for vulnerable children, etc, take-up was not great and the experience was hardly immersive (just three days in total, with one day spent alongside a pupil, teacher and headteacher). Contrast this rather tokenistic experience with Germany where collaboration between national, regional and local government is viewed as so important that they have their own phrase for communities of professionals working together in their service area: *vertikale fachbrüderschaften* (or, loosely translated, 'vertical fraternity').

During my time at the Department for Education I led a collective effort to put a focus on delivery back at the heart of the department. From April 2017 the Education Funding Agency was merged with the Skills Funding Agency to form the Education and Skills Funding Agency which was far more embedded within departmental strategic thinking. Capacity was developed in regional offices, and connections were made to bring staff based outside of London into policy planning and discussions. A cultural change initiative was also launched that put the notion of the 'service user' at the core of everything that happened in the department; and in order to show clear leadership and commitment from the top I attended every induction programme for new staff. Visibility was in this sense a key element of aligning a new culture with a new incentives system. I'm certainly not going to argue that things had been transformed by the time I left the Department for Education in August 2020, and it's self-evident that we really struggled in our efforts to deal with the huge impacts of the pandemic. But progress was made in terms of addressing some of the profound disconnects mentioned above, a degree of positive momentum for change had been established. Morale in the department was higher than in any other Whitehall department, as measured by the annual People Survey, when the Prime Minister announced that there was 'a need for fresh leadership' in the department and I subsequently tendered my resignation.

But the key insight from my experience in Whitehall is that the civil service can change if it chooses to. The key ingredients are: (i) strong, determined, consistent messages from the top downwards that this is the top priority; and (ii) rewarding people who act accordingly, and not those who don't. And the beauty of this approach is that, once you start, it's a self-improving system. The people who get promoted are the ones with the necessary leadership skills, and they in turn promote people with those skills themselves. The government's announcement of a shift towards 'capability-based' pay as part of its wide-ranging Declaration on Government Reform of July 2021 could, in theory, further align incentives with delivery-focused behaviour. The key issue will be how 'capability' is defined and measured and the degree to which the traditional 'upwards' focus on policy is balanced against a more robust and future-focused emphasis on collaborative partnerships, customers and effective implementation. 'It cannot be beyond the wit of the civil service' as Margaret Hodge (2016, 353), herself a longstanding chair of the Public Accounts Committee in the House of Commons 'to devise a career progression ladder with appropriate financial rewards and opportunities for promotion that encourages all civil servants to develop expertise and to stay to see jobs through to their conclusion.' But if officials 'develop expertise' and 'stay to see job through to their conclusion' then a corollary of this process would be a tightening of policy accountability and increased visibility.

C. Visibility

Christopher Hood and his colleagues have developed the notion of a 'new' public service bargain (see, Hood and Lodge 2006). The 'old' public service bargain in this framing revolved around elements such as a job for life, good working conditions, excellent pension arrangements, possibly some form of public honour towards the end of a career and – crucially – anonymity from public criticism and rebuke should things go wrong. The notion of the anonymous bureaucrat working very much 'off stage' to fulfil the wishes of their ministerial masters is, to all intent and purposes, part of the mythology of the British Constitution. But it also has very real and practical implications; the most obvious of which are arguably the rules that define what civil servants can and cannot discuss in front of select committees (known as the Osmotherly Rules). The rules are designed to protect the constitutional position of the civil servant, while also conveniently giving ministers the capacity to control exactly how much information (and about what) a select committee can obtain. Hood's work on the 'new' public service bargain underlines how much has changed, especially for the senior civil service. Permanent employment has very often been replaced by time-limited contracts, moderate pay in some cases replaced by very high levels of remuneration and – critically – the principle of anonymity has to some extent been replaced with an expectation that if things go wrong it will be the lead official rather than the responsible minister who appears in front of the media to explain what went wrong.

This is all broadly accurate and it manages to capture a general pattern of change in fairly broad and accurate terms. But one thing I would say based on my own experience is that the 'new' public service bargain is generally reserved to those officials who lead large and complex executive agencies or arm's-length bodies. Back in the core or hub of departments the 'old' public service bargain is generally still in force and a key element of this is weak policy accountability. It is therefore moving to a 'new' civil service bargain involving clear and visible policy accountability that this sub-section is principally concerned. Putting the same point slightly differently, policy-focused officials will only take responsibility for their role when they are truly connected to the public and feel personally accountable to them. The problem is that the current arrangements are broken: there is no effective accountability for policymaking in practice. The current accountability theory is simple. Ministers account to Parliament, and civil servants account to their ministers. Which means that ministers are supposed to ensure that Parliament is apprised of the facts (accounting to MPs), and to take the credit and blame when policies turn out well or badly (being held to account by them). Civil servants are supposed to ensure that ministers are apprised of the facts (truth to power), but simply to explain their minister's view to Parliament when asked (certainly not offering their own perspective, as to do so would challenge the democratic authority of ministers). They don't take the credit, and are supposed to be shielded from the blame by their minister, who is supposed to rely on civil service management to take disciplinary action if needed.

In practice the theory is corrupted by the irrationalities of partisan politics. This was laid bare by the Scott Report into the 'arms to Iraq' affair in 1996. This is an episode that has been recounted and analysed many times over – 'put under the Scott-light' to paraphrase Thompson and Ridley (1997) – and there is little to be gained from presenting a detailed discussion. What does merit highlighting, however, is the final report's conclusion that governments

> do not submit with enthusiasm to the restraints of accountability … governments are little disposed to volunteer information that may expose them to criticism. The enforcement of accountability depends largely on the ability of Parliament to prise information from governments which are inclined to be defensively secretive where they are most vulnerable to challenge.

As the Commons Liaison Committee in the House of Commons, which consists of all select committee chairs, suggested in its November 2012 report on select committee effectiveness: 'the old doctrine of ministerial accountability … is being stretched to implausibility by the complexity of modern government' (HC 911, 2013, para 114). The argument here is that the 'old doctrine' would be far more plausible if senior civil servants were held to account for the content and quality of the policy advice they gave to ministers by select committees. The notion, however, of connecting policy advice *into* the general framework of parliamentary and public accountability forces us to acknowledge the basic linkage between politics, policy and power.

III. Speaking Truth to Power

There is a political dimension to this chapter's argument about strengthening policy accountability. Political in the 'small 'p' non-partisan sense, but political no less. The benefit of moving from weak to strong policy accountability is not just about ensuring that the specific quality and veracity of that advice is as accurate as it can be, but also in a very different but related manner that the thrust of the advice is, where necessary, challenging ministerial assumptions. The role of the civil service, possibly even part of the 'old' public service bargain that was protected by tenure, has always been to *question and to serve*. But how realistic is it to expect officials to 'speak truth to power', especially in the context of a shift towards a more aggressive form of populist politics? The fact that an individual has progressed to high political office and been appointed a Secretary of State generally belies a fairly strong and determined character. Some ministers enjoy being challenged and relish the opportunity to be pushed and tested when it comes to policy projects, while others see even the merest suggestion of the need to pause for thought as nothing less than treachery. I would not want to overstate this point, but I have seen a number of hard-working, experienced colleagues pushed-out of their jobs as a result of a ministerial meeting that didn't go according to plan.

'The truth is that it is difficult to speak frankly to people in power' Martin Stanley (2021, 7–8) observes correctly 'Many powerful people aren't interested in detail. Experts are indispensable but annoying … no-one likes truly honest feedback.' As a former senior civil servant in the Cabinet Office with experience of working across the regulatory landscape and business community he goes on to note that 'ministers find it harder than people in the private sector to understand or accept challenging advice (18)'. There are undeniably civil servants who rise to the challenge with great expertise; who understand that most ministers actually do want to hear the truth, even if unpalatable. And who have learned how to give it without causing offence, recognising that their approach will need to change according to the tastes of the particular minister they are communicating with. But this skill and confidence is the exception rather than the rule: most civil servants don't take the risk. That they prefer studied neutrality (even with each other, hence groupthink).

It's not that most ministers want to be talked to like this; in fact, they often interpret it as a lack of commitment of the civil service in delivering for them. I remember Justine Greening receiving some written advice when she was Minister for Education (2016–18) telling her she could do either (a) or (b), depending on her preference. Her perfectly reasonable response was to get her private office to ask for the civil servant's view as to which of the two options would better achieve the outcome she sought. To which the response she got was that 'it depends on the minister's steer'. In other words, the civil servant felt quite unable to offer a view even when explicitly asked for one by a minister. I also remember Damian Hinds as Secretary of State for Education (2018–19) going out of his way in meeting after meeting with his civil servants to reinforce the importance of them treating his initial comments not as injunctions to be followed at all costs, but simply as a contribution to the discussion, when the objective was to get as many ideas out onto the table as possible. He did this very well, but it was striking that he needed to say it over and over again.

And I remember induction meetings of new civil servants, when I would explain that it was our job to offer advice without fear or favour – that this was literally what we got paid for. More often than not, I would be asked if that's really what ministers wanted. Wouldn't it be safer simply to give them the advice we thought they wanted? And this from people who'd only just arrived in the department. My reply was partly that none of the ministers I'd worked for had indicated an unwillingness to listen, so long as we understood that it was their right to decide otherwise. Which of course it is. And partly that the law actually requires civil servants to be objective, impartial and honest, ever since the civil service code was written into legislation through the Constitutional Reform and Governance Act 2010. Leadership to support a more dynamic and engaging culture was a very important part of my job as permanent secretary. On arrival in the Department of Education and speaking to senior officials I was struck by what seemed an almost complete lack of organisational confidence. And yet, having the confidence to say what you think, not just to ministers but to your colleagues as well, is absolutely vital if the civil service is going to avoid groupthink. When something goes wrong, it is almost always the case that someone knew it would, but didn't have the confidence to speak up, because they (rightly) feared what might happen to them if they did.

One of the most important attributes of good leadership is promoting a culture which rewards the inconvenient truth, rather than – as is much more typical, certainly in Whitehall – finding such contributions rather embarrassing and to be avoided at nearly all costs. I soon had the opportunity to demonstrate my own commitment to speaking truth to power in the most public of ways. Ministers were committed to developing a completely new post-16 curriculum with a set of new qualifications, assessment system, funding regime and so on – to be called 'T-levels'. They wanted them introduced in three years, significantly less time than it had taken the department to revise A-levels earlier in the decade. Permanent secretaries have been required since 2011 to seek a 'ministerial direction' on grounds of 'feasibility' if they are asked to do something 'where there is a significant doubt about whether [it] can be implemented … to the intended timetable' (for a review of their historical use see Institute for Government 2022). This basically involves the Secretary of State signing a letter in which they acknowledge the advice they have been given and accept the related risks. The minister is essentially taking personal responsibility against the advice of their officials in a very public manner (the letter is shared with the Public Accounts Committee in order to underline the minister's clear responsibility). I had hoped that by requiring a 'ministerial direction' I might encourage both my Secretary of State and the Prime Minister to reflect upon their plans and extend the implementation timetable but in the event this was not to be the case and ministers were clearly within their rights to make this decision. The direction was duly published on the 24 May 2018 and the Secretary of State noted that 'I appreciate the advice I have received about the delivery timetable and have considered this in detail. I recognise your reasons for requesting a ministerial direction and how they align with your responsibilities as the Accounting Officer for DfE' before concluding that in his opinion 'None of the advice has indicated that teaching from 2020 cannot be achieved' and that 'I know that you will now, in the best traditions of the Civil Service, work at all speed to deliver this top Government priority.'

Due process had been followed. Clear and strong policy accountability had been achieved. It was also a small symbolic victory for the department in the sense that my colleagues had seen that I really was committed to 'speaking truth to power'. Certainly during my four years in the department from 2016–19 the proportion of staff who indicated they felt that they worked in an environment where it was safe to challenge others increased from 46 to 61 per cent. Such statistics must always be taken with a large dose of salt, but my sense is that a small but significant shift in the culture of the department had been achieved. But whatever the case the simple fact remains that for a civil servant it is less risky *not* to speak 'truth to power' than to do so; and that emotional detachment, 'under-statedness' and other similar traditional Whitehall idiosyncrasies, as identified so well by the Social Mobility Commission (discussed above), are seen as techniques of self-preservation, of avoiding the risk of disapproval or worse. This is simply not a recipe for good or effective governance. A new model of accountability is needed, opening up the secret world of policymaking. What's more, international experience in other Westminster-style democracies suggests that strong policy accountability is compatible with the UK's constitutional configuration, with New Zealand being the most obvious example of where almost all reports and policy briefings to ministers are published as soon as decisions are made (see Craft and Halligan 2020).

With the emphasis of earlier chapters on issues of measurement, balance, proportionality and 'sweet spots' it's interesting that a debate has emerged in New Zealand as to whether the balance towards strong policy accountability has shifted too far. In 2012 Richard Mulgan opened a roundtable event on 'free and frank advice' in New Zealand with the argument that 'This situation requires a revisiting of the official information legislation.'

> In the adversarial Westminster system there is a strong case for confidentiality in respect of politically sensitive meta-advice. This is a contentious issue. In Australia, recent statutory changes have ruled out political embarrassment for the government as an acceptable reason for withholding disclosure of documents. On the other hand, United Kingdom legislation enables the withholding of 'free and frank exchange of views for the purposes of deliberation' (Freedom of Information Act 2000, s 36 2(b)). The question is 'where to draw the line' (11).

If the line might have moved too far in New Zealand then the central argument of this chapter is that the policy accountability line has not shifted at all and that a new balance needs to be found. The role of permanent secretaries as departmental accounting officers directly accountable to Parliament through the Public Accounts Committee suggests that forms of direct accountability can be operationalised. The personal responsibility that permanent secretaries assume for financial matters also acts as a strong motivation to not only provide 'free and frank' advice to ministers (for some reason always termed 'frank and fearless' in Australia), but also to request a formal ministerial direction when that advice is not followed. Placing policy advice (and in this case its rejection) in the clear light of day is a strong example of positive policy accountability in action. It is very hard, if not impossible, for any minister to try and shift the blame when things go wrong when they have very publicly rejected the advice and warnings of their most senior official. So if permanent secretaries' advice on matters of 'value for money' and financial management are put into the open air in these circumstances, why not on broader matters of policy? Might this not encourage the civil service to speak a bit more 'truth to power'?

The Osmotherly rules (mentioned above) currently provide a key barrier or blockage in strengthening policy accountability. They state that civil servants 'providing evidence to Select Committees do so under Ministerial agreement and instruction' and 'as representatives of their Ministers' (Cabinet Office, 2014, 11). The impact being that officials will generally refuse to answer questions about policy (advice, options, discussions, accuracy, etc) and defer any questions with the stock response, 'That is a matter for the minister.' Discretion is therefore preferred to confrontation but a focus on policy accountability highlights that the existence of clear and transparent evidence and discussion about the information and advice given to ministers would aid good governance. It would reflect the existence of a mature and confident democracy. It is also worth highlighting that the Osmotherly rules have never been formally approved by Parliament. They were a creation of the executive and only came to public attention following the publication of the Procedure Committee report of 1977–78 which recommended the creation of departmental select committees (see HC 588, 1978, paras 7.12–7.16). The rules have evolved into a defensive convention, and one that has been the focus of reform commitments. In 1984, for example, the then leaders of the main opposition parties (Labour, Liberals and SDP) pledged to reform the rules (see Horne 2015). In 1990 the Procedure Committee in the House of Commons reviewed the rules and concluded 'at the risk of accusations of defeatism' that they should not be reformed (see HC19, 1989). Lord St John of Fawlsey, who was leader of the House when the system of 'new' departmental select committees was introduced in 1979, would later describe this conclusion as 'extremely feeble' (see Horne 2015).

It would at this point be possible to highlight the absurdity of public inquiries being able to ask officials about the policy advice they provided while select committees accept deflection, or the extent to which ministers will tie themselves in knots rather than engage in an open discussion about the extent and nature of the policy advice and evidence underpinning their decisions. But the key concluding point it is necessary to underline takes the discussion back to a theme that has now surfaced in a number of preceding chapters and is captured in the notion of 'the trap'. As Monaghan and Welsh (above) note,

> [T]his 'trap' reflects the manner in which reforms that are intended to enable scrutiny and shift the balance of power away from the executive must generally be supported by the executive that they seek to bind or disempower. Few executives are going to voluntarily cede power, strengthen the opposition or make the business of government harder.

This 'trap' has clear implications in terms of strengthening policy accountability for the simple reason that few ministers will want the full rationale for their policy-decisions laid bare, especially when it departs from the official advice or available evidence. And yet that is exactly why shifting the balance would help improve both the quality of democracy and the effectiveness of policy.

Interestingly enough, such a proposal is not without historical precedent. In 1976 the then Prime Minister, James Callaghan, directed Sir Douglas Allen (Cabinet Secretary 1974 –78) to publish more explanatory material and the background advice on which policy decisions had been taken. The Prime Minister announced this shift to the House of Commons on 24 November 1976 by stating,

> [T]he practice of publishing Green Papers will continue, for appropriate subjects, but in addition the question has been raised about what other information can be made available. When the Government make major policy studies, it will be our policy in future to publish as much as possible of the factual and analytical material which is used as the background to these studies.

Although published and the focus of much discussion, the Croham directive was essentially nullified by the content of the Osmotherly Rules just four years later.

But what it does suggest is that change can occur; and to some extent the evolution of the 'new' select committee system over the last 40 years is testament to how much evolutionary change can achieve.

It is in exactly this context that this chapter has raised a set of questions concerning strengthening policy accountability. More importantly, it has proposed a number of solutions to close both the cultural and operational disconnects that too often blight effective public policy design and implementation. These challenges are not particularly unique to the UK but it could be argued that recent concerns about the behaviour of the government, the extent of recent policy failures and the rejection of long-standing constitutional conventions by the executive (see chapter fifteen in this volume) may have opened a 'window of opportunity' within which the case for strengthening policy accountability might be made with fresh vigour.

9

Enforcing the Conventions of Constitutional Monarchy

ROBERT BLACKBURN

Traditionally it has been thought rude to contemplate the idea that a Monarch might ever behave badly and break a rule of constitutional conduct. In fact, one of the problems generally in understanding the law and conventions of the Monarchy today is the legal and political fictions perpetuated by the ceremonial flummery and obsequiousness of communications or forms of address and official descriptions of the Monarch's role and importance in matters of state. So, this chapter addresses a question that is normally unthinkable and indeed is hardly anywhere dealt with in our works of constitutional law: what would happen if a Monarch refused or was unwilling to act in accordance with one of the fundamental conventions of the Constitution?

As well as being of academic interest, this question may be of practical relevance at Westminster with some useful lessons to be drawn, not only on the regulation of royal affairs generally but on the nature of some of the more archaic and unresolved aspects of UK constitutional law. Queen Elizabeth II throughout her long reign was a model constitutional Monarch, strictly complying with ministerial advice and her constitutional duties, and avoiding public controversy and personal involvement in matters of state. However, many politicians and sections of the media have been concerned in recent years that a politically more active Monarch in the new reign could pose dangers to the integrity of our parliamentary democracy and jeopardise the stability of the Monarchy itself.

Conventions are famously of special importance in the regulation of UK politics and government generally, in the absence of a written Constitution, but this is especially so in the case of the Monarchy. This is because they serve to make sense of and modernise what would otherwise be hopelessly out of date laws, whether of a common law or statutory nature. The legal theory of the Monarchy is that its occupants possess great powers of state, collectively known as the royal prerogatives (Blackburn 2022). In today's democratic practice these are routinely exercised on the advice of elected ministers who are then politically accountable to Parliament, or they are performed upon the basis of established conventions.

There are a number of classic expositions on the enforcement of conventions in our academic literature. An early analysis was provided by Albert Dicey at Oxford University in 1885, who more than anyone committed the expression 'conventions' into our modern constitutional law vocabulary as, 'understandings, habits or practices which, though they may regulate the conduct of the several members of the sovereign power … are not in reality laws at all since they are not enforced by the courts' (Dicey 1985, 24; see also Freeman 1872, 109–10 and Marshall 1984). He then went on to argue that conventions are obeyed because, if not, their violation would lead to a breach of the law, citing in support the convention that Parliaments must assemble at least once a year, because otherwise the raising of most taxation and the existence of the armed forces would become unlawful since the necessary parliamentary consents, after the Bill of Rights 1689, have only ever been granted on an annual basis (see Dicey 1985, ch XV and Blackburn 1990, ch 1). However that is virtually the only example that can be given to support his thesis. Later, Ivor Jennings at the London School of Economics provided a clearer analysis of the situation, observing that conventions are followed because of the political difficulties which arise if they are not, and that in reality there is little difference in nature or substance between laws and conventions of the Constitution because both require the acquiescence of our rulers in their recognition, obedience, and enforcement (Jennings 1959, 117 and 134).

Even if conventions were principles of the common law, they could not be enforced through the courts against a Monarch, since it is an ancient common law maxim that 'the King can do no wrong'. Monarchs today remain personally immune from all suits and actions, either civil or criminal, and no legal remedy can be ordered or enforced against them (Halsbury's Laws of England 2019, [56]–[57]). The truth is, therefore, that any serious breach of convention by a Monarch, or the solution to a Monarch being unable to fulfil the constitutional duties expected of them, would of necessity be dealt with politically.

This chapter selects four case studies on the outcome or remedy where a Monarch fails to comply with of a fundamental convention and constitutional duty relating to their work as royal Head of State. The first is on the customary duty to summon Parliaments into existence, where the royal convention is crystal clear to the point of it being inconceivable today that a violation would ever take place.[1] This is still a question worth exploring for what it tells us about the unreal and antiquated state of UK constitutional law at its apex.

The second relates to Royal Assent where the Monarch's signature authorising the passage of Bills into law is by convention performed routinely on ministerial advice. However, from the perspective of the individual on the throne the question

[1] It is worth recalling that five centuries ago the government of King Charles I tried to rule permanently without Parliaments (the 'eleven years' tyranny', 1629–1640) before being compelled to call one out of financial necessity; and five years ago the government of then Prime Minister Boris Johnson tried to terminate parliamentary business and legislative action on Brexit by way of a prorogation of Parliament, ruled unlawful by the Supreme Court in *R (on the application of Miller) v The Prime Minister*.

arises, what is the situation where the duty to give formal approval to the legislation would violate their beliefs and conscience as a human being? This problem could arise, and has done elsewhere (see below), simply because there is no documentary authority that convincingly detaches their private personality from the public act of Assent, as this writer believes there should be.

The third case study raises the question of the removal of a Monarch who is considered by the Prime Minister and Cabinet, taking parliamentary and public opinion into account, to be unsuitable for continuing to hold the office of royal Head of State. This important element of accountability arises, as it has done in the past, for reasons of moral incapacity[2] or an unwillingness to comply with the conventions and public duties of constitutional Monarchy expected of them. In terms of moral incapacity, earlier precedents being James II in 1688 for his religious views that were regarded as incompatible with the protestant settlement, and Edward VIII in 1936 for his determination to marry someone who was twice divorced that was regarded as incompatible with the social and religious norms of the day especially as Head of the Church of England.

The fourth case study selected addresses the role and duty of the Monarch to remove from office a Prime Minister who is acting in violation of one of the core constitutional conditions upon which they hold office. Under the UK's unwritten Constitution, the existence and tenure of the office of Prime Minister is a matter of de facto political practice, with no legal terms that might be enforced by the Supreme Court. As things stand, there is simply no alternative legal mechanism to the Monarch, even Parliament unless it was able to legislate an Act of Attainder, to legally terminate a Prime Minister's tenure of office.

In a final section, some reflections for the future are given, including on possible new methods by which the duties and conventions of constitutional Monarchy might be given greater clarity, force, and legitimacy.

I. Case Study 1: The Duty to Summon Parliaments

It is a fundamental convention of the democratic era that the Monarch will exercise their prerogative power of summoning a new Parliament into existence simultaneously with the legal dissolution of the existing Parliament.

In 2015 for example, Parliament dissolved on 30 March 2015 automatically under the terms of the Fixed-term Parliaments Act 2011, and the form of the Monarch's proclamation summoning a new Parliament the same day was as follows, its language indicating the ceremonial style and nature of this process.

[2] Earlier precedents being James II in 1688 for his religious views that were regarded as incompatible with the protestant settlement, and Edward VIII in 1936 for his determination to marry someone who was twice divorced that was regarded as incompatible with the social and religious norms of the day especially as Head of the Church of England.

> Whereas We, by and with the advice of Our Privy Council, being desirous and resolved, as soon as may be, to meet Our People, and to have their Advice in Parliament, do publish this, Our Royal Proclamation, and do hereby make known to all Our loving Subjects Our Royal Will and Pleasure to call a new Parliament to be holden at Westminster on Monday the eighteenth day of May next … Given at Our Court at Buckingham Palace, this thirtieth day of March in the Year of our Lord two thousand and fifteen and in the sixty-fourth year of Our Reign.

The proclamation triggers the statutory machinery under the Representation of the People Act 1983 for election writs to be sent out for holding a general election.

The same automaticity of calling the newly elected Parliament on the same day as dissolution applied at the two more recent general elections of 2017 (held under the early election procedure in the Fixed-term Parliaments Act section 2(1)–(2)), and 2019 (held under the authority of the Early Parliamentary Election Act 2019).

Today, following the Dissolution and Calling of Parliament Act 2022 that repeals the Fixed-term Parliaments Act 2011, the pre-existing royal prerogative power of dissolution is restored and revived enabling a Prime Minister to call a general election whenever they like within a five-year maximum timeframe. The earlier constitutional practice is therefore also revived in that the royal acts of dissolution and summoning of Parliaments are to be declared in the same royal proclamation. I make no comment here on the erratic policy making of the Conservative Party in office towards its legislation on such an important political and constitutional matter (for the author's views on the law, politics, and reform of general election timing, see Blackburn 1995, ch 2).

Thus in 2010, the last time dissolution and summoning of Parliaments occurred simultaneously under the royal prerogative, the Queen's proclamation was set out as follows:

> Whereas We have thought fit, by and with the advice of Our Privy Council, to dissolve this present Parliament, which stands prorogued to Tuesday, the twentieth day of April: We do, for that End, publish this Our Royal Proclamation, and do hereby dissolve the said Parliament accordingly … And We being desirous and resolved, as soon as may be, to meet Our People, and to have their Advice in Parliament, do hereby make known to all Our loving Subjects Our Royal Will and Pleasure to call a new Parliament … to be duly returned to, and give their Attendance in, Our said Parliament on Tuesday, the eighteenth day of May next … Given at Our Court at Windsor Castle, this twelfth day of April in the Year of our Lord two thousand and ten and in the fifty-ninth year of Our Reign.

However, in strict law as laid down in the Meeting of Parliament Act 1694, formerly known as the third Triennial Act, there is no legal requirement for the Monarch to summon a new Parliament until *three years* after the dissolution of its predecessor. According to its section 1, still in force, 'From henceforth a Parliament shall bee [sic] holden once in Three years att [sic] the least.' So in practice this legal provision is qualified by the important royal convention of modern times for simultaneity, the essential purpose of which is to maintain Parliament in a state of virtual continuous existence. Ideally, in the writer's view, UK constitutional law should be codified in a written Constitution with a provision that Parliament is kept in permanent existence, providing for a recess during election campaigns after which newly elected Members take up the seats of those they have displaced. (See Blackburn 2015. The author was Special Counsel to the House of Commons Political and Constitutional Reform Committee for its inquiry into a written UK Constitution, *A New Magna Carta?* (2014–15) HC 463).

As things stand, if a Monarch ever refused to follow modern convention and summon a Parliament to meet following a dissolution, there would be no legal means to force or compel them to do so. The situation would be treated differently in public law if the Monarch was acting automatically on prime ministerial advice, rather than personally (see *Miller No.2* and the Dissolution and Calling of Parliaments Act 2022, section 3, on non-justiciability of the revived prerogative powers, discussed below). As stated above, Monarchs are personally immune from legal process and enforcement by the courts. And there is no alternative machinery laid down in the Triennial Act or any other legislation to provide for a delinquent Monarch refusing to do their constitutional duty. When the 1694 Act was passed and subsequently, it has simply been thought a discourtesy to imagine such a state of affairs.

Earlier in the seventeenth century when there was huge distrust of Charles I, a first Triennial Act in 1641 (later repealed by a second Triennial Act 1664 that removed the default machinery) did empower other officials to summon Parliament in default of the Monarch failing to do so after three years. This provided for the very real possibility at that time that Charles might fail to do so, following on from the 'eleven years tyranny' of 1629 to 1640 when no Parliament was called. The cast-iron default machinery laid down was for any of the Lord Chancellor or the Lord Keeper of the Great Seal or any Commissioner for the keeping of the Great Seal to issue the necessary writs for attendance; but if they failed to do so, then any 12 peers of the realm should do so under their own seals; then if they failed to do so, the Sheriffs of each country, city and borough were required to hold elections as if such writs had been issued; and the bottom line was for the ordinary freeholds and citizens to proceed to the election of their representatives in the usual manner. Today, such alternative machinery could be re-introduced but minimal, with a statutory provision authorising the Lord Chancellor (Justice Secretary) or other designated government minister to perform the legal acts required in default of the delinquent Monarch.

However, in the absence of this there would be no other recourse than a resort to legal fiction and Parliament to convene itself into existence. This is precisely what occurred in 1688 after the enforced abdication and exile of King James II. Parliament simply assembled de factor and then retrospectively legitimised its actions under William and Mary once they had assumed the throne in response to Parliament's invitation (Crown and Recognition Act 1689).

II. Case Study 2: Royal Assent to Government Legislation

It is an essential element of the legislative process that the Monarch by convention will give their Royal Assent to a government Bill that has duly passed both Houses of Parliament, or the Commons alone if the terms of the Parliament Acts 1911 and 1949 are fulfilled.

The ceremonial act of Royal Assent is part of an elaborate process of formal communications starting with the Clerk of the Parliaments giving notice of Bills that have, or are shortly expected to have, passed both Houses to the Head of the Crown Office who prepares the standard form of Letters Patent with the titles of Bills set out in an attached schedule. This document is delivered, with a covering memorandum of the Lord Chancellor in the customary Red Boxes, to the Monarch wherever they happen to be for simple signature. Notification of Assent is given to each House of Parliament by their Speaker (under the Royal Assent Act 1967), or at the winding up of a session by the Lords Commissioners prior to prorogation.

If the Monarch ever refused to perform this legal ceremony in the face of government insistence to do so,[3] there would be no legal remedy against them. As with the case of a refusal to summon a Parliament into existence, there would be no alternative methods or officials to legitimise the legislation if the Monarch simply refused to give Assent, and there could be no recourse to the Supreme Court for a declaration or injunction because of the Monarch's immunity from legal process.

However, where a Monarch felt incapable of divorcing his personal fundamental beliefs from his duty to give Assent to a Bill – in other words, their objection to the legislation was clearly of an individual rather than political nature – it is possible that a sympathetic and supportive Prime Minister could find resolution of the crisis in the Regency Act 1937. This Act provides for a Regency where the Monarch cannot perform the royal functions due to infirmity of mind or body or is under 18 years.[4] Then in section 2 an additional ground is stated, which is where 'the Sovereign is for some definite cause not available for the performance

[3] This article does not address the different situation where there may be conflicting views between the government and Parliament on whether a Private Member's Bill should receive Royal Assent. In such a situation, which could have arisen in the 2017–19 Brexit Parliament, the convention for royal conduct was not universally agreed upon: see Letters to the Editor, *The Times*, 3–5 April 2019; R Blackburn, 'The Politics of Parliamentary Procedure Revisited' in Blackburn (ed) *Essays in Honour of Emeritus Professor Kostas Mavrias* (Athens, Sakkoulas, 2022) 277–307.

[4] This Act, amended in 1953, provides a permanent statutory system for regencies. It was passed early in the reign of George VI to avoid repetition of the incapacitating illnesses suffered by his father, George V in his final years, frequently too incapacitated even to put his signature to state papers. Earlier Regencies, such as that of the Prince Regent (later George IV) in 1811–20 were created in each case by an ad hoc Act of Parliament. See R Blackburn, 'The Royal Assent to Legislation and a Monarch's Fundamental Human Rights' [2003] *Public Law* 205–10.

of those functions'. This 'non-availability' section has always been unclear and was deliberately drafted to be an avenue left open for unforeseen future eventualities.[5]

In my view, it could therefore be argued that the Human Rights Act 1998, which provides under section 3 that 'so far as it is possible to do so' all statutory provisions 'must be read and given effect in a way which is compatible with' the articles of the European Convention on Human Rights, might facilitate the wording of the Regency Act to be construed broadly enough to encompass non-availability of the Monarch on grounds of fundamental belief and conscience. Under the Regency Acts, the decision on this would be made not by a court but by a panel of three senior establishment figures, drawn from an eligible pool that includes a Cabinet minister (Lord Chancellor), the Lord Chief Justice, the Master of the Rolls, the Speaker of the House of Commons, and the spouse of the Monarch. Regardless of this procedure being non-judicial in character, the panel's reasoning and decision could nonetheless draw support from the principles of the Human Rights Act.

This would not be the first time the Human Rights Act has come to the rescue of a senior member of the Royal Family. In 2005 a supportive government relied on the Human Rights Act to enable King Charles, then Prince of Wales, to resolve an apparent legal impediment to his marriage to Mrs Parker Bowles, now Queen Consort. Their problem was that, because adultery was known to have contributed to their earlier divorces, they were precluded under church rules from a church wedding; but so far as a registry office wedding was concerned, under the Marriage Acts 1836 and 1949 that provided for civil marriages, members of the Royal Family were excluded (see Cretney 2007, 159–164).The crisis was resolved by the Lord Chancellor declaring in a written parliamentary statement that, while there were differing views on the Marriage Act exclusion, in the government's opinion since the Human Rights Act protected the fundamental right to marry and for such right to be enjoyed without discrimination on grounds of 'birth or other status', it was 'beyond doubt' that 'the modern meaning' of the Act enabled the Prince and Mrs Parker Bowles to conduct a civil marriage, which they proceeded to do.[6]

A close analogy can be drawn with the case of the late King Baudouin of Belgium who found himself confronted with a government Bill whose content went against his religious beliefs. In 1990 the King wrote a letter to the Prime Minister informing them of his refusal to give Assent to their abortion law reform Bill on grounds of conscience. Out of respect for the King, the government proceeded to rely on an

[5] When the clause in the Regency Bill was presented to the House of Commons for approval, the then Home Secretary Sir John Simon offered two examples of what might constitute non-availability, being where the Monarch was taken prisoner of war or was shipwrecked when abroad; but he went on to emphasise that the reason for including the broad phrase about non-availability in the legislation rather than attempting to list all the different kinds of event which could give rise to a Regency was to create some flexibility to provide for future circumstances: *House of Commons Debates*, March 1, 1937, cols 107–11.

[6] House of Lords Debates, 24 February 2005, cols WS87–88.

article in the Belgian Constitution providing for situations 'where the King finds himself unable to reign'. Under the procedure agreed, King Baudouin abdicated in response to which the two Houses of Parliament created a Council of Ministers to adopt the royal powers and sign the Bill enabling it to pass into law (Articles 93 and 90 respectively). Two days later, the assembled Houses recognised that Baudouin's 'inability to reign' had terminated and his position as King was restored.

It is important to emphasise that this procedure for a temporary Regency to resolve such a crisis in the UK would require the support and 'advice' of the government of the day. The Prime Minister would need to form a judgement on the matter, no doubt taking parliamentary and public opinion into account. If the Monarch's objection could not be seen as a serious or fundamental matter of conscience, but was on a matter of policy and administration on which the Monarch was attempting to sway public opinion, or if it was the second or third occasion on which the Monarch had claimed a right of refusal on grounds of conscience, the outcome and form of enforcement would need to be an abdication.

As with the royal prerogative of calling Parliaments, the present legal and constitutional position on Royal Assent is archaic and would benefit from some form of agreed codification and clarification. Some solutions are offered in the final section on modernisation and reform below.

III. Case Study 3: Duty of Compliance with Ministerial Advice

A third type of situation, serving as an illustration and precedent on the enforcement of the conventions of constitutional Monarchy, draws on an actual precedent of abdication in our modern history, that of King Edward VIII in 1936.

In this case, the King wished to marry a divorcee, Mrs Wallis Simpson, who had two former husbands still alive. This was a proposition that the then Prime Minister Stanley Baldwin, as well as the unanimous Cabinet, Archbishop of Canterbury, and heads of government in the Dominions, all firmly regarded as being incompatible with a Monarch's public role and function. Special exception was expressed by Baldwin to the idea of Mrs Simpson becoming and taking the title of Queen. In his, and the political and religious establishments' view, irreparable damage would be done to the Monarchy performing its role as a symbol of the nation's values, especially as Head of the Church of England.

In several personal meetings, Edward was advised by Baldwin that if he wished to go ahead with the marriage, this would be in violation of the constitutional expectations of a Monarch and the conventions of royal conduct. He requested the King to relinquish his intention to marry Mrs Simpson, rejecting any suggested compromises such as a morganatic marriage, and making it clear that if this was not complied with, then abdication was the only solution (for a full account see Blackburn 2016).

The procedures followed by Baldwin for the dispatch of the King were masterly. It was of course vitally important for him personally to secure Edward's acquiescence, since if the ministerial advice on abdication was rejected by the King it could have been politically lethal to Baldwin's own political survival. He would have felt obliged to resign at a time when a 'King's party' was being discussed at Westminster, with Winston Churchill a friend and strong supporter of the King.

The submission of formal constitutional advice by the Prime Minister, and its acceptance by the King, came in an exchange of letters on Wednesday 9 December. The first, from Baldwin to Edward, was in the form of a Minute of the Cabinet meeting in the morning, offering a Prayer that the King's intention was not irrevocable, thus avoiding the wording of blunt instruction to abdicate if he continued to maintain his wish to marry Mrs Simpson.[7] The predictable response from Edward was simply to state, 'The King has received the Prime Minister's letter of the 9th December, 1936, informing him of the views of the Cabinet. His Majesty has given the matter his further consideration but regrets that he is unable to alter his decision.'[8]

This letter for the Prime Minister was signed together with a second document that was given to Edward for signature for giving his formal approval to the necessary legislation to remove him from the throne. Edward's memoirs state that this document was a second 'letter' for the Prime Minister, by which he was referring to the Letters Patent signed by a Monarch authorising the Royal Assent to be pronounced in the House of Lords once the Bill for abdication had completed all its parliamentary stages. This was therefore a unique constitutional moment, securing the Royal Assent to legislation that would remove the reigning Monarch from the throne, signed and authorised by the Monarch even before the Bill itself had been introduced and given its First Reading in Parliament. It provided the legal guarantee for ministers that there could be no turning back or second thoughts by the King from then onwards.

The royal abdication was put into effect by an Instrument of Abdication signed by Edward, attached as a schedule to an Act of Parliament, entitled His Majesty's Declaration of Abdication Act 1936, referring to itself as 'An Act to give effect to His Majesty's declaration of abdication.' His brother Albert, next in line to the throne, instantly became King George VI, the late Queen's father, taking the name George to buttress the image of Monarchy as the model of moral and family rectitude their father before them had served. The terminology in the statute was as follows.

> Preamble: Whereas His Majesty by His Royal Message of the tenth day of December in this present year has been pleased to declare that He is irrevocably determined to renounce the Throne for Himself and His descendants, and has for that purpose executed the Instrument of Abdication set out in the Schedule to this Act, and has signified His desire that effect thereto should be given immediately …

[7] For the text of the letter see House of Commons Debates, 10 December 1936, col 2185.

[8] Duke of Windsor, *A King's Story* (1951) 403; House of Commons Debates, 10 December 1936, col 2185.

> Section 1: Immediately upon the Royal Assent being signified to this Act the Instrument of Abdication executed by His present Majesty on the tenth day of December, nineteen hundred and thirty-six … shall have effect, and thereupon His Majesty shall cease to be King and there shall be a demise of the Crown, and accordingly the member of the Royal Family then next in succession to the Throne shall succeed thereto and to all the rights, privileges, and dignities thereunto belonging.

Constitutional advice to a reigning Monarch to abdicate may arise in any situation where the Prime Minister and Cabinet have decided that the individual on the throne is incapable of fulfilling the role and expectations of a modern royal Head of State. This could be for a perceived moral failure as with Edward VIII, or the breach of a clear established convention such as the examples given above on the summoning of Parliament and giving royal assent. It would also arise of course if the Monarch abandoned the doctrine of ministerial responsibility altogether. This would include a scenario where the Monarch is temperamentally driven to 'make a difference' on certain public policy issues that drives them to ignore ministerial requests to refrain, openly criticise ministerial decisions, or even worse support or lead a campaign in opposition to government policy.

As things stand therefore, compliance with a fundamental royal convention and function by a Monarch is enforced primarily through the workings of politics, not law. Ultimately, if a Monarch refuses to acquiesce in prime ministerial advice, they will be required to abdicate. If, unlike Edward VIII, a Monarch refused to accept the advice of the Prime Minister and Cabinet to abdicate, the Prime Minister and their government would almost certainly resign. Then even if the opposition party were willing to assuming office in their place as a minority government, a general election would be precipitated very soon with the central issue of the election campaign being the actions of that Monarch and in all probability the continuing existence of the Monarchy itself.

Any enforced abdication or abolition of the Monarchy would then finally have to be dealt with by de facto political events. The government and Parliament may need to resort to legal fictions similar to those in 1688 following the enforced abdication of James II and enactment of the Bill of Rights by the Convention Parliament, as mentioned above. Subsequently it would almost certainly lead to the creation of a written Constitution as the new legal basis of the Constitution in place of the Crown.

A Monarch stepping out of line with convention, challenging the government, or rejecting prime ministerial advice on their performance of a royal duty or exercise of legal power of state, may seem far-fetched in the context of Queen Elizabeth's 70 years on the throne. We have been accustomed to the stability provided by the late Queen, especially as her reign encompassed the entire lifetime of the great majority of people living today, who therefore associate her personally with the institution of Monarchy itself. She was consistently a model of constitutional self-restraint and detachment from the political process. However, this is no guarantee that her hereditary successors starting with King Charles III will follow a similar political and constitutional pattern of behaviour.

Furthermore, if the years since 2016 have taught us anything about today's world, it is to expect the unexpected.

IV. Case Study 4: Duty to Dismiss a Delinquent Prime Minister

Some complexities remain, however. The most vexed area of royal conventions relates to the situation where a Monarch must follow and give force to a convention that overrides prime ministerial advice or has required a Prime Minister to resign but they have failed to do so.

Thus, what is the situation where a Prime Minister fails to respond to a motion of no confidence in the government passed by the House of Commons? By convention – the most fundamental one of all in the Westminster system of parliamentary government – such a resolution automatically imposes a constitutional duty on the Prime Minister to ask the Monarch for a dissolution of Parliament and general election, or else tender their resignation allowing the Leader of the Opposition to be appointed in their place. The last occasion such a motion was carried was in 1979, tabled by Margaret Thatcher who was then Opposition Leader, and it compelled the Prime Minister James Callaghan to duly call an election (that he lost).

> Mr James Callaghan [Prime Minister]: Mr Speaker, now that the House has declared itself, we shall take our case to the country. Tomorrow I shall propose to Her Majesty that Parliament be dissolved as soon as essential business can be cleared up, and then I shall announce as soon as may be – and that will be as soon as possible – the date of Dissolution, the date of the election and the date of meeting of the new Parliament.
>
> Mrs Margaret Thatcher [Leader of the Opposition]: As the Government no longer have authority to carry on business without the agreement of the Opposition, I make it quite clear that we shall facilitate any business which requires the agreement of the opposition so that the Dissolution can take place at the very earliest opportunity and the uncertainty ended.[9]

Non-compliance with this convention has never occurred in the democratic era. But if it did, an associated royal convention may be said to exist that the Monarch is duty bound to dismiss the Prime Minister and appoint the Leader of the Opposition in their place. The irresistible logic supporting this convention is that the Monarch is the only legal means by which the constitutional effect of a parliamentary resolution of no confidence can be enforced. There is no law on the office of Prime Minister that the courts can enforce, since its existence is itself a mere convention and creature of de factor political practice.

There is some analogy with, and lessons to be learnt from, the situation in the *Miller No. 2* case, where the then Prime Minister Boris Johnson acted unlawfully in advising Queen Elizabeth to prorogue Parliament to prevent further debate

[9] House of Commons Debates, 28 March 1979, cols 589–90.

or legislative action over Brexit in the House of Commons. In this situation, the Monarch chose to act in accordance with the doctrine of ministerial responsibility, wisely and correctly, because the precedents in the democratic era (and therefore convention to rebut the Prime Minister's advice) were none.[10] It was left to private individuals challenging the prorogation by way of judicial review in the courts for the Supreme Court to declare the Prime Minister's actions unlawful and so enforce its unconstitutionality.

To prevent such judicial enforcement of unconstitutionality in the future over the even greater issue of the dissolution of Parliament, Boris Johnson had a section inserted in the subsequent Calling and Dissolution of Parliament Act 2022 that any decision by a Prime Minister to terminate Parliament altogether cannot be the subject of judicial review proceedings. Whether or not that ouster clause would be effective in the courts over such a profound constitutional matter is doubtful,[11] but especially for those who believe it could be, this leaves the Palace as the last resort to deal with a delinquent Prime Minister.

During passage of the legislation, this was usefully pointed out and discussed by the former Cabinet Secretary, Robin (Lord) Butler.

> Under the Bill, Dissolution is not something done by Parliament; like Prorogation, it is something done by the Executive to Parliament. Parliament does not authorise it or have any role in it. If the Executive misuse their power, in my view the exercise of that power should be subject to review by the courts.
>
> But in this case, as has already been pointed out, there is an even more fundamental objection. Let us suppose that the Government do misuse the prerogative power in some way. All commentators agree that, at least in theory, such a situation could happen. What protection would exist if the courts cannot intervene?
>
> There is only one source of protection in that circumstance: the sovereign. The sovereign would have to refuse the Prime Minister's request for Dissolution. That would require the sovereign to do what everyone agrees she should be protected from doing: intervening in party politics, and in the most contentious of circumstances.
>
> If it is necessary to have protection against the Prime Minister's abuse of the power in this Bill, in my view it should be provided either by Parliament or the courts, not by the sovereign.[12]

[10] In 1997 it was widely suspected that prorogation was manipulated for political purposes, to suppress publication of a report from the Committee on Standards that would be embarrassing to the government, by being called over a week before dissolution prior to the general election, when the practice since 1974 had been that a prorogation and dissolution takes place on the same day.

[11] Ministers during parliamentary passage of the legislation sought to justify its ouster clause by arguing it was simply codifying a pre-existing principle of administrative law that the exercise of certain prerogative powers including dissolution was outside the jurisdiction of the courts, citing the case of *Council of Civil Service Unions v Minister for the Civil Service*. This was disingenuous, as over the course of the subsequent 37 years the Supreme Court progressively developed its jurisdiction over prerogative powers, culminating in the *Miller No. 2* case in 2019. As the leading commentator Joshua Rozenberg KC has written, 'Will this be sufficient to protect a Prime Minister against another legal challenge? I wouldn't count on it. Judges have a habit of getting round so-called "ouster clauses" if they think a decision-maker has acted unlawfully' ('Unfixing Parliament', *The Critic*, January/February 2021).

[12] House of Lords Debates, 30 November 2021, col 1296.

So how could, and under present arrangements should, the Monarch act if and when a Prime Minister ever sought to unconstitutionally exploit their power over dissolution? To answer this question, one needs to be clear on the very limited circumstances in which the normal rules of ministerial responsibility, in other words royal compliance with ministerial advice, could be set aside.

This could be, first, where a Prime Minister has lost their authority to govern following a no confidence motion, yet fails to resign or call an election, as referred to above. Second, it could be where a Prime Minister has lost a general election, in the sense that the opposition party has won an overall majority of seats in the House of Commons, but fails to resign and requests a second dissolution. The same applies if the election produces a hung Parliament (no overall majority for any single party) and the Prime Minister remains in office but at the meeting of the new Parliament is defeated on an amendment to the Address expressing no confidence in the government (this was the situation in 1923, causing the Conservative Stanley Baldwin to resign and the Leader of the Opposition Labour's Ramsay MacDonald to be appointed Prime Minister). It is in these scenarios, if the Prime Minister fails to resign and/or requests a second dissolution and general election, that the Monarch would be the only form of enforcement of the fundamental constitutional convention that the Prime Minister must resign. The Monarch would be duty bound to dismiss the Prime Minister and send for the Leader of the Opposition.

Before taking such unprecedented action in the modern democratic era, a Monarch would be wise to cloak themself with parliamentary authority. Procedurally the Monarch could await, or request from the House of Commons, a resolution in the form of a Humble Address to the King requesting he dismiss the Prime Minister from office and appoint the Leader of the Opposition in their place. If the Prime Minister is seeking a dissolution, the message to the King should request that he reject such advice until the new Prime Minister was appointed.

V. Modernising the Chain of Accountability

To better deal with such political crises and enhance the accountability and democratic integrity of the role of the Monarchy, some options could be usefully considered in the new reign of King Charles III, possibly initiated by the Palace and himself.

One would be to remove any pretence that the Monarch as a hereditary office holder possesses the democratic legitimacy to act on their own initiative. A Royal Council might be created, a formal body of six of so persons to guide the Monarch exercising their legal prerogative powers in times of controversy, especially when any question of the constitutionality of a Prime Minister's advice or tenure of office is in issue. This body could operate as a committee of the Privy Council, as Jonathan (Lord) Sumption, the former Supreme Court Justice, has advocated

(Sumption 2019 and 2022). Suitable members selected might be senior government officeholders, such as former Prime Ministers or Cabinet members, current or former senior Palace officials, and current or recent senior judicial officeholders. They could be selected by a process of Palace nomination approved by the government and opposition parties in Parliament. This would then formalise and replace the existing de facto group of advisers who in practice Queen Elizabeth turned to at times of political tension or crisis, known as the 'Warlocks'. In Elizabeth's final years, this informal body included her Private Secretary Sir Edward Young and his predecessors Lord Christopher Geidt, Lord Robin Janvrin, Lord Robert Fellowes, and Sir William Heseltine.

At the same time or independently, a Conference on Royal Affairs might be convened to provide written agreement across the establishment on the principles upon which the Monarch performs their constitutional duties and exercises their prerogative powers. This could include senior representatives from the Palace officials, government and opposition parties, Parliament, and judiciary. The advantage of such a conference would be to agree and where necessary replace any lingering uncertainties or disputed limits of the conventions on the royal powers – which have been encouraged in academe by exponents of out of time theories of 'personal prerogatives' and misconceived doctrines on 'reserve powers' (the leading proponents are Brazier 1999 and Twomey 2019; for a critique see Blackburn (2004) and (2022)) – by ones written down and agreed upon. For example, its report could declare that the constitutional basis on which the Monarch will exercise the Royal Assent to government Bills is limited to one of certification of due process,[13] devoid of personal involvement. It could recognise the force of a Humble Address from the House of Commons that a delinquent Prime Minister should be removed from office following a No Confidence resolution, in circumstances described above. As a modernising process, this Conference would have some analogy with the 1930 Imperial Conference on UK relations with the dominions of its former Empire, settling and declaring the conventions that harmonised their political relationships.

A more radical change would be to codify the royal prerogative powers in legislation, as has been proposed inside and outside Parliament for many years, to provide a much clearer line of accountability to Parliament (see House of Commons Public Administration Committee 2003–04). Such reform could be carried out on an individual basis, dealing with each royal prerogative power in turn, or collectively in a Crown Prerogative Powers Bill. The royal power of dissolution had been codified in the Fixed-term Parliaments Act 2011[14] but,

[13] Special provision could be agreed by the Conference for Private Members' Bills passed by both Houses to which the government objected, a contentious issue for the royal role: see J King, 'Can Royal Assent to a Bill be withheld if so advised by Ministers?', *UK Const. Law Blog*, 5 April 2019.

[14] The statutory framework adopted for the 2011 Act was ill-thought out and at odds with the model and recommendations of the writer: see R Blackburn, *The Electoral System in Britain* (London, Macmillan, 1995) ch 2; R Blackburn, 'The Government's Voting and Parliamentary Reform Proposals: Fixed-term Parliaments Bill', House of Commons Political and Constitutional Reform Committee, *Fixed-term Parliaments Bill*, HC (2010–12) 436, 58–63.

as mentioned above, now stands repealed by the Dissolution and Calling of Parliaments Act 2022. A provision that a Prime Minister's request to the Monarch for a dissolution should be confirmed in advance by a House of Commons resolution had been proposed during passage of the repealing Bill, including by this writer,[15] but was rejected by the government. This is to be regretted, as it would have removed any question of royal involvement, as well as giving the House of Commons control over its own existence.

Similarly, an individual Act of Parliament could codify the de facto office of Prime Minister whose existence is based on pure custom and convention. This could then provide for the tenure as well as powers of a Prime Minister, including provisions for their grounds for appointment and dismissal.[16] As matters of law rather than convention, these would then be enforced by the Supreme Court. The more ambitious solution, advocated by Gordon Brown when in office as Prime Minister,[17] and inquired into at length in a recent parliamentary report,[18] would be to codify the position of the Monarchy and with it the royal prerogatives within a written UK Constitution (Blackburn 2015).

The Crown, a broader concept in law than the institution of the Monarchy (Sunkin and Payne 1999), poses considerable problems in terms of democratic accountability in UK constitutional law, extending beyond the prerogative powers possessed by the royal Head of State to executive power in the hands of elected politicians in government. These problems exist simply because so many and such a wide range of powers remain based on ancient common law theories about the Crown as an autocratic authority. As a former Prime Minister of New Zealand has commented, in making the case for a republican constitution in his country,

> Looked at in terms of a rational distribution of governmental powers, the monarchy is a source of confusion and doubt. It is an opaque obstacle to understanding the ways the powers of government are exercised and by whom. Essentially, the Crown is a mask the Government puts on to disguise itself when it wants. It functions as a barrier to explaining to people how our democracy works and what the limits on power are (Palmer and Butler 2018, 58).

The same is equally true in Britain.

[15] R Blackburn, 'The Fixed-term Parliaments Act 2011: Retain, Repeal or Reform?', written evidence, House of Lords Constitution Committee, A Question of Confidence? The Fixed-term Parliaments Act 2011, 2019–21, HL 121; and Private Letter to Cabinet Office, 10 June 2020.

[16] For a legislative model published as a Private Member's Bill, see Prime Minister (Office, Role and Functions) Bill, HC (2001–02) 60.

[17] 'I personally favour a written constitution. I recognise that this change would represent a historic shift in our constitutional arrangements, so any such proposals will be subject to wide public debate and the drafting of such a constitution should ultimately be a matter for the widest possible consultation with the British people themselves': *House of Commons Debates*, 10 June 2009, col 798; see also *Governance of Britain*, Cm. 7071 (2007).

[18] House of Commons Political and Constitutional Reform Committee, *A New Magna Carta?* (2014–15) HC 463; the author served as Special Counsel for the inquiry.

10

Accountability, Human Rights and Beyond: Lessons from Social Security Law

ALISON YOUNG

Too much, or too little? Too much of the wrong kind? Ex ante or ex post? Hard or soft? Clarity or complexity? Upwards or downwards, horizontal or diagonal? As all of the chapters have in their own way demonstrated, significant 'questions of accountability' abound in a great number of contexts. But there are also common themes and issues, debates and discussions that appear to reach across and connect very different contexts or precise policy problems. Central amongst this connective tissue or intellectual scaffolding would be an awareness of the 'over-supply but under-performance puzzle' and an emphasis on balance, blends and proportionality. These are themes that this chapter explores through a focus on human rights legislation and social security entitlements in the UK. In doing so it explores a complex 'accountability space' containing mutually inter-dependent actors operating within a politically salient policy context. Public accountability therefore to some extent fuels or sustains forms of political and legal accountability and it is in revealing the existence of subtle relationships, intricate interactions and modes of mutual recognition that this chapter is primarily concerned.

This matters because at first glance the congested and inter-woven existence of mutual accountability processes and actors – spanning different governing levels and drawing-upon both statutory and non-statutory foundations – might appear as overly complex, potentially even as a case of multiple-accountabilities disorder (MAD). And yet the central argument of this chapter is that the human rights system vis-à-vis social security entitlements, although undoubtedly multifaceted, has not 'gone MAD' but is in reality an example of how legal accountability structures can utilise their discretion to maintain a delicate point of equilibria. The main conceptual contribution of this chapter is therefore its emphasis on *constitutional counter-balancing* as the courts seek to assess and resolve weaknesses within the political Constitution.

The Human Rights Act 1998 (HRA) was designed to 'bring rights home' (see Cm 3782, 1997). The legislation made it possible for citizens to rely on convention rights in UK courts, rather than having to petition the European Court of Human Rights (ECtHR) in Strasbourg. It also aimed to protect rights without undermining parliamentary sovereignty. UK courts *cannot* strike down legislation which contravenes convention rights. They are, however, required to read and give effect to legislation, so far as it is possible to do so, in a manner compatible with convention rights. When this is not possible, courts may issue a declaration of incompatibility, which does not affect the legality, validity, or force of the legislation declared incompatible with Convention rights. It is also unlawful for a public authority to act contrary to Convention rights. The HRA also created different sources of ex post- and ex ante- constitutional accountability for human rights for both the executive and the legislature. There are political and legal forums of accountability, which take place on both the domestic and the international stage and have until recently generally ensured the existence of a form of *balanced constitutionalism*, ensuring a good protection of human rights. To make this argument is therefore to work within the contours of works including Sir John Laws *The Constitutional Balance* (2021) and Aileen Kavanagh's *The Collaborative Constitution* (2023), not to mention Wheatle's chapter six in this volume (see also Young 2017).

But what this chapter provides is a more specific, detailed and intricate exploration of collaborative constitutionalism in practice. The argument is not that the system is perfect, far from it. But it is that the relationships and mutual respect for certain boundaries creates an accountability ecosystem that is far too complex to be captured in broad arguments concerning the political *or* the judicial Constitution. In many ways what this chapter reveals is the everyday ebb-and-flow of accountability relationships between different parts of the constitutional configuration. It achieves this through a focus on three recent decisions by the Supreme Court, all of which assessed whether different benefit-capping schemes breached convention rights as they discriminated against women or children. The intra-court discussion and decisions regarding these cases, plus their engagement with broader processes of political accountability, underline the existence of a standard of review that is very rarely acknowledged. As such, this chapter seeks to engage with three specific 'questions of accountability':

1. What does the Human Rights Act 'accountability web' actually look like?
2. How is an accountability balance maintained, especially via constitutional counter balancing?
3. How might recent proposals for a British Bill of Rights affect the existing balance?

These three questions also provide a framework for the three main sections of this chapter and, when taken together, what the answers combine to provide is a subtle understanding of why accountability needs to be understood as a multi-dimensional and fluid concept.

I. Setting the Scene: The Human Rights Accountability Web

In recent years the UK has been faced with a growing budget deficit, which the Conservative Government was determined to redress. One of the means of doing so was to restrict spending on socio-economic rights. Some of these measures took the form of capping or removing entitlements to welfare benefits which prompted a series of campaigns and protests and, finally, legal challenges (for a review see Meers 2019). Three of these cases provide the case law on which this chapter draws in order to develop its core argument concerning constitutional counter-balancing.

The first of the legal challenges, *R (SG) v Secretary of State for Work and Pensions*, concerned reductions in housing benefits. Entitlement to housing benefit was removed, or the amount received reduced, when households reached a threshold of income received from other welfare benefits. Concerns were raised as the scheme included benefits related to childcare in the determination of the cap. *SG* and others argued that these provisions breached convention rights – specifically Article 1 of the First Protocol (the right to property) and Article 14, the right against discrimination – as it was a form of indirect discrimination against women. The second case, *R (DA) v Secretary of State for Work and Pensions*, also focused on the benefit capping scheme. However, this time, a different argument was made, focusing on the impact of the working tax credit scheme. Working tax credits were not taken into account when determining benefit caps. However, single parents would need to work 16 hours a week to receive working tax credits. *DA* argued that this breached the right to property and the right against discrimination, focusing the argument on discrimination against women and children. The provisions specifically discriminated against single parent families with children under the age of two, who would not be able to receive free childcare to be able to work 16 hours a week. Finally, in *R (SC, CB and others) v Secretary of State for Work and Pensions*, a legal challenge was brought to the way in which working tax credits were calculated. Working tax credits were capped at two children. Households with more than two children did not receive any further working tax credit, with some narrow exceptions. *SC* and others argued that this breached the same Convention rights, discriminating against women and children in households with more than two children.

All three cases are examples of accountability of the executive and the legislature in a domestic legal forum. They require the government to give an account of its decisions to the court, not merely to explain but also to justify how its actions did not breach legal standards designed to protect human rights. And yet it is important to understand that this legal accountability did not exist or operate in isolation. The government's austerity measures were also subject to ex ante accountability mechanisms in the political or, more specifically, parliamentary sphere. In addition to the ex post accountability in the domestic legal forum, there was also the possibility of ex post accountability to an international domestic and international legal forum. To add to the complications, there were two different international forums in play: the mechanism providing for legal and political accountability under the provisions of the ECHR and those stemming from the United Nations Convention on the Rights of the Child (UNCRC).

These mechanisms also placed a range of demands on the government, both in terms of the standard that it was required to meet and the manner in which it is held to account in order to satisfy the accountability requirement. Some of the standards are required to be met in different forums, making it even harder to unravel the web of accountability. These are probably best explained through an examination of the legal rules challenged in the three cases: the Benefit Cap (Housing) Regulations enacted under the Welfare Reform Act 2012 and the Benefit Cap (Housing, Benefit and Universal Credit) Regulations 2016, both of which were enacted under the Welfare Reform and Work Act 2016, alongside a specific challenge to section 14 of the Welfare Reform and Work Act 2016.

Both the Welfare Reform Act 2012 and the Welfare Reform and Work Act 2016 were subject to ex ante scrutiny requiring the government to give a specific account, and answer questions concerning, the extent to which the Bills complied with Convention rights. Both Acts were government Bills which meant that the first political forum before which a minister would need to give an account is the Parliamentary Business and Legislation Committee (PBL Committee), a cabinet committee which makes recommendations as to the selection of Bills which will appear on the government's legislative agenda. Section 19 HRA requires a minister promoting a Bill to make a statement as to the compatibility of the Bill with Convention rights. This is set out in the explanatory memorandum to the Bill, or in a separate ECHR memorandum (see Cabinet Office 2022). If a satisfactory answer as to compatibility cannot be provided, then this may provide the PBL Committee with a reason to reject a proposed Bill. This may place a minister under political, hierarchical, and even social pressure to provide a good account as to Convention-compatibility. There is also a more indirect pressure on ministers in the sense that the sign of a successful minister is being able to get legislation through the PBL Committee and into the legislative process. If compliance with Convention rights is regarded as valuable, social or cultural pressure may add to the political and hierarchical pressure – or vice versa if these pressures push in the opposite direction.

Having made it on to the legislative agenda, there are further ways in which the minister both directly, and indirectly, will need to provide an account of a Bill's compatibility with Convention rights. Statements as to Convention-compatibility can be found in explanatory notes to the Welfare Bill 2011, and in a separate memorandum to the Welfare Reform and Work Bill. Ministers are also required to produce impact assessments. For the Welfare Bill 2011, this included equality impact assessments, which provided a further means through with ministers gave an account of how the Bill minimised its impact on equality rights. The 2016 Bill did not need to include equality impact assessments, but both Bills did include impact statements, setting out the possible consequences of the Bill. These provide a further indirect means of holding the minister to account as regards compliance with Article 14 ECHR. Both Bills were scrutinised by the Joint Committee on Human Rights, which produced a report on the Convention-compatibility of the 2011 Bill (see HC 1704/HL233, 2011). Debate on the 2016 Bill was cut short due to the snap general election on 8 June 2017, meaning the Committee was unable to produce a report. These reports are designed to help MPs perform their scrutiny of legislation. They may also help stakeholders and public interest groups, providing information to aid their assessment of legislation which may indirectly influence the accountability of the government and Parliament.

In addition to these direct means of holding the government to account for the Convention-compatibility of its legislation, both Bills received a plethora of written evidence at the committee stage. The Public Bill Committee also heard evidence. This provided an opportunity for individuals and groups to provide evidence of the impact of the proposed legislation on women and children, in addition to focusing on potential issues as regards the UK's compliance with the ECHR and the UNCRC. This may place further political pressure on the government to explain why its legislation either does not harm these interests, or is nevertheless justified. The government may be held to account in Parliament for the way in which in responds to these pressures, perhaps even leading to legislative amendments. With regard to the 2011 Act, for example the minister provided assurance to Parliament that the government had considered the impact of the proposed legislation on Convention rights and that the government was satisfied that the restriction on these rights was proportionate (Hansard (HL Debates) 23 November 2011, cols GC415-GC425).

Challenges were also brought to delegated legislation enacted under the Act. In *SG* the applicants challenged the Benefit Cap (Housing) Regulations 2012 which were enacted under the provisions of the 2011 Act. The regulations were laid before Parliament in draft, this draft needing to be approved by both Houses of Parliament for the regulations to be enacted. As with the 2011 Act, Parliament received written evidence setting out the consequences of the benefit cap set out in these regulations, providing another political forum in which the government was required to give an account of the regulations, explaining or justifying the implications of these regulations in terms of their potential compatibility with Convention rights and the UNCRC. The three Supreme Court cases provide examples of ex post accountability taking place in the domestic legal forum. The government can be held to account for the legality of its actions. The regulations could be struck down as unlawful if they breached Convention rights. The provisions of the 2011 or 2016 Act could be reinterpreted so as to ensure their compatibility with Convention rights, or declared incompatible with Convention rights. The latter would then create a possible ex post political form of accountability and a possible further ex post legal and political accountability forum in international law.

Whilst a declaration of incompatibility does not create a domestic legal obligation to modify legislation, it arguably creates a strong political pressure on the government and Parliament to amend legislation to ensure its compatibility with Convention rights. In the period from when the Human Rights Act 1998 entered into force on 2 October 2000 to the end of July 2021, for example, there were 44 declarations of incompatibility concerning human rights of which ten were subsequently overturned on appeal, five related to provisions that had already been amended, eight had been changed by a Remedial Order, 15 had been changed by primary or secondary legislation, one had been addressed through other means, and, of the remaining five declarations the government was proposing to bring in amendments to resolve four, and a final decision was still under consideration (see Ministry of Justice 2021). This political accountability is reinforced by legal accountability before the European Court of Human Rights. Individuals have a right to petition this Court. If the European Court of Human Rights decides against the UK, then Article 46 ECHR places the UK under an obligation in international law to adhere to and implement the final judgments of this Court. The Court may also award damages to those whose rights are harmed. Moreover, the implementation of judgments is overseen by the Committee of Ministers of the Council of Europe, who may adopt final resolutions against states who refuse to implement decisions. This can require the UK Government to explain its actions and to be held to account in the international political arena for failing to implement decisions of the European Court of Human Rights.

There are similar ex ante political forums through which the government can be required to give account for the compliance of its actions to the UNCRC. However, these are less formalised and provide a weaker form of accountability. There is no requirement for a minister to make a statement as to the compatibility of Bills to the UNCRC. The nearest equivalent is a written ministerial statement of 6 December 2010 (HC Hansard, col 7WS) setting out the government's commitment that it will give due consideration to the requirements of the UNCRC when presenting legislation, with a recognition that the government may disagree with the UN Committee concerning how these commitments are to be implemented. This means that ex ante accountability for compliance with the UNCRC in the political arena is weaker. Although issues may still be raised through submissions to the Public Bill Committee, the government is less compelled to give an account of its actions, or a justification when legislative proposals diverge from the provisions of the UNCRC. There is also no specific committee tasked with providing reports as to the compatibility of legislation with the UNCRC, although this can be raised in parliamentary committee reports.

The ex post legal and political controls are also weaker. The ECHR has been incorporated into UK law through the provisions of the HRA. The same is not true of the UNCRC which remains generally unincorporated in the UK, although some of its provisions have been implemented in Wales by the Rights of Children and Young Persons (Wales) Measure 2011. Scotland also enacted legislation to implement the UNCRC in Scotland, but the method of implementation was held to be beyond the scope of the Scottish Parliament (see Cowie 2022). As will be discussed in more depth below, this limits the extent to which courts can hold the government to account in the legal arena for failing to uphold the provisions of the UNCRC. Ex post legal accountability is also unavailable in international law, the UK having not ratified the individual right to petition the UN Committee on the rights of the child. In terms of ex post political accountability in international law, the UK produces a report every five years to the UN Committee, setting out the extent to which the UK upholds the rights of the child. This requires the UK to give account of its actions, with the possibility of critical reports from the UN Committee and non-binding recommendations should the UK fail to uphold its obligations (see Fenton-Glynn 2016).

The human rights accountability web is, as this section has attempted to illustrate, truly web-like in the sense of possessing multiple levels and multiple connects almost locked into a delicate state of inter-dependency. Taken together, what this system serves to ensure is that the government complies with its legal obligations under domestic and international law as regards Convention rights and the UNCRC. The political and legal scrutiny process also exist within a wider web of public pressure and professional expectations which, although less tangible, play a role in bolstering and sustaining the overall system. On occasion these multiple accountability pressures may pull in different directions, the demands of the public or a minister's parliamentary party possibly being out of alignment with judicial reasoning or a sense of professional obligation. But this 'existence in tension' is to some extent a defining feature of the overall accountability ecosystem, or space. The next section looks at how an effective and broadly proportionate accountability balance is maintained, especially through what is termed constitutional counter-balancing.

II. Shifting Sands of Accountability

The previous section's focus on the existence of multiple and inter-dependent accountability processes plus its review of three significant supreme court cases that all took place within a six-year window (ie, 2015–21) could at first glance be interpreted as evidence of imbalance, possibly even of a system riven by multiple-accountabilities disorder. It might also be seen as an example of 'over-supply but under-performance' given the multitude of actors and processes, plus the fact that the court supported the government's position in all three cases. Indeed, many individuals and interest groups, many of whom had provided evidence to Parliament during the legislative process, strongly believed that the legislature had failed to protect Convention rights, or the rights of the child when taking measures to tackle austerity through establishing benefit caps. But this perspective raises its own highly distinctive 'question of accountability': just because all three legal challenges failed does that really mean that human rights are not being adequately protected? The main aim of this section is to argue that the situation is far more complicated than the framing of this question seems able to grasp. Indeed, by returning to the three cases introduced in the previous section a far more complicated and arguably balanced interpretation is generated. Moreover, interpretive variations emerge less due to a failure of the courts and more accurately because of the delicate nature of the balance between legal and political forums in holding the executive to account to ensure. It is this level of detailed texture and tone that is very often from broader debates concerning accountability 'deficits' or 'overloads', while the subjective and contextually dependent nature of relationships add fresh insight to Schilleman's work on 'questions of perspective' (chapter two) and particularly to Rock's arguments concerning 'questions of measurement' (chapter four).

To recap, the HRA provides for a combination of legal and political accountability forums. These are designed to hold the executive and the legislature to account to ensure their measures do not contravene Convention rights. Critically, these different accountability forums aim to provide a legal protection of rights that does not undermine parliamentary sovereignty – thereby explaining why the courts may reinterpret legislation and declare it 'incompatible', but may not strike down primary legislation which breaches Convention rights. This relates back to Se-Shauna Wheatle's discussion of collaborative constitutionalism and how new checks and balances have essentially been created and powers devolved *within* the pre-existing Westminster model (see chapter six). A system of 'modified majoritarianism' (Flinders 2010) therefore utilises forms of judicial accountability while retaining the primacy of parliamentary sovereignty in a system designed to protect human rights.

In short, inter-institutional interactions may facilitate constitutional collaboration. This occurs when the courts, the government, and Parliament work together to provide a better protection of rights. This mechanism is useful in particular when faced with contestable rights-issues, when it can be reasonable to disagree about the content of a Convention right and how it applies in a particular situation. There is, of course, a strong prima facie reason for courts to defer to the legislature. Parliament is better able to hear from a wide range of views, balancing interests to reach a decision that aims to maximise the public good. Parliamentary decisions are arguably also more legitimate due to the existence of a parliamentary mandate within the primary chamber. As such, if the electorate is unhappy with austerity measures or concerned about human rights protections then it can express itself at the ballot box; and if a sufficient level of frustration is displayed then the parliamentary arithmetic will shift in such a way that a new party or collection of parties will be invited to form a government. Such broad and relatively infrequent control mechanisms are, of course, far from perfect but the point being made is that at least in relation to the legislature and executive it is possible to 'throw the rascals out' in a way that is near impossible in relation to the judiciary.

That said, the courts do bring a very specific and arguably complementary set of skills and perspectives to the broader 'questions of accountability' that surround human rights. This allows them if not to correct then at the very least to encourage reflection and amendment on the part of the executive. Court cases are brought by particular individuals. This means that courts can determine when a measure that generally provides a good protection of rights may nevertheless harm the rights of particular individuals. In addition, courts are better-placed to protect minority rights. Legislatures take decisions through voting, the majority of votes cast deciding a particular issue (with votes often cast at the instruction of party managers rather than in the wake of any careful exploration or reflection on the issue). This means that minority groups, particularly those who may exist beyond the political mainstream and are not therefore courted by the main parties, of those 'hard to reach' groups who live, either by choice or necessity, on the edges of society may miss out. It is easier for individuals in minority groups to bring a court case to protect their interests than it is, for example, for them to affect the legislative timetable or secure the attention of the main party leaders. Courts can check for any errors made by the legislature or the executive with regard to the protection of minority rights. Courts are also better equipped to reason about rights, being trained in interpreting legal documents, analysing previous cases and being able to recognise and protect human rights principles that may otherwise be overlooked by busy MPs or junior ministers.

The distinction between the legislature and the executive (ie, between MPs and ministers) is highly relevant to this discussion for the simple reason that neither Parliament nor the government should be treated as homogenous entities. As Anthony King argued back in 1976, *inter*-party and *intra*-party relationships are complex, dynamic and constantly shifting (see also Russell and Cowley 2018). As such the relative strengths of various actors are contextually dependent and constantly contested. The notion of a constitutional 'settlement' therefore veils the existence of a constantly evolving and iterative process, and where actors can reinterpret rules, conventions and even agreements should the balance of power be felt to be becoming inimical to the health of democracy. Modifications in legal tests may provide an example of when the courts can adjust their powers to ensure a better separation of powers between the institutions of the Constitution, or to uphold certain protections which they feel need buttressing. This is a process that can be labelled as *constitutional counter-balancing* and which occurs either when an institution acts to defend its own powers, or those of another institution, or through the exercise of principles of self-restraint and mutual respect (see Young 2017). The three modifications that took place in the decisions of the Supreme Court in the cases outlined above are best understood as constitutional counter-balancing, correcting imbalances in the separation of powers between the legislature, executive, and the courts. The remainder of this section looks at these changes in more detail.

A. Convention Rights and the UNCRC

The first change relates to the circumstances in which UK courts can rely on unincorporated treaties. Later decisions of the Supreme Court corrected a potential broadening of the extent to which UK courts can give effect to the UNCRC in domestic law. Treaties are entered into by the executive. In order to create obligations in international law, treaties need to be ratified. To have effect in domestic law, treaties need to be incorporated through legislation. The UNCRC has not been incorporated into UK law. Nevertheless, in *SG*, Lord Kerr provided three arguments as to why the UNCRC *could* be relied upon. First, he argued that the common law should recognise and enforce unincorporated treaties that protect human rights. Second, he argued, alternatively, that the common law should recognise a substantive legitimate expectation that ministers would not act contrary to international law, including international law protected by unincorporated treaties. Third, he argued that, given that the European Court of Human Rights referred to the UNCRC when determining the content of Convention rights that affected the rights of the child, domestic courts could also refer to the UNCRC in a similar way. Consequently, a measure which contravened the UNCRC would also contravene Convention rights.

Lord Kerr was unable to find support for either of his first two arguments. Nevertheless, Lady Hale did agree with his final argument. The other judges did recognise that the UNCRC could be relevant when determining the scope of Convention rights. However, they argued that all that was required was to show that the legislature or executive had taken account of the UNCRC when determining Convention rights that affected children. They concluded, however, that this could not be applied in the *SG* case, as the case did not concern discrimination against children, but against women. Therefore, the case did not engage the UNCRC as it did not concern the rights of the child.

The later cases of *DA* and *SC* saw the courts retreat from Lord Kerr's and Lady Hale's arguments. Lord Kerr in *DA* recognised that he had been unable to persuade other members of the Supreme Court. Therefore, in *DA*, he concluded that courts should only take account of the UNCRC when determining the content of Convention rights affecting the rights of the child. In *SC*, Lord Reed, giving the agreed judgment of seven Justices of the Supreme Court, affirmed that the UNCRC could only be referred to in domestic law when the court was determining the scope of Convention rights that affected the rights of children. Moreover, he restricted how the courts could use the UNCRC. Lord Kerr and Lady Hale in *SG* had used the UNCRC to determine the content of the Convention right. To be compatible with Convention rights, provisions had to demonstrate that they had prioritised the rights of the child. In *SC*, Lord Reed concluded that all that was required of the government or Parliament was to show that they had taken the UNCRC's requirement to prioritise the rights of the child into account. Domestic law did not require that the executive or legislature act in a manner that was compatible with the UNCRC in order to show that provisions did not breach Convention rights as applied to children.

This proposed change, and later rejection, to the extent to which domestic law can refer to unincorporated treaties weakened the ex post legal accountability forum for the UNCRC. In this sense, it is evidence of a weakening of the protection of the rights of the child, removing a means through which the executive or legislature can be held to account for its actions ex post facto. This, in turn, may weaken the ex ante political accountability forum. Courts will now only check that Parliament and the government took these rights into account, which, in turn, may make it easier for these institutions to satisfy ex ante accountability in the political forum.

However, it can be understood as a means of redressing a perceived imbalance in the separation of powers. The common law has long-recognised that, given parliamentary sovereignty, the UK is best-understood as dualist as opposed to monist. International treaties only take effect in domestic law to the extent that they have been incorporated into domestic law. If the courts were to have followed Lord Kerr's arguments, they would have undermined parliamentary sovereignty by giving effect to international law that had not been implemented into domestic law by Parliament. Principles of mutual respect and self-restraint would have potentially been breached if the courts were to have developed the domestic protection of international law in this manner. Consequently, this change in the case law can best be understood as a means of correcting a potential breach of the separation of powers, helping to maintain a combination of legal and political accountability forums in human rights that respects a key constitutional principle of the UK – parliamentary sovereignty.

B. Manifestly Without Reasonable Foundation?

Article 14 is a non-absolute right. This means that, in order to determine whether there has been a breach of Convention rights, courts have to assess whether a restriction on the right was proportionate. In domestic law, this requires the application of a four-stage test: whether the limit on the right is to achieve a legitimate aim; whether this restriction is necessary; whether it is sufficient; and whether the restriction is proportionate, in the sense of striking the right balance between the right and the restriction (see *Bank Mellat v Her Majesty's Treasury*).The proportionality test can be applied more or less stringently. The more weight given to the assessment of the executive or legislature, the less stringently the proportionality test is applied – and vice-versa. This helps to strike the right balance between legal and political controls.

All three cases concerned socio-economic rights. This is an area in which the courts give great weight to the decisions of elected bodies. Socio-economic rights are regarded as more suited to the political as opposed to the legal arena. These rights are polycentric. This can be illustrated by the context of austerity measures, when budget cuts need to be made. To reverse the decisions on capping as regards child tax credits, or the amount of housing benefit that can be paid to those who are not on working tax credits has consequences. Cuts may have to be made elsewhere – for example, to cold weather payments to pensioners. Parliament is better able to weigh these multiple interests. Courts only see the applicants who appear before them. Consequently, Parliament is more institutionally suited to determining socio-economic rights. This balance is also contestable. It can be reasonable to disagree as to the desirability of different austerity measures. Parliament can be held to account for its choices. The same is not true of the judiciary. This explains why Parliament is constitutionally better suited to making these decisions. In both *SG* and *DA*, the Supreme Court concluded that, as the decision involved socio-economic rights, the correct approach to determining proportionality was to ask whether the restriction of the right was manifestly without reasonable foundation. This reformulation of the proportionality test is designed to give great weight to the decisions of the executive and the legislature. This reflects the constitutional and institutional reasons for courts to defer to decisions of Parliament.

However, two concerns were raised in these decisions. The first concern, raised by Lady Hale in *SG*, is the need to look more closely at whether courts are deferring to Parliament or to the government. The challenge in *SG* looked at the implications of regulations enacted by the government. Although there was some parliamentary scrutiny over this delegated legislation, this is lower than the amount of scrutiny received by Acts of Parliament. Therefore, Lady Hale suggested that the courts should be less deferential. Second, both Lord Kerr and Lady Hale in *DA* were concerned about the scope of application of the manifestly without reasonable foundation test. They both concluded that, particularly when applied to discrimination cases, courts should only apply the manifestly without reasonable foundation test to assessments of a legitimate aim component of the proportionality test. The other stages of the test did not require the same degree of deference.

In *SC*, the Supreme Court modified the manifestly without reasonable foundation test. The judgment recognises that, for the reasons discussed above, the manifestly without reasonable foundation test should be the default test for socio-economic rights. Nevertheless, the Supreme Court also recognised that this is not best understood as a replacement for the proportionality test. Rather, the use of 'manifestly without reasonable foundation' was a means through which courts varied the intensity of the proportionality test. More importantly, even when in the field of socio-economic rights, the proportionality test can still be applied more stringently as regards discrimination in relation to 'suspect categories' – for example, sex or gender, nationality, sexual orientation, religious belief and disabilities. Proportionality is applied less stringently for discrimination against other characteristics or individuals – for example, immigration status, prisoners, and minorities. Courts will also apply proportionality more stringently as regards transitional measures designed to remedy historical discrimination. This change was made not in response to the earlier criticisms of the manifestly without reasonable foundation test expressed by Lord Kerr and Lady Hale. Rather, they stemmed from changes made by the Strasbourg court (see *JD and A v United Kingdom*).

This change, also, can be regarded as a means of making adjustments to the separation of powers, ensuring a balanced set of legal and political checks over decisions of Parliament and the government. Whilst there are good prima facie reasons for preferring legal to political controls over socio-economic decisions, nevertheless situations may arise in which courts are better able to determine when a decision harms minority rights, either generally or in its specific application. Minority voices may not have sufficient weight in political decision-making. General rules may apply in such a way that they indirectly discriminate against a specific minority group. The modifications to the test in *SC*, therefore, may also be better understood as a means of ensuring a better collaboration between legal and political controls, ensuring courts can correct situations where actions of the legislature or the executive harm minority rights, particularly those of protected minorities. In *SC*, however, the case did not concern a protected minority. Rather, it concerned discrimination against those living in homes with more than two children. As this was not a protected characteristic, there was no justification for the courts to modify the manifestly without reasonable foundation approach to the proportionality test.

The case also shows how domestic and international accountability mechanisms can be used to provide a better set of checks and balances. The European Court of Human Rights required these changes to the approach to proportionality. Given the contestable nature of the balance between legal and political forums of accountability, it may be that domestic courts are more able to make changes to this delicate balance when they can rely on a decision of the European Court of Human Rights, lending more weight to the need for the courts to be less deferential when dealing with particularly contestable areas, such as socio-economic rights.

C. Use of Parliamentary Materials

A further theme running through the three cases is the extent to which courts can rely on parliamentary material when assessing whether delegated or primary legislation breaches Convention rights. This affects the interaction between legal and political forums of accountability in two ways. First, it can upset the separation of powers between Parliament and the courts. If courts reassess parliamentary debates, determining their quality or questioning their conclusions, this can undermine the parliamentary privilege of freedom of expression (see Article 9, Bill of Rights 1689). Not only might this undermine the need for MPs to be able to speak freely in debates, but also it might upset the delicate balance of powers between Parliament and the courts, with courts having a form of oversight of democratic debate. Second, it may alter the way in which Parliament reasons about rights, indirectly incentivising Parliament to reason in a manner which is more equivalent to the way in which courts reason about rights. However, to do so would undermine the ability of these institutions to combine the different ways in which they reason about rights. This may damage constitutional collaboration, preventing the legal and political forums of accountability from providing complementary checks over the government and Parliament.

This issue was discussed in depth by the Supreme Court in *SC*. Both the applicant and the government wished to rely on parliamentary material. The government wanted to rely on impact statements and the statement of compatibility provided by the minister introducing the Bill to demonstrate that Parliament had taken Convention rights into account and had concluded that there was no breach. The applicants wished to rely on evidence provided by other organisations to the public Bill committee. This evidence explained the impact on children in particular, and argued that the legislation failed to uphold UNCRC rights by prioritising the interests of children. The applicants argued that this demonstrated that the legislation breached Convention rights. The Court concluded that it was important to be cautious when using parliamentary materials. Parliamentary materials can be used to determine the intention of Parliament and the purpose of legislation. However, it is important to distinguish between statements of Parliament, on the one hand, and of the government, on the other hand. Impact statements and statements of compatibility are made by the executive, not the legislature. The Court also noted that the intention of Parliament is a legal construct, discerned from the wording of legislation, separately from ministerial statements as to compatibility.

Parliamentary materials can also be used when the Court is assessing proportionality. However, the Court should be careful not to assess the quality of democratic deliberation. This would undermine parliamentary privilege. Also, it might hold Parliament to the wrong standards, requiring of Parliament a level of transparency and rationality that was more suited to legal reasoning, failing to recognise that Parliament reasons differently. Instead, courts can use parliamentary material to determine whether Parliament had discussed the impact of legislation on convention rights. If there is evidence that Parliament has deliberated on this issue, then courts can give greater deference to Parliament. However, it did not follow that, if Parliament had failed to discuss Convention rights or the quality of debate had been poor, that the Court could conclude that Convention rights had been breached. Rather, that evidence could be used to argue that less deference was owed to Parliament.

It can be seen, therefore, that this change is also a subtle redressing of the balance between legal and political forums of accountability. It is designed to ensure that legal and political forums of accountability can be complementary, so that they work together to provide a better protection of Convention rights. Here, 'better' is not understood in terms of providing a strong protection of rights. In all of these cases, the applicant did not succeed. Trying to determine whether, substantively, different forums of accountability provide a better or worse protection of Convention rights is difficult to assess. These rights-issues are contestable. It can be reasonable to disagree about the best way of protecting convention rights. Instead, our focus has to be on the extent to which accountability forums may focus on different aspects of the same standard of accountability – here the question as to whether Convention rights have been breached – or provide different standards of accountability. We also have to focus on how far one forum of accountability may be better able to correct mistakes that may be made by the other forum, given their different reasoning processes and expertise. 'Better' is understood in terms of providing a system that facilitates an effective blend of complementary forums of accountability, enabling one forum to check the other for institutional weaknesses whilst respecting constitutional boundaries.

III. Conclusion

The central argument of this chapter is that critical 'questions of accountability' very often overlook the existence of interwoven processes and the capacity for specific actors to engage in constitutional counter-balancing. The previous section illustrated some of the interpretive ways in which the courts could shift the constitutional balance of equilibria. The changes in legal tests illustrated in these key recent Supreme Court cases demonstrate subtle changes made in order to achieve a good balance between legal and political forums of accountability for human rights. The aim of this third and final section is to very briefly reflect on how recent proposals for a British 'Bill of Rights' might affect the capacity of the judiciary to engage counter-balancing behaviours.

'My ministers' read the then Prince of Wales as he gave the May 2022 Queen's Speech in his mother's place 'will restore the balance of power between the legislature and the courts.' The Bill of Rights Bill was introduced to the House of Commons on 22 June 2022 with one main goal: 'This Act reforms the law relating to human rights by repealing and replacing the Human Rights Act 1998' (section1, paragraph 1). It preserves declarations of incompatibility, however, it makes it easier for courts to only declare delegated legislation as incompatible with Convention rights rather than striking down delegated legislation. It is also unclear how far earlier Convention-compatible interpretations of legislation made under section 3 of the HRA will be preserved. Clause 40 of the Bill empowers a minister to make delegated legislation to preserve these interpretations. The explanatory notes state that this is designed as a 'belts and braces' provision, designed to preserve legal certainty. Nevertheless, some have argued that clause 40 implies that all Convention-compatible section 3 interpretations will fall away with the repeal of the HRA and its replacement by the Bill of Rights Act.

In addition to these broad changes that reduce the legal accountability forum for Convention rights, there are two themes running through the Bill which may affect the way in which legal and political accountability forums relate to one another. First the Bill changes the relationship between domestic and international legal forums of accountability. Second, it changes the relationship between domestic legal and domestic political forums of accountability. The Bill makes it clear that decisions of the European Court of Human Rights will have a smaller influence in domestic law. It is for the UK Supreme Court to have the final say over the content of Convention rights for the purposes of domestic law. Moreover, the Supreme Court should interpret convention rights by placing greater emphasis on the text and on *travaux preparatoires* (ie, files containing various documents pertaining to the drafting of a Convention, treaty or agreement such as minutes of discussions, hearings and debates). UK courts can adopt interpretations of Convention rights that diverge from those of the European Court of Human Rights (Clause 3(3)(b)). However, UK courts may only adopt interpretations of Convention rights that go beyond the current case law of the European Court of Human Rights when the court has 'no reasonable doubt' that, were the case to be before that court, it would reach the same interpretation of the Convention right. This may make it harder for domestic courts to protect Convention rights, as well as reducing their ability to rely on decisions of the European Court of Human Rights to remedy circumstances in which the separation of powers has tipped too far in favour of legal accountability forums, as was the case in *SC* when the Court altered the 'manifestly without reasonable foundation' test.

The Bill also alters the separation of powers between Parliament and the courts. Courts are required to give the

> greatest possible weight to the principle that, in a Parliamentary democracy, decisions about the balance between different policy aims, different Convention rights and Convention rights of different persons are properly made by Parliament.

In addition, when determining how to balance rights, courts must 'regard Parliament as having decided, in passing the Act, that the Act strikes an appropriate balance'. It is hard to know how this provision is to be interpreted. At its widest, the clause appears to be instructing courts that, given that Parliament has passed a particular piece of legislation, it must be deemed to be a proportionate restriction on Convention rights. If this is the case, it would radically undermine the delicate balance between political and legal forums of accountability for human rights in UK law. However, it is hard not to accept this interpretation given the further instruction to the court to 'give the greatest possible weight' to the principle that it is for Parliament to balance Convention rights and interests.

The requirement can be interpreted more narrowly, as a means of responding to the use of parliamentary materials approved by the Supreme Court in *SC*. The Supreme Court concluded that an assessment of whether Parliament had considered the implication of legislation on Convention rights would affect the degree of weight given to Parliament when assessing whether legislation had breached convention rights. Less weight is given to the conclusions of Parliament if the impact on Convention rights has not been debated. However, the Bill is now instructing courts to accept that, the mere fact that legislation has been enacted, is to be taken as demonstrating that Parliament has considered the issue and decided that the appropriate balance has been struck. Consequently, the 'greatest possible weight' is due to Parliament. The weight due to Parliament's assessment cannot be lessened because Parliament has not specifically debated the appropriate balance with regard to Convention rights. The flexibility and malleability that allowed the judiciary to play some small but corrective role via constitutional counter-balancing is therefore being removed. The implication and central argument of this chapter being that the proposed Bill of Rights is likely to upset the delicate balance between legal and political modes of accountability in relation to human rights, in particular, but also at a far wider and more general level. From the perspective of collaborative constitutionalism this is a worrying development that is likely to generate even more 'questions of accountability'.

PART III

Futures

11

Accountability in Global Governance

KATE MACDONALD AND TERRY MACDONALD

In recent decades, the ascendance of accountability discourses and practices within national governance settings throughout the Anglosphere has extended to multiple domains of global governance. Scholars examining diverse domains of global governance ranging from the work of international aid and development organisations to the regulation of global business activity have directed increasing analytical scrutiny to processes through which those responsible for the conduct and consequences of such diverse governance activities can be held to account for their actions (Kahler 2004; Scholte 2004; Newell 2008). In the field of international aid and development, calls for 'strengthened accountability' have played a particularly central role within the demands of activist groups for the reform of prominent multilateral development finance institutions (such as the World Bank, European Bank for Reconstruction and Development, International Finance Corporation and the European Investment Bank, etc). In response to periods of intense civil society pressure over the past two to three decades, such global governance institutions have increasingly acknowledged the need for their decisions to be answerable to an expanding array of political constituencies outside their own organisations, through increased transparency, strengthened dialogue with external stakeholders, provision of access to grievance procedures for project-affected people, and expanded mechanisms for monitoring, evaluation and results-based accountability (Suzuki and Nanwani, 2005; Park, 2010; Macdonald 2018; Macdonald 2014a; Koenig-Archibugi 2010).

Evolving accountability discourses have also played an important role in reshaping systems of transnational business governance, through mechanisms of enhanced transparency, stakeholder dialogue, consultation, grievance-handling, and market-led accountability processes involving the mobilisation of investors or consumers in support of accountability claims (Koenig-Archibugi 2010; Macdonald 2014a). While the aims of specific accountability mechanisms have varied, the mobilisation of accountability politics in each of these examples has been underpinned by the core shared purposes of recognising and empowering political constituencies with a legitimate stake in global governance processes –

thereby strengthening the legitimacy of global governance processes in the face of significant power imbalances between participants.

Yet despite the proliferation of new or reformed accountability mechanisms, the promise of strengthened legitimacy has often failed to materialise. In some cases, new accountability mechanisms have helped to patch over some of the continually evolving accountability gaps that persist across multiple sites and scales of global governance. Yet efforts to bridge ongoing accountability deficits have frequently foundered in the face of ambiguity and contestation surrounding *who* such mechanisms should render accountable *to whom*, alongside the inability of many accountability systems to mobilise sufficient leverage to compel powerful governance agencies to respond in meaningful ways to their constituencies (Macdonald 2018). Such challenges produce a distinctive version of the 'overload but underperformance' dilemma outlined in the introduction to this volume in the sense that the proliferation of accountability mechanisms does not seem to have answered the 'questions of accountability' they were designed to address. If anything, the 'accountability explosion' that has to some extent emerged as a key facet of global governance during the last decade appears to have fuelled concerns about fugitive power and the dysfunctions of democracy vis-à-vis international actors and non-governmental organisations.

In this chapter, we aim to probe this dilemma of 'overload but underperformance' as it manifests itself in the domain of global governance by engaging with three specific 'questions of accountability'.

1. What is the political value of global accountability?
2. In what ways are statist accountability assumptions 'uploaded' into the sphere of global governance?
3. To what extent do such assumptions align with the liquidity and flow of global governance?

Our core argument resonates with the notions of 'fluid' or 'fuzzy' accountability that have already been touched-upon in other chapters. We suggest that the 'overload but underperformance' emerges within global governance due to what might be termed an 'accountability alignment issue'. In essence, traditional state-based accountability assumptions are too often assumed to 'fit' what is in reality a pluralist global political order which lacks a constitutionalised institutional structure for governance and is generally defined by dynamic, decentred and distorted relationships. Accountability assumptions based on the existence of clarity and stability between clear political constituencies, plus the presence of transparent and coherent institutional rule-based structures, are likely to flounder when applied in a context where those basic elements are simply absent. This is, we suggest, why the proliferation of new, revised and too often 'uploaded' accountability mechanisms within a pluralist global order cannot address persistent accountability gaps. The implication being that accountability mechanisms need to be more appropriately adapted to the features of this order, through a more systematic and explicit focus on both recognising and empowering plural and dynamic political constituencies.

Our analysis of both the systemic origins of persistent global accountability dilemmas and possible directions for adapting institutional responses to a pluralist order is illustrated with reference to the global governance of international development finance and transnational business. These are closely intertwined governance domains in which accountability discourses and practices have played a central role in shaping ongoing struggles over power and legitimacy in global governance.[1]

I. The Political Value of Global Accountability

Accountability, as we understand it here, is

> a political relation[ship] in which one agent (or group of agents) is accorded entitlements to question, direct, sanction or constrain the actions of another – particularly where these actions involve the exercise of public power or authority within a governance system (Macdonald 2014a).

The value of such accountability is widely recognised in both theoretical analyses and real-world practices of political legitimation in contemporary global governance institutions (Boven 2007; Fox 2018; Mulgan 2003; Grant and Keohane 2005). Accountability is not typically theorised as an instrument of a specific moral ideal of political rights or justice, of the kind that has often been articulated in 'moralist' (Williams 2005) political philosophies over the last half-century. Rather, accountability is typically valued on more pragmatic normative grounds – as the solution to political problems produced by *normative contestation* and *power competition* within the complex operating environments of real-world governance institutions.

The political problem of *normative contestation*, first, arises in contemporary governance systems as a function of the pervasive moral and epistemic disagreements that characterise pluralistic modern societies, and recognition of the difficulty this poses for achieving authoritative resolution of normative disputes. The modern ideas that all individuals have capabilities for moral and epistemic judgment that deserve respect, and conversely that no individual has infallible judgment, preclude the grounding of political authority on appeals to moral or epistemic authority. Instead, these ideas give rise to the new political value of *legitimacy* – which seeks to regulate governance institutions with standards that can attract support from actors with diverse moral and epistemic judgments (Macdonald and Macdonald 2020). *Accountability* then emerges as a political value within this modern theory and practice of legitimacy – embodying a crucial institutional instrument through which the problem of normative contestation can be managed within political governance systems. Accountability instruments can help

[1] Analysis in parts of this chapter draws on ideas elaborated in more detail in previously published work (Macdonald and Macdonald 2017; 2019; 2022; Macdonald 2014a; 2018; 2008).

to manage normative contestation through performing two inter-connected functions. One is the *recognitional* function of highlighting the fallible and contested moral and epistemic judgment of powerholders within a governance system, and conversely the competing judgments of other actors within the system. The other is the *regulative* function of distributing, across this wider plurality of actors, entitlements to question, direct, sanction or constrain power- and authority-holders when they act on the basis of contested normative judgments.

The political problem of *power competition*, second, arises within governance systems as a function of the extent to which political actors are not only diverse and fallible in their moral and epistemic judgments, but also *corruptible* – in the sense of being liable to misuse their power in the pursuit of political self-interest (as distinct from what they judge to be morally or epistemically right). The problem of competing political interests and competitions for power can overlap with the problem of normative contestation and play a role in the pursuit of political legitimacy; but it also has some independence as the central concern of the 'realist' political value of *order*, which seeks to allay risks of political instability or violence that can result from conflicts of interest and competitions for power (Williams 2005). Accountability can achieve further pragmatic value as an institutional instrument for managing this problem of power competition by providing well-ordered institutional processes of political challenge and sanction that can channel and contain the background struggles over competing interests that take place within governance systems and prevent them from degenerating into political domination.

A range of institutional models for performing these valuable political functions have been developed within overlapping realist, republican, liberal, and democratic traditions of theoretical work on the legitimation of modern governance – extending across both domestic and global levels of institutional analysis (Macdonald and Macdonald 2017; Grant and Keohane 2005). In 'realist' traditions of political theory (Rossi and Sleat 2014; Bell 2017), accountability mechanisms focus primarily on institutional instruments for achieving a 'balance of power' among actors with competing interests – typically through institutionalising norms of strategic action within state leadership regimes, operating either domestically or internationally. Republican institutional models of accountability similarly emphasise the importance of balancing the power of competing factional interests within a governance system, but typically seek to institutionalise this balance via some separation of functional powers within the constitutional rules of a state (Pettit 2007), or within the rules of a global institutional scheme providing equivalent political safeguards against insecurity and domination (Laborde and Ronzoni 2006). Liberal accountability models extend these commitments to separated constitutional powers with further institutional instruments of 'social accountability' to domestic and transnational 'civil societies', which function to contest and counterbalance the powers of liberal states (Walzer 1984). Democratic accountability mechanisms, finally, seek to collectivise social accountability through processes of representation for organised democratic publics – in which accountability and authorisation work together to the democratic legitimacy of state or transnational governance processes (Macdonald 2008).

While these established models of global accountability vary somewhat in their prescribed institutional instruments, they typically share in common some important background assumptions, which reflect their common histories as remedies to the legitimacy problems of *statist* (Macdonald and Macdonald 2020) governance systems, centred on the closed societies and public rules characteristic of state governance institutions. The first of these assumptions is that accountability mechanisms can be designed with an expectation of *clarity and stability* in the distinctions and relationships between political constituencies and governance agents, so that it is straightforward to identify who is the governance agent to be held accountable, and who is the political constituency with the entitlement to question, challenge, or sanction. The second assumption is that *governance power is concentrated in transparent and coherent structures of institutional rules*, so that authority relationships and opportunities for accountability can operate through a publicly-articulated and coherently-ordered institutional scheme. These assumptions together amount to the idea that accountability can be successfully achieved through some well-designed set of public institutional rules – which operates in parallel to (and as a check and balance against) the rules that constitute the authority structures and decision-making procedures of political governance processes, operating both within and across the boundaries of states.

II. Pluralist Dilemmas of Global Accountability

Extending these established institutional models of political accountability to global governance systems can help to realise the pragmatic political value of accountability, to the extent that *statist* assumptions about the structural features of governance systems also hold true in the global case – that is, to the extent that the political constituencies holding governance agents to account are stable and well-defined, and that governance power is exercised through transparent and coherent structures of institutional rules. The difficulty, however, is that global governance systems increasingly display structural characteristics that depart significantly from these assumptions – insofar as they are embedded within a global order that is sometimes now described as *pluralist* rather than statist in character (Macdonald and Macdonald 2020). A pluralist political order, as we understand it here, is characterised by complex, interactive, and dynamic governance processes and social collectives, with open and fluid boundaries between governing authorities and their political constituencies, and significant diffusion of governing powers out of rule-based structures of institutionalised authority and into the more complex and dynamic social spaces that lie between them.

This language of political 'pluralism' originates in a range of theoretical critiques directed against the ascendant 'statism' of much late nineteenth- and early twentieth-century political thought, and in particular against its 'monist' ideals of institutional authority and political community (Bevir 2012; Laborde 2000; Runciman and David 1997; Stears 2002). Pluralist and statist imaginaries of political order share common intellectual roots across a number of theoretical traditions – with influences traced to ideas found in older republican constitutional traditions (Levy 2014), 'medieval' or 'organicist' Germanic theories of group personality (Runciman and David 1997, 34–63), and liberal and democratic accounts of civic associations as instruments of freedom (Levy 2014) and political participation (Hirst 1994). While the influence of these late nineteenth- and early twentieth-century pluralist ideals had significantly declined by the 1930s (Runciman and David 1997, 195–222), pluralist imaginaries of political governance and legitimation retained greater currency in the emerging scholarly field of International Relations – influencing the evolution of pluralist internationalism, and pluralist International Relations theory, over the subsequent decades of the twentieth century (Schmidt 2002; Sylvest 2007).

Through the early decades of the twenty-first century, pluralist analyses of international politics have expanded into richer empirical examinations of the 'neomedievalist' (Friedrichs 2001) or 'neopluralist' (Cerny 2010) characteristics of global institutional practices, alongside normative explorations of the distinctive legitimacy challenges arising in 'pluralist' international law (Krisch 2011), transnational authority (Macdonald and Macdonald 2017; Krisch 2017; Zurn 2018) and global democracy (Bohman 2007; Hirst 2013; Macdonald 2008). These pluralist models of world order now provide an increasingly widespread alternative to statism in capturing key structural features of the overarching institutional and societal system in which practices of global accountability must be pursued.

Understanding the contemporary global order as in important respects 'pluralist' rather than 'statist' in its institutional and social structure has two key implications for the functional viability of those accountability mechanisms that have been designed for operation within statist governance systems, yet which are implemented within a pluralist order. We consider each of these distinctive pluralist dilemmas of accountability in turn.

First, it becomes more difficult in a pluralist order to both identify and distinguish between: on the one hand, those agents that exercise *governing authority*, with corresponding responsibilities to *be held* accountable; and on the other hand, those that are *legitimate political constituencies* of governing authorities, with corresponding entitlements to *hold* them to account. Identifying who should be held accountable to whom is an essential first step in the establishment of accountability mechanisms capable of performing valuable functions of managing normative contestation and power competition within a governance system: it is through this basic differentiation that an accountability system must work to restrain the fallible judgment and corruptible power of some (governing authorities), while empowering the legitimate voice and agency of others (political constituencies). The more accountability mechanisms rely for this function on the codification of differentiated political roles, rights, and responsibilities in clear (legal, bureaucratic, or organisational) institutional rules, the more they will be disrupted by the structural features of pluralist global governance systems. In a pluralist order, where a plurality of governance agents and corresponding constituencies interact and overlap through dynamic and continually evolving processes (Zurn 2010; Krisch 2006), there can be significant challenges in identifying which specific governance agents should be held accountable to which political constituencies for which particular outcomes.

It is helpful here to consider some concrete examples. As the roles of intergovernmental bodies such as the International Monetary Fund, the World Bank and a range of regional and bilateral development finance organisations expanded significantly during the latter decades of the twentieth century, these governance agents took on increasingly broad and influential roles in allocating and governing development finance, alongside national and sub-national governments (Macdonald and Miller-Dawkins 2015). Likewise, a wide range of private and hybrid (public-private) multi-stakeholder governance organisations came to play a significant role in governing the social and environmental impacts of global business, including standard-setting and certification bodies such as the Forest Stewardship Council and other multi-stakeholder sustainable commodity roundtables, and transparency and reporting mechanisms such as the Extractive Industries Transparency Initiative (which brings together companies and governments to promote the transparent management of oil, gas and minerals revenues) and the Global Reporting Initiative (which facilitates standard-setting and reporting in relation to a range of issues such as corruption, human rights and environmental management) (De Bakker et al 2019; Utting 2014). These governance domains are therefore characterised by a multiplicity of governing agents and associated constituencies, together with the tendency for these to significantly overlap (so that constituencies are subject to the authority of multiple governing bodies, while governing bodies must juggle multiple competing constituencies).

To the extent that relationships between governing agencies and their constituencies continue to be defined primarily through clear and procedurally-grounded mechanisms such as membership or other institutionalised forms of contractual relationship or affiliation, such plurality does not fundamentally undermine established logics of constituency recognition, though it certainly makes processes of constituency recognition more complicated (Grant and Keohane 2005). The challenge of matching governing agents to political constituencies is significantly intensified, however, when political constituencies instigate demands for recognition and responsiveness in situations where their membership or affiliation is not already institutionally recognised. For example, while global governance organisations like the World Bank and IMF always had clear lines of accountability to Member States (Grant and Keohane 2005; Woods and Narlikar 2001), from the early 1990s, mobilisation began to intensify by and on behalf of broader communities and populations who were affected by their decisions but who lacked these formal accountability relationships. Claims for recognition and responsiveness were increasingly framed in the language of accountability, as affected people and their supporters engaged in protracted political struggles to organise and demand recognition in the form of new or significantly revised accountability mechanisms (O'Brien et al 2000; Grant and Keohane 2005; Goodhard 2014; Fox and Brown 1998).

Such processes of mobilisation and claim-making contributed in important ways to institutional responses such as the creation of the World Bank Inspection Panel, which enables people affected by funded projects to register grievances and initiate investigations into whether the Bank has adhered to its own social and environmental policies in relation to a given project, alongside other new and revised accountability procedures (Fox and Brown 1998; Scholte 2004; Park 2020). Yet such shifts also created increased contestation and uncertainty regarding which of the expanding range of political constituencies affected by the decisions of these international bodies should be entitled to hold them to account for which aspects of their decisions, and on what grounds. Such challenges have been magnified in cases where the effects of decisions taken by these governance bodies play out through complex chains of impact – further compounding challenges of identifying the relevant political constituencies to whom governing agencies have a responsibility to respond. While constituencies can be relatively straightforward to identify in cases where international development agencies are funding large-scale energy or infrastructure projects (for example communities forced to resettle as a result of land appropriation or flooding in the case of dam construction (Fox and Brown 1998)), those constituencies who are either adversely or positively affected as a result of more diffuse and long-term economic or environmental effects of the projects encounter more significant obstacles to recognition. Moreover, affected constituencies are often subject to the authority of a range of interacting governing agencies – national and international, public and private – each applying very different (and sometimes weakly articulated) conceptions of stakeholder or constituency recognition (Olanya 2016). The ways in which communities themselves engage in processes of identify-formation and claim-making also vary significantly between locations and over time – further complicating processes of constituency recognition from the perspective of a given governing agency (Macdonald and Macdonald 2020). Such challenges present significant challenges for reaching agreement or shared understandings regarding who should be accountable to whom for what in a given governance context (Mason 2005; Newell 2008).

The second key implication of pluralist global order for the functional viability of accountability mechanisms is that the diffusion of significant governing powers out of rule-based structures of institutionalised authority, and into the more complex and dynamic social spaces that lie between them, makes it more difficult for political power to be restrained and re-balanced through a framework of publicly-articulated and coherently-ordered institutional rules. Many established accountability instruments for re-distributing power and restraining its abuse – in particular, the republican and liberal constitutional instruments noted above – rely on the assumption that governance power itself is concentrated in clear institutional structures, such that restraint and rebalancing of power can be achieved through separating and balancing the powers assigned through the design of these institutional schemes. In a pluralist global order, however, strong institutionalisation of the relationships between governance agencies and political constituencies is patchy and uneven – with many power contestations playing out in the normative 'wild' (Bicchieri 2016) of weak or overlapping institutional fields. This undermines the capacity of these accountability mechanisms to perform their intended functions with regard to constraining domination and the abuse of power.

This second pluralist dilemma can also be usefully illuminated with reference to some examples. Efforts to regulate the social and environmental impacts of transnational business activity are well-known to confront serious challenges in the face of huge power imbalances between corporations (and their investors and shareholders), governments and citizens, and affected workers and communities dispersed across different parts of the world (Macdonald 2014b). To the extent that the plural political constituencies involved in interactive processes of transnational business governance seek to hold their respective governing agents to account for broadly shared collective purposes, even very significant power imbalances between these groups can have relatively benign implications from the perspective of the role of accountability in managing power competition and conflicting interests, insofar as the power exerted by stronger constituencies and governing agents serves practically to reinforce and amplify the values and purposes of weaker constituencies. Such benign dynamics can emerge for example in the case of those synergistic governance interactions in which collaboration or joint action expands governance capacities in mutually beneficial ways – bringing together diverse governance competencies or facilitating dynamic processes of learning and capacity-building (Abbott and Snidal 2009; Macdonald 2020; Amengual 2010).

In the presence of significantly conflicting aims and priorities between political constituencies, however, such pluralist governance interactions frequently enable more powerful governing agents (and the political constituencies that in turn hold them to account) to influence and constrain the governing capacities of others, thereby constraining the latter's ability to fulfil legitimate obligations of accountability to their own political constituencies. In such circumstances, characterised by conflicting interests alongside significant inequalities of power, the constituencies of weaker governance bodies find that even if they have developed strong accountability mechanisms linking them to governing bodies with whom they have direct institutional relationships, the ability of these authorities to respond effectively to their claims in line with their agreed obligations is undermined by the weakly regulated power of other governing agencies and political constituencies. For example, the influence that corporate shareholders and investors are able to exert over corporate decisions regarding socially and environmentally harmful business practices typically overshadows the leverage of accountability mechanisms available to workers and communities, such as complaints mechanisms linked to voluntary sustainability standards or more informal mechanisms of social accountability (Byrnes 2007; Haines and Macdonald 2020).

In a pluralist order, the weak capacity of any given centralised governance agent to regulate power struggles between plural and decentred governing agents and political constituencies undermines the ability of weaker political constituencies and governing agents to sustain well-functioning accountability mechanisms in relation to their own designated mandates (this problem is not unique to accountability mechanisms in a pluralist order; a similar problem confronts other collective choice mechanisms that are similarly undermined by weakly institutionalised and rule-bound dynamics of interactive power between different political authorities and constituencies, as we have discussed in greater depth elsewhere (Macdonald and Macdonald 2020)). Such dynamics significantly undermine the functional capacity of accountability mechanisms to support the legitimate regulation of power competitions and conflicting interests. In such political spaces, alternative political instruments are required to achieve success in restraining the misuse and over-reach of governing power.

III. Instruments of Accountability in a Pluralist Political Order

How then can we think differently about the kinds of institutional instruments that are most likely to support accountability systems to realise their fundamental purposes amidst the distinctive dilemmas of a pluralist order? Up to a certain point, there is scope for accountability mechanisms to be productively pluralised beyond traditional constitutional or representative models through the use of well-established approaches such as horizontal mechanisms of networked accountability (Slaughter, 2004; Benner et al 2004; Backstrand 2008), alongside a range of other decentred accountability mechanisms involving oversight or review bodies, auditors, ombudsmen and complaints mechanisms, transparency and disclosure requirements and monitoring and evaluation systems (Woods and Narlikar 2001; Chesterman 2008; Kingsbury 2004; Koenig-Archibugi 2010). But as we elaborate below, the structural features of a pluralist order demand reimagined approaches that extend more fundamentally beyond established repertoires of accountability in order to provide more active support for both the recognition and the empowerment of plural and dynamic political constituencies.

Reimagined approaches are required first to provide more support for identification and recognition of the political constituencies associated with a given governing agency, in the face of dynamic, ambiguous and contested boundaries of plural political constituencies. Such approaches need to encompass not only explicit, principled recognition of the legitimacy of fluid and contestable boundaries of political constituencies, but also the creation of institutional mechanisms that actively facilitate inclusion of dynamically shifting constituencies by creating open processes for contested claim-making.

Accommodating dynamic processes of constituency recognition first requires accountability mechanisms that actively facilitate the ongoing entry and exit of constituencies from relevant accountability relationships. For example, while governance agencies often attempt to engage in ex ante mapping of constituencies or stakeholders to whom they are willing to recognise entitlements to hold them to account, a pluralist order demands institutional instruments that provide more systematic means of inviting and facilitating contested claims to such a status, through ongoing processes of negotiation, revision and review (Macdonald and Macdonald 2022).

Second, accountability instruments require organised means of accommodating the qualitatively *different kinds* of constituencies with entitlements to varied forms of recognition and inclusion. At a basic level this requires institutions that are designed explicitly to enable processes of active claim-making, as in the case of the formal accountability mechanisms that have been created by some international development agencies and transnational business governance bodies to enable affected people to participate in deliberative processes or voice their grievances – at least minimally enabling emergent constituencies to mobilise politically and claim a stake in the operation of an existing institution (Macdonald and Macdonald 2017). Accommodating different kinds of constituencies further entails both principles and institutional mechanisms that support recognition of a *diversity* of different kinds of accountability claims, through principled differentiation of the different kinds of claims that can legitimately be made by different groups of affected people. This entails not only plural and flexible inclusion criteria that can be adapted to varied contexts, but also a willingness to consider claims that do not fit neatly into pre-defined criteria. For example, while some accountability mechanisms continue to require specific evidence that pre-defined rules or standards have been violated before affected people are eligible to claim accountability, others (such as the Compliance Advisor Ombudsman (CAO) of the World Bank Group, which handles complaints about projects funded by the International Finance Corporation (IFC) and Multilateral Investment Guarantee Agency (MIGA)), are deliberately open in the way they define eligibility criteria. The Ombudsman arm of the CAO makes access to their accountability mechanism available to anyone who can make a convincing claim to be affected by IFC or MIGA funded projects without imposing pre-defined criteria of affectedness, and allows claims to be brought for any social or environmental problem of concern to affected people, even where these do not relate directly to the World Bank Group's formal International Finance Corporation Performance Standards (Balaton Chrimes and Macdonald 2016).

Openness towards recognising different kinds of constituencies also requires institutional instruments that can accommodate recognition of *indirectly affected* stakeholders. Again, it is possible to find some examples of nascent shifts towards increased openness in principles and practices of constituency recognition that can help to clarify useful directions of change. For instance, governance institutions that regulate the social and environmental impacts of both transnational business activity and international development projects have increasingly been willing to recognise constituencies who are indirectly impacted through distant and highly intermediated supply chain relationships, or through arms-length relationships of international finance (Shavin 2019; Balaton Chrimes and Macdonald 2016; Macdonald and Macdonald 2020). Such examples remain the exception however, reflecting persistent institutional discomfort with the inescapable ambiguities surrounding open approaches to constituency recognition, and there is significant scope for such approaches to be expanded.

Once plural and dynamic political constituencies have been appropriately recognised, revised approaches to accountability are also required to empower these constituencies to hold governance agents to account. Because accountability mechanisms in a pluralist order possess weakened capacity to regulate power imbalances between competing governance agencies and constituencies, such mechanisms need to rely more heavily on *decentred strategies of social empowerment* that harness more dispersed sources of knowledge, power and agency as counterbalances to established and emergent concentrations of social and political power.

First, a pluralist order demands attention to mechanisms designed to empower plural political constituencies directly, thereby helping these groups to engage in accountability claims against a societal background of material inequality and asymmetrical power, and in the absence of an overarching 'state' or unified framework of authoritative rules. For example, formal accountability systems associated with international financial institutions or multi-stakeholder certification schemes can productively be supplemented by more diffuse social empowerment initiatives at the local level, in order to provide affected people with requisite information, resources, relationships and bargaining power to make practical use of formally available accountability mechanisms (Miller-Dawkins, Macdonald and Marshall 2016). Depending on circumstances, such empowerment may be supported for instance through direct institutional facilitation of the participation of marginalised groups (Dingwerth 2008), through establishment and maintenance of public service users' groups or worker or community-based organisations (Gupta 2020, Tanaka 2011), or via outreach and capacity-building designed to directly facilitate access of disempowered workers or communities to specific grievance or accountability mechanisms (Macdonald and Macdonald 2017; Haines and Macdonald 2020; Garvey and Newell 2005).

Second, facilitating decentred processes of social empowerment demands targeted structural interventions that can help to counter background social conditions that impede the empowerment of more marginalised constituencies (Fung et al 2003; Macdonald and Macdonald 2020). For instance, considering again the example of accountability mechanisms in the international development sector, efforts to empower the claim-making capacities of marginalised women or other structurally marginalised groups such as indigenous communities or smallholder farmers in processes of accountability can be facilitated by concurrent interventions oriented toward facilitating immediate subsistence needs and strengthening access to basic services and livelihood opportunities, as a means of building structural capacities to establish and sustain the capacity to engage effectively in processes of political claim-making (Yan et al 2018; Ward and Mouyly 2013; Macdonald and Macdonald 2022).

Third, it can be possible to empower constituencies more indirectly through support for appropriately empowered and authorised intermediaries, who can sometimes act as 'surrogates' or 'proxies' to hold decision makers to account, nominally on behalf of primary accountability-holders (Rubenstein 2007; Koenig-Archibugi and Macdonald 2013). For example, within global systems of voluntary sustainability governance targeting the social and environmental performance of business, NGOs or other civil society actors often take on roles as third-party intermediaries who claim to act on behalf of others, either on the basis of a direct representative mandate, or on their own initiative. In such capacities, intermediaries may play significant roles in shaping or endorsing accountability obligations, receiving information about compliance, sanctioning governing agents, or supporting directly affected constituencies themselves to mobilise and make claims (Macdonald and Macdonald 2022). Intermediated accountability relationships of this kind are particularly common where directly affected political constituencies lack sufficient information, power or institutional access to enforce accountability obligations directly. While use of such intermediated accountability relationships can play an important role in adding leverage to the claims of structurally marginalised groups, such approaches also entail distinctive risks with regard to the accountability of intermediaries to ultimate principals – particularly when such actors have not been explicitly authorised to act in such roles, and where their own organisational values or interests diverge from those of the people they claim to represent (Koenig-Archibugi and Macdonald 2013; Macdonald 2018). Therefore, at the same time that pluralist accountability systems can benefit from strengthened mechanisms of intermediated accountability, attention is also required to mechanisms of transparency, oversight and representation that can help to ensure that intermediaries in turn support rather than undermine the responsiveness of governance agents to the constituencies to whom they ultimately owe obligations of accountability.

IV. Final Thoughts

Despite the ongoing proliferation of new and revised accountability mechanisms in global governance, global accountability agendas have struggled to find workable ways of controlling power imbalances and managing normative disagreements amongst political constituencies within a pluralist global political order that lacks a constitutionalised institutional structure. This has fuelled an ongoing dilemma of overload and underperformance, in which the proliferation of global accountability mechanisms may succeed in partially or temporarily papering over some specific accountability gaps, while failing to address the deeper challenges that are structurally produced by a pluralist order, linked in particular to diffuse and decentred configurations of governing power, and dynamic and ambiguous boundaries of political constituencies.

Because the structural drivers of such paradoxical tensions between accountability overload and underperformance are linked to underlying features of a pluralist political order, the conventional repertoire of statist accountability mechanisms, grounded in assumptions about stable relations between governing agents and their political constituencies, cannot adequately counter persistent global accountability gaps. In some ways the very language of accountability 'gaps' is unhelpful here, insofar as this language reinforces that idea that what we need is *more* and/or better targeted accountability mechanisms to plug the array of enduring accountability deficits. Instead, we have argued that we need to think differently about the structural constitution of accountability instruments within a pluralist political order.

Our analysis has underlined the distinctive value of accountability arrangements that align with a pluralist order not only by recognising multiple sites of global governance authority and associated political constituencies, but also by recognising and seeking actively to accommodate the inescapable dynamism and diversity of relationships between governing agents and political constituencies within complex interactive systems of global governance. We have also highlighted the need for accountability approaches that better accommodate highly decentred configurations of social and institutional power, through supporting more explicit strategies of social empowerment as a basis for establishing the material leverage required to render global accountability systems functionally effective and politically sustainable. In these ways, our analysis has highlighted the importance of the concept of 'rebalancing' not only with regard to the importance of a proportionate balance between democratic scrutiny and governing capacity, as discussed in other chapters in this volume, but also with regard to the importance of *rebalancing social power*. This entails efforts both to counter deeply constituted imbalances between the social and institutional power of different social constituencies, and to support the continual contestation and rebalancing of the ways in which political institutions recognise and empower diverse constituencies. Indeed, it may be that despite the distinctive challenges of accountability associated with a pluralist global order, accountability actually rises in importance under pluralist conditions: while in a rules-based order, legitimacy depends centrally on creating institutional systems that enable the right people to make the rules in the right ways, in the 'normative wilds' of a pluralist order, a more diverse range of mechanisms for regulating and balancing power is required. Precisely because of the ways in which accountability is oriented towards rebalancing power relations in normatively directed ways, its significance is potentially heightened in a pluralist order, at the same time that it becomes ever more challenging to attain.

In these ways, reconceptualising the paradox of overload and underperformance through the lens of a pluralist understanding of global political order not only helps us to understand underlying drivers of persistent accountability gaps and to develop revised accountability repertoires that may be better equipped to support the legitimacy of global governance under pluralist conditions; it also helps us to reflect more deeply on the central purposes of accountability, understood with reference not only to the design of formal governance institutions, but also with regard to the deeper aims of legitimising the ways in which underlying social power struggles can be channelled into and constrained by shared collective governance institutions. This helps to remind us why accountability continues to be of such persistent and fundamental importance despite the accountability deficits and paradoxes that continue to afflict global as well as domestic scales of public governance.

12

Accountability from the Inside-Out

DAVID BLUNKETT

In many ways the 'inside-out' theme of this chapter reflects my own personal experience with 'questions of accountability' and I recognise many of the themes, issues and dilemmas that have been raised in previous chapters. My life has to some extent been based very much within the messy business of practical politics. At the age of just 22 I became the youngest ever councillor elected to Sheffield City Council, and went on to lead the council from 1980–87. Elected to Parliament in 1987, I went on to hold a number of senior ministerial positions including Secretary of State for Education and Employment (1997–2001), Home Secretary (2001–05) and Secretary of State for Work and Pensions (2005). In total I was an MP for 28 years and even now as a working member of the House of Lords I cannot really claim to be 'out' of politics or public life. What's interesting about my move from the lower and democratically accountable chamber to a largely appointed and advisory 'upper House' is that 'questions of accountability' still tend to dominate debates and discussions. These questions tend to be as technically challenging as they are political, and there are no simple answers I can offer in this chapter. But what I can offer is a very specific and generally unheard perspective that uses insights from personal biography and my life in politics. The perspective provided is not defined so much from constitutional theory, public law or scholarly seminar rooms; not even from the position of those of advisers or officials who have supported me over the decades, but from the position of the elected representative who has to answer for the decisions they make.

The perspective I seek to explore is therefore one that looks from the inside-out and from the position of the individual, the person, the man or woman who has stepped 'into the arena' – to paraphrase Theodore Roosevelt – generally based on a commitment and belief in the capacity of collective action to produce positive social change. From this perspective it is worth remembering that political systems in general, and Westminster-style democracies in particular, provide a very clear response to the question of '*who* is accountable?' The answer is *ministers*, and the *secretaries of state*, in particular. It is members of the executive who very often act as lightning rods for public anger, frustration or disappointment irrespective of whether the source of concern could ever reasonably have been within the minister's control. To highlight the social psychological role of politicians serving as societal pressure valves should not be read as an early attempt to engage in presentational blame games. But it does begin to highlight the complexity and multi-layered nature of political life and, as such, serves to focus attention on the politics and management of public expectations. In an age when the business of government is increasingly complex and politicians are, as a result, governing under amplified pressure, disentangling where the controlling 'mind' lies, and therefore who is responsible, is increasingly difficult. When collective decisions are being made, individual cabinet ministers are expected to adhere to the overall policy decision taken. Sometimes this means they will be held to account for things that were either out of their control, or where they were overridden. This is the very essence of collective responsibility.

This brings the discussion back to a topic that was raised in chapter one and whether the concept of accountability should always be viewed as a 'good' thing. As a democrat with a strong, extensive and demonstrable commitment to communitarian thinking I would argue that accountable governance is indeed a *sine qua non* of any truly democratic regime. But my experience looking from the inside-out as a professional politician has also underlined that very few grand statements can be made without at least one or two notes of reservation. The note of caution I would raise is simply one that takes the discussion back to the themes of blend, balance and proportionality that have already emerged as the intellectual glue that binds each of the chapters into a coherent collection. In this chapter I seek to tighten the focus around the impact of accountability on individual politicians in order to broaden out the discussion. The aim is not to develop an 'In Defence of Politicians' position – others have already taken on that notoriously tricky task (see, for example, Riddell 2011; Flinders 2012; Stoker 2016; Hardman 2019) – but simply to outline my perception of the 'lived reality' of political life.

In this regard there is an obvious link back to Jonathan Slater's contribution to this collection (chapter eight) in the sense that his focus on policy accountability emerged out of his professional experience rather than decades of academic study. My arguments are similarly based not on 'scientific' peer-reviewed research but on practical experience. If pushed to dress my comments in the cloak of academic credibility I might suggest that this chapter is derived from an auto-ethnographic approach. According to Adams, Holman Jones and Ellis (2015) autoethnography is a research method that uses an individual's personal experience to critique specific political, cultural or social beliefs, practices or conventions. In doing so it assists those individuals (and research-users) to understand *what* they have done, *why* they did it and *how* to live with and give meaning to challenges that span personal, professional and political boundaries. The researcher or writer uses self-reflection to explore anecdotal and personal experience with the aim of then connecting the insights of this knowledge base to wider political, cultural and social debates. 'The meanings and applications of autoethnography' as Ellingson and Ellis (2008, 449) note 'have evolved in a manner that makes precise definition difficult' but the value of this approach is that it creates a space for different stories to be told.

To date, too many of the 'academic' stories written about the topic of accountability – laden as they are with rich and relevant analyses of 'webs', 'overloads', 'shields' and 'deficits' – are just that: academic analyses written at a distance from the day-to-day messiness and experience of accountability processes. To make this point is not intended to devalue the skill or sophistication of scholarly works written from the relative safety of the university library or seminar room – the *Oxford Handbook of Public Accountability* (Bovens, Goodin and Schillemans 2014) is a particularly impressive text – but it is to suggest that such 'outside-in' analyses might benefit from being both offset and challenged by 'inside-out' accounts that seek to explain the lived experience of those who do at least 'step into the arena' of political life. The benefit of pluralism – in terms of approach, method and perspective – was drilled into me by my friend and university tutor, Sir Bernard Crick. His work as both an academic and as an active mediator in practical politics ranged from promoting citizenship education to supporting the Constitutional Convention in Northern Ireland (see Gormley-Heenan 2012; Walker 2017) which reflected his commitment to understanding and studying politics from the 'outside-in' and 'inside-out'. It's probably also worth noting that for Bernard – as a man who was intellectually brilliant and professionally prickly in equal measure – the existence of a crisis represented an opportunity to get under the skin of practical politics and through this to understand the broader significance of specific issues or tensions.

Evidence of some form of democratic crisis does seem to sum-up the contemporary condition. From global reports of 'democratic backsliding' to Covid-inspired debates concerning the relative merits of authoritarian as opposed to democratic regimes; through to pessimistic analyses of populist pressures and concerns about a basic 'assault on truth'. Even more positive analyses about the achievements of collective responses in the past and the need for a new 'upswing' (see Putnam 2020) today seem relatively light in terms of specific actionable insights.

The extraordinary events of July–October 2022 within the UK political arena graphically demonstrate the interaction between human emotion, hubris, failure of intellectual rigour and understanding of modern sources of economic power, and simple human frailty. Accountability clearly lies with a Prime Minister and Chancellor who translated ideology into practical political action, but what of the 82,000 Conservative Party members who voted for a programme which so many had already predicted would lead to catastrophic outcomes? No wonder questions of accountability occupy a central position within this general pool of democratic discontent. It is in exactly this context that this chapter seeks to explore three very specific questions within a broader and highly unconventional focus on *mess and messiness*.

My basic argument is that this focus adds tone and texture to questions of accountability by adding an inflection born from practical politics. Moreover, although I don't want to fall into the trap of trying to appear too clever in a book consisting largely of academic contributions, I think it is possible to introduce the topic of messiness from three complementary perspectives. The first is intellectual and brings me to a focus on Bernard Crick's classic text *In Defence of Politics*. First published in 1962 and still in print today, this book's central argument is that democratic politics is essentially messy and to some extent prone to failure. This was not, however, a weakness of democratic politics but for Crick was a reflection of its innate beauty – democratic politics revolved around the resolution of often incompatible demands. Resolving these dilemmas demanded compromise, deal-making and horse-trading that could often be very hard to understand from the outside and almost inevitably led to what economists would term 'sub-optimal outcomes'. As so many have reflected in the past, the prioritisation of scarce resources and the contradictions of an electorate that want to pay less but receive more are bound to lead to perceived failure. But that was the price you paid for living in a democracy where transitions of power were peaceful, and where most people were broadly satisfied with how the system worked.

This brings me to a focus on messiness from a second more institutional angle. Put very simply, the institutional structures and processes that were originally designed to deliver a workable level of accountability have to a large extent been overtaken by increasing levels of complexity. This is the transition from 'government to governance' that scholars such as RAW Rhodes (see, for example, Rhodes 1996; 2007; Kjaer 2011) have done so much to explore and understand. The shift from hierarchies to markets and networks is reflected in the structure of the modern state; while the capacity of that system in terms of meta-governance has to some extent also been weakened by transnational flows and forces. Where power lies is always the underlying question which is rarely addressed. Politicians, in particular, do not want to admit that power doesn't lie with them, because otherwise the electorate might be inclined to ask the reasonable question: 'why should I vote for you?'. But without the admission of the reality of global sources of power and their impact on domestic decision-making, we end up debating accountability in a vacuum. Aneurin Bevan's journey from parish council to county council, to Parliament and hence to the cabinet in the post-war Labour Government was a personal search for the exercise of influence. Despite his enormous achievements in that government, he remained frustrated, and at a time when nation states had much greater control, and therefore power, than they possess today.

As Home Secretary in the UK Government at the time of the September 11 attack on the World Trade Centre and beyond in 2001 (also known as '9/11'), did underline, for me, the latent strategic capacity and co-operative structures that can be invoked in moments of crisis. In this regard I was interested to see that analyses of how different countries responded to the Covid crisis are already being framed in the language of 'hollowing-out' and 'filling-in' (see, for example, Jones and Hameiri 2021; Paton 2020; Carter and May 2020). But the point I am making is that governance and governing is messy. As in this case, something that doesn't just dislocate but completely disrupts the planned development of policy and its delivery, the agenda that was proactive, as opposed to reactive. This is what the former Conservative Prime Minister, Harold Macmillan, described in the early 60s as 'events, dear boy, events'. Twenty-five years ago, Vivien Lowndes argued that 'we are learning to accommodate mess' (1997) yet to some extent the scholarly literature on accountability seems unable or unwilling to. This is seen through an emphasis on neat theories, clear frameworks and methodological rigour which too often appears incapable of accommodating the day-to-day realities of political life.

Although our media and our traditional political processes would like to hold just one single person to account, the reality is that both decision-making processes and delivery systems tend to involve a plethora of people and a range of organisations. As such, although our theories and constitutional blueprints for accountability might be nice and simple the real world is (unfortunately) far more multi-faceted. It is the space of contradiction between constitutional clarity and real-world messiness that explains perennial concerns regarding an 'accountability gap'. Can this 'gap' ever be completely closed? I doubt it. Can this 'gap' be better understood? I am sure it can.

And one way of promoting understanding brings me to a third perspective on messiness and back to my adoption of a broadly autoethnographic approach. I am not exactly inexperienced when it comes to writing autobiographies or memoirs (see Blunkett 1995 (updated 2001); 2006; and, for reflections on community politics, see Blunkett and Jackson 1987) but autoethnographic work is very different and not something that I have any real experience of. And yet I am drawn to it as a method for the simple reason that 'Social life is messy, uncertain, and emotional' as Adams, Holman Jones and Ellis (2015) have written, and 'If our desire [is] to research social life, then we must embrace a research method that, to the best of its/our ability, acknowledges and accommodates mess and chaos, uncertainty and emotion.'

The first question to be addressed takes us back to debates concerning accountability 'overloads' and 'deficits' and seeks to express my concern (born of practical experience) that the accountability landscape has become somewhat chaotic. Have we got the balance right or are we in danger of creating an anarchic impression which leads to alienation, mistrust or contempt for the political process (namely falling foul of multiple-accountabilities disorder and its pathological implications)? This brings us to the second theme and to a focus on coping with uncertainty. One of the most obvious risks of any *post-hoc* accountability process is hindsight bias; that is, the failure to acknowledge that events demanded that decisions needed to be taken by politicians or officials who were expected to govern under huge pressure and with imperfect information. Subsequent inquiries, reviews or commissions tend to frame their account-taking activities within a very different context (calm, post-crisis, perfect information, etc). The benefit of hindsight might be a wonderful thing for a vast range of 'monitory bodies' – to adopt John Keane's phrase – to possess but it does little to capture the realities of raw politics (especially when politicians, parties and actors in non-democratic parts of the world proactively seek to sow the seeds of doubt and mistrust). How can hindsight biases be resolved or addressed, especially when scrutiny structures are very often pulled into more partisan game playing? How are ministers to be held to account when the advice they received from 'the experts' was itself unable to cope with uncertainty? Take, for example, decisions which are made by other players but for whom the politician in the driving seat at the time might be blamed. Demutualising building societies could be one example. Government facilitated the process, but individual investors 'voted' – with the promise of financial return – to create banks (rather than mutual societies) which then became vulnerable to global movements, including the financial global meltdown of 2007–08. These are core questions of accountability that the existing research base seems particularly ill-equipped to answer.

This brings us to a third and final focus and to a topic which has for too long evaded detailed analysis – the link between accountability and emotion. There is, of course, significant literature on the social psychological drivers of scrutiny processes. This generally highlights an embedded 'negativity bias' and explores the role of emotional dynamics such as trust, hope, fear and anger in underlining the need for 'effective' accountability processes. Thomas Schilleman's contribution to this volume (chapter two) explores the relevance of this literature alongside attempts to draw-upon the insights of more applied studies of public administration. This fusing of approaches is to be welcomed and to some extent its most stimulating and potentially impactful recent contribution has involved a focus on understanding 'felt accountability' (for a review see Hall, Frink and Buckley 2017). The concept of 'felt accountability', would at first glance appear to offer an intuitive connection to this chapter's emphasis on emotions and to some extent it does, but through a very specific and arguably narrow focus. That is, through a focus on how agency chief executives feel about accounting 'up' to their parent departments in terms of the governing expectations and expertise of the department to credibly assess the content of that account (see Schillemans et al 2021).

This approach, although undoubtedly representing the state-of-the-art, might from the position of this chapter be seen as arguably 'felt-lite' (or possibly more accurately, 'felt-narrow') in the sense that it seeks to gauge how officials feel about accounting in a formal or bureaucratic sense. Whereas this chapter's focus seeks to promote a more 'felt-heavy' (or 'felt-broad') position that would embrace a more rounded approach to how it feels to be accountable. An account, that is, which would include some understanding of the stressors of political life, possibly even some sensitivity towards the mental health and well-being of politicians and public servants. Human beings have private lives. Human beings have a real problem in balancing work and social life, and in the present era, the pressures of social media, greater transparency and scrutiny, and 24-hour news outlets and the demand for instant answers. What this chapter does not address is the issues raised by the Nolan principles. These are about personal behaviour and individuals' responsibility for their actions. Obviously, this raises questions about wider accountability but is very much about the ethical and constitutional behaviour of those involved and, therefore, not addressed in detail here.

With this in mind, if a focus on mess and messiness provides the foundation for this chapter then the following three questions of accountability provide its main pillars.

1. Do we have too much or too little accountability (or too much or too little of the wrong type of accountability)?
2. How can accountability mechanisms cope with uncertainty, in general, and hindsight bias, in particular?
3. How does it *feel* to be the focus of accountability?

Let me be very clear about my reasons for focusing on the topic of emotions and human factors. My interest in focusing on the emotional or psychological impact of *being a politician* is purely intended to help promote the public understanding of politics, and to help contribute to a climate in which a broader range of people might find a career in politics an attractive and feasible option. In engaging with all three of these questions I want to utilise stories, anecdotes and insights from my own career in politics. This begins with a focus on chaos.

I. Chaos: Too Much or Too Little?

The focus of Ellen Rock's chapter was on 'questions of measurement' and the elusive (or illusive) search for some sort of 'normative yardstick' against which debates concerning 'too much' or 'too little' ('deficits' and 'overloads') might be assessed. The challenge, as Rock acknowledges, is that such questions are not only contextually dependent but they are also multi-layered and inevitably contestable. The messiness of public accountability makes the concept difficult to fit into measurable units; there are no easily identifiable 'sweet spots'. There are, of course, proxy indicators that might provide a sense of 'accountability activity' such as numbers of parliamentary questions answered, appearances before legislative scrutiny committees, audit reports, etc, but in reality, I know from good experience that such processes are often part of a performative game and that what counts vis-à-vis accountability can rarely be counted. What's also interesting but rarely discussed in the academic literature is that politicians face different constituent audiences.

There are the formal and well-known audiences, like parliamentary committees or questions on the floor of the chamber, and to some extent you can prepare for those. Ministers will clear significant chunks of their diary in order to practice how they might respond to various questions. But there is a scripted and almost ritualistic process to be gone through and although unexpected questions may well be thrown at you – what we called 'googlies' – for the most part it is a game-like interaction. The aim of the game, moreover, is very often less about finding out what went wrong or to explore the policy-learning opportunities emerging out of an event or incident, and far more about party political point-scoring with the ultimate aim being to embarrass the minister. There were occasions in my own experience where I walked away from either an interchange on the floor of the Chamber or appearance before a Select Committee, and indicate to my own special advisers or private office that 'we had better get that sorted out', or 'that went fine, but I think we should have some better answers next time this topic is raised!' However, when you get into the 'real world' accountability of different audiences, by which I mean serious interviews on radio or television, analysis in the remaining print media, or the occasional outburst on social media, you find yourself on your own. Sometimes, when things have gone badly wrong you can find yourself isolated. There is an old adage that if you want a friend in politics, get a dog. I, of course, have a dog. But what I also have is a range of family, friends and acquaintances who have stuck with me through thick and thin. I am very fortunate in this respect, it isn't all that usual, and it can see you through the most difficult times. In fact, on occasions, it has been an alternative to 'going into therapy'!

In opposition, you do not have a large official team to support you, there are no rules or conventions that limit what you might be asked (or how) and there are no limits on the number of secondary questions that might be levelled straight back at you. All of this is relatively new. The newsreels and recorded interviews from the past indicate a very different world where deference and respect led to what would now seem a very easy time for our predecessors. Perhaps a newspaper interview once every few weeks, or a radio interview on an equally infrequent basis. Yes, there was *That Was the Week That Was*, and eventually there was *Spitting Image*, but this was about satire and attack on the individual rather than any form of meaningful accountability.

In government, you are on your metal because what you say – until the phrase 'misspoken' became a frequent mantra – was taken as government policy! You are in a different realm in terms of the nature of accountability, but this often reverberates back into the more formal constitutional processes. One dimension of this is that politicians will often attempt to use every opportunity to shift the blame on to other people, parties or governments around the world; or they might try and use an event to signal a change in policy or to simply acknowledge that they understand why an issue is attracting public interest.

This is not confined to government. Oppositions endeavour to place the blame on the incumbents when they know, perfectly well, that what they are saying is nothing short of a downright lie. The suggestion that the Labour Government was responsible for what, in reality, was a financial global meltdown initiated in the US back in 2007–08, is a classic example. Knockabout it might be, but very serious knockabout at that!

Politicians will often try and *account back to the public* in ways that represent them trying to regain control of an agenda. When they have a clear narrative, this can work. When they are so busy trying to sort out a major problem, as in

2008, it becomes more difficult. This is reinforced when major action which would otherwise gain enormous credit is overlaid by internal issues that are not the responsibility of government. The 'allowances scandal' of 2009 would be such an example. A successful meeting initiated by then Prime Minister, Gordon Brown, to pull together the G20 of leading countries and institutions in the financial world, was universally acknowledged as successful. However, just weeks later, the revelations published by the *Daily Telegraph* about MPs expenses changed the political landscape almost out of recognition. Any credit that the Prime Minister might have claimed for his leadership at the international level was immediately wiped away by a domestic crisis. Although the roots of this crisis could be traced back many decades and involved the decisions of successive Prime Ministers to allow a lax expenses system to emerge as an excuse not to tackle the thorny issue of MPs pay head on, it was a 'creeping crisis' that erupted at a very specific point in time (see Flinders and Anderson 2022). Historical explanations were unable to assuage understandable public anger, and although party leaders attempted to 'get tough' with their own backbenchers in an attempt to reassure and provide confidence for the public this also had unexpected repercussions.

Trying to engage with the public through formal accountability processes is far harder than is often recognised. Good intentions are easily twisted into accusations of vacuous 'virtue signalling'. The challenge for any politician is that the electorate are never united on any one issue. As such, you cannot please 'all of the people all of the time' but those sections of society who are most against you (or your position) are likely to dominate the subsequent debate. The next issue is that public accountability can be bruising. Visits to schools, hospitals or any form of public event bring with them the obvious risk that an irate member of the public might use your visit as the opportunity to unleash their anger. To some extent, that is all part-and-parcel of political life; it is good for professional politicians to be brought down to earth with a bump sometimes. Open and honest meetings with patients, parents, police officers, etc, can also be invaluable for politicians who want to understand what is happening (or not happening) 'on the ground'. Constituency surgeries and meetings are such an important part of the accountability process – they keep the politician grounded and connected into local community concerns. This is why I personally remain committed to the single-member constituency, and whilst recognising the intellectual validity of the debate around Proportional Representation (PR), remain unconvinced. Whilst this isn't the place to open-up a debate in relation to PR as opposed to the single-member constituencies, it would be remiss not to indicate in this chapter that the nature of coalition government automatically alters lines of responsibility, defining how and where decisions have been taken, and therefore who to hold to account.

Constant boundary changes erode the connection between the individual politician and those they represent. This 'disconnect' can then become a justification for moving to multimember constituencies but, far from increasing the democratic connectivity, such moves emphasise the internalisation of political fixers, insiders' manipulation and negotiation, and confuse, still further, who should be held to account for what. But returning to the human factor, it is always worth remembering that they exist in an environment that is low-trust but blame-heavy, and sometimes they will inevitably let their personal frustrations and failures show. The ubiquity of media coverage and microphones mean that even the most ill-advised comment, born ultimately of tiredness and frustration and uttered beyond the public gaze, may well be picked-up and form the focus of an outcry.

The aim of making this point is not to excuse such behaviour, but to promote understanding about the pressures of public life. The ebb-and-flow of this account-demanding and account-giving is, in many ways, little more than the practical reality of democratic life. It is part of the process, or rich ecosystem. My slight concern, however, is that the biggest waves often don't focus on the most important topics. Small issues and scandals become universalised and sensationalised to the extent that there is far more smoke than fire; or one big issue dominates to the detriment of continuing to scrutinise a host of other equally important issues. Covid was, for example, a 'big' issue and it was completely correct that the government's response was subject to a huge amount of scrutiny (see Flinders 2021). But it's also possible to suggest that an 'accountability over-steer' occurred and that lots of continuing societal challenges and issues did not receive the sustained treatment they deserved. Whilst 'Partygate' was a great opportunity for the Opposition – not only to attack the government but also to gain a hearing, the undoubted cronyism associated with major public expenditure through contracting for PPE and billions of pounds wasted on unusable equipment or uncollected loans, was diminished. The focus was elsewhere, and time is a great friend of any government, as memories fade and attention shifts elsewhere.

Which brings the discussion back to a focus on chaos and the inevitable complexities of public life and getting things done. The focus of the far greater part of the existing literature on accountability adopts a supply-side perspective and generally comes to the conclusion that the system is somehow failing. But this interpretation that politics is failing and that someone must therefore be to blame itself fails to grasp the realities not just of complex and inter-dependent institutional structures but also what might be termed the basic essence of democratic politics. 'Politics often involves a stumbling search to find a collective response to particular problems' Colin Hay and Gerry Stoker (2009, 234) emphasise, '[I]t is not the most edifying human experience. It is rarely an experience of self-actualisation and more often an experience of accepting second-best. The results tend to be messy, contingent and inevitably create a mix of winners and losers.' But we risk losing something, or contaminating our political culture, as those who do not always get what they want begin to decry the underpinning values and principles of democracy itself.

Practical politics is made up of competing priorities. It revolves around reconciling massive demands with limited resources. The neatest, most rational and evidence-based plans are often disrupted by events that could never have been anticipated and I wonder if this might be the root problem with the concept of accountability. Mel Dubnick (2002) has written of the need to get 'beyond the false promises of accountability' as part of his 'seeking salvation' argument and this theme certainly resonates with the 'inside-out' perspective offered in this chapter for the simple reason that 'accountability' is a loaded concept. Loaded in the sense that it implicitly suggests a level of clarity, precision, control that is very rarely present in the messy world of practical politics. The 'quest for responsibility' – to paraphrase the title of Mark Boven's (2008) influential book – is complicated by at least two factors. The first is *temporal in nature* and simply highlights institutional, or more specifically individual, 'churn' (a point discussed by Jonathan Slater in chapter eight). Ministers, far more than their officials, come and go. This means that a minister is rarely responsible for carrying through a policy to eventual implementation, and those who take over often have other agendas even when they are of the same political party as their predecessor. 'Not invented here' applies as much within the political family as it does when there is a change of government. Continuity is often in the hands of the professional Civil Service who collectively have their own likes and dislikes, their own interests and priorities. Even then, the way in which musical chairs takes place within the Service – particularly the disbandment of those who formed the team putting through legislation rather than giving them responsibility for implementation, results in anything but smooth delivery, adequate evaluation, or internal scrutiny of success. Repeated structural changes to the NHS including the two major upheavals since 2010 would be a good example.

Leaving aside the absolute chaos of 2022, the previous decade had seen the most enormous churn in relation to key briefs. The number of Justice Secretaries, the revolving door in Education following Michael Gove's departure, are just two examples of a complete lack of continuity of policy, and subsequent diminution in the quality of delivery. The second element that frustrates any simplistic quest for responsibility is structural and simply emphasises how and why complex societal challenges (ie, 'wicked issues') tend to span governmental structures. Tackling obesity, loneliness, online abuse, homelessness, etc, demands 'joined-up' government or a network-based approach which inevitably complicates the accountability landscape.

This makes holding anyone to account really difficult because the system is just too fluid. This is why simplistic constitutional conventions about individual ministerial responsibility, which were designed in times when the structure of the state was far smaller and simpler, struggle to cope with complexity. Disentangling administrative incompetence from policy ineptitude is incredibly challenging – traditional distinctions about officials being responsible for administration and ministers for policy just doesn't work in reality – especially in a context where the shadow of intense and highlighted personalised blame really does hang over the system. The resignation of Lord Carrington as Foreign Secretary following the Argentine invasion of the Falklands was a classic example of a politician falling on his sword – resulting from the lack of intelligence, diplomatic monitoring and foresight by the Foreign Office, MI6 and GCHQ.

In the modern era with 24/7 news and instant communication, people being held to account by real-time polling and the twitterati, and with much greater transparency and access to government information than we have ever had in the past, the world has changed. Whatever books were written about politics and accountability in the twentieth century are almost irrelevant now, which is why there are so many questions to be examined about the juxtaposition of theory and practice. Yet in office I found it incredibly hard to promote conversations that attempted to explain the link between complexity and accountability. There were at least two dimensions to this challenge. The first revolved around intra-governmental relationships and simply trying to explain things to your fellow cabinet members who didn't always relate to what was going on because their departments might have been part of the problem. If we take a complex topic like immigration, it was surprisingly hard to get across what the nuances of the debate were, especially when you relied on the Foreign Office to do their bit in terms of returning people to safe countries, ensuring an effective visa application process, or undertaking negotiations with other governments, which were all policy elements that affected inward immigration that the Home Secretary would ultimately be held accountable for. But explaining and driving change across government was challenging, and when it came to explaining all of this to the public there was the danger of information overload. Cultivating a calm, evidence-based and mature public debate about any major topic was nearly impossible.

Where are the examples of accountability coping with complexity? Maybe this is a key question that needs to be asked in an attempt to close the 'accountability gap' that has been mentioned so often. The second question might also ask – if accountability cannot always deliver clarity and precision in relation to the 'who?', 'what?', 'when?', 'why?', 'how?' questions, then does that automatically mean that the system is failing or that politicians and their officials have something to hide? On some occasions it may well reflect a willingness to 'carry the can' and all the other features of 'Teflon-coated' politics that have been explored in great detail within the literature on blame-avoidance. But on other occasions the existence of blurred accountability may, as already suggested, reflect the simple scale and complexity of the issue, and the *shared* accountability across a network that simply cannot satisfy the concept's implicit desire for a single focus in the form of a minister or official who 'takes one for the team' or is essentially 'hung out to dry' as the sacrificial lamb or scapegoat.

Too much of the wrong kind of accountability (ie, immature, simplistic, aggressive, often gendered) leads to under-performance for the simple reason that those working within the system tend to adopt highly defensive and risk-averse positions. In fact, my sense of coping with accountability in government was generally synonymous with constant fire-fighting which makes policy-making and open honest conversations far more difficult. This 'tin hats mentality' (see Norton 2017) stifles innovation, creativity and dynamism; but this is a systemic challenge (or question) which is very rarely even discussed. Taking this thought further, it may well be that we need *less* of the wrong kind accountability and *more* of a very different form if we are to progress beyond the questions that currently define the debate.

Let me give a very simple example. In the UK, the Public Accounts Committee (PAC) in the House of Commons is generally viewed as an effective scrutiny tool. Effectiveness in this sense bolstered by the existence of an 800-person strong National Audit Office which reports into the PAC and therefore provides a resource and capacity which is way beyond the handful of staff that service most other select committees in the Commons or the Lords. The PAC is therefore seen as sitting at the apex of parliamentary accountability, and it is very often used as the basis for other broader parliamentary reforms and modernisation. People respect the PAC and yet I'd suggest it's where the most blame-games tend to play out. I've seen people literally skewered when in front of the committee. I've also seen members and chairs of that committee take great delight when they have either been able to embarrass ministers or civil servants, or subject chief executives from across the public and private sector to a particularly uncomfortable grilling in front of the television cameras. This, of course, is not to say that the PAC has not undertaken a huge amount of important scrutiny in recent years or that some witnesses have not deserved to be 'hauled across the coals' but I am just floating the question as to whether such an adversarial approach is really likely to get to the truth about what might have gone wrong, and what needs to happen to put it right. Witnesses will put on their tin hats, adopt a defensive posture, feel unable to speak with candor and may well be tempted to try and place the blame on someone else. So, you have to be very careful that what you are doing – and this goes back to the type or blend of accountability – is forensic and insightful and gets to the truth but in a way that helps to carry policy forward, rather than pushing people back into a bunker where they won't take difficult decisions or dare to innovate. It might also be useful if that approach could acknowledge the existence of uncertainty and the benefit of hindsight.

II. Uncertainty: Beyond the Benefit of Hindsight?

Section I suggested that democratic politics may have evolved to a position where it has become unbalanced. Unbalanced in the sense that it has too much of the 'wrong' type of accountability and too little of the 'right' type. To talk in such 'wrong'/'right', 'black'/'white', 'less'/'more', etc terms is clearly problematic in a chapter dedicated to underlining that practical politics is a world defined by constantly shifting shades of grey, but at a basic level there is something to be said for chapter one's identification of 'two types' or, more precisely 'two modes' of accountability.

Mode I is blame-based, emotionally driven and generally discussed in terms of 'hot rhetoric'. It is vulnerable to partisan game-playing and often mutates into the knee-jerk identification of sacrificial lambs or scapegoats. Mode I is also imbued with highly gendered and equally discriminatory values. Mode II, by contrast adopts a learning-emphasis that is evidence-led, policy-sensitive and more future-focused. This is an approach that asks: 'What happened and what can we learn to build resilience against such failings or challenges in the future?' rather than simply 'Who is to blame?' Mode II is associated with 'cool theory', Mode I with 'hot rhetoric'. This 'two types' dichotomy may well lack the sophistication and complexity of many of the existing categorisations and typologies of accountability that are present within the existing research base. And yet just as Mark Bovens (2012) has identified 'two concepts of accountability' – as a virtue and as a mechanism – then it would seem that articulating two further and highly complementary 'types'– one backward-looking and blame-based, the other forward-focused and learning-orientated – is, at the very least, a legitimate approach. It is also an approach that allows me to link the main argument of the previous section with that developed in this section.

The core argument of the earlier section was that we possibly have far too much of 'hot rhetoric' accountability, and too little of 'cool thinking' within contemporary politics. The balance and blend is therefore wrong and risks simply sustaining and reinforcing a cycle of cynicism that shows no sign of ending. The whole ethos of populist politics also seems highly dependent on a divisive 'us-versus-them' version of 'Mode I' accountability which fails to recognise the inevitable complexities, compromises and messiness that constitute practical politics. But having promoted this simple distinction I want to use it to explore a second question of accountability which introduces a time-based or temporal dimension which, in turn, further focuses attention on the anatomy, contradictions and minutiae (whilst also grappling with the 'governing under pressure' theme of the third and final section). The question, simply put, is can accountability processes cope with the challenge of hindsight bias?

Hindsight bias is the common tendency to exaggerate in retrospect how predictable an event was at the time, either to ourselves or to other people. The 'accountability gap' from this perspective is essentially a 'hindsight bias trap' revolving around the degree to which those enforcing the account appreciate the levels of complexity, possibly even confusion, that existed at the time an event might have occurred or a decision may have been made. Take for example 9/11. Immediate action had to be taken in terms of what legislative changes needed to be brought about through the Anti-Terrorism, Crime and Security Act 2001 that was passed within three months of the attack but, more crucially, we had to make administrative changes that would protect people without destroying the basis of civil liberties and that was, to put it bluntly, very hard. In the weeks leading up to the passing of the legislation, decisions were taken that were queried in the public sphere and in the media and, through those processes, refracted back into the more formal parliamentary accountability processes. In many ways that is what is sometimes labelled the 'accountability ecosystem' working well, and as a minister you want those processes to work well. You want to be challenged, you want your proposals to be stress-tested, you want to hear from a wide range of perspectives in order to try and fine-tune your proposals and prepare the socio-political context for the planned changes you want to bring forward.

You would, if the term can be used without political abuse, draw down upon 'real expertise'. Essentially, this will use the accumulated knowledge within services that are relevant to the particular issue, but vitally from outside formal governmental structures. This is what happened with the establishment of the Scientific Advisory Group for Emergencies (SAGE) at the beginning of the Covid-19 outbreak, but which consequentially raised the issue of 'who are the experts?', was there a wide enough sphere of influence, and did this therefore skew the decision-making process? In the aftermath of 9/11, the expertise of the security and intelligence service was necessary, but crucially, as was the expert advice of the senior judiciary, those familiar with issues relating to Civil Contingencies and advice in respect of social cohesion. That is the 'bright side' of accountability playing a positive role, but very different to a constant crash, crash, crash of negative attack politics or what might be described as the more dominant 'dark side' of accountability.

It is important to understand that in the immediate wake of a crisis there is huge pressure on the government of the day to 'do something' even if it's not immediately clear what that 'something' might be. In these contexts, even doing nothing is a decision which at some point will have to be accounted for and explained. Doing nothing ends up being a decision. The consequences of failure to act, to request, over and over again, 'further information' and the clear indecision that arises from this, will inevitably rebound. Tony Blair said in his Conference speech in 2006 'the worst ministers are those who are incapable of making a decision'. This takes us back to the whole notion of arenas of accountability and implicit assumptions regarding clarity and precision. It is relatively easy for a select committee or public inquiry to review what happened around a certain event, but it is far harder for that arena to understand the informational and emotional context in which decisions had to be taken. The calm, clear and considered environment of the committee room or court is a far cry from the realities of highly pressurised practical politics. In politics decisions generally have to be taken on the basis of imperfect information and with an awareness that some form of unintended consequence is likely. Once again, this is not an argument against accountability. All politicians and public servants should be held to account for the decisions they make – or their non-decision-making – but the arena in which an account is subsequently given must itself take some responsibility for acknowledging the contextual pressures within which those individuals were required to operate.

The late Christopher Meyer (2021) made this point in relation to Covid. 'Hindsight bias' Meyer notes 'is the tendency to exaggerate in retrospect how predictable an event was at the time, either to ourselves or other people'. Also known as the 'knew it all along fallacy', it is well-evidenced in psychological studies of medical diagnoses, auditing decisions and terrorist attacks. What's interesting is that hindsight bias has been shown to not only distort the memories and reasoning of individuals who lived through a specific event, but it can also affect the nature of accountability as individuals and organisations are retrospectively thought to have had far more information that they actually did at the time decisions had to be taken. The highly controversial issue of the UK's decision to join the US in the invasion of Iraq is a good example. The confidence that MI6 placed in Agent 'Curveball', was only discredited in July 2003 – almost four months after the decision was taken by Parliament to go to war. Tony Blair and the government, and not the leadership of MI6, were held to account.

There is an interesting link back to the distinction between 'cool theory' and 'hot rhetoric' modes of accountability in the sense that structures tend to be ex ante processes and therefore operate far beyond the 'heat' of the actual crises or the demands of day-to-day policy making. The issue of uncertainty and being aware of the benefit of hindsight is particularly important in a post-Covid context as many countries around the world establish independent public inquiries to investigate how their respective governments coped with the pandemic. The UK is slightly unique in this regard in having not one but two Covid-focused independent statutory inquiries – one in Scotland chaired by the Hon Lady Poole, and one for the whole of the UK chaired by Baroness Hallett, a former Court of Appeal judge. I do not want to make any specific comment about these inquiries. But they do raise some important questions.

It is appropriate to return to the bimodal distinction outlined in chapter one and the notion that public inquiries too often get drawn towards a more blame-based 'Mode I' model to the detriment of the arguably more important 'Mode II' lesson-learning functions. As a host of studies have demonstrated the blame-allocation role can be detrimental for the learning role for the simple reason that individuals or organisations will be unlikely to speak with candour if they fear that the content of that account may be used to demand their resignation or abolition. 'After all' Resodihardjo notes (2020, 5–6) 'learning requires openness. It requires a willingness to share information about mistakes that have been made – mistakes which might have led or contributed to the crisis.' Reflection in 'the shadow of blame' – to paraphrase Sulitzeanu-Kenan (2010) – is unlikely to foster a future-focused learning-environment. This is not to suggest that public inquiries cannot lead to effective policy learning, the work of Alastair Stark (2018) has shown that they can, but that maintaining a balance between blaming and learning requires very careful and mature management. It is for exactly this reason that in the British context Meyer (2020, 1) suggests the need for two completely separate Covid inquiries:

> The objectives of lesson-learning and holding individual organisations to account are often in tension. Our key recommendation is to prioritise lesson-learning over political

> accountability for a public health-focused inquiry. *We argue for two separate inquiries* [emphasis added].

Learning the right lessons from the Covid pandemic, as it does from any major crisis or challenge, therefore demands that questions are asked about the capacity of our tools of accountability to themselves maintain a sense of balance and proportionality. These questions are very rarely asked which leads, in turn, back to the more specific question of this section: the 'hindsight bias trap'. This tendency to exaggerate in retrospect how predictable an event was or how much knowledge was available at the time risks not only failing to contextualise events but also to an over-reliance on commentators who bring their own bias and partial reflection of past events. It can also affect organisations, scrutiny processes and the media by over-exaggerating levels of blame.

Politicians may, of course, attempt to defend themselves from accusations of failure and blame by highlighting that hindsight is, as William Blake wrote 'a wonderful thing'. In 2020, for example, the British Prime Minister, Boris Johnson, countered criticisms of his government over the Covid-related death toll in care homes by labelling the Leader of the Opposition, Keir Starmer, 'Captain Hindsight' – after the superhero from the South Park series who dishes out useless advice in the immediate aftermath of accidents and disasters. I can do no better than quote the words of the Chair of the enquiry into the Clapham Junction rail disaster in 1988. Anthony Hidden QC said: 'There is almost no human action or decision that cannot be made to look flawed and less sensible in the misleading light-up of hindsight.' But the point being made is that the hindsight bias trap is a serious one. 'It can lead to misinterpretation of cause-effect relations, underestimation of the difficulty of taking decisions during periods of high uncertainty' and Meyer (2021) argued 'pressure to act, and flawed prescriptions of how to overcome problems.' The unfortunate flipside of this is that those leading inquiries are aware that they may be accused of somehow failing (usually in the language of 'cover up', 'façade', 'deception', 'whitewash', etc) if they conclude that an error was unavoidable, fate was at play or that no single individual should be identified for the majority of the blame. This rational concern may serve to amplify this bias, while media campaigns inevitably demand a scapegoat. This, again, risks incentivising highly defensive organisational cultures and working procedures within the public sector which can reduce efficiency and increase the risk to others. Sharon Shoesmith's chapter (chapter thirteen) provides an incredibly powerful example of the possible pathologies of unbalanced accountability.

The main argument of this section is that processes of accountability, especially when relating to crises and emergency situations, somehow need to build in an appreciation of what it was like 'in the moment' for those politicians or officials who had to take critical decisions, in potentially life-or-death situations, under huge pressure and without 'perfect' information. None of this exonerates those who have failed to take advice, put short-termism before long-term perspectives that might benefit the nation, or who knowingly took a shortcut for expediency's sake. Ideologically driven decisions to reduce the size of the state or public expenditure, presented as 'necessary' austerity, cannot be relieved of responsibility if the consequences exacerbate (as clearly happened with the pandemic) the problems faced by those in the here and now. In this case, the policy was intentional, clearly thought through, based on a set of political values and implemented in the full knowledge that one of the outcomes would be the reduction of public services and the capacity to cope with crisis. Culpability clearly lies in situations where those taking the decisions are fully aware of the likely outcome.

III. Emotions: The Mental Health and Wellbeing of Politicians

Since 2015 I have been lucky enough to be able to combine my role as a working peer in the House of Lords with the position of Professor of Politics in Practice at the University of Sheffield. This has allowed me to continue in public life while also allowing me to play a role in connecting teaching and research into the complex world of practical politics that I have attempted to chart in this chapter. Two main arguments have so far been defined: the first was simply that we may have too much of the 'wrong' kind of accountability, and too little of the 'right' kind; the second argument was that significant 'questions of accountability' surround the need for scrutiny mechanisms to somehow reflect the emotional context in which decisions were taken. This brings me to a third and final question: How does it *feel* to be the focus of detailed scrutiny and therefore to be personally held to account? In many ways a valuable reference point that can be used as a bridge between the conclusion of the previous section and this section's core argument is Joanne Warner's (2015) *The Emotional Politics of Social Work and Child Protection*. In this book Warner reveals not only how social work and child protection systems have been subject to accelerating cycles of crisis and reform, with each crisis involving intense media and political scrutiny, but also how within understanding the nature and causes of this cycle little attention has been paid to the importance of collective and individual emotions.

Accountability of a solely destructive or 'Gotcha!' type (see chapter one) is highly unlikely to inspire any individual or organisation to reach their full potential. The All Party Parliamentary Group on Mental Health produced its first report on mental health in Parliament in 2008 and since then a raft of studies have revealed not only the accountability-related pressures that MPs and their staff work under but also the impact it has on their health and wellbeing (see Poulter et al 2019; Rao 2020; Geddes et al 2020). Consideration, here, needs to be given to the staff working for Members of Parliament, and the stress many feel – particularly when they are operating in a constituency office, or when there is a campaign which leads to an avalanche of approaches both on social media, as well as by more traditional means.

I know from personal experience just how draining and distracting public attacks, albeit framed in terms of upholding accountability, can be and my sense from over 50 years of being very much 'in' public life has shown me how these pressures have not only intensified but become more personalised. This is why Warner's scholarship on the 'emotional politics' of social work and child protection piqued my interest; its emphasis on accelerating cycles of crisis and reform, on increasingly intense media and political scrutiny and particularly on the notion of 'collective emotions' resonated with my own perspective. What very few scholars have studied is the emotional politics of *being a politician* at a time when the pressures of governing, of being *in* politics, are increasing at a considerable pace. This explains why Mannevuo, Rinne and Vento's 2022 study of emotional stress and strain amongst professional politicians concluded with an emphasis on 'long hours, uneasy feelings'.

Let me just say very clearly that a life in politics takes a huge emotional toll. The extent of this toll obviously depends on a vast range of variables but at a basic level politics is a brutal game. Of course, each individual handles the situation in their own way. Having a work-life balance, a stable and understanding home life, and a circle of friends makes all the difference. But they too carry the burden. When I left office after eight years in Cabinet, more than one long-standing and close friend, said 'welcome back'. I had no idea that I had 'gone away'!

In surveys the public generally want their politicians to be 'more human' or 'more like us' but then – in what is often referred to as 'the Eagleton Effect' – voters punish politicians who admit to having suffered from depression or anxiety (see Loewen and Rheault 2021). And yet we also know from recent research that the pressure of political life is more likely to increase the stressors that lead to depression and anxiety (see Poulter et al 2019; Rao 2020). These pressures include (inter alia) a combination of high expectations, low resources, very limited direct control or capacity, job insecurity, working in a low-trust-high blame environment, working away from home, plus increasing intimidation and threats of physical violence (see Cm 9543, 2017; Flinders et al 2020). For fairly obvious reasons, no one in senior public office can expect any sympathy from the electorate. You have, after all, chosen to take on the role and, mistaken or otherwise, people believe you are well-rewarded in one form or the other. So, none of my observations should in any way be interpreted as 'crying into my cups'. The rewards have been considerable, and I don't mean in monetary terms. Making a difference, seeing real change happening, knowing you have made a contribution and the world, albeit most often in very small ways, has changed for the better because of the time and effort you have expended. However, research also reveals how these pressures often continue after losing political office (see Roberts 2017), and can be felt not just by elected politicians but those who work in politics and public life more broadly (see, for example, Baldwin et al 2020). Anyone who wants to gain insight into the emotional politics of a life *in* politics would do well to read Michael Ignatieff's memoirs *Fire and Ashes: Success and Failure in Politics:*

> As you submit to the compromises demanded by public life, your public self begins to alter the person inside. Within a year of entering politics, I had the distorted feeling of having been taken over by a doppelganger, a strange new persona I could barely recognize when I looked at myself in the mirror … I had never been so well-dressed in my life and had never felt so hollow (2013, 80).

Ignatieff's position might be extreme but it captures something of the realities of being in politics. This is a dimension of political life that is very hard to know about or understand from the outside-in. The pressures of political life tend to pull in and affect those around the politician – their friends, spouse and children – like a vortex. The impact of social media is a part of this dimension for the simple reason that you can be out with your family enjoying a meal or taking a quiet walk in the park and you suddenly become aware that people are filming you on their phone. A reflective moment or unguarded comment said in jest amongst good friends is suddenly recorded for life and distributed around the world in a millisecond. The intensity and nature of the public gaze has therefore changed in ways that are hard to appreciate or feel from the outside-in. One illustration during the years of coalition was when the then Secretary of State for Business, Innovation and Skills, Vince Cable, a Liberal Democrat, was recorded by the *Daily Telegraph* in his advice surgery. A setting which is often (in order to put the constituent at ease) an environment in which politicians try to display their 'human face'. No longer, if they know that the conversation is going to be played back in the pages of a national newspaper, and the flattery, as in this case, of two young female reporters, would lead to the 'got you' expose. And being on guard, being vigilant, a state of almost constant anxiety is related to operating in the constant shadow *not of sensible scrutiny* of the kind that is the lifeblood of democratic politics *but of blame* which takes an emotional toll. A good thing, therefore, that in order to create a shield to put on the armoury which will at least offer some protection, who have to shut off the immediate tendency to believe that you are constantly on show. Rather, that you have this in the back of your mind but try to go about your business and life as you would have done were you not literally in the public eye. The consequence of living constantly on the edge would drive anyone into a nervous wreck, which is why so many people find public office impossible to take.

The reason I want to end with this focus on *how it feels to be accountable* is to add a new dimension to existing debates concerning the 'pathologies of accountability' or the existence of 'overloads'. The existing literature on these topics tends to adopt an overwhelmingly organisational focus but what I am attempting to emphasise in this section is that accountability can be equally pathological at the individual level. It wears people down. It saps their confidence. Accountability simply as an element of 'attack politics' does not sustain politics but risks almost destroying the essence of democratic life because the lived reality is that accountability often feels disruptive. This matters, as it often comes with highly gendered and discriminatory dimensions; and risks creating a political system in which only those individuals with a very particular personality type are likely to seek a life on the public platform. Isabel Hardman's book – *Why We Get The Wrong Politicians* (2019) – comes to a very similar conclusion. But I don't believe that politics is a place for only the thick-skinned and the bull-headed. Most people will pull out before the pressures of the system destroy them, while others develop ways of counterbalancing and coping with the dangerous forces that suck you into a formula and process that you never wanted to be part of. Where this leaves us is back with a focus on how to achieve a shift in the balance or blend of dominant accountability approaches – from the 'hot rhetoric' and aggression of 'Mode I' towards some of the more considered and 'cooler thinking' that is likely to come with 'Mode II'. How to achieve such positive accountability and shift the balance from 'naming, shaming and blaming' to something very different is the focus of the concluding chapter.

But nothing in this chapter should be seen as concluding that young people should avoid entering the formal political arena like the plague. Active citizenship should lead them to want to be in the right place to make a difference, to exercise whatever power exists in that particular sphere, and to counterweigh unaccountable and unresponsive power from outside the formal landscape. However, to do this we need to ensure that we prepare those going into formal political life for what they can expect, and provide them, therefore, with the resilience and perspective to be able to cope.

It is self-evident that the more we devolve and decentralise political influence and, where possible, power, the less pressure there will be on those at the centre. It is also obvious that the more delegation can take place within the immediate environment in which politics is played out, the less any one individual will have to carry a load themselves. Leading a ministerial team and having excellent special advisers is a task which, undertaken effectively, can make a massive difference. In the end, however, our politics needs to be much more *communautaire*. Building from the bottom-up and ensuring that we share the load allows us to support and challenge not only each other but those who demand the impossible of us. All of this is vital if we are to sustain democracy, which is under constant threat; a constitution that is creaking under the stresses and strains of the moment, and the global environment which constrains even the most dedicated and committed politician from achieving their declared goals. In the end, the teaching of citizenship and the spreading of political literacy is fundamental not only to a greater understanding by the wider electorate, but to reducing the impossible demands on those who put themselves forward in the public arena, who stand on the stage with the spotlight on them, and who, as human beings, so often fail to live up to expectations.

13

Positive Accountability: From Naming, Shaming and Blaming to Lesson Learning

SHARON SHOESMITH

Accountability matters. That is, in essence, the core argument of this book, and several chapters have been dedicated to exploring important 'questions of accountability' from a wide range of perspectives. What's interesting about these contributions – and the wider literature on public governance– is that accountability is at-one-and-the-same-time seen both as a 'good thing' and a 'bad thing'. A 'good thing' in the sense of delivering transparency, quality assurance, responsibility, and the control of power within democratic systems; and a 'bad thing' in the sense of being largely associated with the allocation of blame, criticism and scapegoating. The paradox being that what might be termed the 'dark side' of accountability (see chapter three), with its over-emphasis on blame and defensive reactions prevents the full realisation of the 'bright side' of accountability, in terms of facilitating positive future-focused policy learning.

It is in exactly this context that this chapter makes a significant and original contribution to the accountability debate: it highlights the need to shift away from 'naming, shaming and blaming' towards a stronger and more mature 'lesson learning' emphasis. To make such an argument is not, of course, to suggest that politicians or their officials should never be held responsible when mistakes which they could reasonably have been expected to avoid occur. But it is to make the case for a shifting of the current accountability balance from an almost total and at times highly immature focus on blame, towards a more mature and candid attempt to realise the learning opportunities that emerge when things go wrong. A further focus of this chapter is empirical. Existing academic literature is rich in analyses of forms of accountability but arguably far more limited when it comes to detailed case studies that reveal the 'dark side' of accountability. Moreover, studies that explore the impact of the 'dark side' of accountability that have been written by officials and public servants with practical professional experience of coping with those pathological pressures are particularly rare. This is a critical point. Although the academic analysis of accountability has boomed as a topic of inquiry in recent years (for a bibliometric analysis see Dimova, Dubnick, Flinders and Monaghan 2023) the proportion of contributions or analyses written by public service practitioners remains very low. As such, one of the main aims of this chapter is to provide some insight into *what it feels like to be at the sharp end of accountability*. This is a theme that connects with Lord Blunkett's contribution (chapter twelve) and broader studies of 'felt accountability' which is defined here as 'real-world experiential knowledge about the personal impacts of operating in intense professional accountability contexts'. The 'sharp end' of accountability in this case relates to being or becoming the lightning-rod or scapegoat for volatile public anger and intense societal emotions. To be the focus of 'naming, shaming and blaming', or to work in a profession that exists in 'the shadow of blame' places huge emotional pressures on individuals (and their families) in ways that students of public accountability have generally not studied.

The event explored in this chapter concerns the familial homicide of 16-month-old Peter Connelly – known to the public as Baby P in August 2007 (for an extensive account see Shoesmith 2016; see also Jones 2014). What the events following this case of familial child homicide demonstrate is not the balanced search for a mature understanding of the complex interplay of factors, but a furore of blame and scapegoating. The complex blame-game that followed Baby P's death involved a range of framing techniques and strategies which all served to arguably satisfy the public and the media's demand for sacrificial responsibility. The chapter is informed by an appreciation of the insights of critical realism (see Bhaskar 1975) rather than through a more explicitly auto-ethnographic perspective. Critical realism accepts that a real world exists beyond our thoughts, knowledge and ideas, but it also acknowledges the role of interpretation and subjectivity in understanding and navigating reality. This matters because blaming and false accusations – whether targeted at individuals or organisations – can distort accountability and limit learning while also impacting on the legitimate use of power, the infrastructure of democracy and the safety of society.

This chapter challenges basic notions of accountability as 'a good thing' and demonstrates how what emerges in many contexts and situations as 'a race to blame' not only neglects a more sophisticated understanding of the challenges faced by public services but also acts as a barrier to effective and future-focused positive policy-learning. The three 'questions of accountability' that define this chapter are as follows:

1. How does contemporary cultural affect the nature and impact of accountability?
2. How does the analysis of a specific case study demonstrate the real-world impact of these cultural pressures?
3. How might a stronger focus on positive policy-learning be achieved?

Each question is tackled in each of the three sections that follow. The first section briefly explores the changing socio-political context. Its main argument has two elements. The first element is that early societies coped with fear and uncertainty through ritualistic and performative naming, shaming and blaming. Blame in this sense offering some form of reassurance or control. But the intensity and communicative flow of modern societies has created the second element; a blame-culture which is now as pervasive as it might be thought pathological in modern life. This has major implications for the governance of the public sector where expectations are very high, resources severely limited and the outcomes of some public services often unpredictable. The second section shifts from a broad societal focus to a very specific case study of exactly these public sector pressures through a focus on the Baby P case. The aim of this section is to demonstrate the denial of familial child homicide, the knee-jerk reaction to blame and scapegoat social workers and the embeddedness of blame avoidance strategies in public services as a means of protecting individual and organisational reputations. This pattern of activity has far-reaching consequences that add insight to broader debates about the 'dark side' of accountability. The third section considers the broader implications of these implications for more future-focussed policy learning and considers the new 'questions of accountability' it raises.

I. Contemporary Cultural Context

To talk in terms of the contemporary cultural context of accountability, risks overlooking a long and distinguished historical literature on the relationship between fate and fortuna, crises and catastrophes and the social utilisation of blame-based strategies when things go wrong. What much of this often anthropologically inspired literature underlines is that when things go wrong, or even when natural disasters occur human nature generally demands that someone, something or some group is held personally responsible (for a review see Alaszewski 2015). History reveals that when crops failed, a well ran dry, a volcano erupted, or a disease ravished a community it was common – as Mary Douglas (1992) illustrated – for communities to blame individuals, often through accusations of witchcraft or corrupt morality, in an attempt to explain why a specific event had occurred. Witches would be burned, individuals cast out of communities, or animals sacrificed in order to 'take the blame' for events that might equally have been defined as 'acts of god' or 'bad luck' for which no person or group could credibly be blamed. In ancient Greece, for example, human scapegoats (*pharmakoi*) were used to mitigate a plague or other calamity, often even being sacrificed in the hope of preventing future ills. During the Athenian festival of Thargelia a man and woman were led around the city, draped with figs, whipped with sticks, then stoned and driven out of the city in the belief that having made such a sacrifice to the Gods the health of the city would be ensured for the forthcoming year. The singling-out and casting-out of individuals therefore served to provide a ritualistic sense of order that, at one level, allowed communities to make sense of the uncertain world around them.

Risk, fear and anxiety are therefore to some extent inter-twinned with the mirror-image phenomena of naming, shaming and blaming; the anthropological literature suggesting that the tendency to blame is an integral part of human behaviour. It is a coping strategy driven by a basic instinct for understanding, certainty and control. It is exactly these dimensions of collective human nature that are visible within the contemporary cultural context. When something goes wrong the existence of a powerful societal 'negativity bias' fuels an often immediate, knee-jerk reaction to identify 'who is to blame?' rather than 'how can we stop this happening again?' as the immediate focus of attention. Political witch-hunts seek to identify where fault and culpability should lie, while at the same time providing for the rejuvenation of collective sentiments about morality, service and diligence (see Bergesen 1977). Accountability is, as a result, rarely concerned with the distribution of praise or credit but almost wholly concerned with the attribution of blame. It is of a 'Gotcha!' variety which stimulates a defensive culture and complex blame-avoidance strategies that have been studied at length in the work of scholars including Kent Weaver (1986), Paul Pierson (1996) and Christopher Hood (2002).

Standard accountability practices, the 'cross-pressures' and 'multiple accountabilities' that have been discussed at length in the existing literature are, however, intensified in the aftermath of specific crises or events. The social salience and sensitivity to a specific event increasing the clamour for answers to the question of 'who is to blame?' But shifts in relation to contemporary culture and technological change have also produced a heightened blame-based culture in recent years. The global age of 24/7 media and rolling news has arguably intensified the societal 'negativity bias' (see Douglas et al 2021) and, as such, exerts an ever-greater pressure on political decision-making and public governance. Governments and major public services have, as a result, generally become increasingly adept at utilising blame-avoidance to reduce reputational damage. New 'public service bargains' – as the work of Hood and Lodge (2006) has demonstrated – are agreed in an attempt to pre-determine who will be left 'holding the can' and taking the blame if things go wrong. Added to this are distinct dimensions concerning the emergence of affective polarisation, populist post-truth pressures, the rejection of experts and the promotion of misinformation in the form of 'alt-truths' 'fake news' and 'deepfakes' (see Kunz and Abel 2022). The 'populist signal' provides a seductively simple blame-based narrative '"they" [the elites] are to blame for ignoring and oppressing "us" [the blameless masses].' '*They* did it!' is – as Hameleers, Bos and de Vreese (2017) have illustrated – is a highly effective and particularly emotionalised form of blame-attribution which is central within populist communication strategies.

As a result, (post) modern societies are increasingly blame-based and arguably blame driven. This is fuelled and facilitated by advances in social media that increase reach in real-time and facilitate the social amplification of risk in a way that was simply not possible just two decades ago. At the same time, however, this increased capacity for 'news and views' to travel has not been matched by an increased capacity to reason or reflect. In this context what Evans (2003) labels 'punitive populism' emerges as a real threat and flows through into wider concerns about the emergence of a modern-day version of 'pitchfork politics' (see Mounk 2014; Kane 2019) whereby *the perception* that someone or some group is to blame becomes more important than finding out and understanding what actually happened. This gap between what might be framed as *blame intensity*, on the one hand, and capacity for *evidence-based reasoning*, on the other hand – what has been termed a 'double-dilemma' – provides the simple societal context that needs to be fully acknowledged as the background to what happened in the wake of the familial homicide of Baby P.

It also explains the context within which the public apology has become a focus of intense controversy and contestation. To some extent the corporate or impersonal apology has become a blame-limitation strategy within what Mills (2001) calls a new 'culture of apology' and Taft (2000) describes as the 'commodification of apology'. What's interesting is why public apologies seem to 'work' in some contexts (in terms of reducing media, political and public criticism), but 'fail' in others (simply intensifying negative attention and demands for dismissal). Saying sorry without sincerity or apologising when an intense process of social stigmatisation has already occurred may not lead to forgiveness (see Ward Struthers et al 2008), let alone open-up the political space in which a focus on more future-focused lesson-learning may occur. Further, the nature of the perceived transgression is significant. To apologise for the leaking of important government information compared to the apology for the death of a child, is of a different order in terms of the public response. The existence of a 'tin hats mentality' whereby organisations respond to scrutiny in a defensive manner is, if not excusable, then partially understandable if a capacity for reasoned, open and honest discussion has not been put in place or is virtually impossible given the arguably invidious nature of the service being provided. Creating space for different kinds of accountability, and understanding how and why different processes may or may not deliver the 'cool theory' or 'hot rhetoric' that was discussed in chapter one remain very real questions in search of an answer.

Emotions tend to be very 'hot' in the immediate aftermath of a tragedy, but the passage of time generally allows those immediate emotions to 'cool' in a way that facilitates reflection and reasoning. This is the basic logic of Daniel Kahneman's (2011) influential work on 'thinking, fast and slow'. An accountability-focused example arguably occurred in August 2022 when the former Secretary of State for Health, Jeremy Hunt, gave evidence to the public inquiry into infected blood. In the 1970s and 1980s an estimated 5,000 people were given blood infected with

HIV and hepatitis and around 2,500 of those patients died. Thirty years later the public inquiry concluded that blood contamination had been an avoidable problem and Hunt told the inquiry that 'sometimes institutions and the state close ranks around a lie … and I think that is what happened in this case' before acknowledging that the victims' wait for justice was a 'huge failing of democracy' (see BBC 2022). Hunt's reflections were far more honest and enlightening than those provided by politicians and public servants at the time the scandal occurred, although neither Hunt nor the inquiry provided answers to how and why such misleading responses were made. The problem and paradox this highlights however, is that sometimes crises and scandals are the cause of complex issues that need to be addressed in a calm and reasoned manner. But often there is no time for a 'cooling off' period to occur because immediate steps need to be taken to prevent further harm. But the immediate focus, as the case study provided in this chapter illustrates, is too often dominated by strategic blame-avoidance and scapegoating rather than by the evidence-based and calm review that is actually needed. The emphasis is too often on 'naming, shaming and blaming' and not on positive policy learning.

II. Naming, Shaming, Blaming Not Learning

The aim of this section is to explore how the analysis of a specific case demonstrates the real-world impact of the growing cultural pressures that were highlighted in the previous section. It is written in the first-person narrative since the author of this chapter was the senior local government manager, who, along with others came to be named, shamed and blamed. As this chapter attempts to illustrate, the broader socio-political factors discussed above create a highly politicised and almost ravenous need to identify someone or something to blame. The immediate blame allocation crowded out the space for questions about policy learning or questions of accountability which are at the heart of this book. Questions that might have led to greater knowledge of the complexities of familial child homicide and the pressures facing social workers, health professionals and police in protecting children.

Peter Connelly, named initially in public as Baby P, died in August 2007 aged 16 months at his home in Tottenham in the north London Borough of Haringey. The public learned of his death over a year later in November 2008 when his mother, Tracey Connelly, her boyfriend, Steven Barker, and his brother, Jason Owen (name changed by deed poll) were each convicted of 'causing or allowing' Peter's death. Connelly and Owen were given minimum term sentences of five years, and Barker for 12 years (the maximum sentence was 14 years). All three had pleaded 'not guilty' to the charge of murder. At the time I was the Director of Education and Children's Services in the London Borough of Haringey.

Peter had been known to social workers in my department, to several health professionals including paediatricians from the world-renowned Great Ormond Street Children's Hospital (GOSH), and to police officers from the Child Abuse Investigation Unit (CAIU) of London's Metropolitan Police Service. Twenty days after the news of Peter's death, such was the demand for 'public accountability' that the then Secretary of State for Children, Schools and Families, Ed Balls, without any warning, dismissed me from my statutory role in a live television media briefing, and later that same day Haringey Council announced that I was no longer an employee, again without warning. Four social workers were sacked four months later and a paediatrician from GOSH removed herself from the UK medical register and left the country.

Three years later I won my judicial review in the Court of Appeal which is based in London's Royal Courts of Justice (*R(Shoesmith) v Ofsted*) into the decisions made by the Secretary of State and Haringey Council to sack me. One of the judges hearing the case in the High Court in *R(Shoesmith) v Ofsted* commented that I was 'entitled to be treated lawfully and fairly and not simply summarily scapegoated', another noted that 'public accountability did not mean that heads should roll'. The sacking of me and the social workers had become a high-profile case of blaming and scapegoating.

I had been used by politicians in both national and local government as a scapegoat to satisfy a broader societal need to manage public emotion (*over what happened*) and to restore certainty (*that it would not happen again*). The remainder of this section explores the emergence of not only a worrying form of 'punitive populism' whereby politicians, police and the tabloid media worked together to stoke public anger, but also the existence of complex and at times murky blame-games as different actors and organisations sought to make themselves blame-proof. This is a complex story (a chronology is provided in Box 13.1, below) that sheds light on the real world 'cross-pressures' of accountability in a way that I think very few academic analyses have or can achieve. Put slightly differently, it reveals *the politics and governance of blame* in the rawest of terms, and in ways that create many new 'questions of accountability'. To provide a full account this section is divided into six sub-sections. The first utilises the previous section's focus on punitive populism in order to contextualise the relationship between politicians and sections of the media. The second section focuses on the role and behaviour of London's Metropolitan Police. The third outlines the trial of Baby P's mother, her boyfriend and his brother; the fourth section explores how the judicial review process uncovered a range of anomalies and presentational questions that exposed the 'dark side' of accountability in terms of deflection, denial, deceit and deception. The fifth section focuses on the subsequent conviction of Steven Barker (the mother's boyfriend) for the rape of one of Baby P's siblings. Finally, the sixth section questions why the Metropolitan Police were so committed to preventing a formal inquest into Peter's death. This is a harrowing story, but it also paints an accurate picture of the day-to-day professional lives of those 'street level bureaucrats'– the doctors, nurses, probation workers, carers, teachers and social workers – who care for vulnerable people under massive pressures, limited resources and (critically) uncertainty.

A. Punitive Populism

The notion of 'punitive populism' connects with the previous section's focus on the changing socio-political context within which 'questions of accountability' are asked. It focuses attention on the emergence of an increasingly tough and aggressive stance on crime or misdemeanours especially where public services are involved. It contains a strong anti-intellectual stance which very often rejects the existence of 'evidence' or the opinions of 'experts' in favour of simplistic analyses of both the problem and who is to blame (see, for example, McDevitt and Ferrucci 2018). Punitive populism refers to the idea that public support exists for more severe and immediate punishments for law-breaking, inefficiency or human error. This has, in turn, become a primary driver of policy-making and often (critically) involves politicians, political parties and tabloid media outlets working in unison to frame and fuel public anger. The main argument of this sub-section is that the immediate public controversy surrounding Baby P resonates very clearly with broader concerns about punitive populism: a tragic case of familial homicide arguably co-opted by party leaders and newspaper editors in an attempt to secure votes and readers, with broader public interest dimensions very much a secondary concern.

Peter's death became the immediate focus of opportunist party politics by the official Leader of the Opposition, David Cameron, in an unprecedented attack at Prime Minister's Question Time (PMQs) in the House of Commons, naming me and stating many untruths about the case (see *Hansard* 12 November 2008). The Prime Minister, Gordon Brown, seemed almost completely unprepared as he was attempting to focus attention on his successful management of the international monetary system in the wake of the financial crisis. Such a broad and psychologically distant topic as the global regulation of markets stood in stark contrast to the very direct, tangible and tragic death of a young child. It is at this point, however, that the story takes a deep and complex twist that points to the planned manipulation of public emotions. Evidence would later emerge about the relationship between Cameron and Rupert Murdoch, head of *News International*. Only a few months before the news of Peter's death was reported, Cameron had spent time with Murdoch on his yacht. The Conservative Party desperately needed the support of Murdoch's newspapers, especially from the tabloid newspaper *The Sun* in the run up to the next election. By the time of the Conservative victory in the 2010 election the party had indeed achieved the support of Murdoch's empire.

Box 13.1 The Baby P Tragedy: Timeline of Key Events

1 March 2006	Baby P born.
11 Dec 2006	Social workers refer Baby P to the police for suspect non-accidental injury. Mother and grandmother arrested.
13 March 2007	The case of Baby P has no allocated police officer, and no investigation is taking place.
13 April 2007	Referral by social worker and health visitor to GOSH, informing Peter was subject to child protection but seeking a detailed medical examination that might rule out certain health concerns.
1 June 2007	Social worker refers Baby P to police again for suspect non-accidental injury.
9 July 2007	Andy Coulson appointed Director of Communications for the Conservative Party.
26 July 2007	Last of 14 visits by Peter and his mother to the GP who was later suspended from his post for one year.
27 July 2007	Haringey solicitor advises social workers that Peter's case does not meet the threshold for initiating Care Proceedings.
1 Aug 2007	Baby P examined by GOSH paediatrician after a four-month wait.
2 Aug 2007	Police meet Baby Ps mother and drop all charges again her and her mother.
3 Aug 2007	Baby P found dead.
6 Aug 2007	First Serious Case Review began.
9 June 2008	Murder trial scheduled but then postponed.
11 Aug 2008	Peter's mother and her boyfriend charged with rape at Highgate Magistrates Court.
9 Sept 2008	Murder trial begins.
5 Nov 2008	Police brief press on progress with case, criticising Haringey social workers and Director.
11 Nov 2008	Close of the trial. Defendants found not guilty of murder or manslaughter but of 'causing or allowing Peter's death. Media briefing after the end of the trial.
12 Nov 2008	David Cameron raises issue at PMQs.
17 Nov 2008	Ofsted Inspection begins.
17 Nov 2008	Panorama documentary 1 broadcast.
21 Nov 2008	Ofsted Inspection ends.
21 Nov 2008	Death Threat #1 delivered to my home.
24 Nov 2008	The Home Office and DCSF receive an email from Phoenix associates concerning a MAPPA meeting.

1 Dec 2008	Sharon Shoesmith sacked by the minister, Ed Balls, live on air, Haringey council leader, George Meehan, and the cabinet member for children and young people, Liz Santry, also resign. Balls orders a second SCR.
1 Dec 2008	Ofsted Report published but not signed off by the inspection team or seen by Shoesmith ahead of its publication.
4 Dec 2008	Met Police internal report #1 on Baby P.
Dec 2008	HMIC report made available to police around this time.
15 Dec 2008	Sentencing hearing for Tracy Connelly, Steven Barker and Jason Owen postponed.
8 Jan 2009	Met Police internal report #2 on Baby P.
29 Jan 2009	Death Threat #2 received by Shoesmith at her home.
30 April 2009	Four social workers sacked making media headlines.
1 May 2009	Second Serious Case Review *summary* published.
1 May 2009	Steven Barker given life sentence for rape.
4 May 2009	Panorama documentary #2 broadcast.
11 May 2009	Care Quality Commission publishes critical report about role of GOSH in the case of Baby P – completed in Feb 2009 but held until after the second trial. Much of the criticism not included in the Ofsted Report used to sack Shoesmith and social workers.
7 Oct 2009	Judicial Review proceeding start.
23 April 2010	Shoesmith loses High Court Case but receives permission to Appeal.
10 July 2010	Tim Loughton orders publication of second Serious Case Review *full* report.
30 Nov 2010	Coroner decides not to proceed with an inquest.
8 Dec 2010	Panorama documentary #3 broadcast.
27 May 2011	Shoesmith wins legal case in the Court of Appeal.
2011–2012	Leveson Inquiry into phone hacking.

Soon after their meeting and in an act suggesting an agreement between the men, Cameron appointed Murdoch's former editor of the *News of the World*, Andy Coulson, as his head of communications. Coulson would go on to serve a custodial sentence related to phone hacking while he had been editor. The Leveson Inquiry which ran from 2011 to 2012 scrutinised the culture, practices and ethics of the British press would later reveal the tangled web of relationships between these powerful political and media actors, their shared reasons for attacking the Labour Government and how the death of Baby P was used as little more than a pawn in their plans. Put very simply, Coulson was able to use the death of Baby P to offer his new boss, David Cameron, a powerful story that could be used to attack a Labour Government which by this point had been in power for over a decade and had made major commitments around improving children's social care. Moreover, Coulson had had a close personal relationship with Rebekah Brooks, the editor of *The Sun*, and this story would appeal to her campaigning reputation around sensitive issues. Brooks immediately launched a campaign, 'Justice for Baby P' with an online petition that demanded that four social workers, the paediatrician from GOSH and me to be immediately sacked. The narrative that social workers were to blame for Peter's death was a populist news story subjected to post-truth and false news. The story was rich in anger, outrage, vitriol, and notions of revenge among politicians, tabloid media and the public. Warner (2013) suggested that public anger was mobilised by politicians in conjunction with the press.

The intensity of the media coverage created what might now, on reflection, be interpreted as a bidding contest between the two main parties as both attempted to demonstrate who was the toughest when it came to attacking social workers. Could Balls have gone on television to speak about the dreadful crime of familial child homicide and the fact that 57 other children had died in a similar way to Peter in the same year? Could he have told the public that the last child to die this way was not Victoria Climbié in Haringey as the tabloids claimed but over 400 children had died between Victoria and Peter from all parts of the country? Could he have quoted the NSPCC in estimating that a child dies each week in the UK at the hands of a known adult, a statistic consistent for over 50 years? The answer to all these questions is 'yes' because the statistics were true but if he had publicised the full picture when it comes to familial homicide he would have effectively have been fuelling demands for his own dismissal as the responsible minister. The bigger picture, as it were, pointing to the existence of systemic failings and thereby making it harder to place the blame for the death of Baby P solely on local actors. Instead, Prime Minister Gordon Brown told the country that he would make sure this never happens again. He provided the reassurance and certainty that the public wanted to hear and in doing so prevented any opportunity to learn and to tackle the problem of familial child homicide. By the time of Baby P's death, the Labour Government had been in government for 11 years and had implemented a major policy known as 'Every Child Matters'. Baby P's death gave the Conservatives every opportunity to attack social workers and thereby Labour's record, and Labour defended itself by also attacking social workers. By the time these politicians were engaged in the 'blame-game', 60 further children had become victims of familial homicide since Peter died.

The blaming of social workers when a child known to them is harmed or becomes a victim of familial child homicide is well established in UK culture and is rarely challenged (Shoesmith 2016). Blaming social workers was the well-trodden line of defence from facing-up to or finding a better way to tackle familial child homicide. The role of a social worker at the intersection of the state and people's lives puts them in an arguably invidious position: remove a child and place them in care risks stimulating accusations of insensitivity and authoritarian instincts; the death or abuse of a child that was not foreseen leads to accusations of incompetence and failure. This 'issue-attention cycle' concerning social work as a profession has been well-documented within the academic literature (see, for example, Dominelli 1996; Clapton, Cree and Smith 2013); it is also one that constantly saps the morale of the profession (Eversman and Bird 2017). The 'shadow of blame' (Sulitzeanu-Kenan 2010) that other chapters have highlighted hangs over social work as a profession with both an intensity and a set of real-world effects that are hard to understand from a position *beyond* the community of practice. The positive public administration movement (see Douglas et al 2021) with its focus on policy successes and 'the bright side' of public governance has not, yet, explored the field of social work.

Returning to the case of Baby P, in the wake of his death attacks on social workers in the print and online media became extensive. David Cameron had named and shamed me in the House of Commons, while claiming elsewhere no one had apologised for Peter's death. He even went as far as to suggest in the *Evening Standard* (12 November 2008) that the social workers involved in Baby P's case should be subject to criminal proceedings in an analogous manner to those who had been convicted of causing or allowing his death. *The Sun* published emotive headlines that appeared to support the Conservative Party's aggressive and personalised framing with their petition suggesting not only that social workers had 'Blood on their Hands', but also that Peter had been tortured and that social workers were aware of it but did nothing to prevent it (see, for example, *The Sun*, 12 November 2008, frontpage). This claim was not only a lie, but it became a dangerous, insidious and deeply damaging part of the framing narrative, putting those accused at serious risk of retribution.

Misinformation about me was promulgated by the media, including the BBC. Moreover, in a game of duplicity that resonates with a great deal of the academic scholarship on 'the politics of' making a public apology (see Noble 2008) when I did say sorry, I was held to be not 'properly apologetic' or not expressing 'culpability' (for a discussion see Shoesmith 2016). In an example of what Greer and McLoughlin (2011) has referred to as 'trial by media' and 'the politics of outrage', *The Sun* published daily updates on the growing number of signatories on its petition. The impact on me was extensive. Online intimidation was extensive, a media circus was camped outside my home, and I received a number of death threats – while still working for the council and trying to maintain the morale of a social services department that not only felt under siege but that was also now dealing with an upsurge in referrals of vulnerable children. The literature on 'multiple-accountabilities disorder' (Koppell 2005) cannot really capture the scale of personal and professional intensity that exists around a high-profile public sector tragedy. The Secretary of State's decision to order an emergency inspection by Ofsted only added to a sense of over-load.

For the main players in this blame game – of which I was not one – my removal from office was critical. Brooks had invested her reputation as a newspaper editor in the creation of the public petition; Cameron had worked with Murdoch to focus on Baby P allegedly as little more than a political pressure point to be exploited for partisan gain; and with so much public and media focus on the issue it appeared Balls needed to provide a lightning-rod to prevent him from ultimately 'carrying the can'. Pressure grew on Haringey Council to fire me, but they understood that an evidence-based review of my performance would not support that decision. They did, however, expect me to resign. By this stage the threat level around me of direct violence was making it dangerous for me to walk between council buildings, and travel to work. Headteachers in large number spoke up in my defence but their voices were drowned out. I knew at this early stage that resigning would give legitimacy to all that had been said and that I would be permanently and personally identified as directly responsible for the death of Baby P. I knew that I would not be able to carry on living with that personification. It left me with, on the one hand, suicidal thoughts and, on the other hand, a drive to fight back and to take my case through the courts.

What had emerged were the shocking lengths that the government would go to in order to try and discredit me. Supposedly independent regulatory processes were manipulated for political purposes. As mentioned above, the Secretary of State ordered an emergency Ofsted inspection of child protection agencies of social care, health and police in Haringey. The council had previously been rated as 'Good' by Ofsted but was now suddenly and dramatically down-graded to 'Inadequate' and it was this rating that Balls would subsequently use to justify his decision to sack me. During judicial review proceedings correspondence between Ed Balls's department – the Department for Children, Schools and Families – and the most senior staff at Ofsted were released and revealed that no less than 17 drafts of the final report had been produced. Emails showed that the Head of Ofsted was asked to ensure that the report provided 'definitive evidence on which the Minister can act' and most of the people involved in writing the final report had not been part of the inspection team that had actually visited Haringey. The team that undertook the inspection never signed-off the inspection report. In 2016, an anonymous former Ofsted inspector told the BBC1 documentary, *The Untold Story of Baby P*, that Haringey had originally been graded 'Good' during the emergency inspection but that this had later been altered to 'Inadequate'. The 2008 inspection report has since been removed from the Ofsted website. One of the three Court of Appeal judges commented that the Haringey Panel: 'might not have been quite so confident in their decision … to dismiss (me and others) … had they known the problems with the inspection and the process by which the final report assumed the form it did'.

The Leveson Inquiry would subsequently shed light on the murky relationship between the media and politicians. Rebekah Brooks was questioned under oath as to whether she had telephoned Ed Balls and demanded that he sack me, or the petition would be turned on him. Brooks agreed that she had rung Ed Balls a few days before I was sacked, but denied that she had ordered Balls to sack me. Nick Davies has, however, challenged this denial. In his book *Hack Attack* (2014) he claims that a government official was listening to the call that Brooks made to Balls and that she was blunt and threatening, telling him to sack Shoesmith as 'we don't want to turn this thing [the petition] on you'. It therefore appeared that a Secretary of State was being threatened by the editor of tabloid newspaper, and Lord Justice Leveson would subsequently conclude that the relationship between politicians and the press had become problematic. Although Brooks was acquitted in the Phone Hacking Trials (while Coulson was convicted), she did acknowledge during her testimony that the attacks on social workers and in particular on me – especially her decision to post a photographer outside my home for four months – was 'cruel, harsh and over the top'.

B. The Police and Blame

Whilst party politics and mediated news may have been the initial driver of public anger and frustration there was also a third dynamic that needs to be acknowledged within this case study's analysis of the dynamics of blame – the role of the Metropolitan Police. In summing up his findings in the inquiry, Lord Justice Leveson expressed concern about the relationship between the Metropolitan Police Service and the Murdoch-owned newspapers. With the benefit of hindsight, what is now clear is that the announcement of an emergency Ofsted multi-agency inspection was interpreted by the Metropolitan Police Service as bringing with it significant practical, political and reputational risks. The Metropolitan Police had been defending their conduct in the case as soon as the news of Peter's death was known but with the announcement of the Ofsted inspection, they immediately launched into a campaign of avoiding blame and protecting their reputation by publicly attacking social workers.

Serious Case Reviews (SCR) are processes through which child protection agencies share the details of their engagement with a child who has been harmed or killed in order to understand what happened and to learn lessons. A review had therefore been undertaken, in line with government policy, immediately after the death of Baby P. The SCR made recommendations for improvements for all three agencies; social workers, health professionals and police. Social workers from the Borough of Haringey did not visit Peter's home as often as they should have done, and they were not decisive enough in acting to protect him when medical appointments at GOSH were delayed. That said, it is also worth noting that the police had provided no evidence of a perpetrator living at Baby P's address, and Haringey Council's solicitor had asked the social workers to wait for more evidence from health and police before intervening. Although the social workers were later sacked their independent regulator the General Social Care Council (GSCC), in line with Haringey's disciplinary processes, did not find evidence to sack them or to withdraw their right to practice as social workers. The practice of Great Ormond Street Hospital (GOSH) was criticised, especially the delay of four months to provide a medical appointment for Peter which occurred two days before he died. Later it emerged that GOSH held back a report that outlined the inefficiencies of their clinic in Haringey, and in particular that the paediatrician who saw Peter was not qualified for that clinic and was standing in for an absent colleague. GOSH revealed that it was the police who had asked that the information was held back from the SCR so it could not be used by the defence barrister in the murder trial. The work of Child Abuse Investigation Unit (CAIU) of the Metropolitan Police was also criticised. The CAIU had been aware of Peter's situation for eight months since social workers first referred his case to them and they arrested his mother and grandmother. Despite the arrests, photographic evidence was obtained too late and shortly afterwards, the case – and unknown to Peter's social worker – was unallocated to an investigating police office for a period of four months. It was fully activated only when the social worker made a further referral in June 2007 (discussed below). No evidence of a perpetrator was ever put forward. Peter was found dead on 3 August 2007, and the day before the police had told Peter's mother that they had no case against her despite two arrests. The case against the grandmother was simply not investigated. In effect, by the time Peter died the police had no evidence.

In the days after Peter died the police revealed the existence of a complex and worrying domestic situation. Steven Barker, the mother's boyfriend, had been living in Baby P's house. Barker's brother Jason Owen, accompanied by his three children and a 15-year-old girl who had been reported missing from home, had also moved in (uninvited) six weeks before Baby P's death. Social workers and the CAIU were aware that a boyfriend had been mentioned in interviews, but were not aware that the household had become home to three adults, eight children – and two large dogs. Such knowledge would have led to immediate action when it concerned a child subject to child protection procedures. Information emerged later of a trench dug in the back garden where adults and the missing 15-year-old could hide. At a very early stage in the murder investigation a police officer commented that the house had been under surveillance suggesting to me and senior professional and political leaders in Haringey Council that there was much more to learn about the case, but this information has never been repeated.

Before the murder trial began and while the SCR was being written, tensions grew between Haringey Council and the police. Many demands were made of the SCR panel and the independent writer of the SCR and were generally acceded to, given the weight the police carry in these settings. In retrospect the 'ground was being laid' for blame avoidance but the relevance of many of their demands at the time only became clear as the trial and public debate developed. More specifically, the police requested that the SCR should begin at the point of Baby P's birth and therefore not include any discussion of his mother's early life and her relationship with her mother (Baby P's grandmother). It would later be revealed that the grandmother had a police record for violent behaviour towards her husband and her son from a very early age. She allegedly confessed that she had a problem with violence against men.[1] The police also argued that the SCR should not be published until

[1] The unpublished Social Care Internal Management Review (IMR) submission to the second SCR.

after the murder trial to avoid helping the defence, and it emerged that GOSH withheld information on the advice of the police for the same reason. The police also suggested, well before the criminal trial, that a full inquest should be avoided, especially with north London coroner Andrew Walker.

The blame-game intensified when the police from the murder investigation team got involved. Social workers were accused of tampering with electronic records, but no such evidence was found when the accusation was formally investigated by both Haringey Council and police information technology experts. The independent writer of the SCR revealed (some years later) that the police had told her that I was withholding important documents, in particular the post-mortem report which I had never seen. The murder trial which was to commence on 9 June 2008 was postponed due to lack of evidence and in the weeks that followed the head of the murder investigation team began to undermine the procedures of the SCR, even asking for adjustments to the wording despite not having been a member of the panel. Shortly after the postponement of the trial the Metropolitan Police informed me in the 'margins of a meeting' that Peter's mother, Tracey Connelly, and her boyfriend, Steven Barker, were to be charged with the rape of Peter's sibling but that the case would only go forward if there was no murder conviction in relation to Peter's death. This was odd. Was there a crime or not? If there was it was my responsibility to commence another SCR for the second child, but I was ordered not to do so as the case now rested with the police. I complied, but later I was to be criticised in an Ofsted report for not doing so.

C. On Trial

This section is about the realities of blame and its pathological impact on public governance. But what it is really trying to achieve is to provide a deep and highly detailed of the murky and Machiavellian lengths that different actors and organisations will go to avoid being blamed, even if the outcome of investigations show systemic issues or simply reflect the complexity of a situation. The core insight being that questions regarding positive, future-focused lesson-learning are drowned-out by a clamour for blame or culpability; and the more politically salient or publicly emotive the issue the more intense that clamour is likely to be. By the time the murder trial concerning the death of Baby P began on 9 September 2008 the pressure placed on Haringey Council, its social workers and its solicitors by the Metropolitan Police had led to strained relationships. Claims of withholding documents, threats of individuals being in contempt of court and being summonsed were made by the police but never evidenced.

By 5 November 2008 it became clear that none of the three people charged with Baby P's murder were going to be found guilty. The agreement between the police, GOSH and Haringey Council to jointly brief the media was broken when the police gave their own briefing to the media on the same day and before the verdicts were announced. The content of this briefing later divulged by journalists in anecdotal evidence was that it was openly negative about Haringey Council, blamed social workers and named me. Unaware of the earlier police briefing, at the close of the trial on Tuesday 11 November 2008 the media briefing that I gave alongside the Chief Executive of GOSH was met with hostility and aggression from criminal journalists who had been in the court. My resignation was demanded. In contrast, no hostility was expressed towards the Chief Executive of GOSH.

The events that followed would have been of great concern to the police. The SCR was published at the end of the trial and clearly set out the criticisms and recommendations for each agency, including the police. The unexpected attack the next day from the Prime Minister, David Cameron, at PMQs and the sudden ordering of an emergency Ofsted inspection of Haringey Children's Services including Great Ormond Street Hospital and the Child Abuse Investigation Unit (CAIU) of London's Metropolitan Police Service added to the pressure. The police, however, were already working with BBC's flagship current affairs programme – Panorama – to broadcast a programme that would go out less than a week after the trial ended and on the very first day of the emergency Ofsted multi-agency inspection. The Panorama documentary was little more than an exercise in blame-avoidance designed for the benefit of the Metropolitan Police. Cameras had been given access to Peter's home and the general framing presented the police as 'the good guys' at the expense of Haringey's social workers and me as Director. The fact that the police had no case against Peter's mother only two days before he died never emerged in the programme. At the end of the murder trial a government briefing by a senior civil servant stated:

> [S]o far I think we [Ed Balls's department] have handled this as well as we could and Government is reasonably well positioned ....SoS [Secretary of State Ed Balls] reported to be pleased. Haringey coming under heavy fire. GOSH less so thus far. The police seem to be briefing behind the scenes though publicly coming across as measured and reflective.

The police 'briefing behind the scenes' signifies an acknowledgement and tolerance of the police conduct. Having received several drafts of the SCR, Ed Balls's department was aware not only of police shortcomings but also that the Panorama programme would contain false accusations against Haringey social workers. In her briefing the civil servant referred to the recommendations in the SCR for social care and health, but she made no mention of those for the police. The cultural embeddedness of blame against social workers contrasted with the 'no blame' position apparently held by police.

On the evening of the day that the Ofsted inspection was completed I received the first of two death threats each accurately addressed and containing images of me cut out from newspapers with abusive slurs written across them. The first demanded that I should resign and words to the effect that my daughter was at risk of physical harm if I did not comply. The police responded, my windows were screwed shut and a 'safe space' was created in my home as a secure refuge from which I could ring the police in the case of an attack. (I was advised, however, not to flee my home in the case of an intruder on the basis that I might run straight into the hands of a violent mob waiting outside my home.) The 'realword' meaning of 'felt accountability'; in this situation is almost impossible to describe. My life and that of my family were at risk due to blame-based accountability structures that had fuelled something akin to pitchfork politics. Even my letter box had to be adapted to cope with the possibility that burning materials might be pushed through it. The second death threat was very similar and came three months after I had lost my job and was approaching the deadline to submit my application for a judicial review of the decision to sack me. As events unfolded in the coming months and years, I came to believe that the death threats had been sent by the police in the hope of scaring me into quiet submission. My resignation at that point would have been a topic for credit-claiming by those politicians and media outlets that had pointed the finger of blame at me (by this time *The Sun* newspaper was claiming over 1.4 million signatories on its petition).

My acceptance of dismissal would also have taken the pressure off the Metropolitan Police who knew that the likely sentences for 'causing or allowing' Baby P's death that might be secured were unlikely to sate the public's appetite for justice. A hostile public was demanding life sentences for those convicted of causing or allowing Peter's death, that were simply unlikely to be secured. The pitchfork politics of direct action that had seen my home become a fortress became increasingly visible as social media groups undertook a march from Trafalgar Square. The date for sentencing Tracey Connelly, Steven Barker and Jason Owen was postponed as the police, without any public announcement, brought forward those additional charges of rape against the mother and her boyfriend established some months earlier if no convictions for murder were found.

By the time I was sacked by the Secretary of State live on television without any forewarning and exactly 20 days after the end of the trial, the police had intensified its blame-avoidance strategy. Leaks to the media consistently exonerated themselves and explicitly blamed social workers for the child's death. The presentational and symbolic significance of this strategy reached a new height when the police released computer-generated images of the body of a baby and a close-up of a head that purported to represent Baby P's injuries as they were seen at the post-mortem. These images were published by several media outlets, alongside pictures of Peter's actual blood-stained clothes. Images such as these would not normally be released by the police, especially not in the case of child homicide. It was clearly a strategic decision that appeared to achieve its blame-focusing ambitions when some newspapers chose to publish the images alongside my image and those of the other social workers in the case. Online abuse and threats of violence against me escalated as a result but there was also something about the release of those images by the police that arguably suggested a certain level of desperation.

In May 2009 a second Panorama programme was broadcast that made several false allegations, including that social workers tampered with e-files when a year earlier even the Metropolitan Police's own IT experts had not been able to substantiate these claims. A third programme followed in December 2010 and focused on whether the social workers knew about the men who were living in the house. In a bizarre twist in what was already a twisted story of avoidance and obfuscation the police had gone to great lengths to obtain a video that had been made for training purposes by a private company. The implication made from the existence of this video seemed to be that social workers should have known that at least one man was living in Peter's home. But what made the position and interpretation of this video more interesting within the overall case was the bizarre lengths the police appeared to have gone to in order to secure the film. The head of the company informed me that a man claiming to be a parent arrived demanding a copy of the video, then he claimed to be an MI5 officer, but then identified as a senior detective on the murder team. He was given the video which very soon afterwards was in the hands of BBC 1's Panorama. The video contained a blurred image of Peter's mother mentioning that she liked a man, but no further details. Yet, the programme made allegations that social workers knew about the men living in Baby P's around the time of his death and this seemed to be a strong focus that the police wanted to pursue.

D. Judicial Review

The judicial review of the decisions taken by Ed Balls and Haringey Council to dismiss me, and the role played by Ofsted commenced in October 2009. The evidence provided to the court to fulfil Ofsted's 'duty of candour' opened-up the extent to which blame-avoidance had almost defined the decision-making processes in the wake of Baby B's death. Evidence concerning the Multi-Agency Public Protection Arrangements (MAPPA) which had been problematic in the emergency inspection was particularly informative. The MAPPA makes decisions about dangerous individuals such as paedophiles being released from prison into local areas. Inspecting the MAPPA would be standard procedure in a multi-agency Ofsted inspection but email exchanges between the lead Ofsted inspector and Her Majesty's Inspector of Constabulary (HMIC) show that the latter was unable or unwilling to inspect the MAPPA. The lead Ofsted inspector questions her decision describing it as 'a mystery' as to why the inspection of the MAPPA cannot take place (she copies in senior Ofsted staff but appears to receive no answer). Documents also show that during the emergency inspection the Home Office and then Balls's Department for Children, Schools and Families received an email on 24 November 2008 from Phoenix Associates, which included as one of its leaders Sara Payne, the mother of the murdered child, Sarah Payne. At the time Sara Payne was working closely with the editor of *The Sun*, Rebekah Brooks, as part of its campaign in relation to community safety but the main purpose of the email to a departmental official seems to be to reveal that 'a MAPPA referral was made to Haringey's Children's Service re Barker [mother's boyfriend] and Owen [boyfriend's brother] that was ignored'. If such a referral had been made, then there was no evidence of it in Children's Services. Furthermore, as the MAPPA is a joint police, prison service and probation service structure the police should have acted on any information regarding the release of violent or sexual offenders themselves. It may have been that the police-team linked to the MAPPA were not aware of the involvement of its own Child Abuse Investigation Unit (CAIU) into the Connelly household, but this may explain the comment (noted above) that Baby P's house had been under surveillance around the time of his death. But the revelation also raised questions of accountability about what the MAPPA knew, what action it had taken and especially why HMIC had declined or was prevented from inspecting it.

Second, as well as the emergency Ofsted inspection, Ed Balls ordered a second Serious Case Review which, through unexpected circumstances, was to undo much of the faulty narrative that had endured and shed light on the issues related to the MAPPA. At the time government policy was that a *summary* of a serious case review was published but the *full* more detailed report was kept confidential. But by 2010 and with a new incoming Conservative Government the new Children's Minister, Tim Loughton, ordered the publication of the *full* serious case review that had been demanded by the tabloid newspapers but blocked by Ed Balls. The full report told a very different story than the summary that had been written for public consumption. The full serious case review when read alongside two Metropolitan Police reports and the report of Her Majesty's Inspector of Constabulary (HMIC) revealed not only the shortcomings of the police, but also the attempts to cover up those shortcomings and to blame the social workers. The two Metropolitan Police reports had been submitted to the *Strategic and Operational Policy Committee* both with the title, *MPS Response to the Death of Baby P*, the first dated 4 December 2008 and the second more detailed version dated 8 January 2009. The third was the unpublished report from HMIC outlining her findings from the Ofsted inspection, findings that were not fully reflected in the published Ofsted Inspection report used to dismiss me. For example, the *full* serious case review comments on the police actions when they received a referral from the social worker on 1 June 2008. It states:

> The police held strongly to the view that injuries [to Peter] were non-accidental [in June 2007] but they did not do their duty by accepting the responsibility to investigate the injuries. They left it to the social worker who is not trained in criminal investigation work. Neither did the police undertake a joint investigation with the social worker (para 3.16.2).

Of the same incident the report of HMIC as part of the multi-agency Ofsted report states:

> There was evidence of social workers effectively carrying out initial investigations on behalf of the police. This appeared to be the case in the initial stages of the allegations made on 1 June 2007 [this is the referral from the social worker to the police of suspected abuse] when the social worker did the preliminary work, the investigation not being pro-actively pursued [by the police] until the following Monday morning.

But the serious case review *summary* written for public consumption gave a very different story of the same event suggesting that the police had been overlooked. It stated:

> The police were only informed and involved at two stages. At other times matters were assessed by the social worker alone or by the doctor alone, denying the police the opportunity to assess whether a crime had been committed and deciding whether to investigate it. In relation to the 1 June visit, the police were informed but asked the social worker to assess the situation and inform them of the outcome, when they would decide whether an investigation was justified. This helps to create an unhelpful culture in which other services use discretion about involving the police (para 4.5.1).

At the time the process of producing Serious Case Reviews (SCR) was evaluated by Ofsted. The first SCR had several recommendations for the police but this new SCR, ordered by Ed Balls, had none, while having stark discrepancies between the published summary and the full report. How could the chair nominated by Ed Balls support it and why was it not challenged by Ofsted? Instead, Ofsted evaluated it as 'good' and the police contributions as 'excellent'. Those who sat on the panel for the second SCR included the most senior people, for example, the Haringey Borough Commander of Police and the lead officer for the murder investigation.

The report of the HMIC also raised a wide range of concerns about staffing, supervision, sharing intelligence, oversight of investigations, lack of attendance at referral and strategy meetings and medical examinations, and access to electronic data systems which may well have contributed to the Child Abuse Investigation Unit's problems in managing the case. Importantly, the HMIC report raises concerns about the exchange of information and intelligence between the Metropolitan Police's Child Abuse Investigation Unit (CAIU) and the Violent Crime Directorate (VCD) which included the Multi-Agency Public Protection Arrangements (MAPPA). For example:

> There was no indication of relevant information [from MAPPA] being passed back to practitioners on the CAIU … [T]there was a lack of knowledge amongst CAIU officers of the MAPPA processes, together with those for the identification, assessment and management of Potentially Dangerous Persons, resulting in significant opportunities being missed to include the use of such processes to assist in the management of risks presented to children by individuals falling within these categories' (HMIC, 2008, p 7).

This is critical evidence. During the emergency Ofsted inspection, the same HMIC said she was unable to inspect the MAPPA, but here she presents a detailed and very critical report not fully reflected in the published inspection report that was used as the basis of my dismissal. The 'questions of accountability' are as obvious as they are far-reaching: did the MAPPA have knowledge of the men and the child missing from home who were living in the Connelly home which was not communicated to either the CAIU or the social workers? Was that the evidence in the MAPPA minutes that HMIC avoided declaring in the inspection? Did the fact that the case of Peter Connelly was unallocated for four months mean that details of his family and home were not on the police database for the Violent Crime Directorate to find? Was this a breakdown in intelligence, a case of human error or something more sinister? How might the answers to these questions help explain the extensive efforts of the Metropolitan Police to focus the blame on social workers over several years? The police would certainly have been sensitive to criticism. In 2002 the police had been heavily criticised for a breakdown in communication that had allowed the killer of two young girls to 'slip through the net' in what became known as the Soham murders. The subsequent Bichard Inquiry of 2004 identified serious police errors in the use of intelligence systems and led to extensive changes in relation to both police records and the introduction of a new national Disclosure Barring Service, replacing the former Criminal Records Bureau, in an attempt to protect children from predatory or dangerous adults. Police failures in relation to Soham may well have increased their determination to avoid blame in the case of Baby P for what now seem to be similar issues.

E. The Life Sentence for Rape

In August 2008 at Highgate Magistrate's Court, police had charged Tracey Connelly and Steven Barker with the rape of one of Peter's siblings. The trial took place in early 2009 under strict rules of no press coverage. Connelly was acquitted, and Barker was found guilty and received a life sentence to run concurrently with the 12 years he received for jointly causing or allowing Peter's death. The life sentence for Barker was announced on 1 May 2009 and on the same day, in a seemingly coordinated act, the summary of the new Serious Case Review that Ed Balls had demanded was briefed to the media (by the chairman who Balls had himself appointed). The briefing sought to reinforce the narrative that social workers were to blame, and the fact that the four social workers in Baby P's case had been formally dismissed the day before, seemed to reinforce the logic of this conclusion. Ten days later the Care Quality Commission (CQC 2009) published a highly critical report into the conduct of health services, including the conduct of Great Ormond Street Hospital in the case of Baby P but no connection was made by the report or the media to the social workers or the action taken against them.

F. No Inquest for Peter

Finally, the efforts made by the Metropolitan Police to prevent an inquest into Peter's death from taking place had begun shortly after his death and is the most powerful indicator of not only avoiding blame, but of a potential abuse of power that impacts on democracy. Why was Peter Connelly not entitled to an inquest? The Metropolitan Police submitted over 40 different documents to the pre-inquest hearings arguing that an inquest into Peter's death was unnecessary. Their own reports discussed above ('Metropolitan police response to the Death of Baby P',

December 2008 and January 2009) and that of HMIC were not among them. Nevertheless, the police were clear in their submissions to the coroner that 'those responsible have been identified and made subject to either criminal or professional disciplinary procedures'. Their comment referred to those convicted of 'causing or allowing' Peter's death and my dismissal, those of the four social workers, and the paediatrician who had ended her career. Those responsible for Peter's death, the police claimed, and the coroner appeared to accept, had been punished. This appears as a strange reason to deny an inquest. It is also notable that amongst those who wanted the inquest included Peter's mother and her boyfriend, both of whom were by then in prison. In November 2010 the coroner made the decision not to proceed with an inquest.[2] The next section reflects on the broader implications of this case.

III. Learning from Baby P

The main argument of this chapter has been that too often our accountability systems focus on 'naming, shaming and blaming' instead of focusing on more future-focused and arguably important issues relating to policy-learning, institutional resilience and, in many cases a better-informed public. Building institutional resilience includes robust systems of performance management in which evidence is used to judge individual performance with those found guilty of gross misconduct dismissed. The scapegoating of individuals should not play any part in accountability systems and must be exposed. In many ways the root of the issue takes the discussion back to a distinction that was raised in the opening chapter between Mode I scrutiny (ie, 'hot rhetoric') and Mode II ('cool theory'). What this chapter has attempted to reveal through a detailed case study is the pathological impact of Mode I not just on those individuals who were 'named and shamed' but on society more generally. This is a critical point. The 'hot rhetoric' public and particularly media reaction to the death of Baby P created what might be termed 'a culture of fear' within the social work profession which led to a very sudden and dramatic increase in the number of children taken into care. Indeed, in the ten days after the news of Baby P's death the number of care applications increased by 26 per cent as social workers, in fear of vilification in the media, took immediate risk-aversion measures. As Murphy (2022) has shown, what became known as the 'Baby P effect' was fuelled by the perpetual fear amongst social workers of being named, blamed and shamed. 'I don't want my face on the front page of the Sun' given as a reason by social workers for their concerns about working in child protection.

[2] Inquest into the death of Peter Connelly, Reports/Inquiries/Disciplinary Proceedings. MPS 18/10/10 available from coroners@justice.gsi.gov.uk.

The paradox being that many children were taken into care as an anticipatory blame-deflection strategy, and many would remain in care for the rest of their childhoods. Fewer than 50,000 children were in care when Baby P died but by December 2022 this figure had risen to nearly 108,000. Despite this shift into state care the number of children who become victims of familial child homicide has not altered in a 50-year period. In the year 2020, 53 children died at the hands of a known adult and a further 20 deaths were related to, but not directly caused by maltreatment (The Child Safeguarding Practice Review Panel Executive Summary May 2021). Most often poor children from poor families come into the care sector, and most often poor children become victims of familial child homicide. Given these statistics, the vilification of social workers, the subsequent pressures on services, and the fear parents now have that if they seek help their children will be taken from them, are all indicators that children's social care is a public service in crisis. Did the 'accountability' that surrounded Baby P's death really help to improve public policy? Did we learn anything from the tragedy of Baby P? The resounding answer is no.

In terms of engaging with these questions and situating this chapter within the contours of wider debates and controversies it is possible to make five inter-related points. The first develops the distinction between 'Mode I' and 'Mode II' accountability by injecting a temporal dimension. Put very simply, society needs a stronger emphasis on Mode II (ie, a calm, slow and reflective approach) in the immediate aftermath or wake of a crisis in order to prevent knee-jerk reactions that might actually make the challenge worse in the longer term. Put within the theory of Daniel Kahneman (2012) we need to be able to 'think slow' but quickly. Looking back at the case study of Baby P it was really the judicial review proceedings that were able to inject some slower and more evidence-based thinking into the tragedy. The shift from political accountability to judicial accountability somehow serving to depoliticise and take the heat out of the investigation. But even then, the case of Baby P was not the focus of the judicial review proceedings – the focus was the process by which the decision to sack had been made. It was a full inquest that might have looked in detail at the context and cause of Peter's death. By the time the courts became involved the damage of thinking *too quick*, *too hot*, *too fast*, had already been done. There are examples of 'slow thinking' and lesson-learning within the child safety sector. In the UK around 500 serious case reviews are conducted every year and the broader systemic lessons and insights have been identified through the meta-analysis conducted by the 'Research in Practice' at the University of East Anglia. But even then, the Serious Case Reviews they study will have been subject to different degrees of blame-avoidance.

The work of the University of East Anglia has been superseded by the Child Safeguarding Practice Review Panel, whose focus is on improving learning, professional practice and thereby outcomes for children. They provide the 'slow thinking' but have no broader role in terms of promoting the public understanding of social work and the inevitable challenges that its practitioners face on an almost daily basis given the effects of knee-jerk reactions to familial child homicide. This flows into a second issue and a refocusing on the broader cultural context that formed the focus of the opening section in this chapter. The blaming of social workers has become 'a cultural trope': a habitual response devoid of reason, thought, knowledge or understanding (Shoesmith 2016). Numerous campaigns by social work organisations have attempted to promote a more balanced account of what social workers do and why it matters – see #Respect4SocialWork or 'Stand-Up for Social Workers' – but the societal negativity-bias is simply too intense and apparently so embedded that little progress has been made. The puzzle outlined in chapter one as to why, at a time when we have more accountability systems, structures and processes than ever before, is it that public confidence in political processes and public services appears to be so low is possibly quite simple to answer – our appreciation of the success of public services compared to the response to the very low frequency of things going wrong is out of balance. Accountability generally over-emphasises the latter while almost denying the existence of the former.

But there is also a third and more insidious issue at play. Blame games can cost lives. This chapter began by drawing upon anthropological literature to suggest that human nature possessed a natural desire to be able to understand and control fate. The naming, shaming and blaming of a scapegoat in the form of a politician, doctor, social worker or police officer might therefore fulfil a psychological desire at the societal level to have identified what went wrong and to have taken steps to prevent it happening again. Even if the problems that led to the crisis or disaster are systemic in nature, or even beyond human control, *being able to blame* exerts a cathartic effect or balm upon the affected community. The bigger questions that accountability might unwittingly force us to broach might therefore relate to the limits of the state and to the frailties of human nature. Bringing this thought back to the sphere of social work and caring for vulnerable children, Cooper (2010) suggests 'we know children are harmed and abused but we cannot face it. The pain of knowing [that it happens] is too great … the perceived incompetence of social workers then functions as a defence for society … against having to tolerate knowledge of what is bad.' Cooper (2014) further suggests that society has no discourse to manage such indigestible facts of child murder or torture. At its core is perhaps not blame but denial of what adults, especially mothers, can be capable of. Denial leads to a societal defence mechanism in a context of mediated politics and punitive populism that embeds a belief that social workers failed to save the child. The case of Baby P showed the complex impact that this belief has on protecting vulnerable children and building a resilient workforce.

This flows into a fourth issue and a focus on the tension between assumptions and expectations of individualised blame, on the one hand, against the messier reality of collaborative governance. As the second section of this chapter demonstrates, public policies are often delivered by a range of organisations working together across shared functions. This is particularly true of complex policy areas that reach across traditional policy silos and means that when things go wrong – as they inevitably will – the responsibility for that failing is often shared, but different agencies have different degrees of power and influence to avoid blame. In this case the Metropolitan Police and Great Ormond Street Hospital, both had much more influence in terms of being able to frame the public debate and influence the agenda than Haringey Council. Each had much closer relationships with the media that protected them. Moreover, complex systems that all these agencies experience, tend to break down and fail as more and more pressure and unrealistic expectations are placed upon them. Sometimes it is possible to identify where a specific link in a chain or cog in a machine broke down, but more often it is a combination of failing at the systemic level, of resourcing, of bad basic policy that we fail to identify and learn from, or our inability to predict and therefore prevent the horror that some adults can inflict upon children. Such horrors can be beyond our imagination including beyond the imagination of all those who work in front line services.

In short, accountability expectations generally cannot cope with complexity. They want and demand a simple answer to the question of 'who is to blame?' and this hunt continues. This was demonstrated during the House of Commons' Education Select Committee's evidence hearing into the death of Arthur Labinjo-Hughes and Star Hobson (HC413, Session 2022–23), both victims of familial child homicide in 2020. During evidence sessions local authority chief executives and directors of children's services from the respective local councils where the children died consistently attempted to explain to the members of the committee, how systemic issues with resourcing, recruitment, maintaining and improving services, working with police and other services themselves under pressure, and the impact of the Covid lockdown had created major challenges in monitoring vulnerable children. But the committee was less interested in understanding the underlying causes of these tragedies and more concerned with repeatedly naming the chief executive they thought should take responsibility and resign. The impact of media attention on the local authorities was such that social workers and agency staff resigned in significant numbers; thereby making new recruitment difficult, placing additional pressures on the remaining staff and overall making 'at risk' children even more vulnerable. In January 2023 Ofsted inspected and unsurprisingly judged the respective council services in this case to be 'inadequate' which compounded the problems. At the same time the NHS was in serious breakdown with very poor performance, yet no one would suggest that wholesale sacking of senior NHS staff would have been a sensible solution.

The death of Baby P is clearly an extreme case through which to explore 'questions of accountability'. But that also makes it incredibly valuable because it sheds light on the emotional and moral aspects of accountability (see Shoesmith 2016). The perennial scapegoating of social work suggests that it has some very specific characteristics that render it a very vulnerable profession. This focus on sacrificial accountability, which is almost an obsession, reinforces the 'tin hat mentality' discussed in chapter one but what is almost completely missing in any of the existing academic literature on accountability is an emphasis on emotional labour. Judicial processes and public inquiries may offer the potential for a more evidential approach to be adopted but this too is often at a cost of overlooking systemic issues and the physical, mental, personal and professional exhaustion that being held to account, especially when it involves elements of public vilification and threats of violence, can have upon individuals. There was no 'public service bargain' between myself and the Secretary of State, no 'accountability shield' that I could have hidden behind (even for momentary relief) but operating in high-risk parts of the public sector in 'the shadow of blame' exerts a high emotional and psychological cost that is rarely recognised, let alone studied. This chapter has raised lots of 'questions of accountability' that still require answers. But the answers we do have in terms of the need to emphasise positive lesson-learning and avoid immediate and blame-based reactions may have changed the outcome for me, the social workers, the paediatrician, and several others. It may have also changed the life outcomes for all of those tens of thousands of children that suddenly found themselves placed in care. Nevertheless, the last word and the final questions must surely be about Peter Connelly. Despite millions of words already written, and huge sums of money spent and earned, without an inquest no one knows *how Peter died, why he died, when he died, or who killed him*. It is surely a failure not only of public accountability but also of democracy.

14

Accountability in the Age of Artificial Intelligence

MADALINA BUSUIOC

Decision-making in public organisations is undergoing a profound transformation, with increasing reliance on automation and new generation algorithmic approaches like machine learning in the implementation of public policy (Yeung and Lodge 2019; Veale and Brass 2019; Young et al 2019; Zouridis, van Eck and Bovens 2019; Busuioc 2021). In that process, algorithms take automated or partially automated decisions that used to be the exclusive purview of domain experts and civil servants. We are witnessing the rise of the *artificial public administration* – an administration that is increasingly hybrid in nature, an intermeshing of human and automated decision-making. This is the case not only for so-called 'production agencies' (Wilson 1989) – large-scale bureaucracies that routinely make decisions on benefits, taxes or subsidies – but also for traditionally high discretion tasks. Algorithmic systems are making inroads into the criminal justice systems, shaping the administration of justice (Citron 2016); into law enforcement, police rely ever more on algorithms in the context of predictive policing, shaping the state's use of coercive powers (Ferguson 2017); welfare agencies are also increasingly turning to predictive algorithmic systems for instance, to screen for abuse or child neglect (Ho and Burke 2022). With their adoption spurred by the promise of greater efficiency and effectiveness gains across resource-depleted public sectors, algorithms are becoming a pervasive feature of administrative governance. These developments however, unless carefully managed, can come with serious repercussions: they raise far-reaching 'questions of accountability' (see also Busuioc 2021). Algorithm deployment gone wrong can be exceptionally harmful in administrative contexts.

For instance, in the Netherlands, a recent investigative report revealed large-scale profiling by local municipalities: dozens of low-income neighbourhoods have been subject to data-driven profiling for welfare fraud (Lighthouse Reports 2022). The system pooled together large amounts of data from municipalities and other public bodies such as the tax office or the police. Arbitrary risk criteria such as water consumption, the ownership of a trailer, or being a single woman who has a baby while on welfare – were among the indicators relied on for fraud profiling (Lighthouse Reports 2022; NRC 2022). Those targeted run the risk of having their benefits stopped. This comes shortly in the aftermath of another huge scandal – the so-called 'childcare benefits scandal' (the 'Toeslagenaffaire'), which affected more than 25,000 victims, and where the reliance on an artificial intelligence (AI) algorithm as a decisional aid by the Dutch tax authorities resulted in institutional discrimination. The algorithm used nationality as an indicator in fraud determinations (Dutch Data Protection Authority 2020). Mainly parents with a migration background, single-parent families and families on low incomes were wrongly accused of fraud (Inspectie Justitie en Veiligheid 2022), with benefits stopped and having to be repaid retrospectively, resulting in severe financial problems, bankruptcies, mental health issues and children removed from their families (Geiger 2021; de Volkskrant 2022a). In the context of the large-scale profiling by municipalities, this same biased AI algorithm from the benefits scandal had also reportedly been used (Lighthouse Reports 2022; Ministry of Finance 2022, 7).

As these examples underscore, the transformation of the nature of public authority brought on by the proliferation of AI in government comes with serious consequences. A pressing need for accountability ensues. Can scrutiny structures evolve to control and legitimise the use of complex, computer-based and data driven governance processes? How does the emergence of 'post-human' public administration processes demand a potentially transformative recalibration of how accountability is interpreted in relation to both theory and practice? With these questions in mind, this chapter sets out to investigate what the implications of the growing reliance on AI in government are for public accountability and whether our safeguards are still fit-for-purpose. To that end, this chapter engages with three core questions:

1. How and why does the growing reliance on AI across public sectors challenge the established accountability space?
2. Can the existing architecture of accountability adjust to the challenges posed by artificial intelligence and algorithmic governance?
3. Looking to the future, how can we safeguard and sustain accountability in the age of AI?

Each of these questions are addressed, in turn, in each of the chapter's subsequent sections. In tackling these questions, this chapter speaks to one overarching issue of core concern: with bureaucratic power being eroded and delegated to technological systems, what implications does this have for our understanding of public accountability? As the use of AI in administrative settings proliferates, there is a growing need to take stock of where we stand in matters of public accountability, to assess to what extent our safeguards are still robust, and to retool public accountability to ensure its resilience. The next section begins this process by tackling our first question, exploring how and why the increasing reliance on AI by administrative actors affects central aspects of the administrative process and has crucial implications for public accountability. In light of that, the next two sections speak to the remaining two questions, namely, whether our accountability frameworks are still suited to, and can move in lockstep with, the realities of hybrid governance, and finally, how our oversight structures should be bolstered to sustain accountability in the age of AI-driven governance.

I. Artificial Public Administration: How AI is Transforming the Administrative Process

Bureaucratic legitimacy rests on a triad of bureaucratic expertise (the bureaucracy's claim to superior expertise or know-how as the 'selling point' of the bureaucratic model); the ability to leverage that expertise to act upon it in policymaking processes (discretion); coupled with the presence of institutional accountability mechanisms and constraints to ensure administrative behaviour remains within mandated parameters of desirable public action. Precisely because powers are delegated, and because bureaucratic agents have the ability to exercise discretion, accountability is central as a means to ensure that administrative action is democratically legitimate (Bertelli and Busuioc 2021). The central argument of this section is that as administrative actors increasingly rely on AI to carry out public sector tasks and responsibilities, this is eroding the established foundations of bureaucratic legitimacy and in the process, reshaping the building blocks that inform our theories of political control and accountability.

A. Artificial Administration and Dismissing Discretion

Reflecting established scholarship consensus, Sowa and Selden (2003, 700) describe administrative discretion as 'a fact of life'. On a similar note, Krause (2003, 43) notes that: 'Discretion is obviously part and parcel of the administrative process, and sufficient discretion is essential for an agency to perform its tasks.' Public administrators are endowed with discretion – the freedom or leeway to choose among alternative courses of action – in order to bring their expertise to bear in the implementation of public policy. No amount of legislative foresight can anticipate and hardwire the choices and trade-offs administrators are faced with when implementing open-ended mandates, nor would in fact the necessary expertise to specify such choices reside with legislators in the first place.

The reality of bureaucratic discretion, however, gives rise to a central dilemma for accountability and political control scholarship: on the one hand, as noted above, discretion is a staple of effective public service provision. The ability of public administrators to draw on their expertise to tailor policy to specific circumstances is crucial for administering programmes and executing public policy. Street-level bureaucrats for instance, exercise a large degree of discretion in their interactions with clients as they deploy their professional knowledge to translate general rules to the complex realities of frontline work and to local and individual circumstances (Lipsky 1980). Bureaucratic discretion can be critical in this context, to ensuring fair and equitable outcomes in administrative processes (Bovens and Zouridis 2002), to encouraging effective expertise acquisition in the bureaucracy (Gailmard and Patty 2007) and to overall successful policy implementation (Bartels 2013; Thomann, van Engen and Tummers 2018), playing a critical role to enhancing the quality of services, decisions and outcomes.

On the other hand, discretion brings with it a control problem. By its very existence, administrative discretion creates opportunities for unsanctioned deviations in policy away from the wishes of elected representatives – to the extent that administrative actors make choices that are not consistent or aligned with political preferences. This can result in variation across like cases and the possibility that administrative agents act upon their own preferences, or even biases and stereotypes:

> With greater discretion granted to administrative agents comes more normatively troubling opportunities for those public administrators to engage in racially discriminatory or other discriminatory behavior that emanates from their personal, behavioral biases (Bertelli et al 2022).

When abused, discretion can thus give rise to policy inconsistency, unequal treatment, beneficial treatment of some clients (perceived as 'deserving') to the detriment of others, and even discrimination in frontline work. While the hazards of bureaucratic discretion gone awry are well-recognised, discretion is nevertheless an indispensable feature of the administrative process: 'for all the accountability problems it presents, the value of high-quality information cannot be seriously doubted. (…) we must reconcile ourselves to institutional forms that leverage the information necessary for policymaking through the power to act on it' (Gailmard and Patty 2013, 2). Discretion, in other words, is an inevitable element of democratic governance. This is a truism of the *analogue administration*.

With the rise of what is for the purposes of this chapter labelled 'artificial public administration', this axiom is being challenged. Bureaucratic processes are increasingly (fully or partially) automated. The professional judgment of judges, police officers and social care workers is being curtailed (or even replaced) by algorithmic decision-making systems. As decision-making gets relegated to sophisticated data-driven technologies, the discretionary power of 'street-level bureaucrats' is being eroded as digital tools that discipline or even supplant bureaucratic discretion in public service provision are utilised (Busch and Henriksen 2018; Bullock 2019; Peeters 2020; Busuioc 2021; de Boer and Raaphorst 2021; Zouridis, van Eck and Bovens 2020). A clear 'trend toward throwing away expertise, discretion, and flexibility with both hands' (Calo and Citron 2022, 804) is visible in the administrative state.

While some scholars have raised concerns as to the implications of the rise of so-called 'automated' (Zouridis, van Eck and Bovens 2019) or 'artificial discretion' (Young et al 2019) when it comes to usurping professional leeway and discretion in decision-making (eg, Bovens and Zouridis 2002; Young, Bullock and Lecy 2019; Peeters 2020; Calo and Citron 2022; see also Eubanks 2018 on the automation of welfare), others herald it precisely as a possible solution, even a panacea, for long-standing questions of control and compliance. As data-driven technologies, AI algorithms are said to bring about more accurate, 'neutral' and reliable predictions, allowing us to overcome human biases and the inconsistencies and variability of human judgement (or 'noise') (Kahneman, Sibony and Sunstein 2021; Sunstein 2021). In this understanding, AI amounts to a technological solution to the 'pesky' problem of bureaucratic discretion – a computational fix envisaged to address the liabilities of human discretion (and human decision-making, more broadly). Accordingly, automation is said to usher in a less 'noisy' and as such, more uniform and consistent decision-making: a new dawn in governmental decision-making, where discretion makes way to standardisation through the mediation of algorithmic expert systems. The 'truism' of analogue administration (discretion as 'a fact of life') *seemingly* no longer holds in its digital iteration.

B. The Rise of Synthetic Expertise

The reliance on AI in administrative decision-making simultaneously brings with it unprecedented changes to the nature of bureaucratic expertise. As bureaucracies are increasingly incorporating synthetic or artificial expertise in the form of AI algorithms to inform, or in some cases, even replace traditional decision-making, these new forms of knowledge production are not merely instrumental but can become constitutive.

The biggest subset of AI is machine learning (ML) which is an approach whereby algorithms learn from data. They deduce (and modify) the rules that govern their behaviour – essentially how to classify new, yet-unseen inputs from seeing lots and lots of examples. This is not to say that many consequential choices in terms of algorithm design and functioning are not determined by human actors – to the contrary, developers make key choices (from choice of data, model, hyper-parameters tuning etc) that will determine algorithm functioning or (malfunctioning) in critical ways. Nevertheless, by virtue of the way they learn, analysing large amounts of training data, linking inputs to outputs, ML algorithms can come to learn unwanted patterns and behaviours that were not anticipated by their designers. In that process, algorithms can come to reproduce, automate and exacerbate insidious, undesirable, possibly imperceptible (to us) patterns present within (historic) administrative data. And in this context, these behaviours, now encoded in mathematical code, can be especially difficult to diagnose and correct, given algorithm architectural complexity and convoluted decisional pathways.

Machine learning models such as neural networks (or 'deep learning') – currently the most advanced type of AI – can be extremely complex in their operation: hundreds of layers deep, thousands of features and millions (and even billions) of weights that contribute to one predictive outcome. In fact, popular ML technologies such as large language models can have hundreds of billions of parameters (GPT-3.5, the language model behind the now famous ChatGPT, successor to GPT-3 which had 175 billion parameters, will be followed by GPT-4 which could have as many as 1 trillion parameters). By virtue of the sheer size of the parameter space and complexity of feature interactions of deep learning models, understanding the decisional pathways of how such models arrive at their predictions can be next to impossible (also for their developers). Such algorithms are therefore *technical black boxes* (Burell 2016; Rudin 2019) – algorithmic decisional systems that are effectively opaque in their decision-making by virtue of their technical complexity.

These specificities of complex AI algorithms – opaqueness and convoluted decisional pathways – limit our ability to retrieve how an algorithmic decision came about and to *understand the reasons* behind a specific algorithmic decision or recommendation. This differentiates them from both earlier algorithmic systems relied upon in the past as well as from *traditional forms of expertise*, where experts, when asked, are able to articulate the reasons behind their decisions and recommendations. This significantly curtails our ability to ascertain to which extent algorithmic decisions or recommendations are reached 'for the right reasons' – as opposed to indicative of spurious correlations or unwanted patterns in the data that entrench systemic biases. And while algorithms can be tested for bias, bias can still arise in real-life deployments if predicting on cases that are different from what the algorithm was trained on, with such failures going undetected – exposed as flawed only when mounting evidence of systematic discrepancies accumulates (such as large-scale evidence of algorithmic harm), at a high cost for those adversely affected.

In its artificial or synthetic iteration, expertise (and indeed the merits thereof) thus becomes opaque and impervious to challenge. It is not open to refutation on the merits of its arguments because it does not provide reasons – at least none that are easily understood. Expertise that cannot explain its reasons and in fact, whose very merits often lie outside our ability to interrogate, comes closer to blind faith. It also comes at an exceedingly high price: difficulty in identifying error, delays in diagnosing failures and malfunction to being with, and diminished opportunities for redress. In the case of the Dutch childcare benefits affair for instance, it took years before the bias was exposed – after tremendous damage had already been perpetrated against tens of thousands of victims. The 'quest for responsibility' (Bovens 2014) in government, which always sought to look within the 'black box' of policymaking is now further frustrated by highly complex technological 'black boxes' that withhold their decisional logics.

C. Informational Asymmetries in the Artificial Administration – Looming Large

The inscrutability of artificial expertise simultaneously stands to exacerbate informational asymmetries pertaining to bureaucratic decision-making in its technologically-clad iteration. Informational asymmetries – working to the administrative agent's benefit – are the primordial source of control problems within traditional understandings of political control and accountability. Armed with superior knowledge and expertise, as well as privileged insight into their own actions and motivations, bureaucratic agents are at a considerable informational advantage vis-à-vis their overseers. A vast literature on political control of the bureaucracy, in general, and on principal-agent relationships, in particular, has studied the administrative procedures and institutional mechanisms (such as monitoring and reporting requirements) that may mitigate informational asymmetries and compel bureaucratic agents to relinquish (at least in part) their informational advantage (eg, Weingast and Moran 1983; McCubbins, Noll and Weingast 1987; Moe 2006). In the context of the rise of the artificial public administration, informational asymmetries compound pre-existing and well-recognised challenges (albeit in a different form), with the ultimate outcome being that accountability is further obfuscated.

Technically opaque algorithms do not reveal the reasons for their decision-making. While techniques have been developed to 'compel' black boxes to reveal their logics, these techniques fall short of meaningful transparency of their decision logics (see further, Busuioc, Curtin and Almada 2022, 19–21). While an in-depth exploration of the topic is beyond the scope of this contribution, such techniques essentially amount to the generation of algorithm-made explanations for underlying black boxes (for different techniques see, eg, Ribeiro, Singh and Guestrin 2016; Lundberg and Lee 2017; Wachter, Mittelstadt and Russell 2018) – essentially, deploying an explainer algorithm that 'regurgitates' the black box into something we can understand. Suffice to say, that such techniques are only 'approximations' of underlying black boxes rather that accurate or complete renditions of the underlying algorithmic decisional logic: 'Explainable ML methods provide explanations that are not faithful to what the original model computes' (Rudin 2019, 207; see also, Rudin, Wang and Coker 2020). The features in the explanation are often different to the underlying model (Ribeiro, Singh and Guestrin 2016) – in other words, a different decision logic altogether, and different explanation techniques also produce different explanations for the same outcome (Bordt et al 2022). What is more, recent studies show such techniques can be manipulated and developed to mislead users (Lakkaraju and Bastani 2019;

Slack et al 2021). From an oversight perspective, the risk is that explanations of black boxes offer little more than post hoc rationalisations that provide a false sense of security (Kostick-Quenet and Gerke 2022). Indeed, recent research warns of relying on explanations of black box ML models (see, eg, in healthcare, Babic et al 2021; in adversarial contexts, Bordt et al 2022; or as a substitution for transparency, Busuioc, Curtin and Almada 2022), and relatedly, against reliance on black box algorithms in high-stakes decision-making given their inherent opacity (Rudin 2019). As it stands, black box algorithms and their decisional logics are not reliably understandable.

This becomes highly problematic when such algorithms are relied on in administrative contexts affecting individuals' lives in consequential ways. Reason-giving is a hallmark of bureaucratic legitimacy, and a key safeguard against arbitrary administrative decisions and actions. A key component of public accountability is that of justification (or answerability) – where public actors are required to render transparent, and explain, the reasons behind their actions and decisions (Bovens 2007). Bred by opacity, informational asymmetries in the age of artificial public administration loom large – the rationale for an algorithmic decision, and indeed whether this is based on legitimate or to the contrary, spurious or arbitrary reasons, remains hidden. Under the cloak of impenetrability, algorithms can become a source of oppression (Noble 2018).

What is more, many AI algorithms are not only *technically opaque* but often also *legally opaque* – that is, subject to proprietary protections, including when used in the public sector, further limiting information availability that could inform adequate monitoring of their functioning. For instance, the now infamous MiDAS algorithm that wreaked havoc in the US with its inaccurate unemployment fraud determinations (it is assessed the algorithm was wrong 93 per cent of the time, with 40,000 incorrect fraud determinations, see Angwin 2022) was proprietary (Elyounes 2021, 492); as are predictive systems used in criminal justice (Citron 2016; Rudin, Wang and Coker 2020) as well as numerous predictive policing systems of dubious quality mushrooming across jurisdictions (see for instance, Richardson et al 2019). In the Netherlands, investigations by the Court of Audit found that when algorithms are developed by, or outsourced to, external providers both the responsible ministry as well as the public body concerned have little insight into the algorithms' functioning: 'We found that outsourced algorithms become black boxes, and that it is unclear which aspects of the data are taken into account in arriving at a decision' (Algemene Rekenkamer 2022, 37; see also Algemene Rekenkamer 2021, 42). Even when algorithms are developed in house by public bodies, the details of their design and functioning are not publicly disclosed. Algorithms deployed for highly consequential tasks such as benefits fraud detection (by the tax office and municipalities) or predictive policing (the so-called 'Crime Anticipation System', CAS) are not publicly transparent. The coupling of legal, organisational and technical opacity poses unprecedented challenges from an accountability perspective precluding meaningful external scrutiny.

To sum up, the adoption of AI by administrative bodies is reshaping central characteristics of the bureaucratic process: administrative *discretion, expertise* and the nature of *informational asymmetries* residing with the bureaucracy. As will be demonstrated below, these changes and their interplay come with fundamental implications for public accountability. Our institutional mechanisms and administrative procedures are poorly tailored for the realities of the rise of *artificial public administration.*

II. What Implications? Public Accountability, Still Fit-for-Purpose?

A. Revisiting Discretion: Value Slippage, a Technological 'Shell Game'

The previous section argued that the adoption of data technologies in public services stands to do away with bureaucratic discretion as computational systems and automated decision rules strip away the decisional leeway of case workers, frontline professionals and other bureaucratic actors. This gives rise to a simple but fundamental question for democratic governance: as bureaucratic discretion is removed and replaced by sophisticated algorithmic systems, where does this leave us when it comes to public accountability? Is public accountability on the way to becoming an outdated, archaic value in the age of the artificial administration? The central argument of this section is that nothing could be further from the truth.

In the digital administrative state, discretion does not disappear. It is simply 'moved' (Eubanks 2018), it switches places as it gets displaced to different actors: a high-tech switcheroo. The professional freedom of administrative agents is now replaced by (implicit) choices made by system engineers, designers and providers of algorithmic systems (Bovens and Zouridis 2002; Busuioc 2021, 831–32). Data scientists, engineers and system providers effectively become policymakers, the 'new equivalents of the former street-level bureaucrats', as Bovens and Zouridis (2002, 181) characterise them. This shift in the nature of governance resonates with the notion of 'arena shifting' within the literature on depoliticisation (see Flinders and Buller 2006). Although focused on administrative delegation to arm's-length expert bodies, the argument is that issues or decisions are no less political but have simply been transferred into a new decision-making arena that exists beyond direct scrutiny structures. The reliance on algorithmic technologies and artificial administration reflects a similar pattern but, in this case, it is a form of technological rather than institutional delegation that takes place (although both processes can occur in parallel).

As technical experts translate analogue policy into digital code, they exercise broad discretionary power: seemingly innocuous 'technical' choices can fundamentally alter underlying policy outcomes – and these choices are often made with little (if any) outside scrutiny. The content of rules and public policies can get modified and reorientated in the process, 'lost in translation' to code:

> Although programmers building automated systems may not intend to engage in rulemaking, they in fact do so. Programmers routinely change the substance of rules when translating them from human language into computer code. The resulting distorted rules effectively constitute new policy that can affect large numbers of people (Citron 2008, 1254).

Harmful examples of failed automated systems due to inaccurate 'translation' of rules, policies and administrative programmes into digital code abound, with dire consequences for affected individuals (ranging from false fraud determinations, denial of benefits, inaccurate recidivism predictions), with victims sometimes running into the hundreds of thousands (see, for example, Citron 2008; Calo and Citron 2022; Elyounes 2021; Whiteford 2021; Angwin 2022).

Algorithmic outputs are to a significant extent the product of value choices designed within them. To the extent that, through their choices, system designers promote unintended values and make unsanctioned trade-offs that alter policy intent, 'a shift in public values outside the control of public managers and public policy-makers' (Busch and Henriksen 2018, 19) occurs. As individuals are aggregated into 'predictive categories', improper design and incorrect translation, coupled with standardisation, which leaves little room for affordances to individual considerations, can lead to injustices. The 'excessive rigidity' brought on by automation can become a source of arbitrariness in decision-making in its own right (Bovens and Zouridis 2002, 182). It is therefore crucial that such choices are understood and interrogated. However, in the case of AI algorithms, such trade-offs, are often *implicit* in system design and obscured by complex layers of code and mathematical computations, shading them from closer scrutiny (Busuioc 2021).

It is also important to note that policy distortions and value slippage can occur both unintentionally (as a result of implicit, unsanctioned designer choices that are not aligned with policy goals) but also intentionally – by design, under of the cover of neutrality. For instance, in the case of the 'Toeslagenaffaire' in the Netherlands, subsequent investigations revealed the algorithm functioning echoed engrained organisational practices and problematic aspects of the bureaucratic culture within the tax office itself (eg, PwC 2021, 19, 17; Algemene Rekenkamer 2022, 32) (and the deeper political climate) – geared at a highly punitive approach that explicitly targeted citizens of foreign descent. As data-driven devices, the introduction of algorithms in public services can serve to create the perception of neutrality, statistical certainty, and inevitability of courses of actions that are political rather than neutral in nature. They can serve to 'sanitise', rationalise and package as seemingly 'objective' (ie, they appear to depoliticise) what are in fact deeply political choices, involving normative trade-offs in public values. As seen in the Dutch childcare benefits scandal (but also in the automation of welfare more broadly, see Eubanks 2018, Larsson 2021; Schou and Hjelholt 2018;

Calo and Citron 2022; UN Special Rapporteur on Extreme Poverty and Human Rights 2019), the introduction of automation can bring about the prioritisation of 'sigma-type' values (such as frugality, efficiency) at the cost of other critical public values such as equal treatment, non-discrimination or due process.

All in all, the inescapable conclusion is that discretion does not disappear, but rather much like a technological version of a 'shell game', it is displaced and reappears elsewhere – relegated to data scientists, system engineers and developers. At other times however, in the manner of a magician's disappearing act, discretion remains right where it was all along, now obscured under a cloak of neutrality and objectivity. The result, one could argue, is a more problematic state of affairs than the questions of accountability that have traditionally surrounded public administration and the exercise of bureaucratic discretion. In its technological iterations, disguised discretion, hidden under the guise of neutrality and mathematical certainty, can misdirect and deter scrutiny while displaced discretion, too, can escape accountability as it moves to actors outside traditional scrutiny structures. For one, the legitimate chain of delegation within democracies does not envisage a discretionary role for these actors (often situated in the private realm), and one which, what is more, they exercise in the absence of adequate domain expertise or policy knowledge. Second, and relatedly, our systems of accountability and our constitutional checks are not designed with these actors in mind. They are not tailored to monitor and oversee these 'new street-level (system-level) bureaucrats' to keep their discretion in check and ensure that their choices do not end up effectively reshaping policy, thereby usurping legislative preferences.

B. Governing by Algorithm, Errors and Biases Galore: Accountability, Where Art Thou?

One of the promises of AI is that it should lead to more objective, 'neutral' and accurate decision-making doing away with many of the 'ills' of human decision-making and discretion. According to advocates, governing by algorithm will remove 'unwanted variability', 'prevent unequal treatment' and 'reduce errors' (Sunstein 2022, 1175): 'Algorithms eliminate noise, and that is important; to the extent that they do so, they prevent unequal treatment and reduce errors. (…) they can counteract or even eliminate cognitive biases.' As previous sections have argued, the realities of algorithmic adoption across public services reveal a very different picture. Widespread failures pertaining to algorithmic deployment have been diagnosed across jurisdictions, including in critical domains, with algorithms found to reproduce and automate bias due to the way they learn, are designed, or implemented. Often, it is already marginalised and vulnerable communities that bear the brunt of harmful deployments (Eubanks 2018; O'Neil 2016; Benjamin 2019) – highlighting yet again the pressing need for accountability in the age of automation.

An often-heard argument deployed by proponents, is that while algorithms harbour bias these at least can be technologically-mended, biases spotted and expunged. This, the argument goes, stands in contrast with human decision-making: humans display entrenched biases and may well ex post rationalise their decisions and fabricate their arguments rather than reveal their true reasons, rendering the actual reasons for their decision-making non-transparent (Coglianese and Lai 2022). Leaving aside the fact that this is precisely why we have checks against arbitrary administrative decision-making – reason-giving must align with the facts of the case at hand and be based on legitimate arguments applicable and pertinent to the specific circumstances at hand, the case for the ease with which algorithmic bias can be spotted, removed and corrected is severely overstated. To give an illustrative example, in 2015, Google Photos' image recognition software infamously labelled black people as gorillas. Google apologised and claimed to have fixed the problem. A few years later, it was discovered that 'Google hasn't really fixed anything. The company has simply blocked its image recognition algorithms from identifying gorillas altogether' (Vincent 2018). Unable to fix the algorithm, Google engineers instead found a clumsy work-around: they removed gorillas from the algorithms' search terms and labels (along with other primates and monkeys for good measure) so it could not be used as an image tag by the system (Simonite 2018).

Six years later, in 2021, the same bias re-emerged elsewhere. This time around it was Facebook that issued an apology when its AI recommender system labelled videos of black men as videos 'with primates' (Mac 2021). Recurrent examples of the iteration of the same algorithmic biases emerging on repeat – ranging from failures in large language models that are reiterations of problems flagged since 2016 (see Birhane and Raji 2022) to recurrent issues with biases of facial recognition systems that have been flagged for years (Buolamwini and Gebru 2018) and simply will not let up, including re-enactments of 'Coded Bias' for instance, in the use of proctoring equipment in education (see de Volkskrant 2022b) – belie techno-optimist claims of easy technical fixes to algorithmic bias. Like a high-tech 'whack-a-mole' game that never ends, algorithmic bias remerges over and over in familiar iterations.

The reality is that algorithms are a poor solution to human bias. AI algorithms draw on training data to learn the rules that govern their behaviour. As a result, they can come to learn and entrench discriminatory practices present in the data (in addition to the biases and heuristics of their designers), with resulting models automating human biases and discrimination. They are *made by us* and *learn from us* – as such, inescapably bound up with our cognitive biases, shortcomings and limitations. Paradoxically, as a result, algorithms will exacerbate and reinforce *on a large scale* some of the very biases they were meant to remedy, this time however, under the guise of objectivity, coupled with intractable difficulties in diagnosing failures and diminished opportunities for redress.

The adoption of AI algorithms in government decision-making effectively multiplies the decision points where failures can occur. Biases occur not only at the *algorithm level* in the form of algorithmic bias (arising due to data and/or model inaccuracies, as discussed above) but also in the *human-AI interaction*, in how human decision-makers interact with AI, giving rise to specific cognitive biases brought on by the interaction with automation. Such biases can range from: user overreliance on algorithmic systems irrespective of their actual quality or *'automation bias'* to confirmation biases, so-called *'selective adherence'* to algorithmic advice (see further, Alon-Barkat and Busuioc 2023). The former raises the prospect of uncritical deference to algorithmic systems (essentially 'blind trust' in automation) especially disconcerting in light of algorithmic bias concerns, whereas the latter raises the prospect of biased adherence to algorithmic recommendations, with decision-makers deferring to algorithms selectively, when algorithmic recommendations confirm their priors, beliefs or biases. While our understanding of AI-induced cognitive biases is still in its early days and evidence remains mixed, instances of both types of cognitive biases have been documented empirically in algorithmic decision-making (see, eg, Alon-Barkat and Busuioc 2023; Chen and Green 2019a,b; Kennedy, Waggoner and Ward 2022; Liel and Zalmanson 2022), underlining the high relevance of thoroughly investigating these aspects given critical implications thereof. For instance, in a recent study, Alon-Barkat and Busuioc 2023 find decision-makers tend to follow algorithmic advice selectively, when predictions align with prevalent social stereotypes, compounding bias in decision-making at the expense of already marginalised communities and individuals.

The presence of cognitive biases arising in the human-algorithm interaction is especially concerning as keeping humans in-the-loop is one of our main safeguards against algorithmic failure. Many algorithmic systems in sensitive domains serve as decisional aides, precisely so that humans can act as backstops on algorithmic errors and biases, as checks on the quality of algorithmic recommendations that inform their decisions. It is critical, therefore, to understand how administrative decision-makers interact with AI technologies, the factors that shape their reliance thereon and cognitive biases that arise in the interaction with automation. This pertains directly to the quality of decision-making in this context as well as to the effectiveness of our safeguards against algorithmic harm.

C. The Hollowing out of Bureaucratic Expertise – Who will Keep Watch?

The continued presence of institutionalised expertise is vital to the meaningful oversight of algorithmic processes in administrative contexts. However, as automated systems are taking over tasks traditionally exercised by domain experts, bureaucratic expertise is itself hollowed-out and breaks down. Specialist skills, professional instincts, tacit knowledge, etc, are gradually being lost as a consequence of automation. Even in cases where algorithms serve 'only' as decisional aides, with decision-makers retaining final decision-making power, they will often lack insight as to the reasons behind a particular algorithmic recommendation and/or the ability to assess the merits and quality of that recommendation in light of technical, organisational and/or legal opaqueness that often characterises models in use. For instance, in the Netherlands, in the case of the childcare benefits scandal, victims who attempted to challenge decisions were told that civil servants could not access the algorithmic inputs, with public officials reportedly justifying decisions 'because the algorithm said so' (Hadwick and Lan 2021). Decision-making becomes separated from the information that serves as its basis (Peeters and Widlak 2021), with domain experts lacking insight into the evidence that informs their decisions. Professionals become caretakers of 'decision factories' whose functioning they do not understand, relegated to information management tasks – shaping the nature of administrative and professional work in unprecedented ways.

This has direct implications for (the prospect of) oversight of algorithmic decision-making. With human actors lacking insight into how such systems operate, reach decisions and for what reasons, the prospect of meaningful oversight withers away. Moreover, over time, as opaque algorithmic systems become increasingly embedded within administrative processes and systems, and as we grow to defer to their recommendations in the absence of understanding the rationale for their decisions, this is likely to compromise the expert nature of the bureaucracy itself – exhausting its reservoir of superior know-how.

Within our dominant models of political control and accountability, the source of the bureaucratic actors' power stems from their expertise. As Weber once noted: 'The power position of all bureaucrats rests on knowledge' (Weber 1972, 854–55). As this source of power wanes, what is left to sustain and justify the added value of the bureaucratic model and bureaucracy's very claim to legitimacy? As Calo and Citron (2022, 797) astutely note: 'Automation abdicates the expertise and nimbleness that justify the administrative state, undermining the very case for the existence and authority of agencies.'

Bureaucratic actors themselves certainly bear a large share of the blame for this state of affairs. Administrators are effectively complicit in undermining their continued relevance in the age of automation. In the name of efficiency, opaque algorithmic systems are being assimilated at unprecedented speed, often without proper vetting or due diligence as to their impact for citizens as well as to how they align with administrators' own responsibilities towards citizens and with the values they are meant to uphold in the provision of public services. Recurrent failures involving AI algorithm deployment for public tasks, including models deployed in high-stakes areas without being checked for bias (Margetts and Dorobantu 2019; Algemene Rekenkamer 2022), failure to meet basic requirements (Algemene Rekenkamer 2022), the deployment of non-transparent models over transparent alternatives of equivalent performance for high-stakes tasks (Rudin 2019), as well as a barrage of algorithmic failures across public sectors in critical domains demonstrate that this duty of care is often not undertaken. For instance, in its audit of algorithms used in the public sector, the Netherlands Court of Audit found that 'in most cases, no checks are made to identify the presence and consequences of bias and hence the inaccurate overrepresentation or underrepresentation of certain groups of people' (Algemene Rekenkamer 2022, 26). And reiterated:

> Our audit revealed that organisations do not check whether the algorithms they use contain this type of error. This means that they do not know for certain whether their algorithms generate the same results for all groups of people (Algemene Rekenkamer 2022, 5).

Among the algorithms investigated was the AI predictive policing algorithm used by the Dutch police – an especially disconcerting finding given the high sensitivity of the public task at hand, as well as by now well-established risks of bias predictive policing systems have been shown to harbour (see, eg, Ferguson 2017; Richardson et al 2019). This flows into a final focus on the need to safeguard accountability.

III. Safeguarding Accountability

A growing need to retool public accountability in the era of automation is emerging, to ensure our safeguards are still fit for purpose. In the alternative, accountability in the age of artificial intelligence stands to become a faded carbon copy of its former self. Safeguarding accountability and ensuring that scrutiny structures keep pace with a rapidly shifting technological context demands that a number of steps are taken. First and foremost, it requires the thoughtful and incremental adoption of AI tools coupled with the introduction of robust organisational and institutional checks. The adoption of AI within bureaucratic systems must be accompanied by adequate safeguards as a pre-requisite for use: checks for bias both pre-deployment and in an ongoing manner to ensure systems operate accurately and fairly, incremental adoption with dry run piloting of algorithmic decision-making in parallel with human decision-making, segmented rollout of algorithmic systems, to thoroughly understand – in context! – system failures and inconsistencies. Beyond thoroughly testing and investigating specific technologies' technical features and functioning, it is important to understand in context how algorithms are actually used in public organisations and deployed for real-life uses (see also Meijer, Lorenz and Wessels 2021).

At a broader level, the creation and promotion of clear requirements for the use of algorithmic tools is also required. The aim being to ensure that artificial administration, and the choice of specific algorithmic technologies being deployed in this context, are well-aligned with the obligations of public bodies towards the general public, and the public values that the administration is required to uphold (such as transparency, reason-giving, equity, non-discrimination etc). Reliance on proprietary systems and/or systems outsourced to external providers, and where public administrators lack insight into the actual quality and functioning of such systems, raises serious risk of arbitrary and opaque administrative decision-making. This could be averted through the in-house development of transparent models or in the event externally purchased models are relied upon, the introduction of contractual clauses stipulating strong disclosure requirements by private providers is necessary (see also Busuioc, Curtin and Almada 2022). Similarly, the reliance on deep learning technologies whose decision-making (and in fact the merits thereof) are not understandable is highly problematic in administrative domains that affect individuals' lives in critical ways (see also, Rudin 2019). Computer scientists have shown that ML technologies of equivalent performance that are inherently interpretable (or transparent and understandable from the outset) exist or can be developed for many public sector applications (ibid). What is more, where technical limitations prevent the development of inherently interpretable ML models, the obvious alternative is not reliance on a black box model in administrative contexts. It is instead to forgo the use of automation in order to be able to safeguard citizens' rights. AI is not a silver bullet, a panacea to all of society's problems – to the contrary, in some cases, as exemplified by multiple examples of algorithmic harm referenced throughout this chapter, it can stand to exacerbate problems and be a cause of grave injustices.

An issue of especially critical importance in this context will also be the proper investigation of how civils servants (as users) interact with AI systems in real-world settings, as well as the assessment of the extent to which they are able to understand and scrutinise the systems they rely on and where cognitive biases intervene in human-AI interactions (see further, Alon-Barkat and Busuioc 2023). These critical aspects remain thus-far severely understudied. Yet, a better understanding of our limitations in interacting with AI will be vital to developing mitigation measures that ensure critical and reflective use of algorithmic tools, imperative both to the quality of decision-making in the context of hybrid administrative decision-making as well as for the effectiveness of our oversight measures of AI technologies. To ensure that human oversight, one of our key safeguards against algorithmic failures, is effective, we need to understand the factors that shape our reliance on AI technologies (or repudiation thereof), where blind spots intervene, and what cognitive biases materialise in our interactions with automation. This will allow us to move forward in developing solutions to mitigate these. To the contrary, human oversight of AI risks being a misnomer, a band aid that provides little in the way of a meaningful remedy to algorithmic harm. These aspects require careful investigation and consideration before AI is introduced further across the public sector.

Careful safeguarding of bureaucratic expertise, too, is critical in this context. The development of algorithmic systems for deployment in the public sector should take place with the close involvement of domain experts so as to ensure their suitability to the task at hand as well as in order to avoid slippage and ensure that digital systems do not invertedly alter public policy, nor result in unsanctioned value trade-offs. This requires nurturing (rather than side-lining) domain expertise, coupled with simultaneous investments by bureaucracies in developing inhouse technical knowledge to be able to oversee and interrogate such systems as well as ask critical questions of system providers and designers. Going back to the theme of this book, *accountability matters*. This is no less true in the age of artificial intelligence. The stakes could not be higher: as reliance on AI by administrative actors becomes increasingly ubiquitous, safeguarding accountability in this context will bear on the continued legitimacy of the administrative state, and the preservation of our most cherished rights and entitlements as citizens.

PART IV

Where Next?

15

Questions Still to be Answered

MATTHEW FLINDERS AND CHRIS MONAGHAN

The aim of this book was never to 'quench this thirst' for accountability, but to explore *why* accountability matters and *how* social, political, international, economic, cultural and technological factors this concept seeks to embrace have and continue to change. As the opening chapter emphasised, this collection sought to cast a net across a highly fragmented intellectual terrain through the provision of a clear definitional statement as a starting point and a flexible but unifying framing that focused attention on two themes or puzzles. The first was the 'overload but under-performance' puzzle whereby the emergence of increasingly dense and multi-levelled accountability systems does not seem to have fostered greater faith or public confidence in politicians, political institutions, or policy-making systems. The second theme was the notion of proportionality and balance – not just in the sense of the tricky question of measuring overloads or identifying trigger-points but also in terms of the core aims, ambitions or objectives of different accountability processes. These two topics have combined to offer the connective tissue that has allowed each contributor – academics and practitioners – to range widely and to engage with a multitude of 'questions of accountability' while working within a shared intellectual framework.

The phrase 'engage with a multitude of "questions of accountability"' has been carefully crafted. Very few, if any, 'questions' have been answered in a direct or simple sense because there are no simple (accountability) answers to complex questions. As Romzek (2015, 29) noted, '[A]ccountability is not a puzzle or a formula to be solved. In both the political and governance arenas accountability is a complex dynamic to be *managed at best* [italics in original].' With Romzek's emphasis on 'a complex dynamic' in mind, if this collection has made a significant contribution, it has been to illustrate from a range of perspectives and viewpoints exactly *why* accountability continues to be such a 'chameleon', if not always 'golden', concept. It has also emphasised that many 'questions of accountability' are structurally strategic. Or to put the same point slightly differently, the creation and maintenance of strategic ambiguity is very often not accidental. Fuzzy or blurred accountability is very often a beneficial resource to be exploited by those who seek to deny or delegate blame. The *politics of* accountability is one of the underlying foundational factors that this collection has attempted to expose and interrogate. With this in mind, the aim of this final concluding chapter is *not* to provide a descriptive or integrated review of the collection but simply to tease-out some of the main contributions in terms of *theory*, *themes* and *territory*. In line with the approach adopted in this book, this chapter's structure is defined by three interwoven questions.

1. How has this collection contribution to the study of accountability in terms of theory?
2. What are some of the distinctive themes emerging out of this collection?
3. What does the contents of this collection suggest in terms of territorial questions of accountability?

Teasing topics out of a collection like this inevitably involves a high degree of subjective selection. Contributors and readers may have chosen a very different set of areas to highlight and focus on, but the benefit of the adopted approach is that it does allow us to knit-together and work across the chapters in a way that displays the 'added value' of viewing this collection as a coherent body of work and not as a set of standalone contributions. In doing so we hope to go some way to address Bovens (2010, 946–47) criticism that

> [E]very newly edited volume on accountability – and, even worse, each of the individual chapters within these edited volumes – uses its own concepts, conceptualisations and frames for studying accountability. Some use the concept very loosely, other produce a more narrow definition, but few of these definitions are fully compatible, which makes it very hard to produce cumulative or commensurable research … there are many scholars who talk about accountability, but few who study it rigorously.

Whether this collection has studied accountability with quite the 'rigor' demanded by Boven's critique is debatable, but what is has delivered is an explicit thematic framework for studying accountability which spans *theory*, *themes* and *territory* in distinctive and original ways. This is exactly what this concluding chapter seeks to demonstrate.

I. Accounting for Theory

The opening chapter framed this book very much in terms of an exercise in conceptual cartography in the sense that it was intended to work across and integrate what has traditionally been a highly fragmented scholarly landscape. The collection's emphasis on 'overload but underperformance' and 'balance and proportionality' therefore operated as the intellectual glue or net that bound the chapters together. But to what extent did these focal points actually add value to the collection or facilitate the emergence of any clear answers? What were the theoretical frameworks or key reference points that arose in the collection and where significant analytical leverage and traction might still be secured? How might these perspectives dovetail with or be used to develop existing approaches, such as Brandsma and Schillemans (2013) 'accountability cube'. These questions stimulate a number of, if not answers, then replies.

First and foremost, what was interesting is that the twin-focus on 'overload but underperformance' and 'balance and proportionality' *did* provide a broad and flexible framework that all of the contributors could relate to. This is a not insignificant achievement given the range of issues and authors included in this book. The 'overload but underperformance' puzzle led to a focus on whether it was possible to identify a 'sweet spot' as the optimum point within the delicate balance between accountability-efficiency (see Figure 1.1). Whether it was possible to identify, let alone maintain a governing equilibrium at an optimal point, was discussed directly and indirectly in a number of chapters. At least two insights emerge around the 'sweet spot' theory. The first is more scientific, epistemological, and methodological. It highlights, as Rock did in chapter three, that 'questions of balance' – or more specifically the absence of an agreed conceptual unit of analysis of 'yardstick' – frustrates any formal focus on such questions. The second insight linked to this lack of a 'yardstick' but is more political and subjective in emphasis. It basically underlines that different actors within accountability relationships or networks are likely to have very different views on whether a 'sweet spot' exists and, if it does, where it might be found in terms of operational governance. A third follow-on point might also simply highlight that when it comes to accountability *context matters.* An effective, efficient and broadly balanced accountability relationship may emerge in 'normal' times but then become completely disrupted by unexpected events. Specific failures, tragedies and crises may have systemic and structural effects.

The emphasis in this collection on 'balance and proportionality' also seemed to resonate across a broad range of themes, issues and topics. There was also an obvious dovetailing into the discussion regarding 'overload but underperformance' but the key emergent theoretical contribution that emerged and gained increasing traction as the collection went on was the emphasis not on 'more or less' but on how different 'modes' of accountability not only exist but bring with them very different objectives and implications. Indeed, as the collection progressed three core distinctions also took form and substance (see Table 15.1).

Table 15.1 Contributions to Theorising Accountability

DISTINCTION	MEANING
'Mode I' Accountability	Aggressive, blame-based and forged around 'hot rhetoric'. Focused on the past and associated with sacrificial accountability. Highly emotive but arguably immature.
'Mode II' Accountability	Reflective, learning-based and defined by 'cool thinking'. Focused on the future and associated with lesson-learning and building resilience. Possibly technocratic but arguably mature.
'Type I' Accountability	Formal, process-based and generally top-down accountability frameworks. Often constitutional or legal requirements delivered via report, accounts, oral hearings, etc.

(continued)

Table 15.1 ***(Continued)***

DISTINCTION	MEANING
'Type II' Accountability	Informal, creative, monitory and bottom-up forms of account-demanding. Frequently on-line, participatory and ideally complementary to Type I processes.
'Dark Side' of Accountability	The acknowledgement that accountability can have perverse and highly negative consequences unless carefully calibrated (inefficiency, risk-aversion, blame-games, etc).
'Bright Side' of Accountability	An awareness that accountability connects the governors and the governed and can facilitate democratic engagement, public understanding, governing efficiency, institutional resilience, etc.

The distinctions presented in Table 15.1 are clearly intended to be broad reference points from which more sophisticated and specific studies can be undertaken. Indeed, the great danger of any binary polarisation or theoretical framework is that they risk painting a picture of emergent processes of accountable governance in monochrome when in many ways the whole essence of this collection has been to emphasise the existence of a broad palette of shades of grey. That said, the distinctions in Table 15.1 are incredibly useful at a basic level in terms of helping to dissect ongoing accountability debates. Different actors essentially emphasising different dimensions of the 'Mode I/Mode II', 'Type I/Type II', 'Dark side /Bright side' as the assumed but often unspoken starting point for their position. The distinctions, again at a very basic and tentative level, also add value in underscoring the basic point that 'more accountability does not necessarily equal better democracy'. Seeking salvation for accountability, as Dubnick (2002) has emphasised, demands an appreciation of the need to mix-and-match processes and procedures to suit specific roles, objectives and contexts.

Moving through each of the three distinctions outlined in Table 15.1, possibly the most striking insight of this whole collection was not simply a focus on the pathologies of an *over*-emphasis on blame-based 'Mode I' accountability, nor was it really the argument that there is a distinctive politics of accountability as actors utilise scrutiny structures for partisan or self-interested ambitions. A key insight was to be found in Tetlock's explanation (in chapter four) for why 'it is easy to look down on those who look soft on accountability' with the emphasis being on the relationship between 'tolerance of false positives', on the one hand, and levels of 'default trust' in those being held to account, on the other hand. Put very simply, if A: (i) does not trust (or like) B (a person or organisation); and (ii) A has something to gain from identifying failings or under-performance – or even just creating the perception that something might be wrong; and (iii) the costs to A of holding B to account are either low, marginal or predominantly fall upon those being held to account then A has a systemic incentive to operate towards the top end of what Diagram 4.1 presented as a 'Hypo-to-Hyper Accountability Continuum'.

The argument against accountability which emphasises the need for balance and proportionality is therefore possibly too technical and 'academic' to explain. This is especially true in a socio-political context that is almost defined by low levels of public trust in politics and which, in turn, fuels the assumption that anyone who urges caution must, by definition, have something to hide.

The 'Type I' and 'Type II' distinction with its emphasis on top-down formal as opposed to bottom-up informal processes connects to a seam of scholarship with a very rich intellectual heritage. That is, the literature on multi-level governance (see Bache and Flinders 2004), in general, and Hooghe and Marks' (2003) influential work on 'unravelling the central state' with its own 'two types' distinction, in particular. The link from multi-level governance back into accountability revolves around the emergence of networks and complexity over hierarchies and more traditional state-centric modes of administration. What Hooghe and Marks refer to as the emergence as a complex and over-lapping 'marble-cake' (see, for example, Entwistle et al 2014) in which governing boundaries and organisational responsibilities are often unclear connects across into Taylor and Buranelli's (2007) focus on 'ending up in Pizza' when accountability processes become too cumbersome and congested.

And yet the 'Type I' and 'Type II' also connects more directly into the issues and areas examined in this chapter. Kate and Terry Macdonald's chapter on global governance provided possibly the most direct analysis of how and when very different types of accountability can essentially be grafted on to each other. This led to their argument concerning the existence of a serious 'accountability alignment issue'. 'In essence, traditional state-based accountability assumptions are too often assumed to "fit" what is in reality a pluralist global political order which lacks a constitutionalized institutional structure for governance and is generally defined by dynamic, decentred and distorted relationships' Kate and Terry Macdonald argue

> Accountability assumptions based on the existence of clarity and stability between clear political constituencies, plus the presence of transparent and coherent institutional rule-based structures, are likely to flounder when applied in a context where those basic elements are simply absent.

The notion of 'grafting' new accountability processes onto pre-existing structures is also a theme that resonates with the debate concerning the 'dark side' of accountability and particularly whether John Keane's far brighter analysis of the emergence of 'monitory accountability' (see chapter four). The grafting of new forms of 'thicker', bottom-up and more deliberative forms of accountability onto the far 'thinner' traditional structures of representative democracy may represent an attempt to keep pace with both public expectations and changing administrative structures but it also brings with it the attendant risk of overlaying layer-upon-layer and form-upon-form in a form of accountability accretion that *may* in time become highly problematic.

And yet this problematisation of accountability is itself an element of the debate and discussion that demands some reflection. The language in which debates take place is itself arguably imbued with a negativity and pessimism which, in turn, reflects dominant assumptions about rational self-interested behaviour. To account for accountability is therefore often to talk in terms of traps and gaps, barriers and blockages, denial and delegation, complication and confusion, boomerangs and blame, etc. On reflection it is therefore interesting that this collection's explicit attempt to underline the 'dark side' of accountability has not been balanced by any similar attempt to outline the 'bright side' or 'what works' when it comes to 'good scrutiny'. The emergence of a novel and potentially transformative strand of 'positive public administration' (see Scott et al 2021) that focuses on learning from examples of policy 'success' *as well as* policy 'failure' (ie, a balanced analysis) could therefore provide huge insights if expanded to incorporate the analysis of 'successful scrutiny'. To make this point is not to deny the existence of inevitable tensions concerning criticality, credit and challenge (see Ostaijen and Jhagroe 2022; Flinders 2023) but it is to take the study of accountability and associated questions into a far more evidence-based and solution-orientated intellectual terrain than has arguably existed in the past (see Flinders and Van Der Arend 2023). This brings the discussion to a focus on themes.

II. Thematic Analysis and Accountability

The previous section attempted to identify some of the contributions this collection has made to theory, while also highlighting how those contributions connect to wider debates and discussions. The aim of this section is to explore some of the dominant themes that have surfaced repeatedly during this collection, and which therefore provides consistent thematic threads that warrant brief discussion. Accountability is – as Fox's (2022) extensive analysis demonstrated – generally associated with a fairly stable family of keywords. These include blame, responsibility, answerability, responsiveness, guilt, impeachment, audit, shame, etc. With lexicon in mind, what is interesting and distinctive about the contributions in this collection is the way that, although these common thematic keywords have undoubtedly featured, a broader number of more novel themes have also been discussed (in different ways and from different disciplinary or practitioner perspectives) throughout the collection (see Table 15.2).

Table 15.2 Contributions to Thematic Analysis

THEME	MEANING
Complexity/ Precision	Accountability is a loaded concept in the sense that it brings with it expectations of precision, clarity and clear lines of responsibility that rarely exist within the messy world of everyday politics and policymaking.
Populism/ Realism	Populism promises to reduce complexity and increase precision. It accuses 'elites' of hiding behind complexity and offers clear and direct accountability through a focus on the 'strong leader'. This brings risks of authoritarian accountability.
Emotions/ Structures	Populists understand the role and power of emotions. They castigate 'unaccountable elites', utilise emotive triggers, promote nostalgic framings. They understand that 'feelings trump facts' in ways that can be connected to a broader 'accountability space'.
Understanding/ Ignorance	Where the public understand the challenges faced by politicians and public servants they tend to be more empathetic and understanding. This has implications in terms of promoting 'thinking slow' and potentially an emphasis on 'Mode II' accountability.

Many of the themes outlined in Table 15.2 offer a clear connection across into the more theoretical distinctions included in Table 15.1, just as many of them will relate to some of the territorial issues highlighted in Table 15.3 (below). Aspects of theory, theme and territory are therefore inter-connected in ways that speak to the multi-dimensional complexity of the concept. And it is this theme – complexity – that arguably provides an implicit and foundation component of the accountability debate. As a concept accountability brings with it notions of precision, clarity and accuracy that are matched by the messy realities of governance. Even where legislation is approved or conventions amended in an attempt to specify *who* is responsible for *what, how* and *when*, as Cohn's chapter underlined, an element of fuzziness in not only possibly inevitable but may also be built in by those expected to provide an account in order to ensure an element of flexibility. Lord Blunkett's (chapter twelve) contribution underlined the messy reality of day-to-day governing and the rhetoric-reality gap created by naïve accountability assumptions.

But might complexity as a theme be the root issue of the 'questions of accountability' that have informed this book, as they have many others? Moreover, if complexity is increasing – as suggested in sociological analyses relating to the emergence of 'liquid modernity' and post-political structures – then so too is the rhetoric-reality gap surrounding accountability processes likely to become increasingly problematic. The notion of 'liquidity' is, in this context, interesting due to the manner in which it highlights the evisceration and gradual melting away of social and political structures that once offered forms of anchorage, stability, assurance and stable relationships. Traditional, state-based forms of accountability, like the convention of ministerial responsibility to Parliament, were forged upon the principle of a simpler and stable bureaucratic structure. As the state has not only grown but also become more complex then so too have questions as to where responsibility lies also become more fluid. To put the same point slightly differently, the anchorage provided by traditional tools of accountability have slipped and remain to some extent adrift. And yet as Shoesmith (chapter thirteen) reminds us by delving into the anthropological literature on naming, shaming and blaming, there is a powerful social psychological need in times of crisis to identify a scapegoat.

No matter how irrational the identification of a single point of culpability might be in the context of a complex inter-organisational failing, the creation of a lightning-rod is at the same time arguably completely rationale in the sense that although largely symbolic the process of naming, shaming and blaming allows the community or society to *feel* as if the matter has been taken seriously and that steps have been taken to prevent a recurrence. Of course, the major argument of the 'Mode I/Mode II' distinction is that an aggressive blame-based, thinking-fast approach that forces someone to 'carry the can' or 'take one for the team' is highly unlikely to create the conditions in which lesson-learning takes place and future resilience emphasised. The flip-side, however, is that arguments concerning shared liability, the need for slow-thinking or the complexity of network governance are unlikely to satisfy cotemporary demands for rapid redress. Where this takes the discussion is to a focus not only on the existence of 'redundant accountability architecture' but also to Cohn's (chapter five) 'future fuzzy' argument about the need to design and develop forms of 'fuzzy accountability' that can cope with disaggregated and dynamic structures. That such forms of 'fuzzy accountability' need to incorporate vertical and horizontal governance dimensions was underlined in the work of Kate and Terry Macdonald's on global governance in chapter eleven, and especially in their critique of the automatic 'uploading' of state-based accountability assumptions and structures to a context which was by definition fluid and pluricentric.

With debates about the non-accountability of global elites in mind (and returning to Table 15.2), what is the link between complexity and populism in the context of accountability?

One response is that the logic of populism provides a reassuringly simple answer to questions of complexity. Populist politicians *do* provide simple answers to complex questions of accountability. Why are systems so complex? Because elites, experts and 'the establishment' like to hide behind the veil of bureaucratic complexity. Can clear lines of accountability be re-established? Yes, by joining 'us' and supporting a 'strong leader' model? In essence, the promises of populism contain a form of nostalgia vis-a-vis accountability in ways that link back to the earlier focus on the notion of 'liquid modernity'. The promise is really to reinstate traditional forms of clear and stable (accountability) anchorage – the strong leader will be responsible for everything and all you (ie, the public) needs to do is trust them. Plebiscites, referenda and other forms of direct democracy are promised as adjunct structures but, as Kurt Weyland (2018) has illustrated at length, these processes are very often manipulated from the top and emerge to become performative aspects of more authoritarian modes of governance. Dispelling the populist myth about reinvigorating accountability – to paraphrase John Haskell (2018) – remains a global challenge with the flipside being a more realist perspective that accepts and acknowledges that existence of complex challenges in relation to accountable governance which – as the chapters in this collection have each in their own ways underlined – demand subtle, sophisticated and systemic innovations.

There is, however, a second connection between populism and accountability that demands brief discussion: the role of emotions. The political sociology of emotions is not a term that is generally used in relation to 'questions of accountability' but if accountability is essentially about the management of relationships then emotions will play a defining role. At the macro-political level, the rhetoric of populist parties and leaders is designed to promote emotive triggers and nostalgic memories. Populism is forged on both the funnelling and framing of anger, fear and frustration, alongside the nurturing of hope, belief and confidence. The fact that 'feelings tend to trump facts' (see Flinders 2020) pulls the discussion back not only towards Tetlock's focus on political psychology. It also resonates with Dubnick's emphasis on the 'accountability space' and, more specifically, his criticism of Flinders analysis of 'the dark side' of accountability' (see chapter four). Dubnick argues that Flinders works within a narrow reformist agenda that sees accountability in terms of structures (ie, institutions, mechanisms, and processes) whereas, according to Dubnick, this approach 'blinds us to an even more significant place for accountability in our lives'. That 'significant place' (or 'ontological world') is one in which account-demanding and account-giving *relationships* constitute the very essence of social arrangements that comprise governance.

There is a link here back to the distinction between 'Type I' and 'Type II' accountability in the sense that for Dubnick, 'Type I' institutional structures exist within a broader 'accountability space' (or 'accountability ecosystem') that consists of a multitude of more informal 'Type II' relationships. The key to his argument being that the constant creation of 'Type I' structures risks damaging or destroying the more intricate and interwoven fabric of social relationships that exist not on the basis of laws, constitutions or statute but on the basis of respect, trust, loyalty, love, etc. 'Seeking salvation for accountability' is therefore concerned with acknowledging that simply responding to every challenge, problem or weakness in modern governance through the insertion of new or reinforced ('Type I') accountability processes is ultimately highly unlikely to be an effective response. This in itself might provide a clue to the 'overload but underperformance puzzle' that has developed throughout this collection. The issue is not so much one of 'overload' but one that focuses attention on too much of the wrong kind of accountability (too much 'Mode I/Type I', not enough 'Mode II/Type II').

This leads to a fourth theme (Table 15.2, above) which although not discussed directly in any of the chapters in this collection does emerge out of their collective sentiment. If 'increasing supply' is not the answer to an emergent set of 'questions of accountability' then maybe an alternative approach would be to focus on 'reducing demand'. The idea being that if the public had a more sophisticated understanding of the realities of modern political life (ie, limited resources, growing demand, complex delivery chains, imperfect information, increasing uncertainty, etc) then their 'unquenchable thirst for accountability' (Moore and Gates 1986, 2) might be if not sated then possibly less intense. The thematic argument being that instead of always seeking to 'increase supply' through the creation of or grafting on of new accountability processes or institutions maybe a parallel process might also think about 'reducing demand'. This rebalancing could dovetail with an emphasis on *more* 'Mode II' calm, reflective lesson-learning orientated accountability, and *less* 'Mode I' aggressive, loud and blame-orientated accountability (see Table 15.1, above).

One source of empirical evidence for the potential value of a focus on if not 'reducing demand' then 'increasing public understanding' is Szdlowski, de Boer and Tummers' (2022) work on empathy, compassion and 'bureaucrat bashing'. What this study revealed is that where members of the public had a clear and evidence-based understanding of the real-world challenges faced by street-level bureaucrats, in this case social workers, then they were far more inclined to be less hostile, aggressive and blame-focused than those who lacked such knowledge. Studies have shown that experiencing compassion at work has clear benefits, such as that workers have less stress, are more client-oriented, have higher job satisfaction, higher commitment, less burnout, and better overall performance (Choudhary, Ismail, and Hanif 2017; Dutton, Workman, and Hardin 2014; Eldor 2018; Lilius et al 2008). Shoesmith's chapter provides a clear link back into this focus on empathy, and a focus on increasing public understanding about the challenges of modern governance might also complement Kahneman's emphasis on 'thinking slow'.

Whether phrased in terms of 'bureaucrat bashing' or not, Tetlock's research underlines the challenges faced by anyone who might seek to promote proportionality and understanding in relation to concerns about too much accountability. He states that it will be 'impossible to curb these excesses via Flinders well-intentioned but inadequate pleas for proportionality (2011, 694)'. The always implicit assumption being that anyone who argues against accountability must by definition have something to hide; plus numerous actors have low-cost or zero-cost incentives to co-opt and to some extent corrupt accountability processes and mechanisms for self-interested or highly partisan reasons. Dealing with ignorance and promoting understanding when it comes to the complexities of accountable governance are therefore not only far from straight-forward but also further complicated by the emergence of new governing processes and what might be thought of as new public spaces. This leads us to shift from a focus on themes towards one on territories.

III. Territorial Questions of Accountability

This concluding chapter does not attempt to provide an exhaustive review (or account) of each-and-every chapter in this collection. Instead, it seeks to identify just a few of the emergent themes and issues that this collection has – when viewed in the round – served to identify and emphasise. This has been undertaken through a focus on *theory*, *themes* and now *territory*. It would, however, be a mistake to view these dimensions in isolation; they are, in fact as inter-related as they are interwoven. More broadly, this collection has attempted to fulfil the role of the conceptual cartographer in the sense of mapping and tracing the existence of and relationship between different bodies of research (perspectives, methods and theories) and writing (scientific, experiential, practitioner, etc). With this in mind, the aim of this final section is to focus on *terra incognita* and areas that appear to: (i) warrant further analysis; or (ii) where bridges need to be built between what are currently islands of research and theorising. Territory in this sense is used in both an informal and more formal sense – the former indicating little more than an area of intellectual inquiry, the latter suggesting a more formal 'territory' in a geographical or spatial sense.

Table 15.3 Territorial Questions of Accountability

TERRITORY	SCOPE
Global Governance	Modes and methods of accountability appear unable to cope with the fluidity of transnational governance. But could a 'fuzzy accountability framework' solve or even address long-standing concerns? Will reactions like Brexit increase accountability?
Policy Making	Even in the absence of agreed conceptual 'yardsticks' the sphere of policy-making appears to demonstrate serious questions of under-supply. Quite why policy advice to ministers should remain a scrutiny free zone appears unclear.

(continued)

Table 15.3 ***(Continued)***

TERRITORY	SCOPE
Artificial Intelligence	The evolution of artificial public administration which utilise machine learning processes and algorithmic accountability creates a whole new set of questions concerning balance, blame and behaviour.
Emotional Impacts	Recent advances in the analysis of 'felt accountability' have deepened understandings of how individuals and organisations respond to external demands for information and potential penalties. But this is different to emotional accountability.
Beyond Terra Firma	Existing analyses of accountability understandably focus on the governance of land-based countries. New territorial frontiers are, however, being opened-up. Examples include issues around the ownership of the sea floor and governance of space.

As with the theories and themes examined in this chapter, a multitude of territorial types could have been discussed in this section but Table 15.3 (above) highlights just five. These have been selected as they emerge out of chapters in this collection, they can be folded-back into the theories and themes discussed above, while at the same time raising novel and distinctive 'question of accountability' that might usefully inform future research agendas.

The first territorial focus reintroduces the themes and issues covered by Kate and Terry Macdonald's chapter on global governance (chapter eleven). The basic point being that the 'questions of accountability' that have surrounded debates about supra-national bodies and non-governmental organisations at the international level seem no closer to being resolved to when they first emerged in the twentieth century. The scaling-up of assumptions and approaches from the governance of nation states seem incapable of filling the 'grey holes' (see Dyzenhaus 2006) or dimensions of 'fugitive power' (see Boggs 2021) which almost define forms of transnational governance. At least two questions flow out of this focus. The first takes the discussion back to Cohn's contribution (chapter five) and ask what a 'fuzzy accountability framework' might actually look like and how it would work at the transnational level. The second question focuses on where concerns about a lack of accountability have led to the explicit transfer of powers back to the nation state. Will Brexit, for example, actually deliver increased and clearer lines of accountability as promised by those who promoted leaving the European Union?

This in itself raises questions of policy that connect to this sub-section's second territorial focus and Jonathan Slater's contribution in chapter eight. Policy-making has traditionally remained the territory of the senior civil service. Officials have also carefully guarded their control of this domain and acted as not only the primary purveyors of policy-advice but also as the guardians or gatekeepers of alternative sources of information. What Slater's arguments serve to focus attention on is the need to think about the quality of the advice provided to ministers and how accountability (in this case secured through post-decision transparency) might improve the overall level of decision-making. At least three further questions emerge out of this focus. The first relates to candour: why is accountability so frequently thought to exist in direct opposition to the facilitation of 'free and frank' conversations? As this collection has underlined, the dominant mode of 'Gotcha!' 'Mode I' accountability does tend to prevent open and honest conversation due to the contextual pressures imposed by the 'shadow of blame'. The publication of the policy-advice provided to ministers by their officials is for some reason generally viewed as likely to lead to a narrowing and moderating of the counsel provided. An alternative argument, however, might suggest that transparency would in effect bolster the position of officials and ensure that they provided a portfolio that was as broad and evidence-based as it was honest and direct. 'Speaking truth to power' would from this perspective be reinforced by the introduction of accountability for policy advice. Not only would officials be held to account for the quality of their advice (thereby exerting a powerful anticipatory effect), but ministers would also be expected to account for their decisions in a context where the full 'choice architecture' is clear.

It is at this point, however, that the politics of accountability resurfaces, especially in terms of what might be termed the 'accountability trap'. That is, the introduction of any significant reforms or measures that are designed to strengthen accountability generally require the implicit or direct support of those who are likely to be subject to those strengthened scrutiny structures. In essence, an element of engineered strategic ambiguity provides those who are being held to account with a little capacity for negotiation as to the specific nature of boundaries of those issues for which they can be held directly responsible. This is particularly problematic in those more majoritarian democracies where the executive is drawn from the legislature and simple-plurality systems create artificial parliamentary majorities. In essence, those polities with power-hoarding constitutional configurations have adopted a very specific position on the integrity/efficiency trade-off with an emphasis that weights the latter about the former. The third and final point on policy-making accountability is simply that there is very little research on this topic at all which is not something that could be said about our fourth territorial foci, artificial intelligence and algorithmic governance.

In many ways this focus on technological territory and its relationship with contemporary public governance.

The manner in which powers, responsibilities and resources have shifted above the nation state and through this away from the direct control of national politicians offers a clear connection to the notion of fluidity. With this in mind a related but at the same time very different process was discussed in Madalina Busuioc's (chapter fourteen) exploration of artificial public administration and algorithmic governance. The utilisation of technology adds not just another link in the chain of delegation but more importantly the nature of machine learning makes the internal dimensions of decision-making processes almost impervious to challenge. 'It is not open to refutation on the merits of its arguments because it does not provide reasons' Busuioc writes 'at least none we can understand. Expertise that cannot explain its reasons and in fact, whose very merits often lie outside our ability to interrogate, comes closer to blind faith.' The challenges of algorithmic governance and artificial intelligence open-up a whole new domain to 'questions of accountability' as they have traditionally been conceived and approached. As bureaucratic discretion is replaced by sophisticated algorithmic systems what future is there for public accountability? How does algorithmic accountability fit within broader debates concerning post-human, post-democratic and post-political governance? How does artificial intelligence, returning to Table 15.2, connect with complexity, populism, emotions, understanding and other key themes? How does it demand the development of new theories, methods and approaches – and frustrate simplistic two-dimensional approaches like those included in Table 15.1 (above).

But possibly the most significant question to be asked is how best to unite and integrate two fields of scholarship that have, as yet, evolved with very little obvious cross-fertilisation of knowledge. This is a critical point. Although there are a small number of scholars working at the intersection, for the most part the analysis of artificial intelligence and algorithmic accountability has been constrained to the disciplines of computer studies, engineering and technology, with the fields of socio-legal studies, philosophy and data analysis offering important secondary studies. The key point being that the 'mainstream' literature on public accountability which spans political science, public administration and governance studies has generally not recognised the implications of artificial public administration and system-level bureaucrats to the extent that is arguable needed.

What is interesting about technological advances and their potential application to administrative processes is the way in which they are assumed to make rational decisions. This explains their relevance to, as Sætra (2020) has illustrated, the concept of depoliticisation and also to the theme of emotions. But what the practitioner perspectives brought to this collection (chapters eight, twelve and thirteen) was a much sharper focus on how it feels to be a decision-maker, either as a senior public servant or elected politician. Johnathan Slater's personal experience of having to attend school meetings in order to explain local educational decisions, Lord Blunkett's focus on the mental health and wellbeing of politicians and their staff, and notably Sharon Shoesmith's description of online abuse and death threats underlined with increasing intensity what was referred to as 'the sharp end' of accountability. The key point being made is that the existing research base contains very little data or insight on how it feels to be named, shamed and blamed. How does it feel to become a lightning rod for public anger or frustration? Where are the support structures or what are the self-preservation methods?

There is, of course, a growing literature on 'felt accountability' which seeks to utilise psychological insights (see chapter two) to explore how and why people or organisations respond to the demand to account for their performance in different ways (see, for example, Overman and Schillemans 2022). This has delivered significant findings in relation to reputational dimensions and also in relation to the management of the 'cross pressures' of accountability. But it is an institutionally and process-orientated approach: 'Felt accountability denotes the expectation that one's decisions and behaviors will be evaluated by an "able" accountability forum with authority' (Schillemans et al 2021, 893). The focus of what might be termed 'emotional accountability' is less concerned with institutions and processes and is instead centred on *how people feel* about managing the emotional pressures of being held to account. This, for example, might lead into a focus on the gendered nature of accountability and the manner in which politicians from different backgrounds tend to be held to higher standards and/or be subject to higher levels of abuse (see, for example, Eggers, Vivyan and Wagner 2018; Waylen and Southern 2021). The dimension this focus on 'emotional accountability' would bring to existing analyses is a thicker description of the psychological effects of working in a low-trust, high-blame environment. This would complement but is very different to existing work on 'felt accountability'.

This brings us to a final focus and to a truly 'territorial' perspective in a classically geographical or spatial nature. The simple argument is that the vast majority of research, writing and analyses focuses on traditional dimensions of government and governance. It is therefore implicitly linked to *terra firma* (ie, dry land, solid ground). Just as developments in relation to technology have opened-up new digital vistas then so too have they created new territories that raise equally pressing questions of accountability. The governance of deep seabed mining raises major questions that do not fit easily within traditional ways of thinking. New institutions, such as the International Seabed Authority, and new advisory structures, such as the United Nation's Commission on the Limits of the Continental Shelf, have been established in the hope of establishing frameworks for accountable governance (see Ardron 2018). But these innovations are themselves problematic in the sense that they are expert-led, transnational and operate at an arm's-length from elected politicians. They therefore risk exacerbating pre-existing questions about global governance than they do addressing, let alone solving, questions of accountability. The same argument could be made about the governance of space in the context of astro-politics and emerging debates about, for example, ownership and control of potential inter-planetary resources or even responsibility for space waste. The Outer Space Treaty and Moon Agreement – even the evolution of space debris mitigation guidelines and 'space law' (see Rajapaksa and Wijerathna 2017) – were not only influenced by debates and discussions concerning the exploitation of the seabed but also raise linked and yet distinctive questions of accountability which have so far received relatively little attention (see Khatwani 2019). With this and the broader contribution of this collection in mind it appears that there are still many 'questions of accountability' to be answered.

BIBLIOGRAPHY

Abbott, K.W. and Snidal, D. 2009. 'The governance triangle: regulatory standards institutions and the shadow of the state', in Mattli, W. and Woods, N (eds), *The Politics of Global Regulation*. Princeton: Princeton University Press. 44–88.

Adams, T. E., Holman Jones, S. and Ellis, C. 2015. *Autoethnography: Understanding Qualitative Research*. New York: Oxford University Press.

Akter, S. McCarthy, G. Sajib, S. Michael, K. Dwivedi, Y. D'Ambra, J. and Shen, K. 2021. 'Algorithmic bias in data-driven innovation in the age of AI', *International Journal of Information Management*, 60.

Alaszewski, A. 2015. 'Anthropology and risk: insights into uncertainty, danger and blame from other cultures – A review essay', *Health, Risk & Society*, 17(3-4), 205–225.

Aleksovska, M and Schillemans, T. 2021. 'Dissecting multiple accountabilities', *Public Administration*, online advance.

Aleksovska, M. 2021. 'Accountable for What? The Effect of Accountability Standard Specification on Decision-Making Behavior in the Public Sector', *Public Performance & Management Review*, 44(4), 1–28.

Aleksovska, M. Schillemans, T. and Grimmelikhuijsen, S. 2022. 'Management of Multiple Accountabilities Through Setting Priorities: Evidence from a Cross-National Conjoint Experiment', *Public Administration Review*, 82(1), 132–146.

Aleksovska, M., Schillemans, T. and Grimmelikhuijsen, S. 2019. 'Lessons from five decades of experimental and behavioral research on accountability', *Journal of Behavioral Public Administration*, 2(2), 1–18.

Algemene Rekenkamer (Netherlands Court of Audit). 2021. *Understanding Algorithms*. 26/01/2021. Available at: english.rekenkamer.nl/publications/reports/2021/01/26/understanding-algorithms.

Algemene Rekenkamer (Netherlands Court of Audit). 2022. *An Audit of Algorithms*. 18/05/2022. Available at: english.rekenkamer.nl/publications/reports/2022/05/18/an-audit-of-9-algorithms-used-by-the-dutch-government.

All-Party Parliamentary Group on Democracy and the Constitution. 2022/ *An Independent Judiciary – Challenges since 2016*. Report, London: APPG/ICDR.

Allan, A. 'Functional Apologies in Law' (2008) 15 *Psychiatry, Psychology and Law* 369.

Allan, T. 2013. 'Accountability to Law' in Bamforth, N and Leyland, P. *Accountability in the Contemporary Constitution*. Oxford: Oxford University Press.

Alon-Barkat, S. and Busuioc, M. 2023. 'Human–AI Interactions in Public Sector Decision Making: "Automation Bias" and "Selective Adherence" to Algorithmic Advice', *Journal of Public Administration Research and Theory* 33(1), 153–169.

Amengual, M., 2010. 'Complementary labor regulation: The uncoordinated combination of state and private regulators in the Dominican Republic', *World Development*, 38(3), 405–414.

Anderson, D. 2012. *The Terrorism Acts in 2001: Report of the Independent Reviewer on the Operation of the Terrorism Act 2000 and Part 1 of the Terrorism Act 2006*. London, The Stationary Office.

Anechiarico, F and Jacobs, J. 1996. *The Pursuit of Absolute Integrity*. Cambridge: Cambridge University Press.

Angwin, J. 2022. 'The Seven-Year Struggle to Hold an Out-of-Control Algorithm to Account', The Markup.

Ardron, J. 2018. 'Transparency in the operations of the International Seabed Authority: An initial assessment', *Marine Policy*, 95, 324–331.

Aspalter, C. 2008. 'Towards a More People-Centered Paradigm in Social Development' in Singh, S. and Aspalter, C. (eds) *Debating Social Development: Strategies For Social Development*. Taipei: Casa Verde Publishing.

Auditor General of Australia. 2020. *Award of Funding under the Community Sport Infrastructure Program*, Report 23 of 2019–2020. Canberra: Australian National Audit Office.

Aziz, SF. 2011. 'Countering Religion or Terrorism? Selective Enforcement of Material Support Laws Against Muslim Charities'. Institute for Social Policy and Understanding, Policy Brief #47, September 2011, available at ssrn.com/abstract=2022748.

Babic, B., Gerke, S., Evgeniou, T. and Cohen, I.G. 2021. 'Beware explanations from AI in health care', *Science* 373, 284–286.

Bache, I. and Flinders, M. 2004. *Multi-Level Governance*. Oxford: Oxford University Press.

Bache, I. Flinders, M., Marsden, G. and Bartle, I. 2015. 'Blame Games and Climate Change', *British Journal of Politics and International Relations*, 17(1), 64–88.

Bäckstrand, K. 2008. 'Accountability of networked climate governance: The rise of transnational climate partnerships', *Global Environmental Politics* 8(3), 74–102.

Bagehot, W. 1858 (2001 edn). *The British Constitution*. Oxford, UK: Oxford's World Classics.

Baker, J. 2021. *English Law Under Two Elizabeths: The Late Tudor Legal World and the Present*. Cambridge: Cambridge University Press, 44–46.

Balaton-Chrimes, S. and Macdonald, K. 2016. *The Compliance Advisor Ombudsman for IFC/MIGA*, October 2016, available at: corporateaccountabilityresearch.net/njm-report-xvii-cao, 79 pages.

Baldwin, A, Pinto, C, Perriard-Abdoh, S and Weinberg, A. 2020. *Cognitive Strain in Parliament*. London: The British Psychological Society.

Barendrecht, M. 2011. 'Rule of Law, Measuring and Accountability: Problems To Be Solved Bottom Up', *Hague Journal on the Rule of Law*, 3, 281, 294.

Barnard, F. 2001. *Democratic Legitimacy: Plural Values and Political Power*. McGill-Queen's University Press, xi.

Barron, D. and Lederman, M. 2008. 'The Commander in Chief at the Lowest Ebb—Framing the Problem, Doctrine, and Original Understanding', *Harvard Law Review*, 121, 689.

Bartels K. 2013. 'Public encounters: The history and future of face-to-face contact between public professionals and citizens', *Public Administration*, 91, 469–483.

Basler, R. (ed). 1953. *Abraham Lincoln, The Collected Works*. New Brunswick, Rutgers University Press.

Battaglio Jr, R. P., Belardinelli, P., Bellé, N., and Cantarelli, P. (2019). 'Behavioral Public Administration *ad fontes*: A Synthesis of Research on Bounded Rationality, Cognitive Biases, and Nudging in Public Organizations', *Public Administration Review*, 79(3), 304–320.

BBC. 2022. 'Jeremy Hunt calls contaminated-blood scandal a huge failing of democracy', www.bbc.co.uk/news/health-62325578.

Beck, U. 1992. *Risk Society: Towards a New Modernity*. New Delhi: Sage.

Behn, R. 2001. *Rethinking Democratic Accountability*. Washington DC: Brookings.

Bell, D. 2017. 'Political realism and international relations', *Philosophy Compass*, 12(2), p.e12403.

Bellamy, B. 2007. *Political Constitutionalism: A Republican Defence of the Constitutionality of Democracy*. Cambridge: Cambridge University Press.

Benhabib, S. 1994. 'Deliberative Rationality and Models of Democratic Legitimacy', *Constellations* 1(1), 26–52.

Benjamin, R. 2019. *Race After Technology: Abolitionist Tools for the New Jim Code*. Cambridge: Polity Press.

Benner, T., Reinicke, W.H., and Witte, J.M. 2004. 'Multisectoral Networks in Global Governance: Towards a Pluralistic System of Accountability', *Government and Opposition*, 39(2), 191–210.

Bennett, W.L. and Entman, R.M (eds). 2001. *Mediated Politics, Communication in the Future of Democracy*. Cambridge, New York, Melbourne, Madrid: Cambridge University Press.

Bertelli, A. and Busuioc, M. 2021. 'Reputation-Sourced Authority and the Prospect of Unchecked Bureaucratic Power', *Public Administration Review*, 81(1), 38–48.

Bertelli, A.M., and Van Ryzin, G.G. 2020. 'Heuristics and political accountability in complex governance: An experimental test', *Research & Politics*, 7(3), 1–5.

Bertelli, A., Riccucci, N., Canterelli, P., Cucciniello, M., Grose, C., John, P., Linos, E., Thomas, A., and Williams, M. (2022). 'The (Missing?) Role of Institutions in Behavioral Public Administration: A Roundtable Discourse', *Journal of Behavioral Public Administration,* 5(1), 1–25.

Bevir, M. (ed). 2012. *Modern Pluralism: Anglo-American Debates Since 1880.* Cambridge: Cambridge University Press.

Beynon, HJ. 1987. Prerogative to Supply Plastic Baton Rounds and CS to the Police. *Public Law* 146.

Bhasker, R. 1975. *A Realist Theory of Science.* Routledge: London and New York.

Bicchieri, C. 2016. *Norms in the Wild: How to Diagnose, Measure, and Change Social Norms.* Oxford: Oxford University Press.

Birch, A. 1964. *Representative and Responsible Government.* London: Unwin.

Birhane, A. and Raji, D. 2022. 'ChatGPT, Galactica, and the Progress Trap: When large language models fall short, the consequences can be serious. Why is it so hard to acknowledge that?' *Wired.* Available at: www.wired.com/story/large-language-models-critique/.

Blackburn, R. 1995. *The Electoral System in Britain.* London: Macmillan, ch 2.

Blackburn, R. 2015. 'Enacting a Written Constitution for the United Kingdom', *Statute Law Review,* 36(1), 1–27.

Blackburn, R. 2022. 'The Politics of Parliamentary Procedure Revisited' in *Essays in Honour of Emeritus Professor Kostas Mavrias.* Athens: Sakkoulas, 277–307.

Blackburn, R. 2003. 'The Royal Assent to Legislation and a Monarch's Fundamental Human Rights', *Public Law,* 205–210.

Blackburn, R. 2019–21. 'The Fixed-term Parliaments Act 2011: Retain, Repeal or Reform?', written evidence, House of Lords Constitution Committee, A Question of Confidence? The Fixed-term Parliaments Act 2011, 2019–21, HL 121.

Blackburn, R. 2020. Private Letter to Cabinet Office, 10 June.

Blackburn, R. 2004. 'Monarchy and the Personal Prerogatives', *Public Law,* 546–563.

Blackburn, R. 2016. 'The Abdication of Edward VIII: Legal and Constitutional Perspectives' Glencross, M. et al (eds). *The Windsor Dynasty 1910 to the Present.* London: Palgrave.

Blackburn, R. 2022. 'The Constitutional Role and Working of the Monarchy in the United Kingdom', in Lepsius, O, Nußberger, A Schönberger, C, Waldhoff, C. and Walter, C. *Yearbook of Contemporary Public Law,* Vol. 70, ed. Mohr Siebeck, 181–202.

Blunkett, D. 1995. *On a Clear Day.* London: O'Mara.

Blunkett, D. 2006. *The Blunkett Tapes.* London: Bloomsbury.

Boggs, C. 2021. *Fugitive Politics.* New York: Routledge.

Bohman J. 2007. *Democracy Across Borders.* Cambridge, MA, MIT Press.

Boin, A., 't Hart, P. and McConnell, A. 2009. 'Crisis exploitation', *Journal of European Public Policy,* 16(1), 81–106.

Borah P. 2014. 'Does it matter where you read the news story?', *Communication Research,* 41, 809–827.

Bordt, S., Finck, M., Raidl, E. and von Luxburg, U. 2022. 'Post-Hoc Explanations Fail to Achieve their Purpose in Adversarial Contexts', *Proceedings of the 2022 ACM Conference on Fairness, Accountability, and Transparency* (Association for Computing Machinery 2022). doi.org/10.1145/3531146.3533153.

Bostrom, M. and Garsten, C. 2008. *Organising Transnational Accountability.* London: Edward Elgar.

Boughey, J. and Miller, K. (eds). 2021. *The Automated State: Implications, Challenges and Opportunities for Public Law.* Federation Press.

Bouwman, R., and Grimmelikhuijsen, S. 2016. 'Experimental public administration from 1992 to 2014: A systematic literature review and ways forward', *International Journal of Public Sector Management,* 29 (2), 110–131.

Bouwman, R., Van Thiel, S., van Deemen, A., and Rouwette, E. 2018. 'Accountability and coalitions: Evidence from a negotiation experiment', *Public Administration Review,* 78, 1, 37–47.

Bovens, B. Curtin, D. and 't Hart, P. (eds), 2010. *The Real World of EU Accountability: What Deficit?.* Oxford: Oxford University Press.

Bovens, M. 2007. 'Analysing and Assessing Accountability: A Conceptual Framework', *European Law Journal,* 13, 447, 448.

Bovens, M, R.E. Goodin, and Schillemans, T. 2014. *The Oxford Handbook of Public Accountability.* Oxford: Oxford University Press.

Bovens, M. 2005. 'Public Accountability' in Ferlie, E. Lynn Jr, L. and Pollitt, C. (eds), *The Oxford Handbook of Public Management.* Oxford: Oxford University Press, 194.

Bovens, M. 2010. 'Two Concepts of Accountability: Accountability as a Virtue and as a Mechanism', *West European Politics* 33, 946.

Bovens, M. 2010. *The Blame Game: Spin, Bureaucracy and Self-Preservation in Government.* Princeton University Press, Princeton and Oxford.

Bovens, M. 1998. *The Quest for Responsibility.* Cambridge: Cambridge University Press.

Bovens, M. 2007. 'Analysing and Assessing Accountability: A Conceptual Framework', *European Law Journal*, 13(4), 447–468.

Bovens, M. and Zouridis, S. 2002. 'From street-level to system-level bureaucracies: How information and communication technology is transforming administrative discretion and constitutional control', *Public Administration Review*, 62 (2), 174–184.

Bovens, M. Curtin, D. and 't Hart, P. 2010. 'Studying the Real World of EU Accountability: Framework and Design' in Mark Bovens, Deirdre Curtin and Paul 't Hart (eds), *The Real World of EU Accountability: What Deficit?* Oxford: Oxford University Press, 49.

Bovens, M. Schillemans, T. and 't Hart, P. 2008. 'Does Public Accountability Work? An Assessment Tool', *Public Administration*, 86, 225, 227–28.

Burnett (Lord Burnett of Maldon), 2018. 'Foreword to Judicial Power and the Balance of Our Constitution' Judicial Power Project.

Bradley, AW. 1988. 'Police Powers and the Prerogative', *Public Law*, 298.

Braithwaite, J. 1997. 'On Speaking Softly and Carrying Big Sticks: Neglected Dimensions of a Republican Separation of Powers', *University of Toronto Law Journal,* 47, 305, 314–22.

Braithwaite, V. 2020. 'Beyond the bubble that is Robo-debt: How governments that lose integrity threaten democracy', *Australian Journal of Social Issues*, 55(3), 242–259.

Brandsma, G. and Schillemans, T. 2013. 'The Accountability Cube: Measuring Accountability', *Journal of Public Administration Research and Theory,* 23(4), 953–975.

Brazier, R. 1999. *Constitutional Practice.* 3rd edn, Oxford: Oxford University Press.

Brehm, J. 1966. *A Theory of Psychological Reactance*, Academic Press.

Brewer, MB., and Crano, WD. 2000. 'Research design and issues of validity', *Handbook of Research Methods in Social and Personality Psychology.* Cambridge: Cambridge University Press, 3–16.

Brummel, L. 2021. 'Social Accountability Between Consensus and Confrontation: Developing a Theoretical Framework for Societal Accountability Relationships of Public Sector Organizations', *Administration & Society*, 53, 7.

Brummel, L. 2022, 'Drawing attention. The effects of social accountability via social media and formal mechanisms on agency-CEO's horizontal orientation', *Paper currently under review.*

Brummel, L., Overman, S., and Schillemans, T. 2021. Uitvoeringsorganisaties tussen staat en straat. *Bestuurswetenschappen.*

Buell, E. and Sigelman, L. 2009. *Attack Politics.* Lawrence: University Press of Kansas.

Bullock, J. 2019. 'Artificial intelligence, discretion, and bureaucracy', *The American Review of Public Administration* 49(7), 751–61.

Buolamwini, J. and Gebru, T. 2018. 'Gender shades: Intersectional accuracy disparities in commercial gender classification', *Proceedings of Machine Learning Research* 81, 1–15.

Burrell, J. 2016. 'How the machine 'thinks': Understanding opacity in machine learning algorithms', *Big Data & Society,* 3(1), 2053951715622512.

Busch, P.A. and Henriksen, H. Z. 2018. 'Digital Discretion: A Systematic Literature Review of ICT and Street-Level Discretion', *Information Polity,* 23(1), 3–28.

Busuioc, M., and Lodge, M. 2017. 'Reputation and accountability relationships: Managing accountability expectations through reputation', *Public Administration Review*, 77(1), 91–100.

Busuioc, M., Curtin, D. and Almada, M. 2022. 'Reclaiming Transparency: Contesting the Logics of Secrecy within the AI Act', *European Law Open*. doi:10.1017/elo.2022.47.

Busuioc, M. 2021. 'Accountable Artificial Intelligence: Holding Algorithms to Account', *Public Administration Review*, 81, 5, 825–826. doi.org/10.1111/puar.13293.

Butler, I and Drakeford, M. 2012. *Social Work on Trial*, Bristol: Policy Press.

Byrnes, SJ., 2007. 'Balancing Investor Rights and Environmental Protection Investor-State Dispute Settlement under CAFTA: Lessons from the NAFTA Legitimacy Crisis', *UC Davis Bus. LJ*, 8, 102.

Cabinet Office. 2013. 'Guide to Making Legislation'. London: HMSO.

Cabinet Office. 2014. *Giving Evidence to Select Committees*. London: Cabinet Office.

Calo, R. and Citron, DK. 2021. 'The Automated Administrative State: A Crisis of Legitimacy', *Emory Law Journal*, 70, 4. Available at: scholarlycommons.law.emory.edu/elj/vol70/iss4/1.

Cane, P. 1999. 'Damages in Public Law', *Otago Law Review*, 9, 489, 491.

Carolan, E. 2015. 'Dialogue isn't working: the case for collaboration as a model of legislative-judicial relations', *Legal Studies*, 36(2), 209–229.

Carter, D. and May, P. 2020. 'Making sense of the U.S. COVID-19 pandemic response: A policy regime perspective', *Administrative Theory & Praxis*, 42(2), 265–277.

Cerny, P.G. 2010. *Rethinking World Politics: A Theory of Transnational Neopluralism*. New York: Oxford University Press.

Chesterman, S. 2008. 'Accountability Rules: Accountability, Power and the Prospects for Global Administrative Law', *Global Governance*, 14, 39–52.

Chitty, J. 1820. *A Treatise on the Law of the Prerogatives of the Crown*. London: Butterworth.

Choudhary, S., Ismail, A. and Hanif, R. 2017. 'Individual Compassion Leading to employees' Performance: An Empirical Study from Pakistan', *Journal of Management Research*, 4, 1, 114–48.

Christensen, T. and Lægreid, P. 2015. 'Performance and Accountability – A Theoretical Discussion and an Empirical Assessment', *Public Organiz Rev*, 15, 207–225.

Christiansen, T and Fromage, D. 2019. *Brexit and Democracy*. London: Palgrave.

Citron, DK. 2008. 'Technological Due Process', *Washington University Law Review*, 85(6), 1249–1313.

Citron, D. 2016. '(Un)Fairness of Risk Scores in Criminal Sentencing', *Forbes*, www.forbes.com/sites/daniellecitron/2016/07/13/unfairness-of-risk-scores-in-criminal-sentencing/?sh=65ee9c734ad2.

Cladi, L. 2022. 'Damned If You Do and Damned If You Don't', *Parliamentary Affairs*, 75(1), 174–194.

Clapton, G. Cree, V. and Smith, M. 2013. 'Moral Panics, Claims-Making and Child Protection in the UK', *The British Journal of Social Work*, 43(4), 803–812.

Cm.3782, 1997. *Rights Brought Home: The Human Rights Bill*. London: HMSO.

Cm.9543, 2017, *Intimidation in Public Life*, London: Committee on Standards in Public Life.

Cm.8181. 2011. *The Process of Constitutional Change*: The Government Response to the House of Lords Constitution Committee Report, 15th Report of Session 2010–12.

Cmnd.3638. 1968. *The Civil Service*, London: HMSO. [The Fulton Report].

Coglianese, C. and Lai, A. 2022. 'Algorithm vs. Algorithm', *Duke Law Journal* 72, 1281.

Cohn, M. 2009. 'Judicial Review of Non-Statutory Executive Powers after *Bancoult*: A Unified Anxious Model', *Public Law*, 260.

Collier, D and Levitsky, S. 1997. 'Democracy with Adjectives', *World Politics*, 49, 3, 430–451.

Cooper, A.2010. '*Deep down They're Really Good People: Social Work Now – The State of Mind We're In*', Unpublished discussion document compiled by Professor Cooper. The Tavistock Institute of Human Relations.

Cooper, A. 2005. 'Surface and depth in the Victoria Climbié Inquiry Report', *Child and Family Social Work*, 10, 1–9.

Cooper, A. 2014. 'A short psychological history of British child abuse and protection: case studies in problems of mourning in the public sphere', *Journal of Social Work Practice*, 8, 3, 271–285.

Cowan, D and Mumford, A. (eds). 2021. *Pandemic Legalities*. Bristol: Policy Press.

Cowans, G. and Cygan, A. 2020. *Commons Library Briefing Paper- The Prorogation Dispute of 2019: One Year On*, House of Commons Library Research Briefing, No.9006.

Cowie, G. 2022. 'The power to make laws for Scotland: The "Treaty Incorporation Bills Reference"', *Public Law*, 2, 189–199.

Craft, J. and Halligan, J. 2020. *Advising Governments in the Westminster Tradition: Policy Advisory Systems*. Cambridge: Cambridge University Press.

Craig, P. 2021. 'IRAL: The Panel Report and the Government's Response', UK Constitutional Law Association blog, 22 March.

Cretney, S. 2007. Royal Weddings, Legality and the Rule of Law, *Family Law*, 159–164.

Cygan, A. Lynch, P. and Whitaker, R. 2020. 'UK Parliamentary Scrutiny of the EU Political and Legal Space after Brexit', *JCMS*, 58(6), 1605–1620.

Daintith, T. and Ng, Y-F., 'Legal Form and Function in the Public Sector: The Government-Owned Company in the United Kingdom and Australia' (2020) 136 (April) *Law Quarterly Review* 292.

Darbyshire, P. 2010. *Sitting Judgment: The Working Lives of Judges*. Oxford: Hart Publishing.

Davies, N. 2014. *Hack Attack, how the truth caught up with Rupert Murdoch*. London: Chatto and Windus.

Davis, K. 1969. *Discretionary Justice*. Baton Rouge: Louisiana State University Press.

De Bakker, F.G., Rasche, A. and Ponte, S. 2019. Multi-stakeholder initiatives on sustainability: A cross-disciplinary review and research agenda for business ethics, *Business Ethics Quarterly*, 29(3), 343–383.

de Boer, N. and Raaphorst, N. 2023. Automation and discretion: explaining the effect of automation on how street-level bureaucrats enforce, *Public Management Review* 25(1), 42–62.

De Cleen, B., Moffitt, B., Panayotu, P., and Stavrakakis, Y. 2020. 'The Potentials and Difficulties of Transnational Populism', *Political Studies*, 68(1), 146–166.

de Volkskrant. 2022a. CBS: Toeslagenaffaire trof veel eenoudergezinnen en ouders van buitenlandse afkomst. 28/06/2022. Available at: www.volkskrant.nl/nieuws-achtergrond/cbs-toeslagenaffaire-trof-veel-eenoudergezinnen-en-ouders-van-buitenlandse-afkomst-b183ffcc/?referrer=https%3A%2F%2Fwww.google.com%2F.

de Volkskrant. 2022b. De antispieksoftware herkende haar niet als mens omdat ze zwart is, maar bij de VU vond ze geen gehoor. 15/07/2022. Available at: www.volkskrant.nl/nieuws-achtergrond/de-antispieksoftware-herkende-haar-niet-als-mens-omdat-ze-zwart-is-maar-bij-de-vu-vond-ze-geen-gehoor-b6810279/.

Dekker, S. 2002. *The Field Guide to Human Error Investigations*. London and New York: Routledge.

Dicey, AV. 1915. *Introduction to the Study of the Law of the Constitution*. Liberty Fund.

Dimova, G. 2019. *Democracy Beyond Elections*. London: Palgrave.

Dimova, G., Dubnick, M., Flinders, M., and Monaghan, C. (eds). 2023. *Accountability with Adjectives*. London: Routledge.

Dingwerth, K. 2008. 'North-South parity in global governance: The affirmative procedures of the Forest Stewardship Council', *Global Governance*, 14, 53.

Dominelli, L. 1996. 'Deprofessionalizing Social Work', *The British Journal of Social Work*, 26(2), 153–175.

Douglas, M. 1992. *Risk and Blame*. London: Routledge.

Douglas, S. Schillemans, T. 't Hart, P. Ansell, C. Bøgh Andersen, L. Flinders, M. Head, B. Moynihan, D. Nabatchi, T. O'Flynn, J. Peters, B. Guy. Raadschelders, J. Sancino, A. Sørensen, E. and Torfing, J. 2021. 'Rising to Ostrom's challenge: an invitation to walk on the bright side of public governance and public service', *Policy Design and Practice*, 4(4), 441–451.

Dubnick, M. 2002. 'Seeking Salvation for Accountability', prepared for delivery at the 2002 Annual Meeting of the American Political Science Association, August 29-September 1.

Dubnick, M. 2005. 'Accountability and the Promise of Performance', *Public Performance & Management Review*, 28(3), 376–417.

Dubnick, M. 2011. 'Move Over Daniel: We Need some Accountability Space', *Administration & Society*, 43(6),704–716.

Dubnick, M. and Frederickson, H.G. 2011. *Accountable Governance: Problems and Promises*. Armonk, NY: M.E. Sharpe.

Dubnick, M. and Romzek, B.S. 1991. *American Public Administration*. New York, NY: Macmillan.

Dubnick, M. and Romzek, B.S. 1993. 'Accountability and the centrality of expectations in American public administration', in Perry, J.L. (ed), *Research in public administration*. Greenwich, CT: JAI, 37–78.

Dudley, SE., and Xie, Z. 2020. 'Designing a choice architecture for regulators', *Public Administration Review*, 80(1), 151–156.

Duke of Windsor, 1951. *A King's Story*. London: Cassell and Co.

Dutch Data Protection Authority (Autoriteit Persoonsgegevens). 2020. Belastingdienst/Toeslagen: De verwerking van de nationaliteit van aanvragers kinderopvangtoeslag Research Report z2018-2244. Available at: autoriteitpersoonsgegevens.nl/sites/default/files/atoms/files/onderzoek_belastingdienst_kinderopvangtoeslag.pdf.

Dutton, J., Workman, K. and Hardin, A. 2014. 'Compassion at Work', *Annual Review of Organizational Psychology and Organizational Behaviour*, 1(1), 277–304.

Dyzenhaus, D. 2006. *The Constitution of Law: Legality in a Time of Emergency*. Cambridge, Cambridge University Press.

Eberlein, B., Abbott, K.W., Black, J., Meidinger, E. and Wood, S. 2014. 'Transnational business governance interactions: Conceptualization and framework for analysis', *Regulation & governance*, 8(1), 1–21.

Eckersley, P. and Ferry, L. 2020. 'Public service outsourcing: the implications of 'known unknowns' and 'unknown unknowns' for accountability and policy-making', *Public Money & Management*, 40(1), 72–80.

Eggers, A., Vivyan, N. and Wagner, M. 2018. 'Corruption, Accountability, and Gender: Do Female Politicians Face Higher Standards in Public Life?', *Journal of Politics*, 80(1), 321–326.

Ekins, R. 2016. 'Brexit and Judicial Power', Judicial Power Project blog 21 July 2016.

Ekins, R. 2019. *Protecting the Constitution*, London: Policy Exchange.

Ekins, R. and Gee, G. 2018. '*Miller*, Constitutional Realism and the Politics of Brexit' in Elliott, M. Williams, J. and Young, A. (eds), *The UK Constitution After Miller*. London: Hart Publishing.

Ekins, R. and Laws, S. 2019 'The Supreme Court has done lasting damage to our constitution: No principle justifies last week's radical legal intervention in high politics', *Prospect*, 4 October 2019.

Ekins R. 2019. 'Written Evidence from Professor Richard Ekins- The Supreme Court's prorogation judgment and its constitutional implications': data.parliament.uk/writtenevidence/committeeevidence.svc/evidencedocument/public-administration-and-constitutional-affairs-committee/prorogation-and-the-implications-of-the-supreme-court-judgment/written/106116.html.

Eldor, L. 2018. 'Public Service Sector: The Compassionate Workplace – The Effect of Compassion and Stress on Employee Engagement, Burnout, and Performance', *Journal of Public Administration Research and Theory*, 28(1), 86–103.

Elliott, M. 2013. 'Ombudsmen, Tribunals, Inquiries: Re-fashioning Accountability Beyond the Courts' in Bamforth, N and Leyland, P. (eds), *Accountability in the Contemporary Constitution*. Oxford: Oxford University Press, 258.

Elliott, M. 2017. 'Judicial Power and the United Kingdom's Changing Constitution', Paper No. 49/2017 Legal Studies Research Paper Series.

Elliott, M. 2020. *The Judicial Review Review – I: The Reform Agenda and its Potential Scope*. London: Public Law for Everyone.

Elyounes, D.A. 2021. '"Computer Says No!": The Impact of Automation on the Discretionary Power of Public Officers', *Vanderbilt Journal of Entertainment and Technology Law* 23, 451.

Entwistle, T., Downe, J., Guarneros-Meza, V., and Martin, S. 2014. 'The Multi-Level Governance of Wales: Layer Cake or Marble Cake? *The British Journal of Politics and International Relations*', 16(2), 310–325.

Eriksen, A. 2021a. 'Accountability and the Multidimensional Mandate', *Political Research Quarterly*, 74(2), online advance.

Eriksen, E. 2021b. *The Accountability of Expertise*. London: Routledge.

Eubanks, V. 2018. *Automating Inequality: How High-tech Tools Profile, Police, and Punish the Poor*. New York: St. Martin's Press.

Evans, J. 2003. 'Vigilance and Vigilantes: thinking psychoanalytically about anti-paedophile action', *Theoretical Criminology* 7, 163–189.

Evans, P. 2019. 'So, What Is Good Scrutiny Good For?', *Parliamentary Affairs*, 72(4), 987–995.

Eversman, M and Bird, J. 2017. 'Moral Panic and Social Justice: A Guide for Analyzing Social Problems', *Social Work*, 62(1), 29–36.

Ewing, K. 2013. 'The Resilience of the Political Constitution', *German Law Journal*, 14(12), 2,111– 2,136.

Fagan, J., Davies, G. and Carlis, A. 2012. 'Race and Selective Enforcement in Public Housing', *Journal of Empirical Legal Studies*, 9(4), 697–728.

Faircloth, C. 2011. '"It feels right in my heart": Affective accountability in narratives of attachment,' *Sociological Review*, 59, 283–302.

Falaschetti, D. 2009. *Democratic governance and economic performance*. New York, NY: Springer.

Fawcett, P., Wood, M., Hay, C. and Flinders, M. (eds). 2017. *Anti-Politics, Depoliticisation and Governance*. Oxford: Oxford University Press.

Fenton-Glynn, C. 2016. 'Reviewing the UK's implementation of human rights obligations', *Family Law*, 1201.

Ferguson, A.G. 2017. *The Rise of Big Data Policing: Surveillance, Race, and the Future of Law Enforcement*. New York: NYU Press.

Finnis, J. 2019. *The Unconstitutionality of the Supreme Court's Prorogation Judgment*. London: Policy Exchange.

Haines, F and Macdonald, K. 2020. 'Non-judicial business regulation and community access to remedy', *Regulation & Governance*, 14(4), 840–860.

Flaherty, M. 1996. 'The Most Dangerous Branch', *Yale Law Journal*, 105(7), 1,725–1,841.

Flinders M. and Kelso A. 2011. 'Mind the Gap: Political Analysis, Public Expectations and the Parliamentary Decline Thesis', *British Journal of Politics and International Relations*, 13(2), 249–268.

Flinders, M. 2023. 'Keep walking on the bright side: criticality, credit and challenge', *Policy Design and Practice*.

Flinders, M. 2001. *The Politics of Accountability in the Modern State*. London: Routledge.

Flinders, M. 2008. 'Bi-Constitutionality: Unravelling New Labour's Constitutional Orientations', *Parliamentary Affairs*, 61(1), 99–121.

Flinders, M. 2009. *Democratic Drift*. Oxford: Oxford University Press.

Flinders, M. 2011. 'Daring to be a Daniel: The Pathology of Politicized Accountability in a Monitory Democracy', *Administration & Society*, 43(5), 595–619.

Flinders, M. 2012. *Defending Politics*. Oxford: Oxford University Press.

Flinders, M. 2013. 'Flinders on What is Governance?', The *Governance* Blog, 11 March 2013.

Flinders, M. 2020. 'Why feelings trump facts: anti-politics, citizenship and emotion', *Emotions and Society*, *2*(1), 21–40.

Flinders, M. 2021. 'Democracy and the Politics of Coronavirus: Trust, Blame and Understanding', *Parliamentary Affairs*, 74(2), 483–502.

Flinders, M. and Judge, D. 2017. 'Fifty Years of Representative and Responsible Government', *Representation*, 53(2), 97–116.

Flinders, M. and Van Der Arend, J. 2023. 'From Policy to Scrutiny: Exploring Positive Public Accountability' in Nabatchi, T, O'Flynn, J. and 't Hart, P. (eds). *Positive Public Administration: New Directions for Theory and Practice*. London: Edward Elgar.

Flinders, M., Weinberg, A., Weinberg, J., Geddes, M. and Kwiatkowski, R. 2020. 'Governing under Pressure? The Mental Wellbeing of Politicians', *Parliamentary Affairs*, 73(2), 253–273.

Flinders, M. and Anderson, A. 2022. 'MPs' expenses: the legacy of a scandal 10 years on', *British Politics*, 17, 119–143.

Flinders, M., Mulgan G. and Stark, A. 2021. Range and variety of models of public inquiry: how to stimulate innovative inquiry design, process and practice, in IPPO: IPPO (covidandsociety.com)

Ford, J.B., and Zelditch Jr, M. 1988. 'A test of the law of anticipated reactions', *Social psychology quarterly*, 164–171.

Foreman, S. 2004. 'Managing Customers and Information for Improved Performance', *Henley Manager Update*, 16(1), 12–19.

Forsyth, C. 1996. 'Of Fig Leaves and Fairy Tales: The Ultra Vires Doctrine, the Sovereignty of Parliament and Judicial Review', *Cambridge Law Journal*, 55(1), 122–140.

Fox, J. (2022). 'Accountability Keywords', Accountability Working Paper 11, Accountability Research Centre.

Fox, J. and Brown, L. (eds). 1998. *The Struggle for Accountability: The World Bank, NGOs and Grassroots Movements.* Cambridge, MIT Press.

Fox, J., 2018. 'The political construction of accountability keywords', *IDS Bulletin*, 49(2), 65–80.

Fredman, S. 2013. 'From dialogue to deliberation: Human rights adjudication and prisoners' rights to vote', *Public Law*, 292–311.

Friedrich, C.J. 1937. *Man and his Government.* Toronto: University of Toronto Press.

Friedrichs J. 2001. 'The meaning of new medievalism', *European Journal of International Relations* 7(4), 475–501.

Fukuyama, F. 2013. 'What is governance?', *Governance*, 26(3), 347–368.

Fung, A., Wright, EO. and Abers, R. 2003. *Deepening Democracy: Institutional Innovations in Empowered Participatory Governance.* London: Verso.

Gailmard, S. and Patty, J. 2007. 'Slackers and Zealots: Civil Service, Policy Discretion, and Bureaucratic Expertise', *American Journal of Political Science* 51(4), 873–889.

Gailmard, S. and Patty, J. 2013. *Learning while Governing: Expertise and Accountability in the Executive Branch.* Chicago: University of Chicago Press.

Galligan, D. 1997. *Discretionary Powers.* Oxford: Oxford, Clarendon Press.

Gardbaum, S. 2020. 'Comparative Political Process Theory', *International Journal of Constitutional Law*, 18(4), 1,429–1,457.

Garvey, N and Newell, P. 2005. 'Corporate accountability to the poor? Assessing the effectiveness of community-based strategies', *Development in Practice*, 15(3&4), 389–404.

Gearty, G. 2022. 'In the Shallow End', *London Review of Books*, 44(2), www.lrb.co.uk/the-paper/v44/n02/conor-gearty/in-the-shallow-end.

Gee, G. and Webber, G. 2010. 'What Is a Political Constitution?', *Oxford Journal of Legal Studies*, 30(2), 273–299.

Geiger, G. 2021. 'How a discriminatory algorithm wrongly accused thousands of families of fraud', *Vice*, March 1. Available at: www.vice.com/en/article/jgq35d/how-a-discriminatory-algorithm-wrongly-accused-thousands-of-families-of-fraud.

Goldoni, M. and McCorkindale, C. 2019. 'Three Waves of Political Constitutionalism', *King's Law Journal*, 30(1), 74–96.

Goldsmith, J. and Manning, J. 2016. 'The Protean Take Care Clause', *University of Pennsylvania Law Review*, 164, 1835.

Goodhart, M. 2014. 'Accountable International Relations', in Bovens, M, Goodin, R.E., and Schillemans, T. *The Oxford Handbook of Public Accountability.* Oxford: Oxford University Press.

Gordon, M. 2019. 'Parliamentary Sovereignty and the Political Constitution(s): From Griffith to Brexit', *King's Law Journal*, 30(1), 125–147.

Gormley-Heenan, C and Aughey, A. 2012. 'Freedom, Peace and Politics: Crick and Northern Ireland', *Political Quarterly*, 83(4), 653–659.

Graham, L. 2022. 'The Reed Court by Numbers. How Shallow is the Shallow End?' *U.K. Const. L. Blog.* 4 April 2022.

Grant, R. and Keohane R. 2005. 'Accountability and abuses of power in world politics', *American Political Science Review* 99(1), 29–43.

Green, B. and Chen, Y. 2019a. 'Disparate Interactions: An Algorithm-in-the-Loop Analysis of Fairness in Risk Assessments' in *Proceedings of the Conference on Fairness, Accountability, and Transparency*' '–FAT*'19, 90–99. New York: ACM Press. doi:10.1145/3287560.3287563.

Green, B. and Chen, Y. 2019b. 'The Principles and Limits of Algorithm-in-the-Loop Decision Making' in *Proceedings of the ACM on Human-Computer Interaction*, 3(CSCW), 1–24.

Greer, C., and McLaughlin, E. 2011. '"Trial by media": Policing, the 24-7 news mediasphere and the "politics of outrage"', *Theoretical Criminology*, 15(1), 23–46.

Griffith, J.A.G. 2000. 'The Brave New World of Sir John Laws', *Modern Law Review*, 63(2), 159–176.

Griffith, J.A.G. 1979. 'The Political Constitution', *Modern Law Review*, 42, 1, 16.

Griffith, J.A.G. 2001. 'The common law and the political constitution', *Law Quarterly Review*, 117, 42–67.

Griffith, J.A.G. 2010. *Politics of the Judiciary*. London: Fontana Press.
Gritsenko, D. and Wood, M. 2022. 'Algorithmic Governance: A modes of governance approach', *Regulation & Governance*, 16, 45–62.
Grossi, G. and Thomason, A. 2015. 'Bridging the accountability gap in hybrid organizations: the case of Copenhagen Malmö Port', *International Review of Administrative Sciences*, 81(3), 604–620.
Grossi, G., Kallio, K.-M., Sargiacomo, M. and Skoog, M. 2020. 'Accounting, performance management systems and accountability changes in knowledge-intensive public organizations,' *Accounting, Auditing & Accountability Journal*, 33(1), 256–280.
Grzymala-Busse, A. 2019. 'How populists rule: the consequences for democratic governance', *Polity*, 51(4), 707–717.
Guasti, P. 2020. 'Populism in Power and Democracy', *Politics and Governance*, 8(4), online open-access.
Gupta, D., Sharachchandra, L. and Geetanjoy, S. 2020. 'Promoting a Responsive State: The Role of NGOs in Decentralized Forest Governance in India', *Forest Policy and Economics* 111, art 102066.
Hadwick, D. and Lan, S. 2021. 'Lessons to be learned from the Dutch childcare allowance scandal: A comparative review of algorithmic governance by tax administrations in the Netherlands, France and Germany', *World Tax Journal* 13(4).
Haggard, S. and Kaufman, R. 2021. *Backsliding Democratic Regress in the Contemporary World.* Cambridge: Cambridge University Press.
Halachmi, A. 2014. 'Accountability Overloads' in Bovens, M, Goodin, R.E. and Schillemans, T. *The Oxford Handbook of Public Accountability*. Oxford: Oxford University Press.
Hale (Baroness Hale of Richmond), 2022. *Spiderwoman: A Life*. London: Bodley Head.
Hall, A. Frink, D. and Buckley, R. 2017. 'An accountability account: A review and synthesis of the theoretical and empirical research on felt accountability', *Journal of Organizational Behaviour*, 38, 204–224.
Hall, A.T., Bowen, M.G., Ferris, G.R., Royle, M.T. and Fitzgibbons, D.E. 2007. 'The accountability lens', *Business Horizons*, 50, 405–413.
Halloran, B. 2016. *Accountability ecosystems: directions of accountability and points of engagement.* Brighton: IDS.
Hameleers, M., Bos, L. and de Vreese, C.H. 2017. '"They Did It": The Effects of Emotionalized Blame Attribution in Populist Communication', *Communication Research*, 44(6), 870–900.
Han, Y. 2020. 'The impact of accountability deficit on agency performance: Performance-accountability regime', *Public Management Review*, 22(6), 927–948.
Han, Y. and Hong, S. 2019. 'The impact of accountability on organizational performance in the US federal government: The moderating role of autonomy', *Review of Public Personnel Administration*, 39(1), 3–23.
Han, Y. and Perry, J.L. 2020a. 'Conceptual bases of employee accountability: A psychological approach', *Perspectives on Public Management and Governance*, 3(4), 288–304.
Han, Y. and Perry, J.L. 2020b. 'Employee accountability: development of a multidimensional scale', *International Public Management Journal*, 23(2), 224–251.
Harari, M.B. and Rudolph, C.W. 2017. 'The effect of rater accountability on performance ratings: A meta-analytic review', *Human Resource Management Review*, 27(1), 121–133.
Hardman, I. 2019. *Why we get the Wrong Politicians*. London: Atlantic Books.
Harlow, C. 2002. *Accountability in the European Union*. Oxford: Oxford University Press.
Harlow, C. 2004. *State Liability: Tort Law and Beyond*. Oxford: Oxford University Press.
Harris, B. 2007. 'The "Third Source" of Authority for Government Action Revisited', *Law Quarterly Review* 113(2), 225–250.
Hart, HLA. 2008. *Punishment and Responsibility: Essays in the Philosophy of Law*, 2nd edn. Oxford: Oxford University Press.
Haskell, J. 2018. *Direct Democracy or Representative Government? Dispelling The Populist Myth.* New York: Routledge.
Hay C. 2020. 'Brexistential Angst and the Paradoxes of Populism: On the Contingency, Predictability and Intelligibility of Seismic Shifts', *Political Studies*, 68(1), 187–206.

Hay, C and Stoker, G. 2009. 'Revitalising Politics: Have we lost the plot', *Representation*, 45(3), 225–236.

Hay, C. 2004. 'Theory, stylized heuristic or self-fulfilling prophecy?', *Public Administration*, 82(1), 39–62.

HC 123 *Assessment of the Capability Review Programme*, Report by the Comptroller and Auditor General, Session 2008–2009, London: HMSO.

HC 1704/HL233, *Legislative Scrutiny: Welfare Reform Bill*, 21st Report from the Joint Committee on Human Rights, Session 2010–2012.

HC 19 Procedure Committee, Report 1989–1990.

HC 224. 2004. *Taming the Prerogative: Strengthening Ministerial Accountability to Parliament*, House of Commons, Public Administration Select Committee.

HC 544 *Individual Learning Accounts*, Tenth Report of the Public Accounts Committee, Session 2002–2003, London: HMSO.

HC 588 Procedure Committee, First Report 1977–78.

HC 911 *Select committee effectiveness, resources and powers*, Third report of Session 2012–2013, London: HMSO.

HC89/HL31, *The Government's Independent Review of the Human Rights Act*, Third Report of Session 2021–22, London: HMSO.

House of Commons Political and Constitutional Reform Committee for its inquiry into a written UK constitution, *A New Magna Carta?* (2014–15) HC 463.

He, G and Peng, W. 2022. 'Guns and roses: Police complicity in organized prostitution', *Journal of Public Economics*, 207(C).

Hennessy, P and Blick, A. 2020. *Good Chaps No More?* London: The Constitution Society. consoc.org.uk/wp-content/uploads/2019/11/FINAL-Blick-Hennessy-Good-Chaps-No-More.pdf.

Hennessy, P and Blick, A. 2022. *The Bonfires of the Decencies: Repairing and Restoring the British Constitution*. London: Haus Publishing.

Hickman, T, *Abracadabra Law-Making and Accountability to Parliament for the Coronavirus Regulations* (17 November 2020).

Higgins, M. 2019. 'The Donald: Media, Celebrity, Authenticity, and Accountability', in Happer, C., Hoskins, A. and Merrin, W. (eds). *Trump's Media War*. London: Palgrave, 129–141.

Hinterleitner, M. 2020. *Policy controversies and political blame games*. New York: Cambridge University Press.

Hirst P. 1994. *Associative Democracy: New Forms of Economic and Social Governance*. London: Polity Press.

Hirst P. 2013. *From Statism to Pluralism: Democracy, Civil Society and Global Politics*. Abingdon: Routledge.

HL 10 /HC 92. *Human Rights Joint Committee – Work of the committee in 2008–2009*, Second Report of Session 2009–2010, London: HMSO.

HL 47/HC 38 *Eighth Report of threw Joint Committee on Statutory Instruments*, Session 2007–2008, London, HMSO.

Ho, S. and Burke, G. 2022. An algorithm that screens for child neglect raises concerns. *AP news*. (20 April 2022).

Hochwarter, W.A., Ferris, G.R., Gavin, M.B., Perrewé, P.L, Hall, A.T. and Frink. D.D. 2007. 'Political Skill as Neutralizer of Felt Accountability – job Tension Effects on Job Performance Ratings: A Longitudinal Investigation', *Organizational Behaviour and Human Decision Processes*, 102(2), 226–239. doi:10.1016/j.obhdp.2006.09.003.

Hochwarter, W.A., Perrewé, P.L., Hall, A.T. and Ferris, G. 2005. 'Negative affectivity as a moderator of the form and magnitude of the relationship between felt accountability and job tension', *Journal of Organizational Behavior*, 26(5), 517–534.

Hodge, M. 2016. *Called to Account*. London: Little Brown.

Högberg, B. and Lindgren, J. 2021. 'Outcome-based accountability regimes in OECD countries: a global policy model?', *Comparative Education*, 57(3), 301–321.

Hong, S. 2017. 'What are the areas of competence for central and local governments? Accountability mechanisms in multi-level governance', *Journal of Public Administration Research and Theory*, 27(1), 120–134.

Hood, C. 2010. *The Blame Game: Spin, Bureaucracy and Self-Preservation in Government.* Princeton University Press, Princeton and Oxford.

Hood, C. 2002. 'The Risk Game and the Blame Game', *Government and Opposition*, 37(1), 15–37.

Hood, C. and Heald, D. 2006. *Transparency.* Oxford: Oxford University Press.

Hood, C. and Lodge, M. 2006. *The Politics of Public Service Bargains.* Oxford: Oxford University Press.

Hooghe, L. and Marks, G. 2003. 'Unraveling the Central State, but How? Types of Multi-level Governance', *American Political Science Review*, 97(2), 233–243.

Horne, A. 2015. *The Osmotherly Rules*, London, House of Commons Library, SN/PC/2671.

House of Commons Library 2017. *The Royal Prerogative*, Briefing Paper 03861.

House of Representatives Standing Committee of Privileges and Members' Interests, Register of Members' Interests Complaint concerning the Member for Pearce (November 2021).

Hughes, J. 2017. 'Algorithms and Posthuman Governance', *Journal of Posthuman Studies*, 1(2), 166–184.

IDEA. 2021. *The Global State of Democracy*, www.idea.int/gsod/sites/default/files/2021-11/the-global-state-of-democracy-2021_1.pdf.

Ignatieff, M. 2013. *Fire and Ashes: Success and Failure in Politics.* Cambridge MA: Harvard University Press.

Inspectie Justitie en Veiligheid. 2022. Toeslagenaffaire trof vooral eenoudergezinnen.

Institute for Government. 2019. *Moving On: The Costs of High Turnover in the Civil Service.* London: IfG.

Institute for Government. 2022. *Ministerial Directions*, London: IfG. www.instituteforgovernment.org.uk/explainers/ministerial-directions.

Jaffe, L. 1965. *Judicial Control of Administrative Action.* Little, Brown & Company, 245.

Jarman, H. Greer, S. and McKee, M. 2020. 'Brexit is just a symptom: the constitutional weaknesses it reveals have serious consequences for health', *Journal of Public Health*, 42(4), 778–783.

JCHR, Third Report of Session 2008–09, 13.

Jenkins, K. Caines, K. and Jackson, A 1988. *Improving Management in Government: The Next Steps.* London, HMSO.

Jenkins, S. 1996. *Accountable to None.* London: Penguin.

Jilke, S., Van de Walle, S. and Kim, S. 2016. 'Generating usable knowledge through an experimental approach to public administration', *Public Administration Review* 76(1) 69–72.

Johnston, J.M. and Romzek, B.S. 1999. 'Contracting and accountability in state Medicaid reform', *Public Administration Review*, 59(5), 383–399.

Johnston, J.M. and Romzek, B.S. 2000. *Implementing state contracts for social services.* Arlington, VA: The PricewaterhouseCoopers Endowment for the Business of Government.

Joint Committee on Human Rights, 'The Government's Independent Review of the Human Rights Act' (Third Report of Session 2021–22, 8 July 2021) 36.

Jones-Jang, S.M., Kim, D.H. and Kenski, K. 2021. 'Perceptions of mis- or disinformation exposure predict political cynicism', *New Media & Society*, 23(10), 3105–3125.

Jones, L. and Hameiri, S. 2021. 'COVID-19 and the failure of the neoliberal regulatory state', *Review of International Political Economy*, 29(4) 1027–1052.

Jones, R. 2014. *The Story of Baby P.* Bristol: Policy Press.

Jos, P and Tompkins, M. 2004. 'The Accountability Paradox in an Age of Reinvention', *Administration & Society*, 36(3), 255–281.

Kahler, M. 2004. 'Defining Accountability Up: the Global Economic Multilaterals', *Government and Opposition* 39(2), 132–158.

Kahneman, D. 2011, *Thinking Fast and Slow.* New York: Farrar, Straus and Giroux.

Kahneman, D., Sibony, O. and Sunstein, C. 2021. *Noise: A Flaw in Human Judgment.* Little, Brown and Company.

Kane, B. 2019. *Pitchfork Politics.* New York, Prometheus.

Kavanagh, A. 2019. 'Recasting the Political Constitution: From Rivals to Relationships', *King's Law Journal*, 30(1), 43–73.

Keane, J. 2009. *The Life and Death of Democracy*. London: Simon & Schuster.

Kelly, J. 2007. 'The Accountability Trap', *National Civic Review*, 96(3), 46–51.

Kennedy, R.P., Waggoner, P.D. and Ward, M.M. 2022. 'Trust in Public Policy Algorithms', *The Journal of Politics* 84(2), 1132–1148.

Kerr, J. 1999. 'More than missing metric doomed orbiter', *Science*, 286(5438). www.science.org/doi/full/10.1126/science.286.5438.207a.

Khaitan, T. 2019. 'Executive Aggrandizement in established democracies', *International Journal of Constitutional Law*, 17(1), 342–356.

Khatwani, N. 2019. 'Common Heritage of Mankind for Outer Space', *Astropolitics*, 17(2), 89–103.

Kim, S.E. 2005. 'Balancing competing accountability requirements', *Public Performance & Management Review*, 29(2), 145–163.

Kim, S.E. and Lee, J.W. 2010. 'Impact of competing accountability requirements on perceived work performance', *American Review of Public Administration*, 40(1), 100–118.

King, A. 2009. *The British Constitution*. Oxford: Oxford University Press.

King, A. 1976. 'Modes of Executive-Legislative Relations: Great Britain, France, and West Germany', *Legislative Studies Quarterly*, 1(1), 11–36.

King, J. 2019. Can Royal Assent to a Bill be withheld if so advised by Ministers?', *UK Const. L. Blog*.

Kingsbury, B., Krisch, N. and Stewart, R.B. 2004. The Emergence of Global Administrative Law. *IILJ Working Paper (Global Administrative Law Series)*, 2004/1.

Kippin, S. and Cairney, P. 2022. 'The COVID-19 exams fiasco across the UK: four nations and two windows of opportunity', *British Politics*, 17(1), 1–23.

Kirton, J. and Larionova, M. (eds). 2018. *Accountability for Effectiveness in Global Governance*. Abingdon: Routledge.

Kjaer, A. 2011. 'Rhodes' Contribution to Governance Theory: Praise, Criticism and the Future Governance Debate', *Public Administration*, 89(1), 101–113.

Klein, E, and Robison, J. 2020. 'Like, Post, and Distrust?', *Political Communication*, 37(1), 46–64.

Kleinnijenhuis, J., van Hoof, A. and Oegema, D. 2006. 'Negative News and the Sleeper Effect of Distrust', *Harvard International Journal of Press/Politics*, 11(2), 86–104.

Kloby, K. 2012. 'Lost in Translation: Exploring Stakeholder Perceptions of Accountability', *Journal of Public Management & Social Policy*, 18(1), 27–45.

Klug, F. and Wildbore, H. 2007. 'Breaking New Ground: the Joint Committee on Human Rights and the role of Parliament in Human Rights Compliance', *European Human Rights Law Review*, 3(1), 361–1, 526.

Koch, C. 2021. 'Varieties of populism and the challenges to Global Constitutionalism: Dangers, promises and implications', *Global Constitutionalism*, 10(3), 400–438.

Kocourek, A. 1914. 'Formal Relation between Law and Discretion', *Illinois Law Review*, 9(4), 225–246.

Koenig-Archibugi, M. 2010. 'Accountability in transnational relations: how distinctive is it?' *West European Politics* 33(5), 1142–1164.

Koenig-Archibugi, M. and Macdonald, K. 2013. 'Accountability-by-proxy in transnational governance', *Governance: An International Journal of Policy, Administration, and Institutions*, 26(3), 499–522.

Koppell, J. 2005. 'Pathologies of Accountability', *Public Administration Review*, 65(1), 94–108.

Körösényi, A. 2019. 'The Theory and Practice of Plebiscitary Leadership', *East European Politics and Societies*, 33(2), 280–301.

Korten, D. 1995. *Steps Toward People-Centred Development: Vision and Strategies in Government-NGO relations in Asia: prospects and challenges for people-centred development*. London: Macmillan.

Kostick-Quenet, K.M., Gerke, S. 2022. 'AI in the hands of imperfect users', *npj Digit. Med.* 5, 197. doi.org/10.1038/s41746-022-00737-z.

Krause, G.A. 2003. 'Agency Risk Propensities Involving the Demand for Bureaucratic Discretion' in *Politics, Policy, and Organizations: Frontiers in the Scientific Study of Public Bureaucracy*, Krause, G.A. and Meier, K.J. (eds). Ann Arbor, MI: University of Michigan Press.

Krisch N. 2011. *Beyond Constitutionalism: The Pluralist Structure of Postnational Law*. Oxford: Oxford University Press.

Krisch N. 2017. 'Liquid authority in global governance', *International Theory* 9(2), 237–260.

Krisch, N. 2006. 'The pluralism of global administrative law', *European Journal of International Law* 17(1), 247–278.

Kumarasingham, H. 2020. 'The Role and Powers of the Queen in the 2019 Brexit Political Crises', *Journal of Imperial and Commonwealth History*, 48(1), 1–14.

Kunz, K. and Abel, C.F. 2022. 'Politics, governance and the ethics of belief', *Philosophy & Social Criticism*, 48, 10.

Laborde, C. 2000. *Pluralist thought and the State in Britain and France, 1900–25*. Basingstoke: Macmillan.

Laborde, C. and Ronzoni, M. 2016. What is a free state? Republican internationalism and globalisation, *Political Studies*, 64(2), 279–296.

Lakkaraju, H. and Bastani, O. 2020. 'How Do I Fool You?': Manipulating User Trustvia Misleading Black Box Explanations. In Proceedings of the 2020 AAAI/ACM Conference onAI, Ethics, and Society (AIES '20), 7–8 February 2020, New York.

Langford, J. 1984. 'Responsibility in the senior public service: marching to several drummers', *Canadian Public Administration*, 27(4), 513–521.

Larsson, K. 2021. 'Digitization or equality: When government automation covers some, but not all citizens', *Government Information Quarterly*, 38(1), 101–547.

Laws, J. 2021. *The Constitutional Balance*. London: Bloomsbury.

Lee, M. 2017. 'Accountability for Environmental Standards after Brexit', *Environmental Law Review*, 19(2), 89–92.

Leland, S., Mohr, Z. and Piatak, J. (2021). 'Accountability in Government Contracting Arrangements: Experimental Analysis of Blame Attribution Across Levels of Government', *The American Review of Public Administration*, 51(4), 251–262.

Lerner, J.S., and Tetlock, P.E. (1999). 'Accounting for the effects of accountability', *Psychological Bulletin*, 125(2), 255.

Lester, A. and Weait, M. 2003. 'The Use of Ministerial Powers without Parliamentary Authority: The Ram Doctrine', *Public Law*, 415–428.

Levy, J.T. (2014) *Rationalism, Pluralism, and Freedom*. Oxford: Oxford University Press.

Li, Y., Qin, X. and Koppenjan, J. 2022. 'Accountability through public participation?', *Journal of Public Policy*, 42(1), 43–62.

Liel, Y. and Zalmanson, L. 2020. 'What If an AI Told You That 2 + 2 Is 5? Conformity to Algorithmic Recommendations', *ICIS 2020 Proceedings* 17.

Lighthouse Reports. 2022. The Algorithm Addiction: Mass profiling system SyRI resurfaces in the Netherlands despite ban and landmark court ruling. 20/12/2022. Available at: www.lighthousereports.nl/investigation/the-algorithm-addiction/.

Lijphart, A. 1999. *Patterns of Democracy*. Yale: Yale University Press.

Lijphart, A. 2007. *Thinking About Democracy*. London: Routledge.

Lilius, J., Worline, M., Maitlis, S., Kanov, J., Dutton, J. and Frost, P. 2008. 'The Contours and Consequences of Compassion at Work', *Journal of Organizational Behaviour*, 29(2), 193–218.

Lindberg, S. 2013. 'Mapping Accountability: Core concepts and subtypes', *International Review of Administrative Sciences*, 79(2), 202–226.

Lipsky, M. 1980. *Street-level bureaucracy. Dilemmas of the individual in public services*. New York: Russell Sage.

Loewen, P. and Rheault, L. 2021. 'Voters Punish Politicians with Depression', *British Journal of Political Science*, 51(1), 427–436.

Loughlin, M. 2019. *The Case of Prorogation*. London: Policy Exchange.

Loveland, I. 2021. *Constitutional Law, Administrative Law and Human Rights: A Critical Introduction*. Oxford, Oxford University Press.

Lowndes, V. 1997. '"We are learning to accommodate mess": Four propositions about management change in local governance', *Public Policy and Administration*, 12(2), 80–94.

Lührmann, A., Marquardt, K. and Mechkova, V. 2020. 'Constraining Governments: New Indices of Vertical, Horizontal, and Diagonal Accountability', *American Political Science Review*, 114(3), 811–820.

Lundberg, S.M. and Lee, S-I. 2017. 'A Unified Approach to Interpreting Model Predictions' in *NIPS'17: Proceedings of the 31st International Conference on Neural Information Processing Systems* December 2017, 4768–77.

Lupia, A. 2003. 'Delegation and its Perils' in Strom, K., Muller, W. and Bergman, T. (eds), *Delegation and Accountability in Parliamentary Democracies*. Oxford: Oxford University Press.

Mac. R. 2021. Facebook Apologizes After A.I. Puts 'Primates' Label on Video of Black Men. *New York Times*. 3 September 2021. Available at: www.nytimes.com/2021/09/03/technology/facebook-ai-race-primates.html.

Macdonald, K. and Miller-Dawkins, M. 2015, Accountability in Public International Development Finance, *Global Policy*, 6(4), 429–434.

Macdonald, K. and Macdonald, T. 2017. 'Liquid Authority and Political Legitimacy in Transnational Governance', *International Theory*, 9(2), 329–351.

Macdonald, T. and Macdonald K. 2022. NGOs as Agents of Global Justice: Cosmopolitan Activism for Political Realists, *Ethics and International Affairs*.

Macdonald, T. and Macdonald, K. 2020. 'The idea of a "pluralist" world order: Creating legitimate global institutions without "world government"?', *European Journal of International Relations*, 26(2), 518–544.

Macdonald, T. 2008. *Global Stakeholder Democracy: Power and Representation Beyond Liberal States*. New York: Oxford University Press.

Macdonald, K. 2018. Accountability in Global Economic Governance, *The Oxford Handbook of International Political Theory*, Brown, C. and Eckersley, R. (eds). Oxford: Oxford University Press, 453–466.

Macdonald, K. 2014a. 'The Meaning and Purposes of Transnational Accountability', *Australian Journal of Public Administration*, 73(4), 426–436.

Macdonald, K. 2014b. *The Politics of Global Supply Chains: Power and Governance Beyond the State*. Polity Press, Cambridge.

Macdonald, K. 2020. 'Private sustainability standards as tools for empowering southern pro-regulatory coalitions? Collaboration, conflict and the pursuit of sustainable palm oil', *Ecological Economics*, 167, 106439.

Malleson, K. 1999. *The New Judiciary: the effects of expansion and activism*. London: Dartmouth Publishing.

Margetts, H. and Dorobantu, C. 2019. Rethink Government with AI, *Nature* 568 (7751), 163–165.

Mason, M. 2005. *The New Accountability: Environmental Responsibility Across Borders*. London, Earthscan.

Masterman, R. and Wheatle, S. 2019. 'Miller/Cherry and Constitutional Principle', *UK Const. L. Blog*, 14 October 2019.

McCubbins and Schwartz. 1984. 'Congressional oversight overlooked: Police patrols versus fire alarms', *American Journal of Political Science* 28(1), 165–79.

McCubbins, M.D., Noll, R.G. and Weingast, B.R. 1987. 'Administrative Procedures as Instruments of Political Control', *Journal of Law, Economics and Organization* 3(2), 243–77.

McDevitt, M. and Ferrucci, P. 2018. 'Populism, Journalism, and the Limits of Reflexivity', *Journalism Studies*, 19(4), 512–526.

McLaughlin, K. Osborne, S. and Ferlie, E. (eds). 2002 *New Public Management*. London: Routledge.

Meers, J. 2019. 'Families and challenges to social welfare policies: key themes in the case law', *Fam Law*, 1300.

Meijer, A., Lorenz, L. and Wessels, M. 2021. 'Algorithmization of Bureaucratic Organizations: Using a Practice Lens to Study How Context Shapes Predictive Policing Systems', *Public Administration Review* 81(5), 837–846.

Mettler, S. 2021. *Four threats*. New York: Griffin.

Meyer, C et al. 2020. *Learning the right lessons from the pandemic*. London: King's College.

Meyer, C. 2021. 'How can Covid-19 public inquiries avoid the hindsight bias trap', IPPO Blog, 16 November: covidandsociety.com/covid-19-public-inquiries-avoid-hindsight-bias-trap/.

Meyer, C., Ikani, N., Avendano, P. and Kelly, A. 2020. *Learning the right lessons for the next pandemic*, London: King's College.

Mikuli, P and Kuca, G. (eds). 2021. *Accountability and the Law*. London: Taylor and Francis.

Miller-Dawkins, M. Macdonald, K. and Marshall, S. 2016. *Beyond Effectiveness Criteria: The Possibilities and Limits of Transnational Non-Judicial Redress Mechanisms*, Non-Judicial Redress Mechanisms Report Series 1, Corporate Accountability Research, available at: corporateaccountabilityresearch.net/njm-report-i-beyond-the-uns-effectiveness-criteria.

Mills, N. 2001. 'The new culture of apology', *Dissent* 48, 113–116.

Ministry of Finance. 2022. Answers to Parliamentary Questions about LSI. *Antwoorden op Kamervragen over LSI*. Kamerbrief 13/12/2022. Available at: www.rijksoverheid.nl/documenten/kamerstukken/2022/12/13/antwoorden-op-kamervragen-over-landelijke-stuurgroep-interventieteams-lsi.

Ministry of Justice, 2009. *The Governance of Britain, Review of the Executive Royal Prerogative Powers: Final Report*, London.

Ministry of Justice, 2021. *Responding to Human Rights Judgments*', CP 562, MoJ, London.

Minow, M. 2007. 'Between Vengeance and Forgiveness: South Africa's Truth and Reconciliation Commission', *Negotiation Journal*, 14(4), 319–355.

Moe, T. 2006. Political Control and the Power of the Agent. *Journal of Law, Economics, & Organization*, 22(1), 1–29.

Moffitt, B. 2016. *The Global Rise of Populism*. Stanford: Stanford University Press.

Monaghan, C. 2022. *Accountability, Impeachment and the Constitution: The Case for a Modernised Process in the United Kingdom*. Abingdon: Routledge.

Monaghan, C. 2018, 'An imperfect legacy: the significance of the *Bancoult* litigation on the development of domestic constitutional jurisprudence' in Allen, S and Monaghan, C. (eds). *Fifty Years of the British Indian Ocean Territory: Legal Perspectives*. New York: Springer.

Monaghan, C. 2019. 'The prorogation litigation: "which was as if the Commissioners had walked into Parliament with a blank piece of paper"', *Coventry Law Journal*, 24(2), 7–24.

Moore, M. and Gates, J. 1986. *Inspectors General*. New York, NY: Russell Sage.

Moravcsik, A. 2000. 'In defence of the democratic deficit', *Journal of Common Market Studies*, 40(4), 603–624.

Moseley, A. and Thomann, E. 2021. 'A behavioural model of heuristics and biases in frontline policy implementation', *Policy & Politics*, 49(1), 49–67.

Mounk, Y. 2014. Pitchfork Politics, *Foreign Affairs*, Sept./Oct. www.foreignaffairs.com/articles/united-states/2014-08-18/pitchfork-politics.

Mudde C. 2010. 'The populist radical right', *West European Politics*, 33(6), 1167–1186.

Mulgan, G. 2021. 'The Synthesis Gap: reducing the imbalance between advice and absorption in handling big challenges', 1 December. www.geoffmulgan.com/post/the-synthesis-gap-reducing-the-imbalance-between-advice-and-absorption-in-handling-big-challenges.

Mulgan, R. 2014. 'Accountability Deficits' in Bovens, M., Goodin, R.E. and. Schillemans, T. (eds), *The Oxford Handbook of Public Accountability*. Oxford: Oxford University Press, 548–49.

Mulgan, R. 2003. 'One Cheer for Hierarchy – Accountability in Disjointed Governance', *Political Science* 55(2), 6, 10.

Mulgan, R. 2000. 'Accountability: An Ever Expanding Concept', *Public Administration*, 78(3), 555–573.

Mulgan, R. 2003. *Holding Power to Account: Accountability in Modern Democracies*. Houndsmill, Palgrave Macmillan.

Mulgan, R. and Uhr, J. (2001). 'Accountability and Governance' in Davis, G. and Weller, P. (eds), *Are You Being Served? State, Citizens and Governance*. Allen and Unwin, 153.

Murphy, C. 2022, '"I don't want my face on the front page of The Sun": the "Baby P effect" as a barrier to social worker discretion', *Journal of Children's Services*, 17(1), 45–58.

Nagtegaal, R., Tummers, L., Noordegraaf, M. and Bekkers, V. 2020. 'Designing to debias: Measuring and reducing public managers' anchoring bias', *Public Administration Review*, 80(4), 565–576.

Neal, A. 2012. 'Terrorism, Lawmaking, and Democratic Politics: Legislators as Security Actors', *Terrorism and Political Violence*, 24(3), 357–374.

Neundorf, A. and Pardos-Prado, S. 2022. 'The Impact of COVID-19 on Trump's Electoral Demise', *Perspectives on Politics*, 20(1), 170–186.

Newell, P. 2008. 'Civil society, corporate accountability and the politics of climate change', *Global Environmental Politics* 8(3), 122–153.

Ng, Y. 2020. 'Political Constitutionalism: Individual Responsibility and Collective Restraint', *Federal Law Review* 48(4), 455, 465–67.

Nieuwsbericht, 28 June 2022. Available at: www.inspectie-jenv.nl/actueel/nieuws/2022/06/28/toeslagenaffaire-trof-vooral-eenoudergezinnen.

Noble, S.U. 2018. *Algorithms of Oppression: How Search Engines Reinforce Racism*. New York: New York University Press.

Norton, P. 2017. 'Speaking for Parliament', *Parliamentary Affairs*, 70(2), 191–206.

NRC. 2022. Een uitkering én een aanhangwagen? Dat is verdacht, volgens dit fraudesleepnet. 20 December 2022. Available at: www.nrc.nl/nieuws/2022/12/19/een-uitkering-en-een-aanhangwagen-dat-is-verdacht-volgens-dit-fraudesleepnet-a4151997.

O'Brien, R., Goetz, A., Scholte, J.A. and Williams, M. 2000. *Contesting global governance: Multilateral economic institutions and global social movements*. Cambridge: Cambridge University Press.

O'Kelly, C and Dubnick, M. 2014. 'Accountability and its Metaphors', Paper given to the Quality and Integrity of Governance Panel, EGPA Annual Conference, Speyer, Germany.

O'Neill, O. 2002. *A Question of Trust*. Cambridge: Cambridge University Press, 19.

O'Neil, C. 2016. *Weapons of Math Destruction: How Big Data Increases Inequality and Threatens Democracy*. New York: Crown Books.

Oborne, P. 2021. *The Assault on the Truth*. London: Simon & Schuster.

Olanya, D.R. 2016. 'Dams, water and accountability in Uganda', *Land and Hydropolitics in the Nile River Basin*, 166–181.

Oliver, D. 1991. *Government in the United Kingdom: the Search for Accountability, Effectiveness, and Citizenship*, Open University Press, 22.

Olsen, J.P. 2015. 'Democratic order, autonomy, and accountability', *Governance*, 28(4), 425–440.

Orhan, Y. 2022. 'The relationship between affective polarization and democratic backsliding', *Democratization*, 29(4), 714–735.

Ossege, C. 2012. 'Accountability–are We Better off Without It? An empirical study on the effects of accountability on public managers' work behaviour', *Public Management Review*, 14(5), 585–607.

Ostaijen, Van, M. and Jhagroe, S. 2022. 'Making Public Administration great again', *Policy Design and Practice*, 5(3), 261–275.

Ostiguy, P. 2017. 'Populism: A Socio-Cultural Approach', in Rovira Kaltwasser, C. et al (eds). *The Oxford Handbook of Populism*. Oxford: Oxford University Press, 73–101.

Ostrom, E. 2000. 'The Danger of Self-Evident Truths', *PS: Political Science and Politics*, 33(1), 33–44.

Overman, S. 2021. 'Aligning accountability arrangements for ambiguous goals: the case of museums', *Public Management Review*, 23(8), 1139–1159.

Overman, S., Schillemans, T. and Grimmelikhuijsen, S. 2021. 'A validated measurement for felt relational accountability in the public sector', *Public Management Review*, 23(12), 1748–1767.

Overman, S., and Schillemans, T. 2022. 'Toward a Public Administration Theory of Felt Accountability', *Public Administration Review* 82(1), 12–22.

Palmer, G and Butler, A. 2018. *Towards Democratic Renewal: Ideas for Constitutional Change in New Zealand*. Victoria University Press, 8.

Palmer, G. 1989. *Unbridled Power: Study of New Zealand's Constitution and Government*. Oxford: Oxford University Press.

Palmer, G. 2004. *Bridled Power: New Zealand's Constitution and Government*. Oxford: Oxford University Press.

Palumbo, A., and Bellamy, R. 2017. *Political accountability*. London: Routledge.

Panetta, R. 1999. 'Damages for Wrongful Administrative Decisions', *Australian Journal of Administrative Law* 6(4), 163, 179.

Papadopoulos, Y. 2010. 'Accountability and Multi-level Governance: More Accountability, Less Democracy?', *West European Politics*, 33(5), 1030–1049.

Papadopoulos, Y. 2012. 'Daring to be a Daniel: How Much Does it Contribute to a 'More Fine Grained Understanding of the Pathologies of Accountability', *Administration & Society*, 44(2), 238–252.

Park, S. 2020. *Environmental Recourse at the Multilateral Development Banks*. Cambridge: Cambridge University Press.

Park, S. 2010. 'Designing accountability, international economic organisations and the World Bank's Inspection Panel', *Australian Journal of International Affairs* 64(1), 13–36.

Parton, N. 1985. *The Politics of Child Abuse*. London: Macmillan.

Parton, N. 1986. 'The Beckford Report: a critical appraisal', *British Journal of Social Work* 16(5), 511–530.

Pasquino, G and Pelizzo, R. 2023. *The Culture of Accountability: A Democratic Virtue*. Abingdon: Routledge.

Paton, C. 2022. 'World-beating? Testing Britain's Covid response and tracing the explanation', *Health Economics, Policy and Law*, 17(2), 238–245.

Patterson, T. 2003. *The Vanishing Voter*. New York, NY: Random House.

Peeters, R. 2020. 'The agency of algorithms: Understanding human–algorithm interaction in administrative decision-making', *Information Polity* 25(4), 507–522.

Peeters, R. and Widlak, A. 2021. Automation Hubris: An Institutional Analysis of Administrative Burdens in Automated Decision Factories – The Case of the Dutch Daycare Benefit Scandal, *Paper for the Workshop on Administrative Burden at the NoPSA conference*, August 2021.

Perreau-Saussine, A. 2002. 'A Tale of Two Supremacies, Four Greengrocers, A Fishmonger, and the Seeds of a Constitutional Court', *Cambridge Law Journal*, 61(3), 527–530.

Pettit, P. 1997. *Republicanism: a theory of freedom and government*. Oxford: Oxford University Press.

Philp, M. 2009. 'Delimiting Democratic Accountability', *Political Studies*, 57(1), 28–53.

Piatak, J., Mohr, Z. and Leland, S. 2017. 'Bureaucratic accountability in third-party governance: Experimental evidence of blame attribution during times of budgetary crisis', *Public Administration*, 95(4), 976–989.

Pierson, P. 1996. 'The new politics of the welfare state', *World Politics*, 48(2), 143–179.

Pollack, D. 2009. 'Legal Risk, Accountability and Transparency in Social Work', *International Social Work*, 52(6), 837–842.

Pollmann, M., Potters, J. and Trautmann, S. 2014. 'Risk taking by agents: The role of ex-ante and ex-post accountability', *Economics Letters*, 123(3), 387–390.

Poulter, D., Votruba, N., Bakolis, I., Debell, F., Das-Munshi, J. and Thornicroft, G. 'Mental health of UK Members of Parliament in the House of Commons: a cross-sectional survey'. BMJ Open. 2019 Jul 1;9(7):e027892. doi: 10.1136/bmjopen-2018-027892.

Przeworski, A, 2019. *Crises of Democracy*. Cambridge: Cambridge University Press.

PwC. 2021. *Onderzoek effecten FSV Particulieren*. Amsterdam.

Questiaux, N. 1982. *Study of the implications for human rights of recent developments concerning situations known as states of siege or emergency*, UN ESC, E/CN.4/Sub.2/1982/15.

Rajapaksa, C. and Wijerathna, J. 2017. 'Adaptation to Space Debris Mitigation Guidelines and Space Law', *Astropolitics*, 15(1), 65–76.

Rao, R., Bakolis, I. and Das-Munshi, J., et al. 'Alcohol consumption of UK members of parliament: cross-sectional survey' *BMJ Open* 2020;10:e034929. doi: 10.1136/bmjopen-2019-03492.

Reason, J. (1990) *Human Error*. Cambridge: Cambridge University Press.

Resodihardjo, S. 2020. *Crises, Inquiries and the Politics of Blame*. London: Palgrave.

Rhodes, R.A.W. 1996. 'The New Governance: Governing without Government', *Political Studies*, 44(4), 652–667.

Rhodes, R.A.W. 2007. 'Understanding Governance: Ten Years On', *Organization Studies*, 28(8), 1,243–1,264.

Ribeiro, M.T., Singh, S. and Guestrin, C. 2016. 'Why Should I Trust You?' Explaining the Predictions of Any Classifier' in *Proceedings of the 22nd ACM SIGKDD International Conference on Knowledge Discovery and Data Mining* (Association for Computing Machinery 2016).

Richard, E. 2021. 'Written Evidence from Professor Richard Ekins- The Supreme Court's prorogation judgment and its constitutional implications': data.parliament.uk/writtenevidence/committeeevidence.svc/evidencedocument/public-administration-and-constitutional-affairs-committee/prorogation-and-the-implications-of-the-supreme-court-judgment/written/106116.html.

Richardson, R., Schultz, J. and Crawford, K. 2019. 'Dirty Data, Bad Predictions: How Civil Rights Violations Impact Police Data, Predictive Policing Systems, and Justice', *New York University Law Review Online* 94, 192–233.

Rickard, E. and Gee, G. 2018. 'Putting Judicial Power in its Place', *University of Queensland Law Journal* 36(2) 375.

Riddell, P. 2011. *In Defence of Politicians*. London: Biteback.

Roberts, A. 2017. *Four Crises of American Democracy*. Oxford: Oxford University Press.

Roberts, J. 2017. *Losing Political Office*. London: Palgrave.

Rock, E. 2020. *Measuring Accountability in Public Governance Regimes*. Cambridge: Cambridge University Press, 13–20.

Rock, E. 2020. 'Resolving Conflicts at the Interface of Public and Private Law', *Australian Law Journal* 94(5), 381.

Rock, E. and Weeks, G. 'Monetary Awards for Public Law Wrongs: Australia's Resistant Legal Landscape' (2018) 41(4) *University of New South Wales Law Journal* 1159.

Romzek, B. 2015. 'Living Accountability: Hot Rhetoric, Cool Theory, and Uneven Practice', *PS – Political Science and Politics*, 48(1), 27–34.

Romzek, B. and Ingraham, P. 2000. 'Cross pressures of accountability', *Public Administration Review*, 60(3), 240–253.

Romzek, B.S. and Dubnick, M. 1987. 'Accountability in the Public Sector: Lessons from the Challenger Tragedy', *Public Administration Review*, 47(3), 227–238.

Rooduijn, M. 2018. 'How to study populism and adjacent topics?', *European Journal of Political Research*, 58(1), 362–372.

Rose-Ackerman, S. 2005a. 'Policy-Making Accountability and Democratic Consolidation', in *From Elections to Democracy: Building Accountable Government in Hungary and Poland*. Cambridge: Cambridge University Press, 1–13.

Rossi, E. and Sleat, M. 2014. 'Realism in normative political theory', *Philosophy Compass* 9(10), 689–701.

Rozenberg, J. 2020. *Enemies of the People? How Judges Shape Society*. Bristol: Bristol University Press.

Rozenberg, J. 2021. 'Unfixing Parliament', *The Critic*.

Roosevelt, T. (1916). *An Autobiography*. Basingstoke, Macmillan.

Rubenstein, J. 2007. 'Accountability in an Unequal World', *Journal of Politics* 69(3), 616–632.

Rudin, C. 2019. 'Stop Explaining Black Box Machine Learning Models for High Stakes Decisions and Use Interpretable Models Instead', *Nature Machine Intelligence* 1(5), 206–215. doi:10.1038/s42256-019-0048-x.

Rudin, C., Wang, C. and Coker, B. 2020. 'The Age of Secrecy and Unfairness in Recidivism Prediction', *Harvard Data Science Review* 2(1). doi.org/10.1162/99608f92.6ed64b30.

Runciman, D. and David, R. 1997. *Pluralism and the Personality of the State*. Cambridge: Cambridge University Press.

Russell, M and Cowley, P. 2016. 'The Policy Power of the Westminster Parliament', *Governance*, 29(1), 121–137.

Russell, M. and Cowley, P. 2018. 'Modes of Executive-Legislative Relations Revisited', *Political Quarterly*, 89(1), 18–28.

Ruth, S.P. 2018. 'Populism and the Erosion of Horizontal Accountability in Latin America', *Political Studies*, 66(2), 356–375.

Sætra, H. 2020. 'A shallow defence of a technocracy of artificial intelligence', *Technology in Society*, 62.

Saffon, M.P. and Gonzalez Bertomeu, J. 2018. 'What/Whose Property Rights? The Selective Enforcement of Land Rights Under Mexican Liberalism' in Brinks, D., Murillo, M.V. and Steven Levitsky, S. (eds), *Understanding Weak Institutions in Latin America*.

Schedler, A. 1999. 'Conceptualizing Accountability', in Schedler, A., Diamond, L. and Plattner, M. (eds), *The Self-Restraining State*. London: Lynne Reinner, 13–28.

Schillemans, T. 2013. 'The Public Accountability Review. A Meta-Analysis of Public Accountability Research in Six Academic Disciplines', Working Paper, Utrecht University School of Governance. igitur-archive.library.uu.nl/USBO/2013-0517-200614/UUindex.html.

Schillemans, T. 2016. 'Calibrating Public Sector Accountability: Translating experimental findings to public sector accountability', *Public Management Review*, 18(9), 1400–1420.

Schillemans, T. and Giesen, I. 2020. 'De kwaliteit van (juridische) oordelen. Verslag van een experiment over verantwoording, bias en de kwaliteit van beoordelingen bij toezichthouders en in de rechtspraak', *Nederlands Juristen Blad*, 24-01, 182–193.

Schillemans, T., and Kremers, G. 2020. 'New development: The unknown world of transnational organizations in Europe – challenges for accountability', *Public Money & Management*, 40(4), 330–334.

Schillemans, T., and Smulders, R. 2016. 'Learning from accountability?! Whether, what, and when', *Public Performance & Management Review*, 39(1), 248–271.

Schillemans, T., Aleksovska, M. and Brummel, L. 2022. 'Accountability beyond hierarchy. A conjoint experiment exploring three logics of accountability behaviour', *Unfinished paper*.

Schillemans, T., Overman, S., Fawcett, P., Flinders, M., Fredriksson, M., Laegreid, P., Maggetti, M., Papadopoulos, Y., Rubecksen, K., Hellebø Rykkja, L., Houlberg Salomonsen, H., Smullen, A. and Wood, M. 2021a. 'Understanding Felt Accountability: The institutional antecedents of the felt accountability of agency-CEO's to central government', *Governance*, 34(3), 893–916.

Schillemans, T., S. Overman, S., Fawcett, P., Flinders, M., Fredriksson, M., Laegreid, P., Maggetti, M., Papadopoulos, Y., Rubecksen, K., Hellebø Rykkja, L., Houlberg Salomonsen, H., Smullen, A. and Wood, M. 2021b. 'Conflictual Accountability. Behavioral Responses to Conflictual Accountability of Agencies', *Administration & Society*. doi: 10.1177/00953997211004606.

Schmidt, BC. 2002. 'Anarchy, world politics and the birth of a discipline: American international relations, pluralist theory and the myth of interwar idealism', *International Relations* 16(1), 9–31.

Schmidt, V. and Wood, M. 2019. 'Conceptualizing throughput legitimacy', *Public Administration*, 97(4), 727–740.

Schmitter, P. 2004. 'The quality of democracy: The ambiguous virtues of accountability', *Journal of Democracy*, 15(4), 47–60.

Scholte, J.A. 2004. 'Civil society and democratically accountable global governance', *Government and Opposition*, 39(2), 211–233.

Schou, J. and Hjelholt, M. 2018. 'Digital citizenship and neoliberalization: governing digital citizens in Denmark', *Citizenship Studies* 22(5), 507–522.

Scott D., Schillemans, T., 't Hart, P., Ansell, C., Bøgh Andersen, L., Flinders, M., Head, B., Moynihan, D., Nabatchi, T., O'Flynn, J., Peters, BG., Raadschelders, J., Sancino, A., Sørensen, E. and Torfing, J. 2021. 'Rising to Ostrom's challenge: an invitation to walk on the bright side of public governance and public service', *Policy Design and Practice*, 4(4), 441–451.

Scott, C. 2000. 'Accountability in the Regulatory State', *Journal of Law and Society* 27(1), 38, 52–53.

Sebastiao, D. 2021. 'Covid-19: A Different Economic Crisis but the Same Paradigm of Democratic Deficit in the EU', *Politics and Governance*, 9(2), 252–264.

Self, P. 1972. *Administrative Theories and Politics*. London: Allen & Unwin.

Shavin, C. 2019. 'Unlocking the potential of the new OECD due diligence guidance on responsible business conduct', *Business and Human Rights Journal*, 4(1), 139–145.

Shoesmith, S. 2016. *Learning from Baby P; the politics of blame, fear and denial.* London and Philadelphia: Jessica Kingsley Publishers.

Simonite, T. 2018. 'When It Comes to Gorillas, Google Photos Remains Blind', *Wired.* 11 January 2018. Available at: www.wired.com/story/when-it-comes-to-gorillas-google-photos-remains-blind/.

Sinclair, A. 1995. 'The chameleon of accountability: Forms and discourses', *Accounting, Organizations and Society*, 20(2–3), 219–237.

Sinclair, A. and Tomlinson, J. 2019. 'Eliminating Effective Scrutiny: Prorogation, No Deal Brexit, and Statutory Instruments', *UK Const. L. Blog*, 4 September 2019.

Slack, D., Hilgard, S., Lakkaraju, H. and Singh, S. 2021. 'Counterfactual Explanations Can Be Manipulated', *35th Conference on Neural Information Processing Systems (NeurIPS 2021)*. arXiv:2106.02666.

Slaughter, A.M. 2004. 'Disaggregated sovereignty: Towards the public accountability of global government networks', *Government and Opposition*, 39(2), 159–190.

Smyth, C. 2021. 'Kate Bingham says Britain is "put at risk by civil service groupthink"', *The Times*, 23 November.

Social Mobility Commission. 2021. *Navigating the Labyrinth: Socioeconomic background and career progression within the Civil Service*. London: Social Mobility Commission.

Sowa, J. and Selden, S.C. 2003. 'Administrative Discretion and Active Representation: An Expansion of the Theory of Representative Bureaucracy', *Public Administration Review* 63(6), 700–710.

Stanley, M. 2021. *Speaking Truth to Power*. London: Nielsen.

Stark, A. 2018. *Public Inquiries, Policy Learning and the Threat of Future Crises*. Oxford: Oxford University Press.

Stears M. 2002. *Progressives, Pluralists, and the Problems of the State: Ideologies of Reform in the United States and Britain, 1909–1926*. Oxford: Oxford University Press.

Stoker, G. 2013. 'Designing Politics: A Neglected Justification for Political Science', *Political Studies Review*, 11(2), 174–181.

Stoker, G. 2016. *Why Politics Matters*. London: Palgrave.

Strom, K. (2003). 'Parliamentary Democracy and Delegation' in Strom, K., Muller, W. and Bergman, T. (eds), *Delegation and Accountability in Parliamentary Democracies*. Oxford: Oxford University Press.

Strong, J. 2018. 'The war powers of the British parliament: What has been established and what remains unclear?', *The British Journal of Politics and International Relations*, 20(1), 19–34.

Subedi, D. and Scott, A. 2021. 'Populism, authoritarianism, and charismatic-plebiscitary leadership in contemporary Asia', *Contemporary Politics*, 27(5), 487–507.

Suiter, J. and Fletcher, R. 2020. 'Polarization and partisanship', *European Journal of Communication*, 35(5), 484–501.

Sulitzeanu-Kenan, R. 2010. 'Reflection in the Shadow of Blame', *British Journal of Political Science*, 40(3), 613–634.

Sumption, J. 2019. *Trials of the State: Law and the Decline of Politics*. London: Profile Books.

Sumption, J. 2019. 'Special Privy Council can solve Crown's conundrum', *The Times*, 18 July.

Sumption, J. 2022. 'Our system of conventions won out this time, but if Johnson had been mad as well as bad, the whole edifice could have fallen', *The Sunday Times*, 10 July.

Sunkin, M and Payne, S. (eds). 1999. *The Legal Nature of the Crown*. Oxford: Oxford University Press.

Sunstein, C. 2021. 'Governing by algorithm? No Noise and (Potentially) Less Bias', *Duke Law Journal* 71(6), 1175–1205.

Suzuki, E. and Nanwani, S. 2005. 'Responsibility of international organizations: the accountability mechanisms of multilateral development banks', *Mich. J. Int'l L.*, 27(1), 177.

Sylvest, C. 2007. 'Beyond the state? Pluralism and internationalism in early twentieth-century Britain', *International Relations* 21(1), 67–85.

Szydlowski, G., de Boer, N. and Tummers, L. 2022. 'Compassion, Bureaucrat Bashing and Public Administration', *Public Administration Review*, 82(4), 619–633.

Taft, L. 2000. Apology subverted: the commodification of apology', *Yale Law Journal* 109(5), 1135–2000.

Tamanaha, B. 2004. *On the Rule of Law: History, Politics, Theory*. Cambridge: Cambridge University Press.

Tamanaha, B. 2009. 'A Concise Guide to the Rule of Law' in Palombella, G. and Walker, N. (eds), *Relocating the Rule of Law*. Oxford: Hart Publishing.

Tanaka, M. 2011. 'The Changing Roles of NGOs in Nepal: Promoting Emerging Rights-Holder Organizations for Inclusive Aid', *Voluntas: International Journal of Voluntary and Nonprofit Organizations* 22 (3), 494–517.

Taylor, M. and Buranelli, V. 2007 'Ending up in Pizza: Accountability as a Problem of Institutional Arrangement in Brazil', *Latin American Politics and Society*, 49(1), 59–87.

Tetlock, P. 1983. 'Accountability and complexity of thought', *Journal of Personality and Social Psychology*, 45(1), 74–83.

Tetlock, P. 2011. 'Vying for Rhetorical High Ground in Accountability Debates: It is Easy to Look Down on those who Look Soft on', *Administration & Society*, 43(6), 693–703.

Tetlock, P. 1992. 'The impact of accountability on judgment and choice: Toward a social contingency model', in Zanna, M.P. (ed), *Advances in experimental social psychology*, 25, 331–376.

Tetlock, P. 2002. 'Social functionalist frameworks for judgment and choice: intuitive politicians, theologians, and prosecutors', *Psychological review*, 109(3), 451.

TheMarkup. 8 October 2022. Available at: themarkup.org/newsletter/hello-world/the-seven-year-struggle-to-hold-an-out-of-control-algorithm-to-account.

Thomann, E., Hupe, P. and Sager, F. 2018. 'Serving many masters: Public accountability in private policy implementation', *Governance*, 31(2), 299–319.

Thomann, E., van Engen, N. and Tummers, L. 2018. 'The Necessity of Discretion: A Behavioral Evaluation of Bottom-Up Implementation Theory', *Journal of Public Administration Research and Theory* 28(4), 583–601.

Tilly, C. 2008. *Credit and Blame*. Princeton: Princeton University Press.

Tomkins, A. 2013. 'What's Left of the Political Constitution', *German Law Journal*, 14(12), 2,275–2,292.

Tu, W. and Gong, T. 2022. 'Accountability intensity and bureaucrats' response to conflicting expectations', *Public Management Review*, 24(11), 1779–1801.

Twomey, A. 2019. *The Veiled Sceptre: Reserve Powers of Heads of State in Westminster Systems*. Cambridge: Cambridge University Press.

UN Special Rapporteur on Extreme Poverty and Human Rights. 2019. *Report of the UN Special Rapporteur on extreme poverty and human rights, Philip Alston of 11 October 2019* (UN doc. A/74/493). Available at: documents-dds-ny.un.org/doc/UNDOC/GEN/N19/312/13/PDF/N1931213.pdf?OpenElement.

Utting, P., 2014. 'Multistakeholder regulation of business: Assessing the pros and cons', in *International business and sustainable development*. Emerald Group Publishing Limited, 8, 425–446.

Van de Walle, S. 2016. 'The experimental turn in public management: How methodological preferences drive substantive choices', in James, O., Jilke, S. and Van Ryzin, O. (eds), *Experiments in public management research*. Cambridge: Cambridge University Press.

Van Slyke, D.M. 2007. 'Agents or stewards: Using theory to understand the government-nonprofit social service contracting relationship', *Journal of Public Administration Research and Theory*, 17(2), 157–187.

Veale, M. and Brass, I. 2019. "Administration by Algorithm? Public Management meets Public Sector Machine Learning" in Yeung, K. and Lodge, M. (eds), *Algorithmic Regulation*. Oxford: Oxford University Press, 121–149.

Verbruggen, P. and Havinga, T. 2015. 'Food safety meta-controls in the Netherlands', *European Journal of Risk Regulation*, 6(4), 512–524.

Vincent, J. 2018. 'Google 'fixed' its racist algorithm by removing gorillas from its image-labeling tech', *The Verge*. 12 January 2018. Available at: www.theverge.com/2018/1/12/16882408/google-racist-gorillas-photo-recognition-algorithm-ai.

Wachter, S., Mittelstad, B. and Russell, C. 2018. 'Counterfactual Explanations without Opening the Black Box: Automated Decisions and the GDPR', *Harvard Journal of Law & Technology* 31(2), 841.

Walker, G. 2017. 'A Place Apart? The Interventions of John P. Mackintosh and Bernard Crick on Northern Ireland', *Contemporary British History*, 31(4), 1–18.

Walker, N. 2010. 'Beyond the Holistic Constitution?', in Dobner, P. and Loughlin, M. (eds), *The Twilight of Constitutionalism?* Oxford: Oxford University Press, 291–308.

Walker, R.M., Brewer, G.A., Lee, M.J., Petrovsky, N. and Van Witteloostuijn, A. 2019. 'Best practice recommendations for replicating experiments in public administration', *Journal of Public Administration Research and Theory*, 29(4), 609–626.

Walzer, M. 1984. 'Liberalism and the Art of Separation', *Political theory*, 12(3), 315–330.

Wang, E.H. (2022). 'Frightened Mandarins: The Adverse Effects of Fighting Corruption on Local Bureaucracy', *Comparative Political Studies*, 55(11), 1807–1843.

Ward, K. and Vichhra, M. 2013. 'The Importance of Being Connected: Urban Poor Women's Experience of Self-Help Discourse in Cambodia, in "Feminist Solidarity and Collective Action,"' *Gender and Development* 21(2), 313–26.

Ward Struthers, C., Eaton, J., Santelli, A., Uchiyama, M. and Shirvani, N. 2008. 'The effects of attributions of intent and apology on forgiveness', *Journal of Experimental Social Psychology*, 44(4), 983–992.

Warner, J. 2013. 'Social work, class politics and risk in the moral panic over Baby P', *Health, Risk & Society*, 15(3), 217–233.

Warner, J. 2015. *The Emotional Politics of Social Work and Child Protection*. Bristol: Policy Press.

Waylen, G. and Southern, R. 2021. 'When Are Women as Corrupt as Men? Gender, Corruption, and Accountability in the UK Parliamentary Expenses Scandal', *Social Politics: International Studies in Gender, State & Society*, 28(1) 119–142.

Weaver, R.K. 2013. 'Policy Leadership and the Blame Trap: Seven Strategies for Avoiding Policy Stalemate'. *Governance Studies at Brooking*, available from: weaverpolicy-leadership-and-the-blame-trapv5032813.pdf (brookings.edu).

Weaver, R.K. 1986. 'The Politics of Blame Avoidance', *Journal of Public Policy*, 6(4), 371–398.

Weingast, B.R. and Moran, M. 1983. 'Bureaucratic Discretion or Congressional Control: Regulatory Policymaking by the Federal Trade Commission', *Journal of Political Economy* 91(5), 765–800.

Weyland, K. 2018. 'Populism and Authoritarianism' in de la Torre, C. (ed), *Routledge Handbook of Global Capitalism*. London: Routledge.

Wheatle, S. 2020. 'Access to Justice: From Judicial Empowerment to Public Empowerment' in Elliott, M. and Hughes, K. (eds), *Common Law Constitutional Rights*. London: Hart Publishing.

White, H. 2022. *Held in Contempt: What's Wrong with the House of Commons?* Manchester: Manchester University Press.

Whiteford, P. 2021. 'Debt by Design: The anatomy of a social policy fiasco– Or was it something worse?', *Australian Journal of Public Administration*, 80(2), 340–60.

Wieringa, M. 2020. 'What to account for when accounting for algorithms: a systematic literature review on algorithmic accountability', Proceedings of the 2020 Conference on Fairness, Accountability, and Transparency, New York: United States.

Wilkins, P. 2002. 'Accountability and Joined-Up Government', *Australian Journal of Public Administration*, 61(1), 114–119.

Williams, B. 2005. *In the Beginning was the Deed: Realism and Moralism in Political Argument*. Princeton, NJ: Princeton University Press.

Wilson, J.Q. 1989. *Bureaucracy: What government agencies do and why they do it*. New York: Basic Books.

Wittgenstein, L. 2013 [1921]. *Tractatus logico-philosophicus*. London: Routledge.

Wood, M., Matthews, F., Overman, S. and Schillemans, T. 2022. 'Enacting Accountability Under Populist Pressures', *Administration & Society*, 54(2), 311–334.

Woods, N. and Amrita, N. 2001. 'Governance and the limits of accountability: The WTO, the IMF and the World Bank', *International Social Science Journal*, 53(170), 569–583.

Woon, J. 2012. 'Democratic accountability and retrospective voting: A laboratory experiment', *American Journal of Political Science*, 56(4), 913–930.

Xinya, Y., Haiying, L. and Clarke, A. 2018. 'Cross-Sector Social Partnerships for Social Change: The Roles of Non-Governmental Organizations', *Sustainability* 10(2), 558–75.

Yeung, K. and Lodge, M. 2019. 'Algorithmic Regulation: An Introduction' in Yeung, K. and Lodge, M. (eds), *Algorithmic Regulation*. Oxford: Oxford University Press, 1–18.

Young, A. 2017. '*R. (Miller) v Secretary of State for Exiting the European Union*: Thriller or Vanilla?', *European Law Review*, 42(2), 280–95.

Young, A. 2017. *Democratic Dialogue and the Constitution*. Oxford: Oxford University Press.

Young, M., Bullock, J. and Lecy, J. 2019. 'Artificial Discretion as a Tool of Governance: A Framework for Understanding the Impact of Artificial Intelligence on Public Administration', *Perspectives on Public Management and Governance* 2(4), 301–313.

Zaibert, L. 2006. *Punishment and Retribution.* Ashgate Publishing 7.

Zouridis, S., van Eck, M. and Bovens, M. 2020. 'Automated Discretion', in H Hupe, P. and Evens, T. (eds), *Discretion and The Quest for Controlled Freedom.* Palgrave Macmillan, 313–329.

Zürn, M. 2018. *A Theory of Global Governance: Authority, Legitimacy, and Contestation.* Oxford: Oxford University Press.

Zurn, M. 2004. 'Global Governance and Legitimacy Problems', *Government and Opposition* 39(2), 260–287.

INDEX

www.ingramcontent.com/pod-product-compliance
Ingram Content Group UK Ltd.
Pitfield, Milton Keynes, MK11 3LW, UK
UKHW020238290926
15470UKWH00002B/596